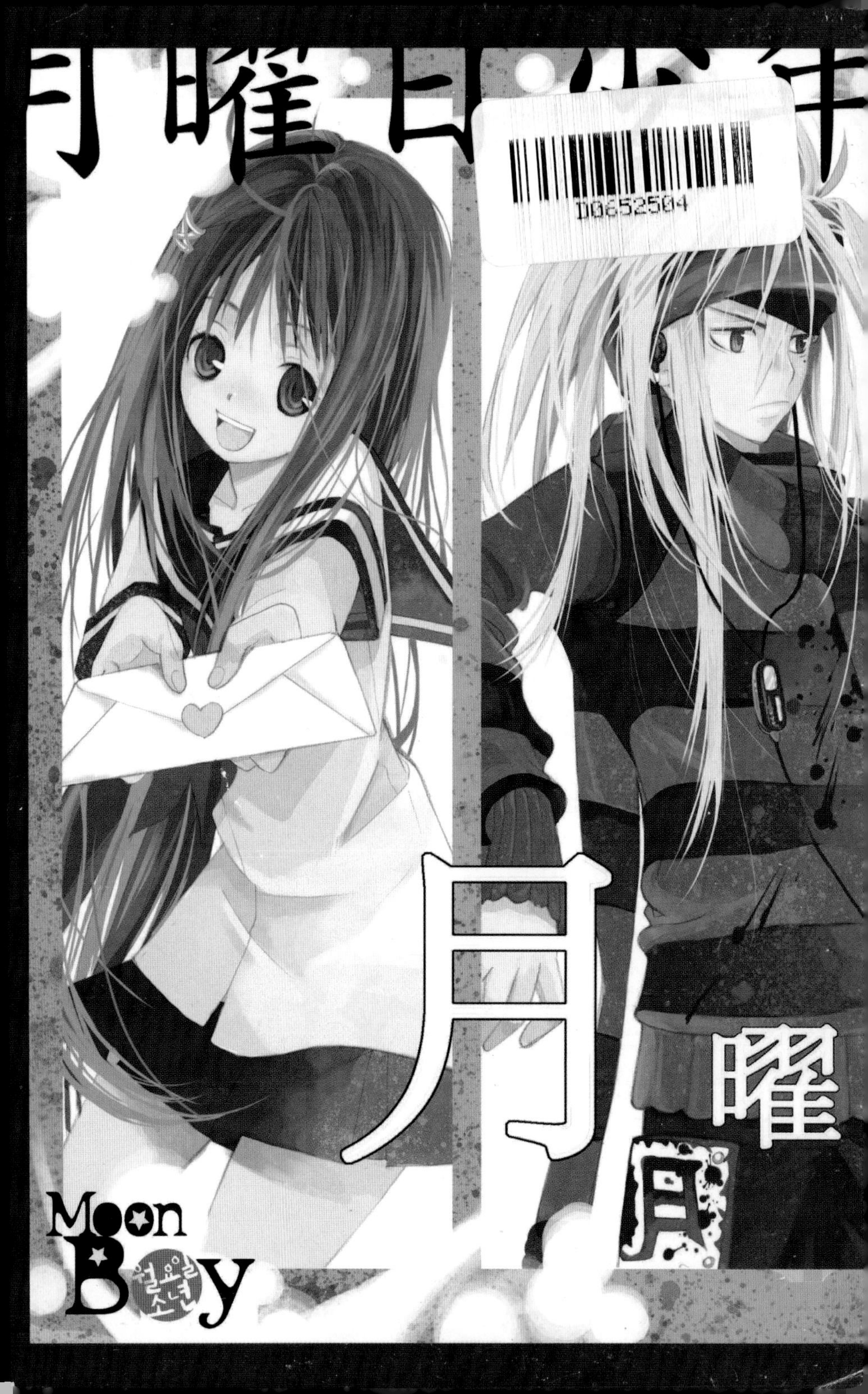
月曜日
月
曜
日
Moon
Boy
월요일
소년

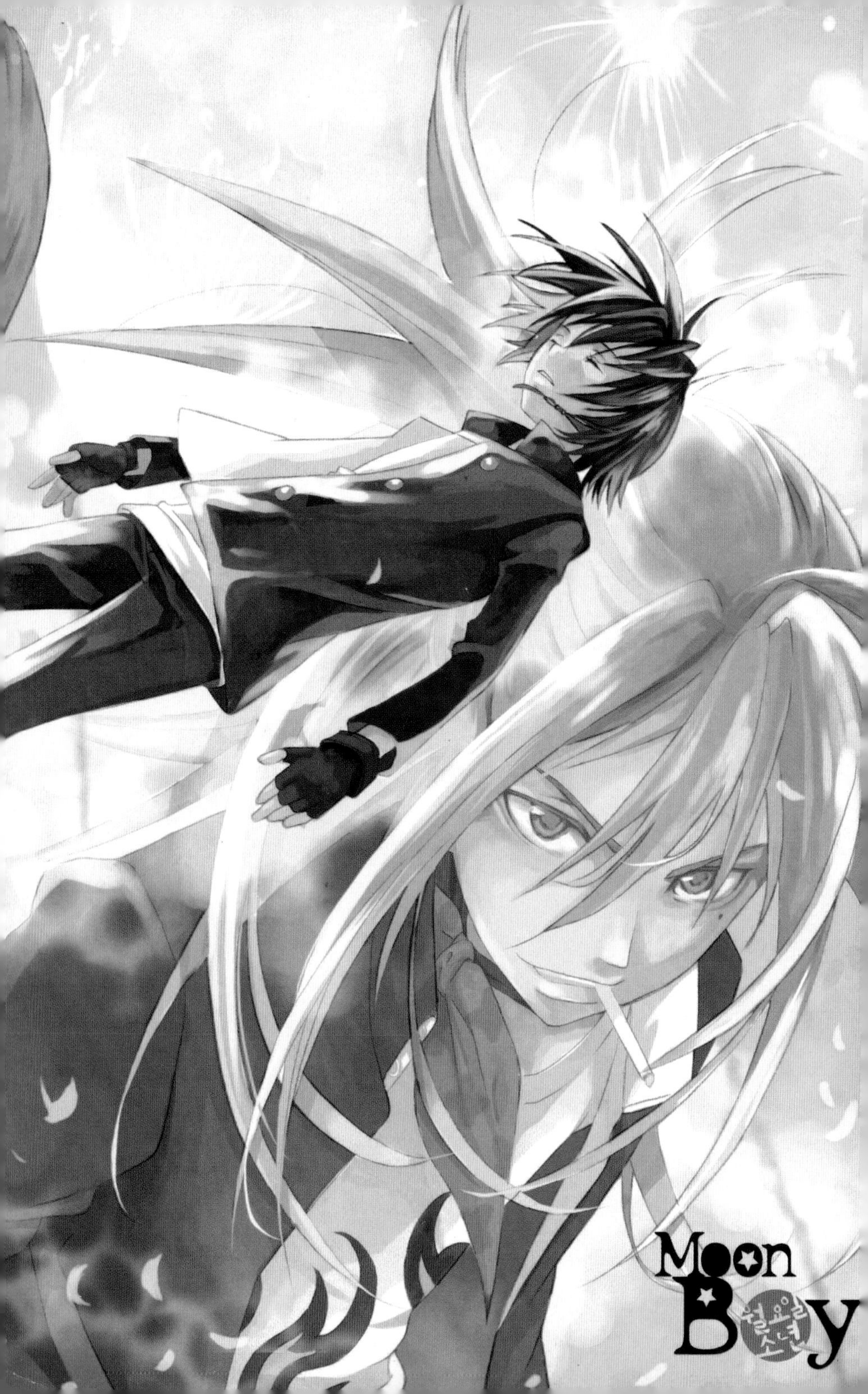
Moon Boy
월요일 소년

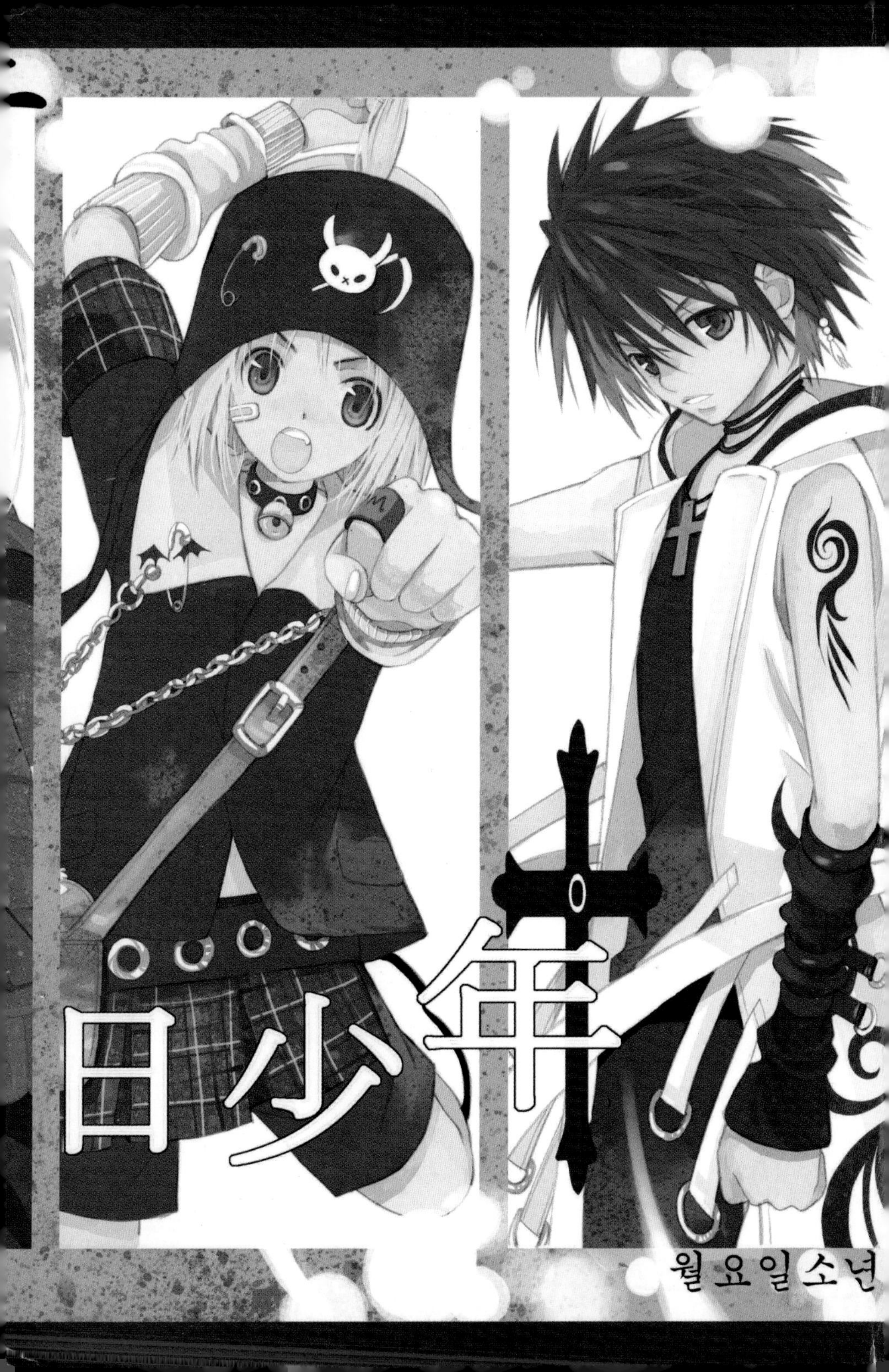
日少年
월요일소년

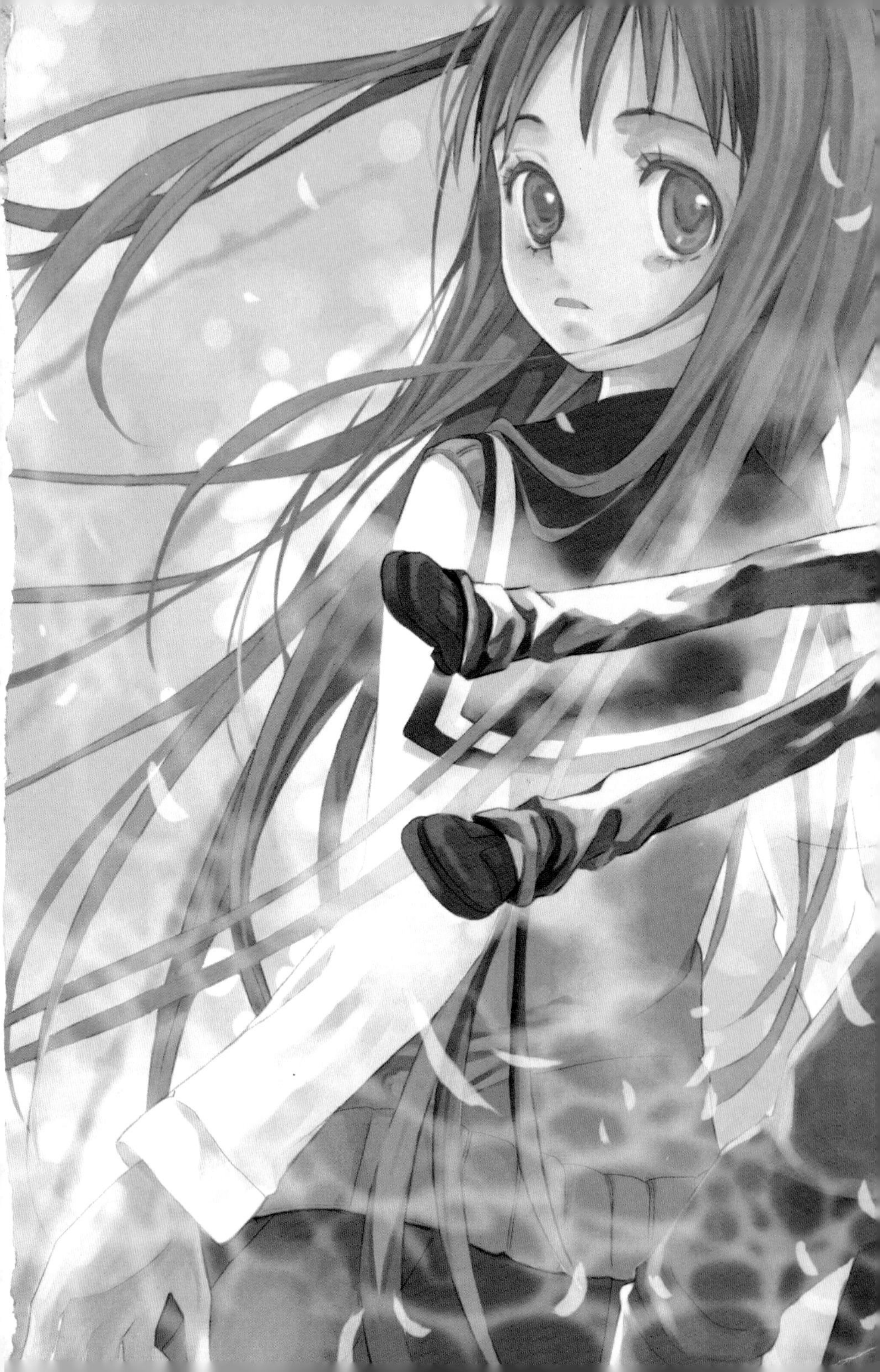

riginal · Danbi Original · Danbi Original · Danbi Original · Danbi Original · Danbi Original ·

MoonBoy 월요일 소년

vol.1

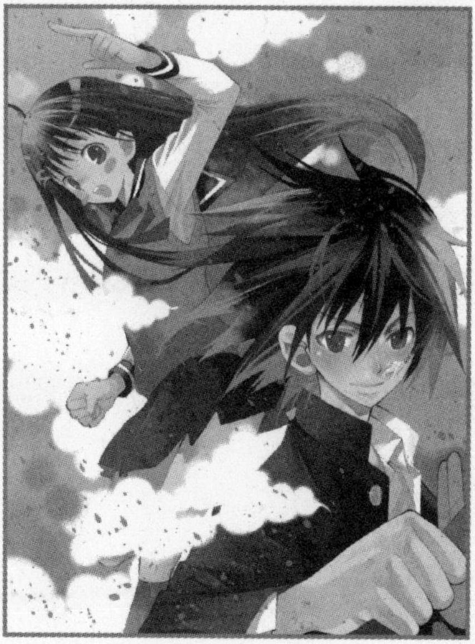

Lee YoungYou

ice
Kunion

Young-You Lee

- Born April 11(Aries), 1977 in Seoul

- Blood type : AB

- Debuted in 1998

- Major works: <K2>, <Spring, Spring>, <In the Flower Garden>

- She was a popular indy comic book writer before making her professional debut. She still writes indy comics under the penname "Yu-Gi Boy". Among her works, <K2> was her biggest hit abroad and made her a name overseas.

As I do my work, Ne-Chi lies down beneath my legs and watches me - just like in the picture below. I feel the primal energy of the universe in his gaze. In other words... Ne-Chi is so lovable. This is the first volume. But it's only the beginning...

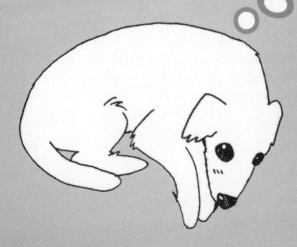

ONCE UPON A TIME...
...RABBITS LIVED ON THE MOON.
ONE DAY, GRAY-HAIRED FOXES WITH BIG MOUTHS APPEARED AND STARTED DRINKING THE RABBITS' BLOOD AND FEASTING ON THEIR LIVERS.
HWOOOOOSH
SO THE RABBITS...
...LEFT THE MOON AND CAME TO EARTH.

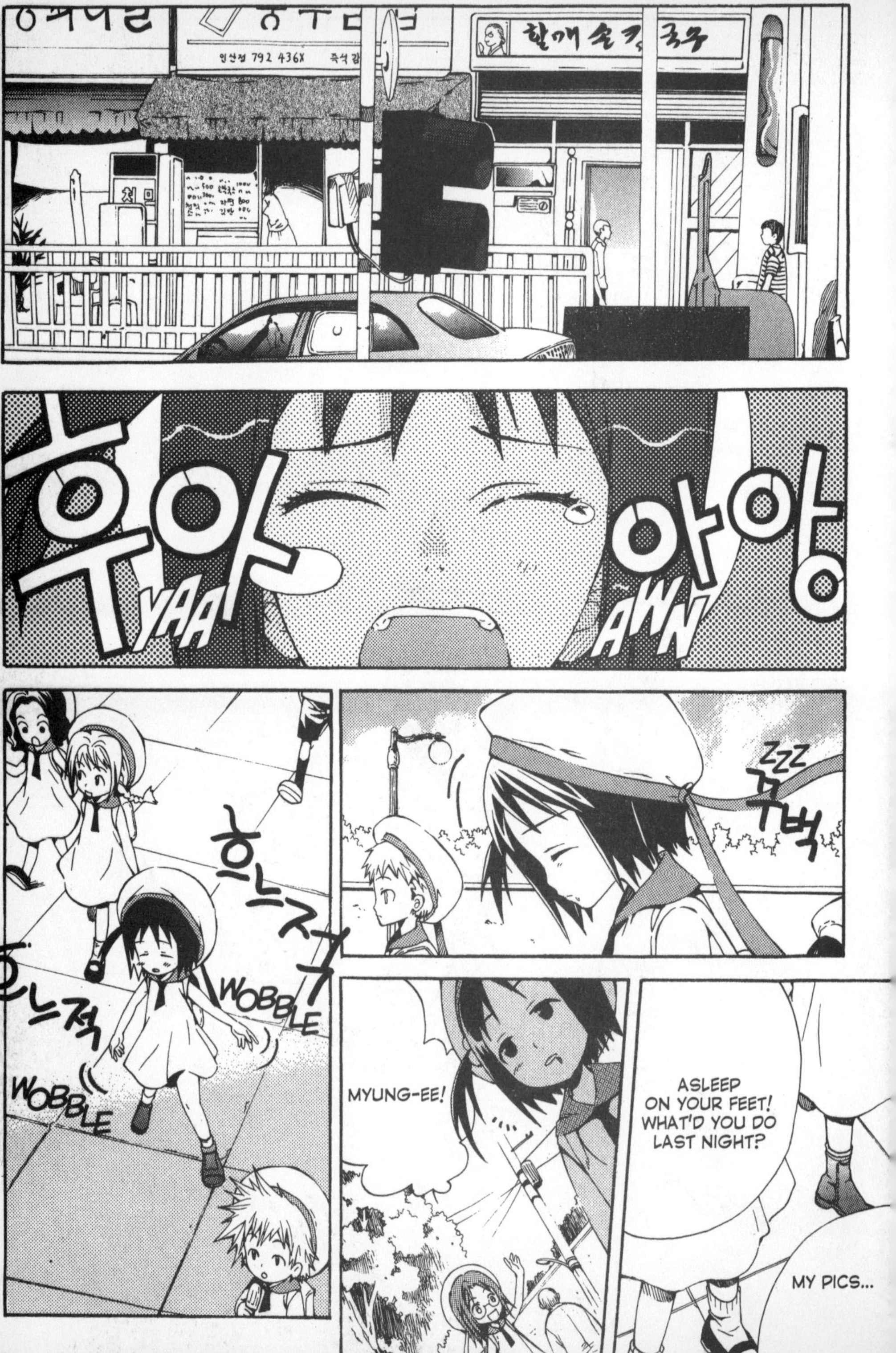

할매손칼국수
후아
YAA
AWN
아앙
흐느적
WOBBLE
흐느적
WOBBLE
ZZZ
꾸벅
MYUNG-EE!
...
ASLEEP ON YOUR FEET! WHAT'D YOU DO LAST NIGHT?
MY PICS...

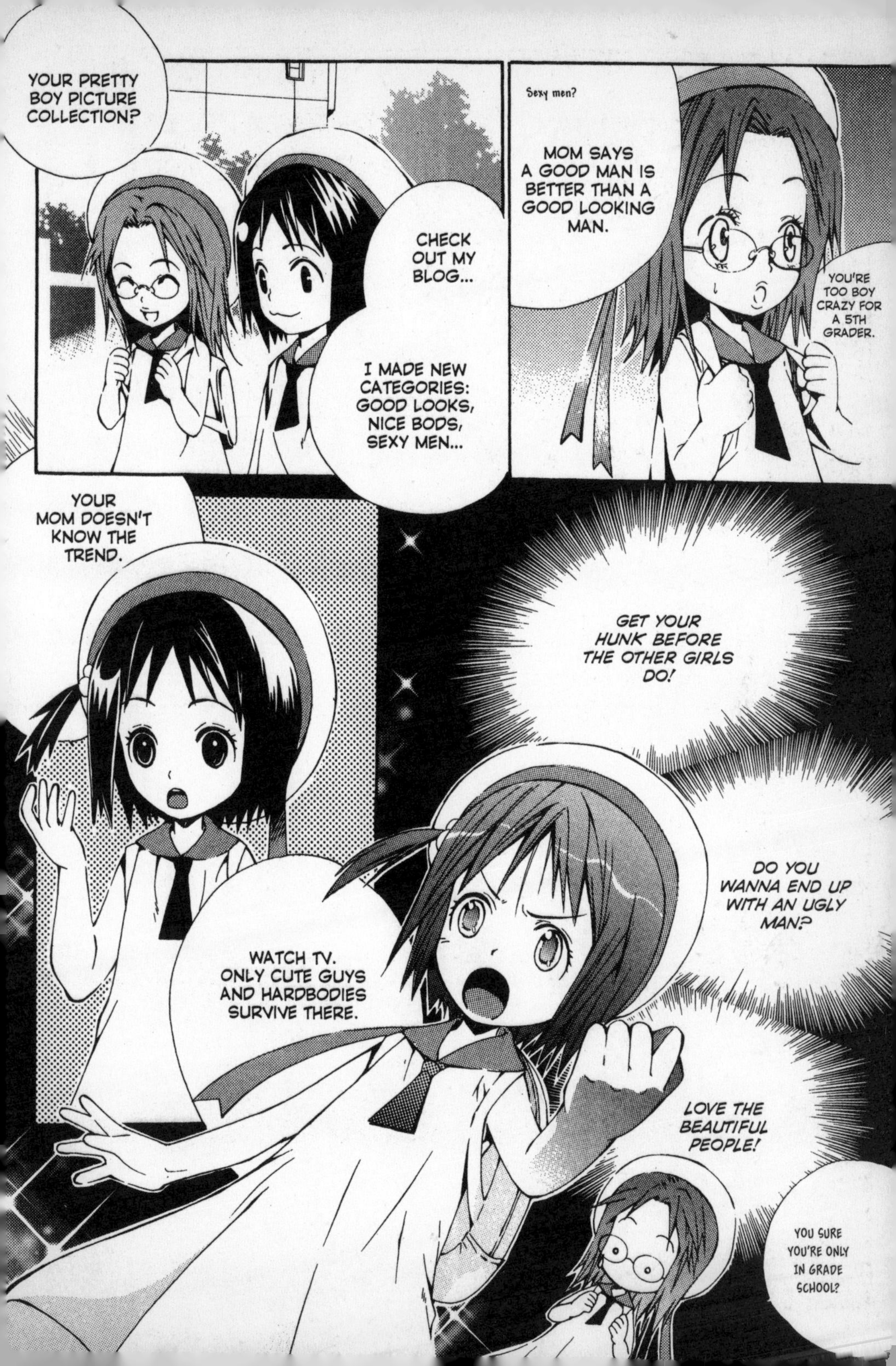
YOUR PRETTY BOY PICTURE COLLECTION?
CHECK OUT MY BLOG...
I MADE NEW CATEGORIES: GOOD LOOKS, NICE BODS, SEXY MEN...
Sexy men?
MOM SAYS A GOOD MAN IS BETTER THAN A GOOD LOOKING MAN.
YOU'RE TOO BOY CRAZY FOR A 5TH GRADER.
YOUR MOM DOESN'T KNOW THE TREND.
WATCH TV. ONLY CUTE GUYS AND HARDBODIES SURVIVE THERE.
GET YOUR HUNK BEFORE THE OTHER GIRLS DO!
DO YOU WANNA END UP WITH AN UGLY MAN?
LOVE THE BEAUTIFUL PEOPLE!
YOU SURE YOU'RE ONLY IN GRADE SCHOOL?

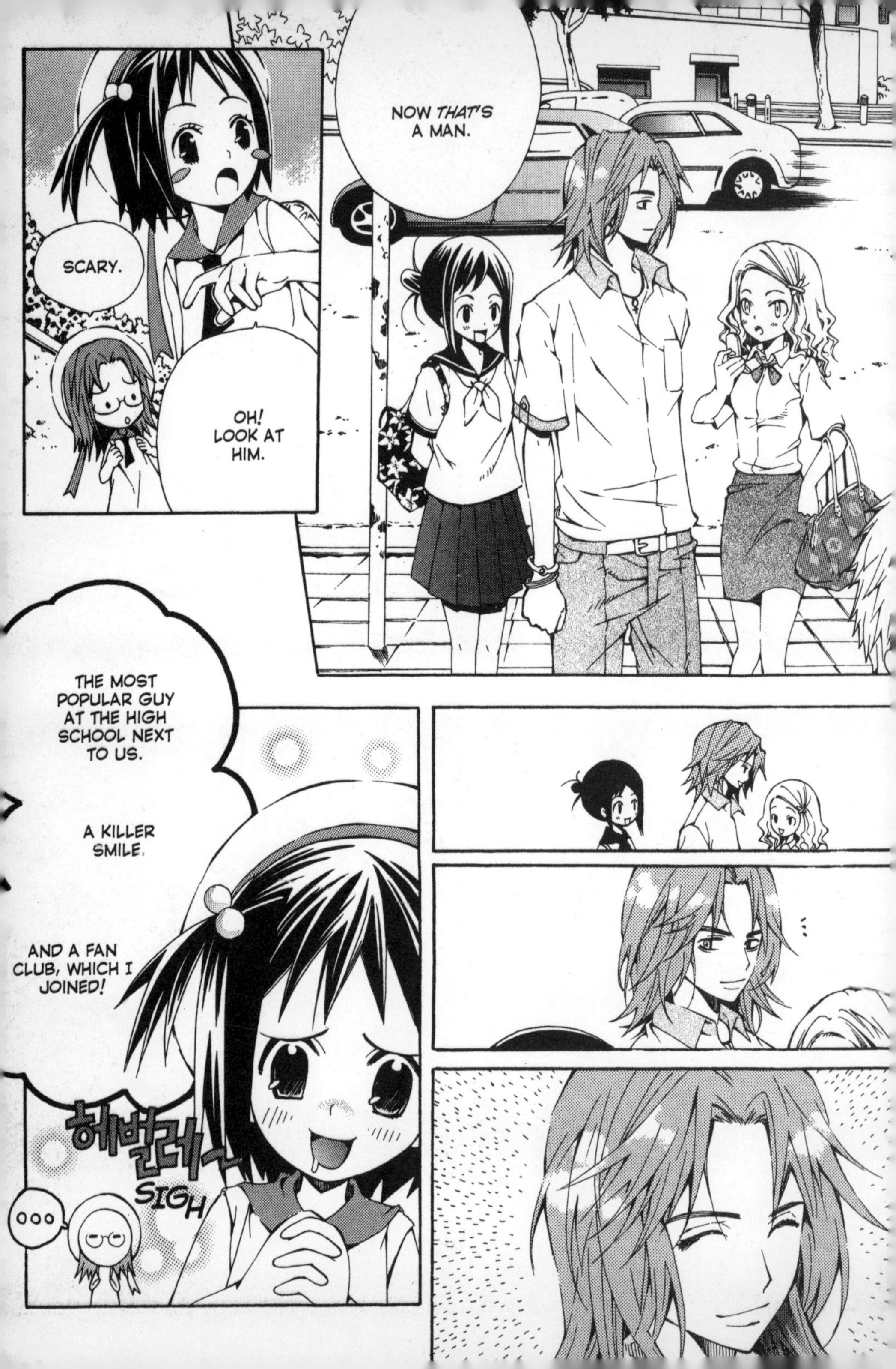

SCARY.
NOW THAT'S A MAN.
OH! LOOK AT HIM.
THE MOST POPULAR GUY AT THE HIGH SCHOOL NEXT TO US.
A KILLER SMILE.
AND A FAN CLUB, WHICH I JOINED!
헤벌레~
SIGH
...

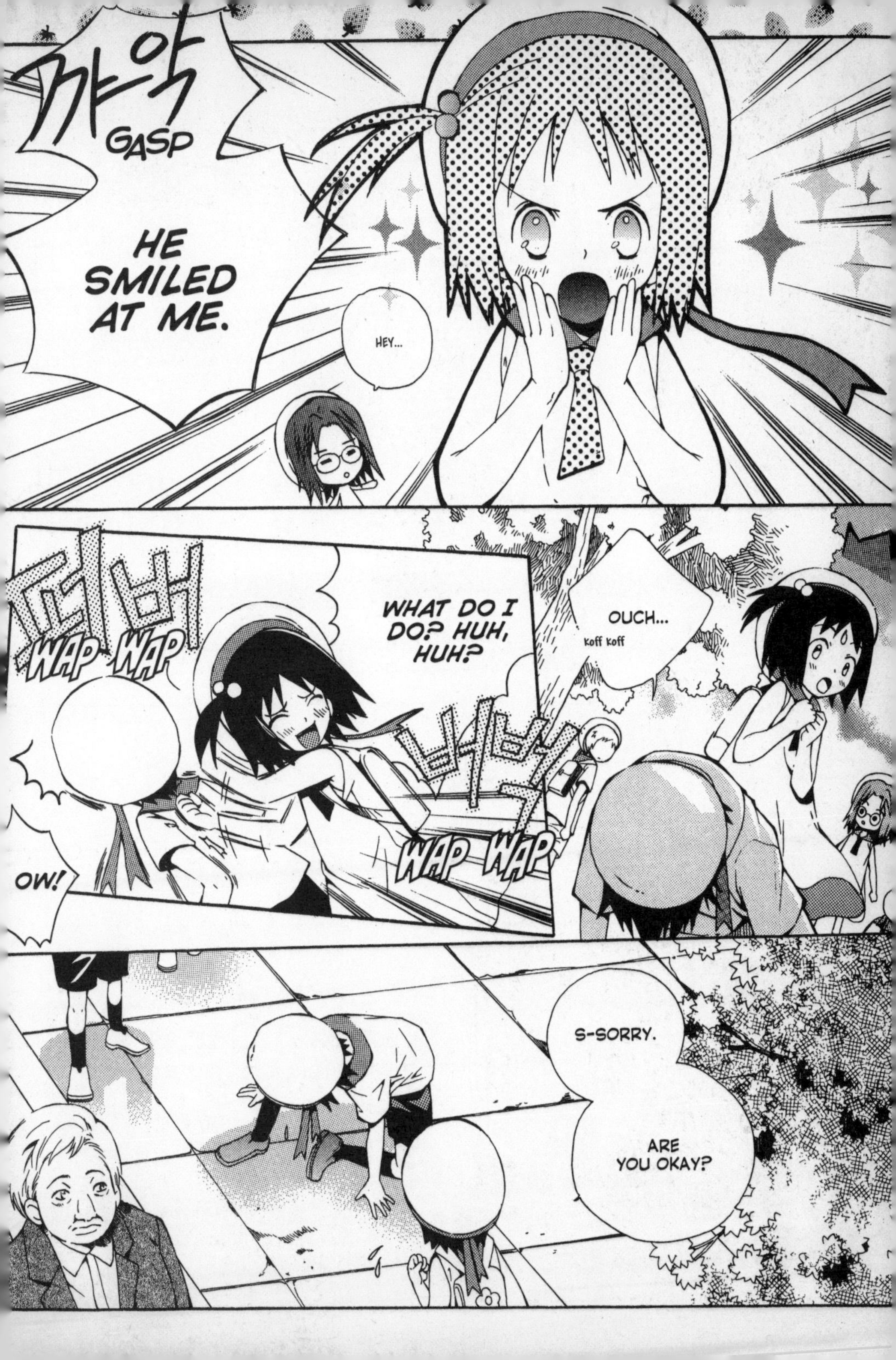
꺄악
GASP
HE SMILED AT ME.
HEY...
WAP WAP
OW!
WHAT DO I DO? HUH, HUH?
WAP WAP
OUCH...
Koff Koff
S-SORRY.
ARE YOU OKAY?

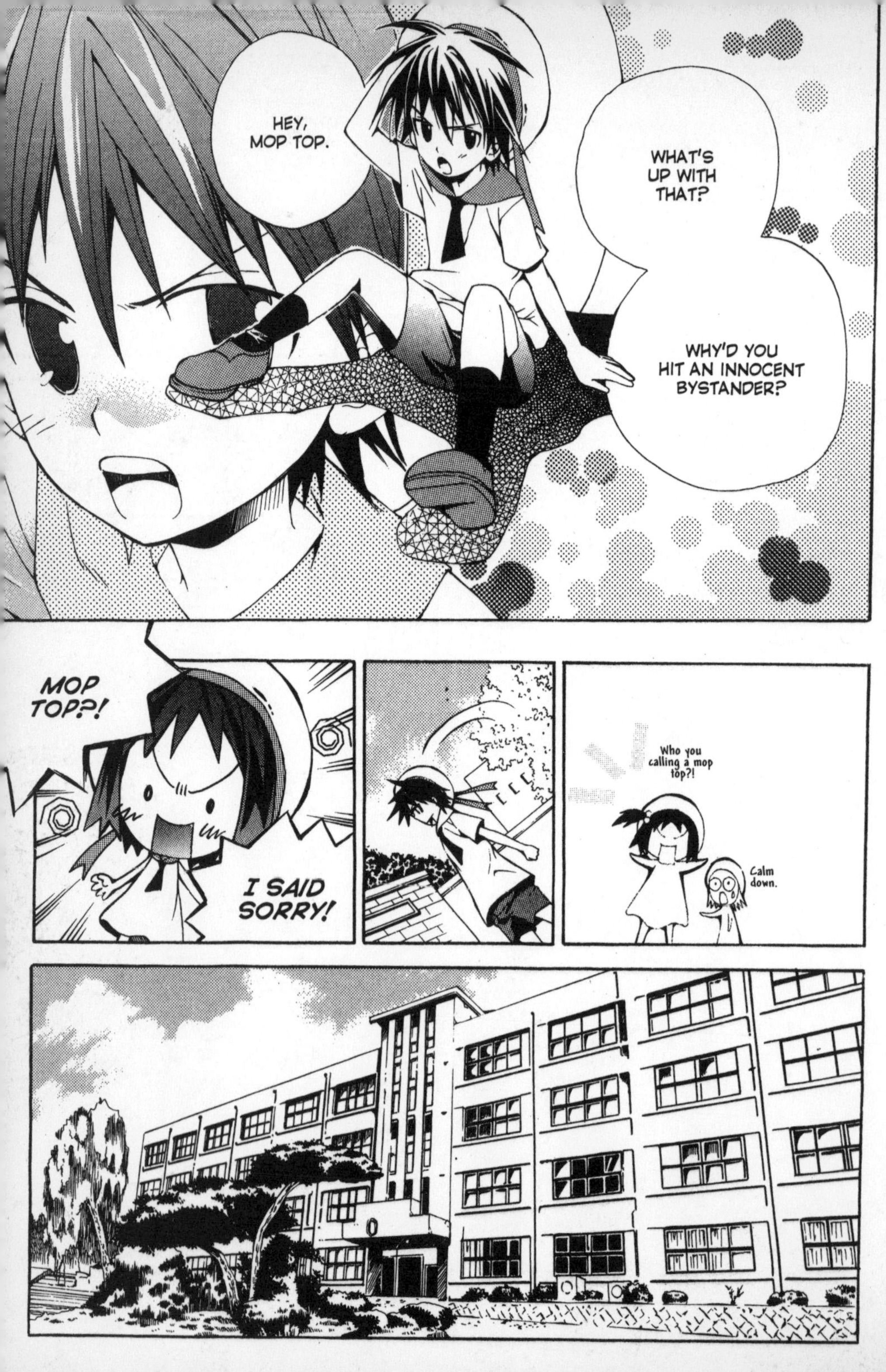
HEY, MOP TOP.
WHAT'S UP WITH THAT?
WHY'D YOU HIT AN INNOCENT BYSTANDER?
MOP TOP?!
I SAID SORRY!
Who you calling a mop top?!
Calm down.

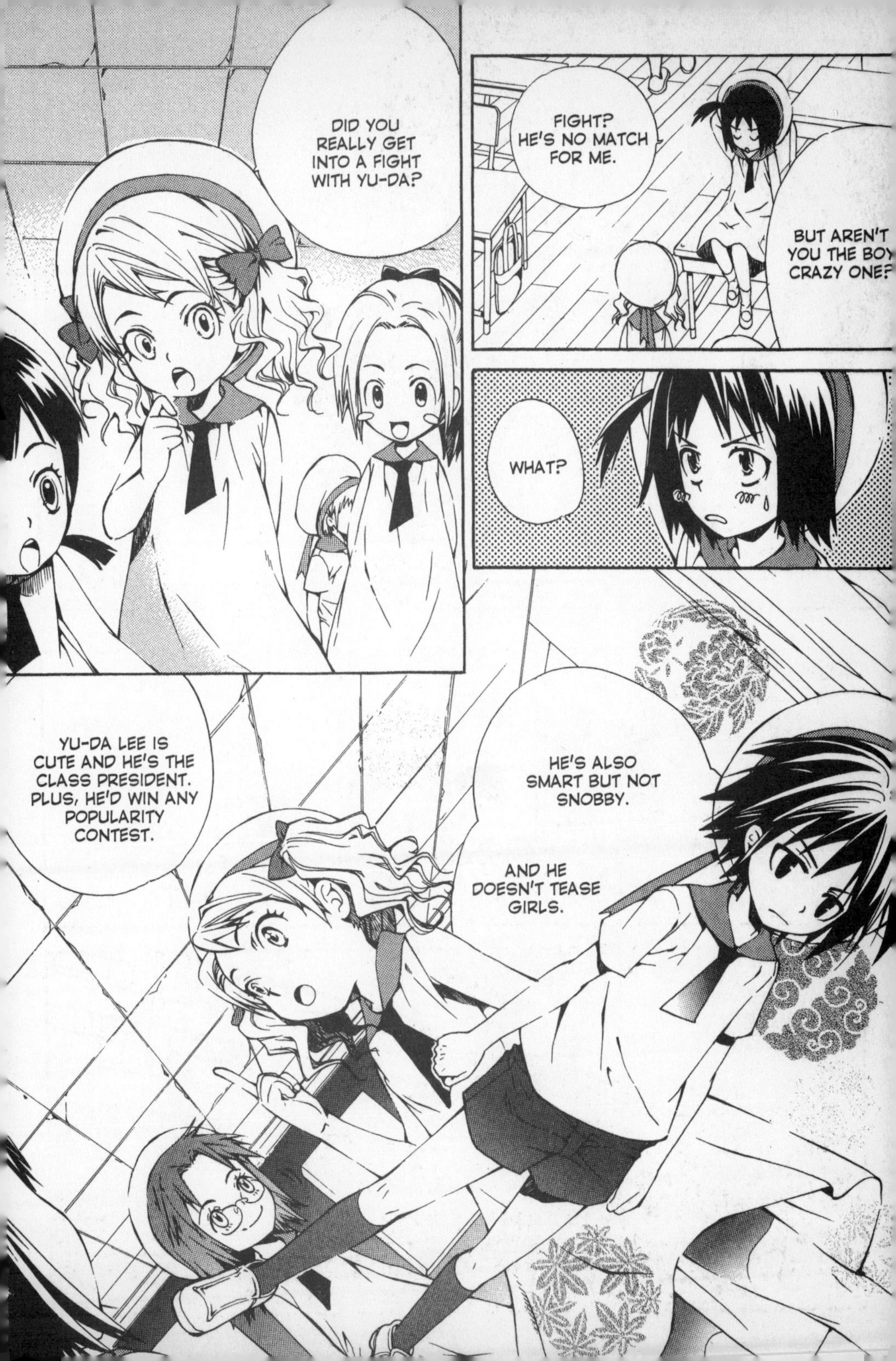
FIGHT? HE'S NO MATCH FOR ME.
BUT AREN'T YOU THE BOY CRAZY ONE?
DID YOU REALLY GET INTO A FIGHT WITH YU-DA?
WHAT?
HE'S ALSO SMART BUT NOT SNOBBY.
AND HE DOESN'T TEASE GIRLS.
YU-DA LEE IS CUTE AND HE'S THE CLASS PRESIDENT. PLUS, HE'D WIN ANY POPULARITY CONTEST.

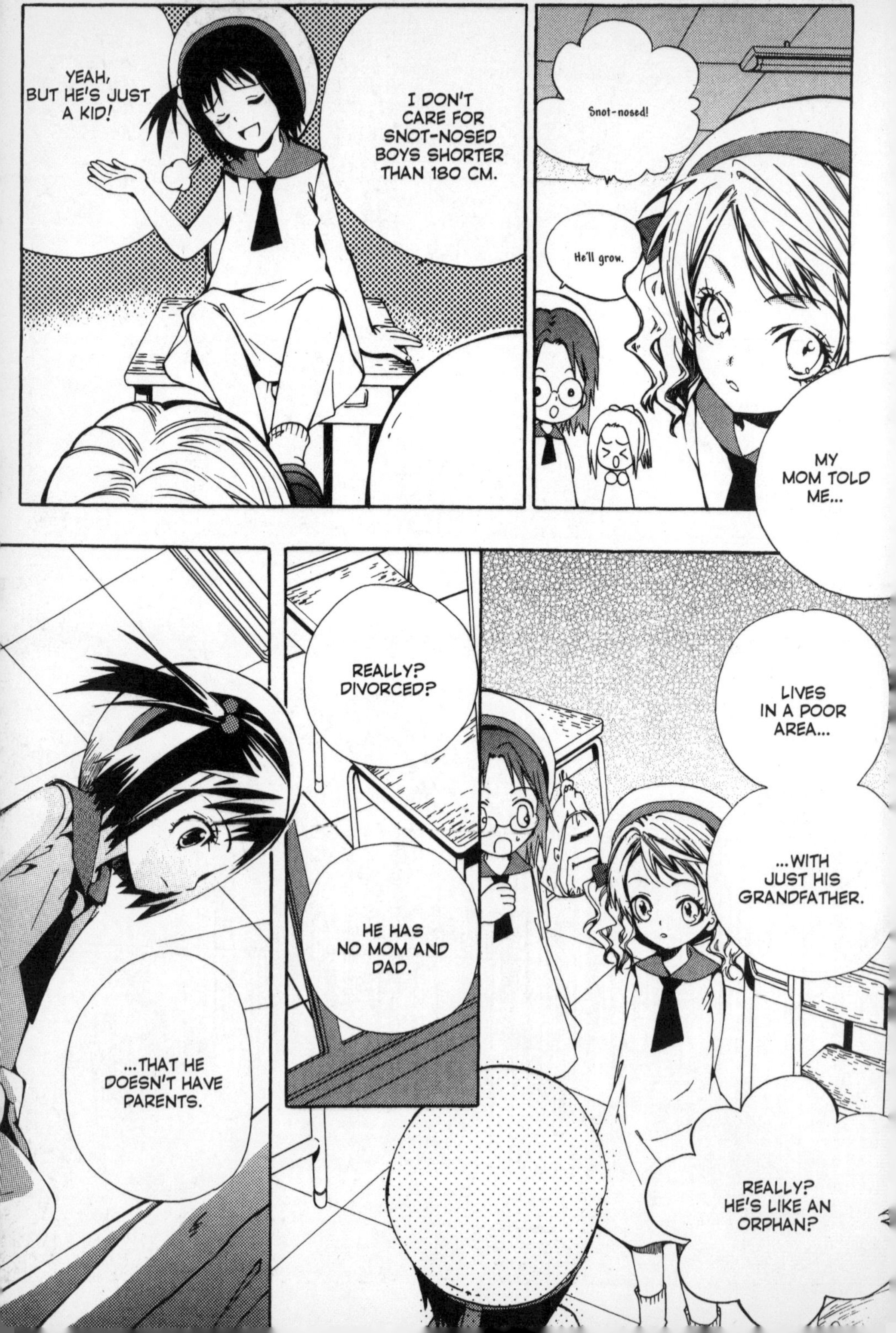
YEAH, BUT HE'S JUST A KID!
I DON'T CARE FOR SNOT-NOSED BOYS SHORTER THAN 180 CM.
Snot-nosed!
He'll grow.
MY MOM TOLD ME...
...THAT HE DOESN'T HAVE PARENTS.
REALLY? DIVORCED?
HE HAS NO MOM AND DAD.
LIVES IN A POOR AREA...
...WITH JUST HIS GRANDFATHER.
REALLY? HE'S LIKE AN ORPHAN?

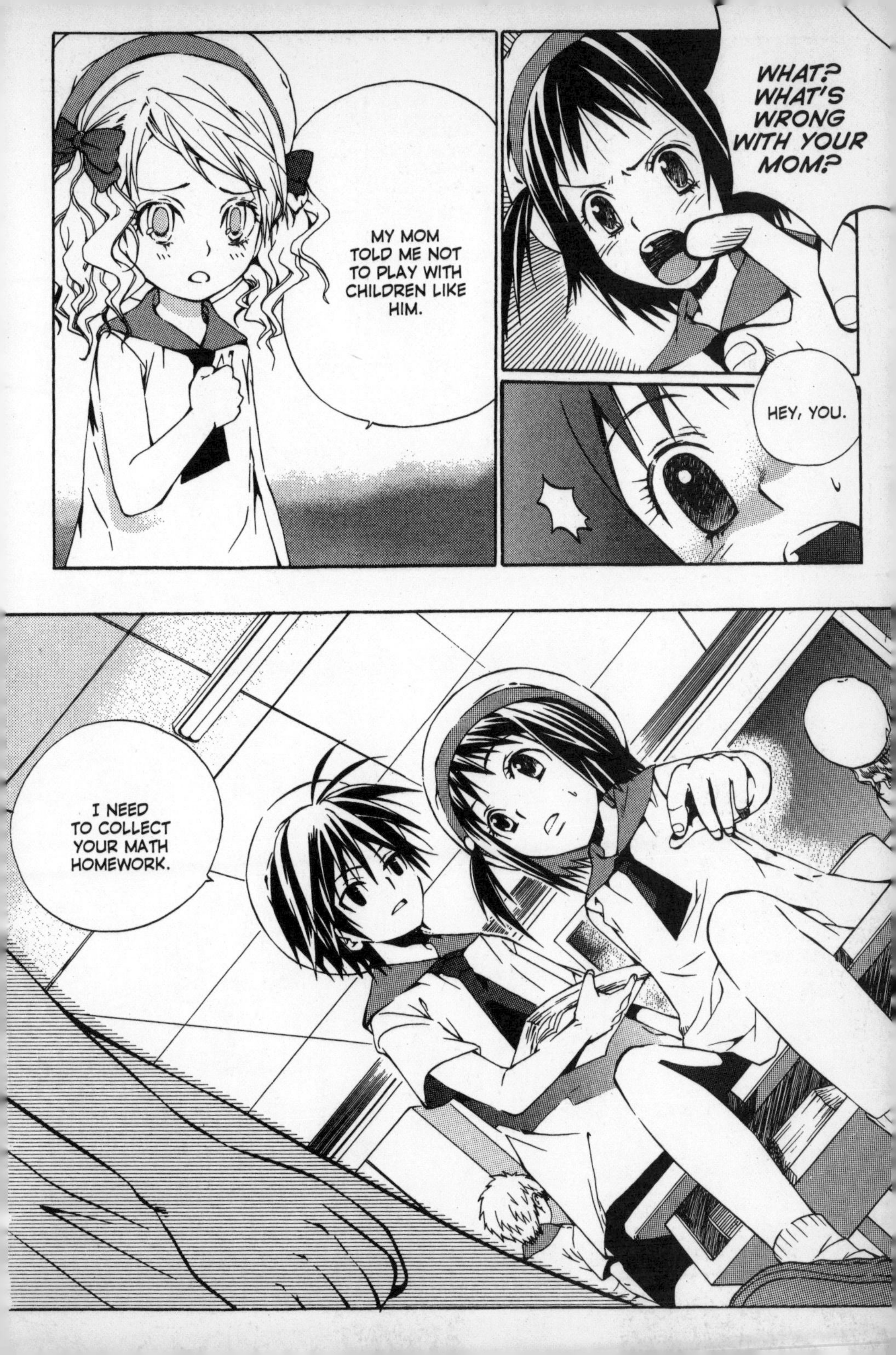
WHAT? WHAT'S WRONG WITH YOUR MOM?
MY MOM TOLD ME NOT TO PLAY WITH CHILDREN LIKE HIM.
HEY, YOU.
I NEED TO COLLECT YOUR MATH HOMEWORK.

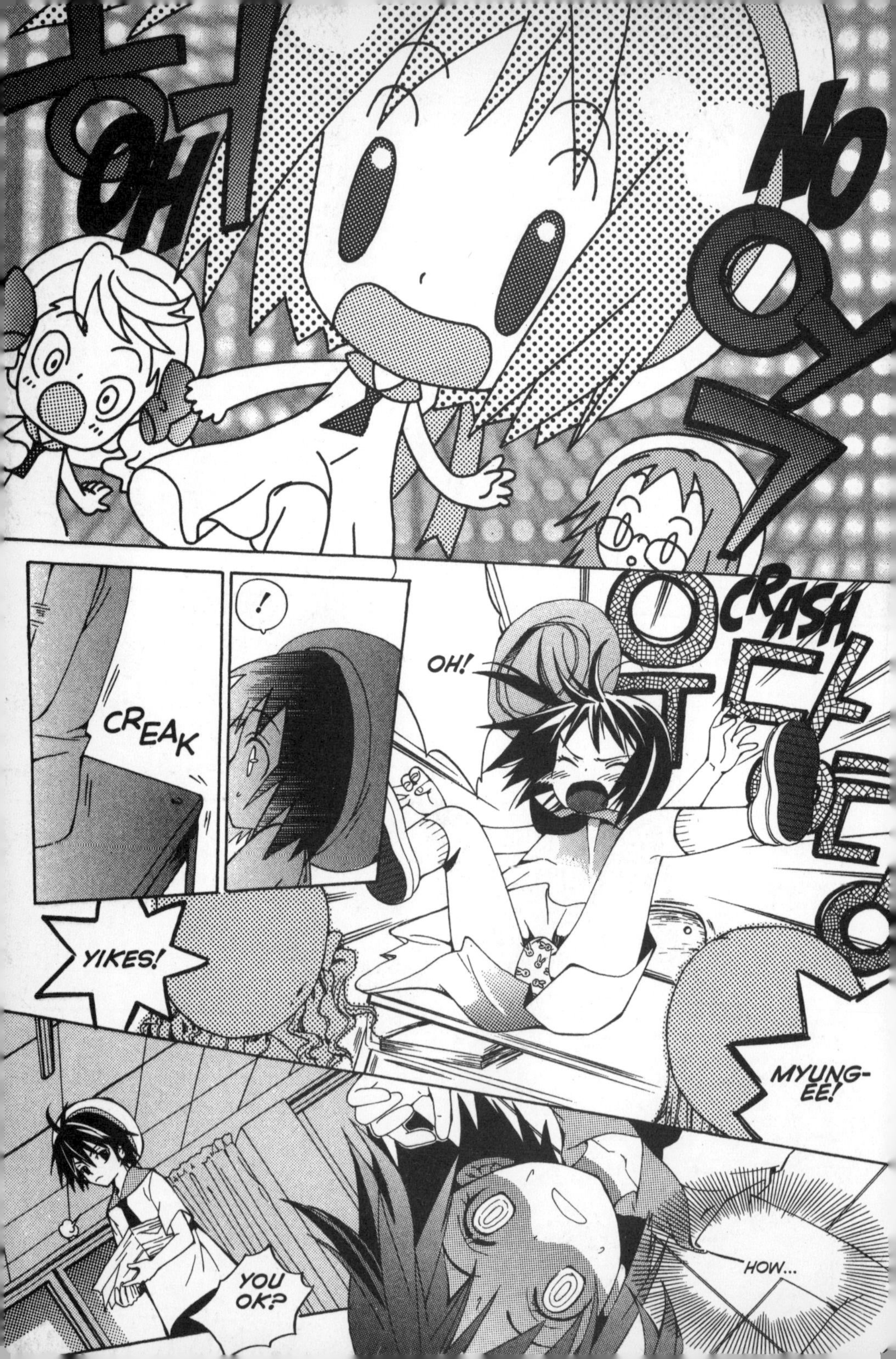
NO
OH!
!
CREAK
CRASH
OH!
YIKES!
MYUNG-EE!
HOW...
YOU OK?

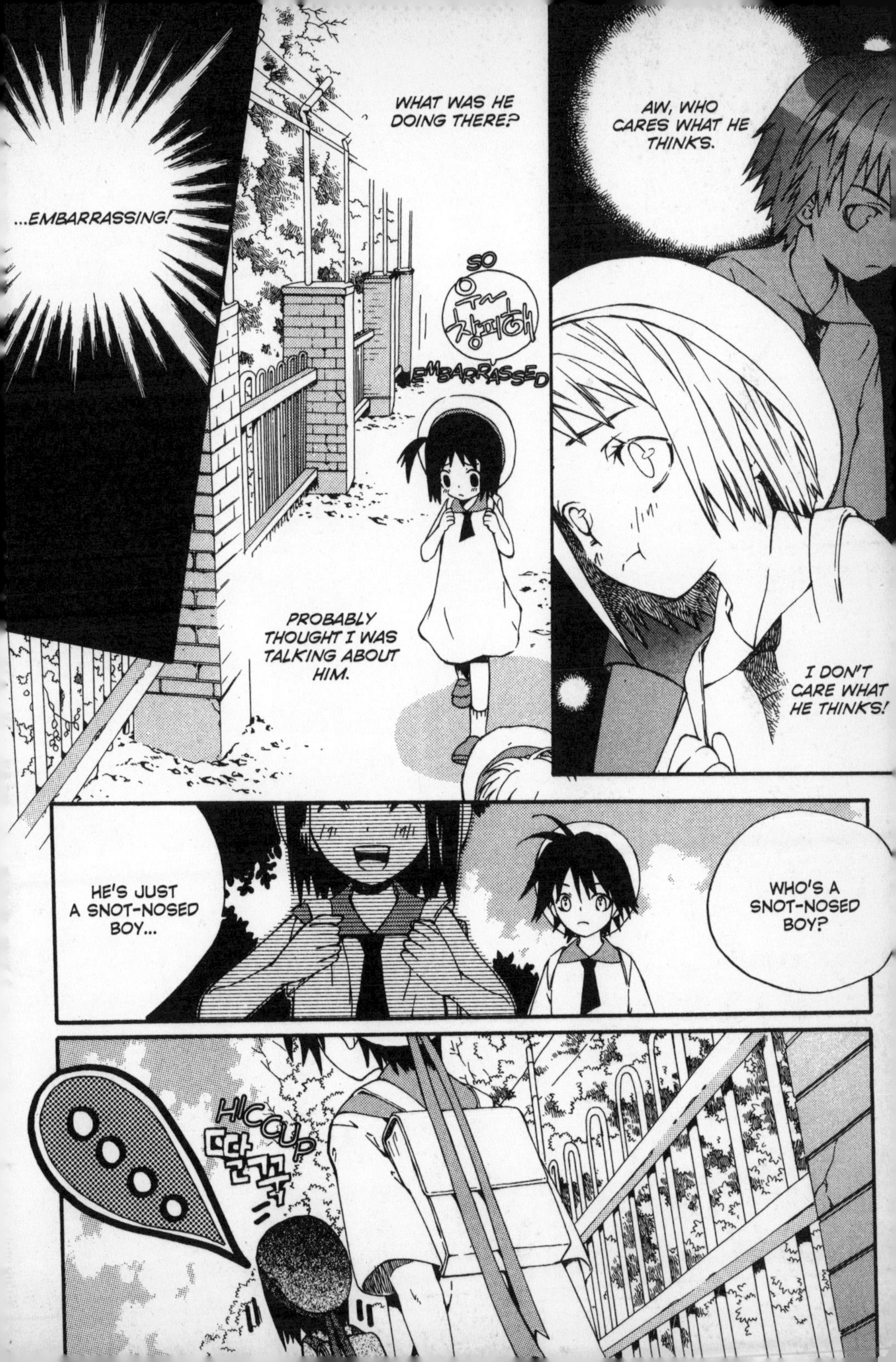

...EMBARRASSING!
WHAT WAS HE DOING THERE?
SO 우~ 창피해 EMBARRASSED
PROBABLY THOUGHT I WAS TALKING ABOUT HIM.
AW, WHO CARES WHAT HE THINKS.
I DON'T CARE WHAT HE THINKS!
HE'S JUST A SNOT-NOSED BOY...
WHO'S A SNOT-NOSED BOY?
HICCUP 딸꾹

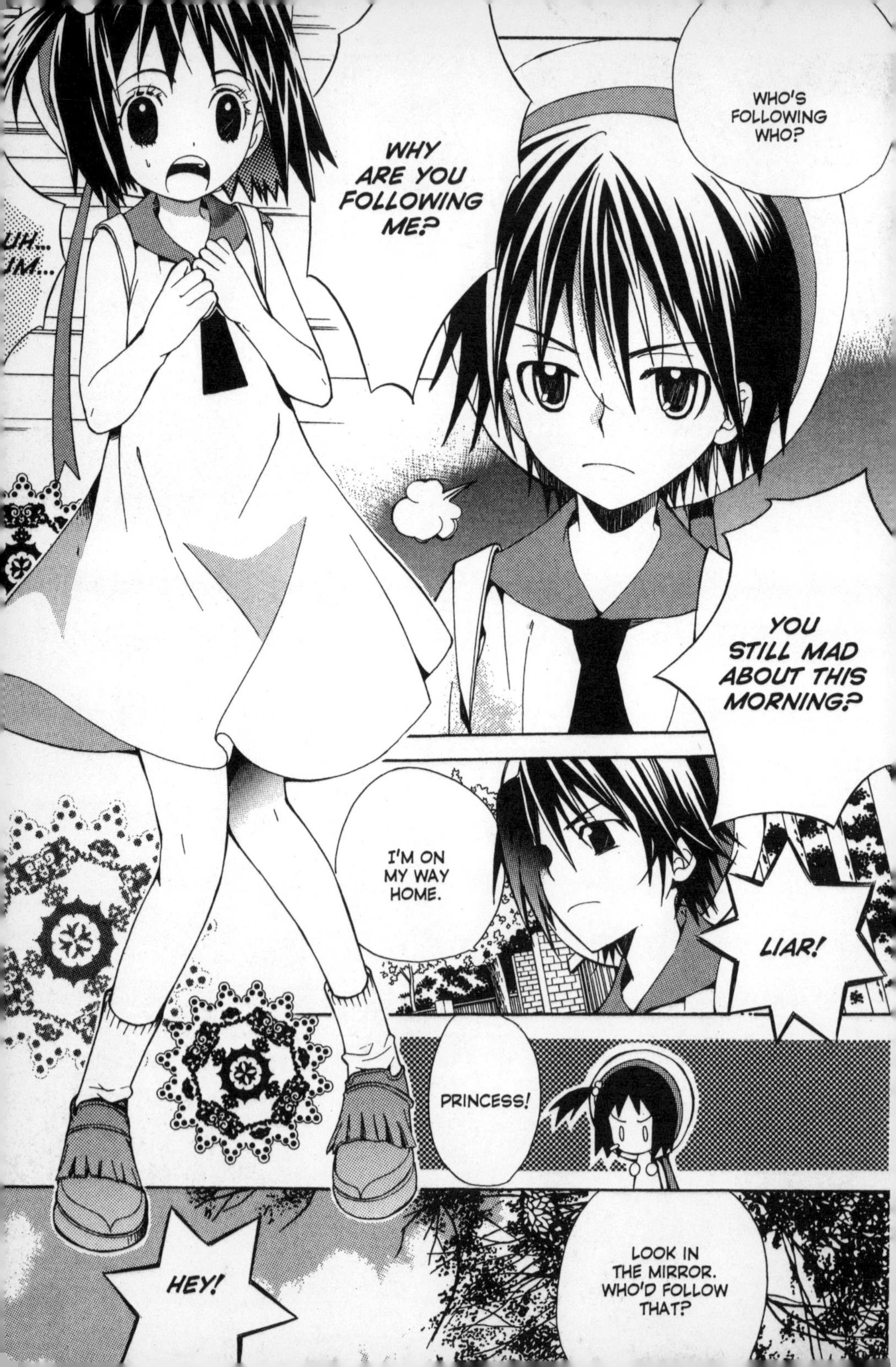
UH... UM...
WHY ARE YOU FOLLOWING ME?
WHO'S FOLLOWING WHO?
YOU STILL MAD ABOUT THIS MORNING?
LIAR!
I'M ON MY WAY HOME.
PRINCESS!
LOOK IN THE MIRROR. WHO'D FOLLOW THAT?
HEY!

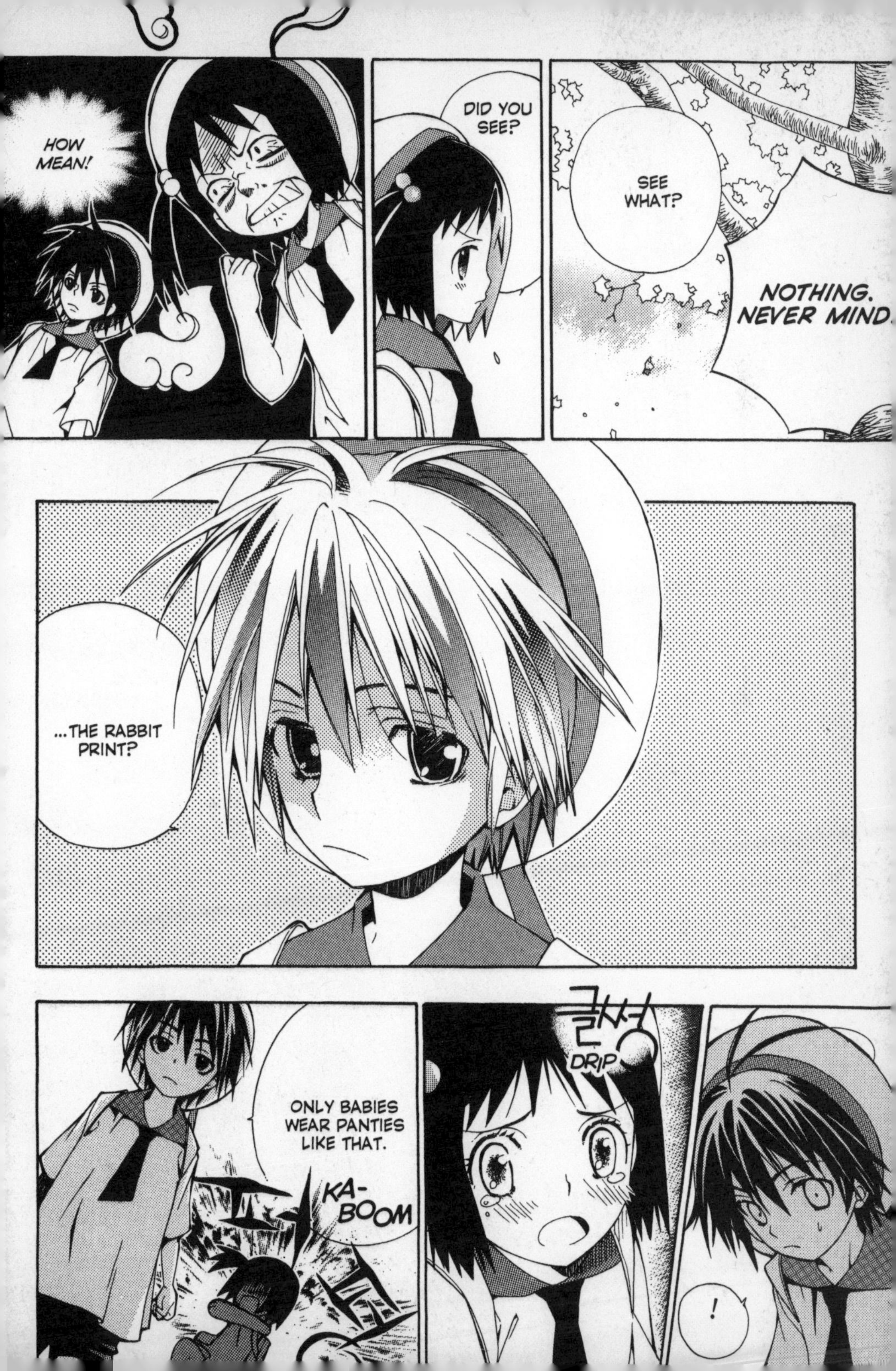
HOW MEAN!
DID YOU SEE?
SEE WHAT?
NOTHING. NEVER MIND.
...THE RABBIT PRINT?
ONLY BABIES WEAR PANTIES LIKE THAT.
KA-BOOM
글썽
DRIP
!

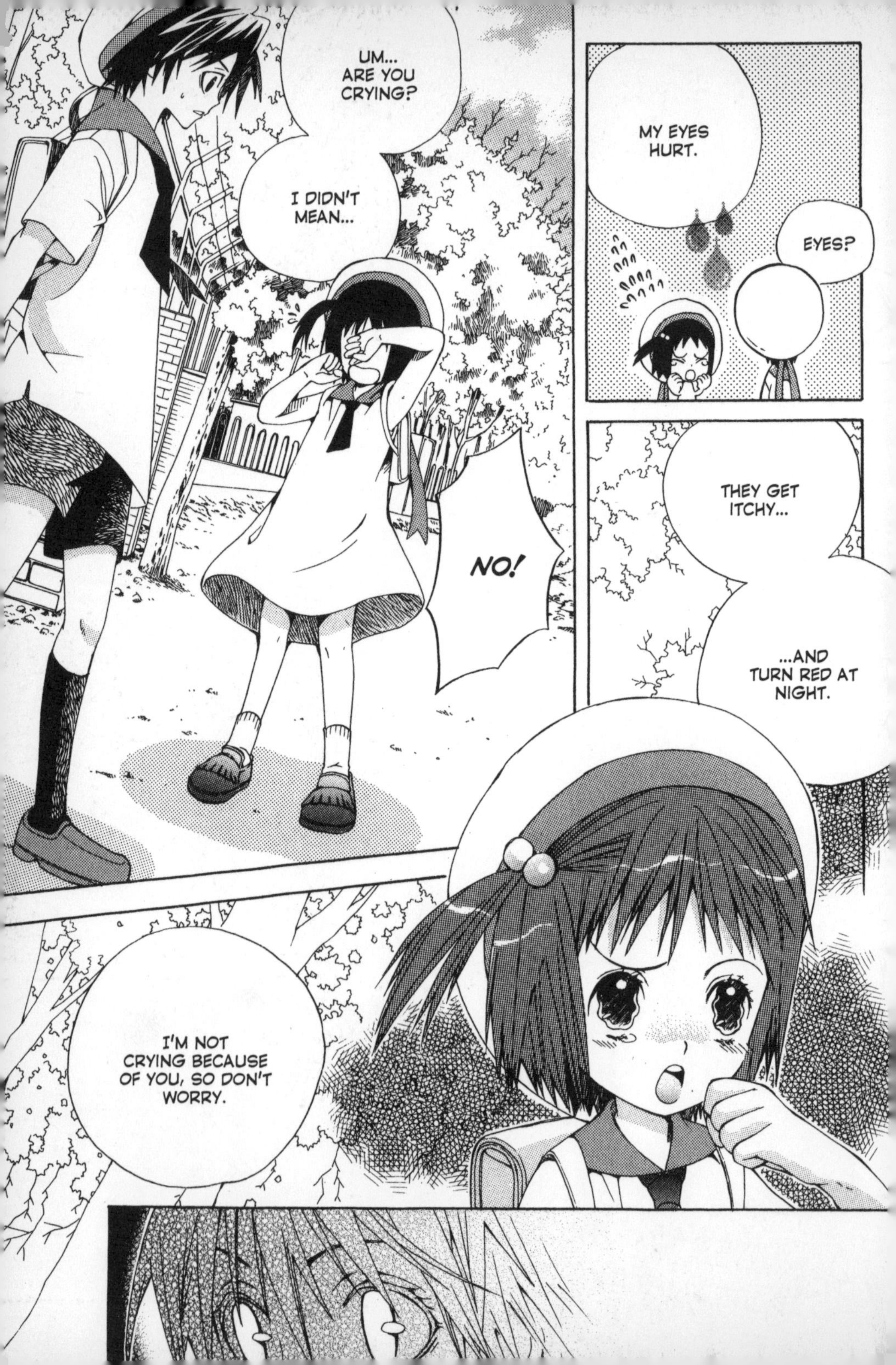
UM... ARE YOU CRYING?
I DIDN'T MEAN...
NO!
MY EYES HURT.
EYES?
THEY GET ITCHY...
...AND TURN RED AT NIGHT.
I'M NOT CRYING BECAUSE OF YOU, SO DON'T WORRY.

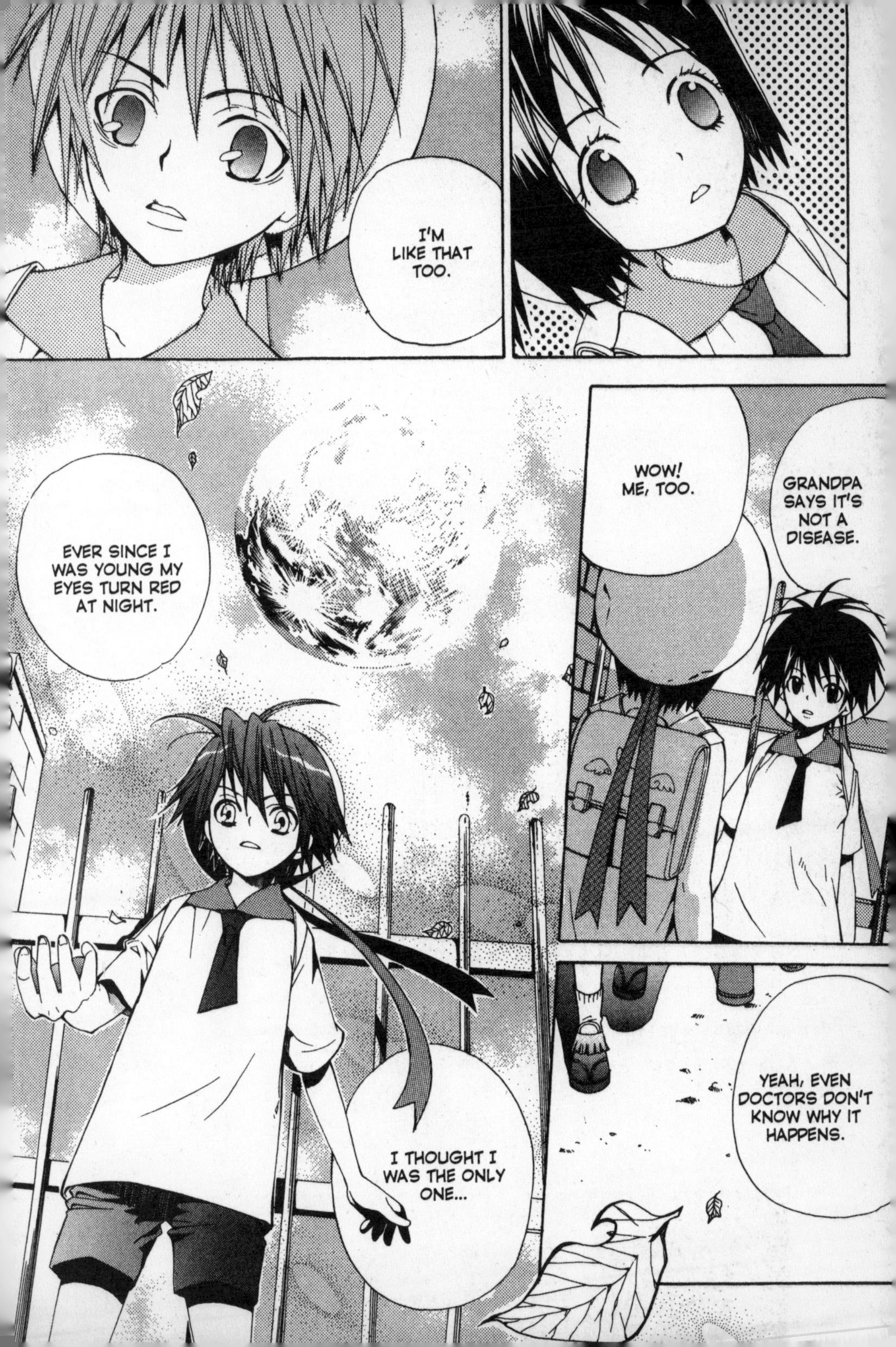
I'M LIKE THAT TOO.
EVER SINCE I WAS YOUNG MY EYES TURN RED AT NIGHT.
WOW! ME, TOO.
GRANDPA SAYS IT'S NOT A DISEASE.
YEAH, EVEN DOCTORS DON'T KNOW WHY IT HAPPENS.
I THOUGHT I WAS THE ONLY ONE...

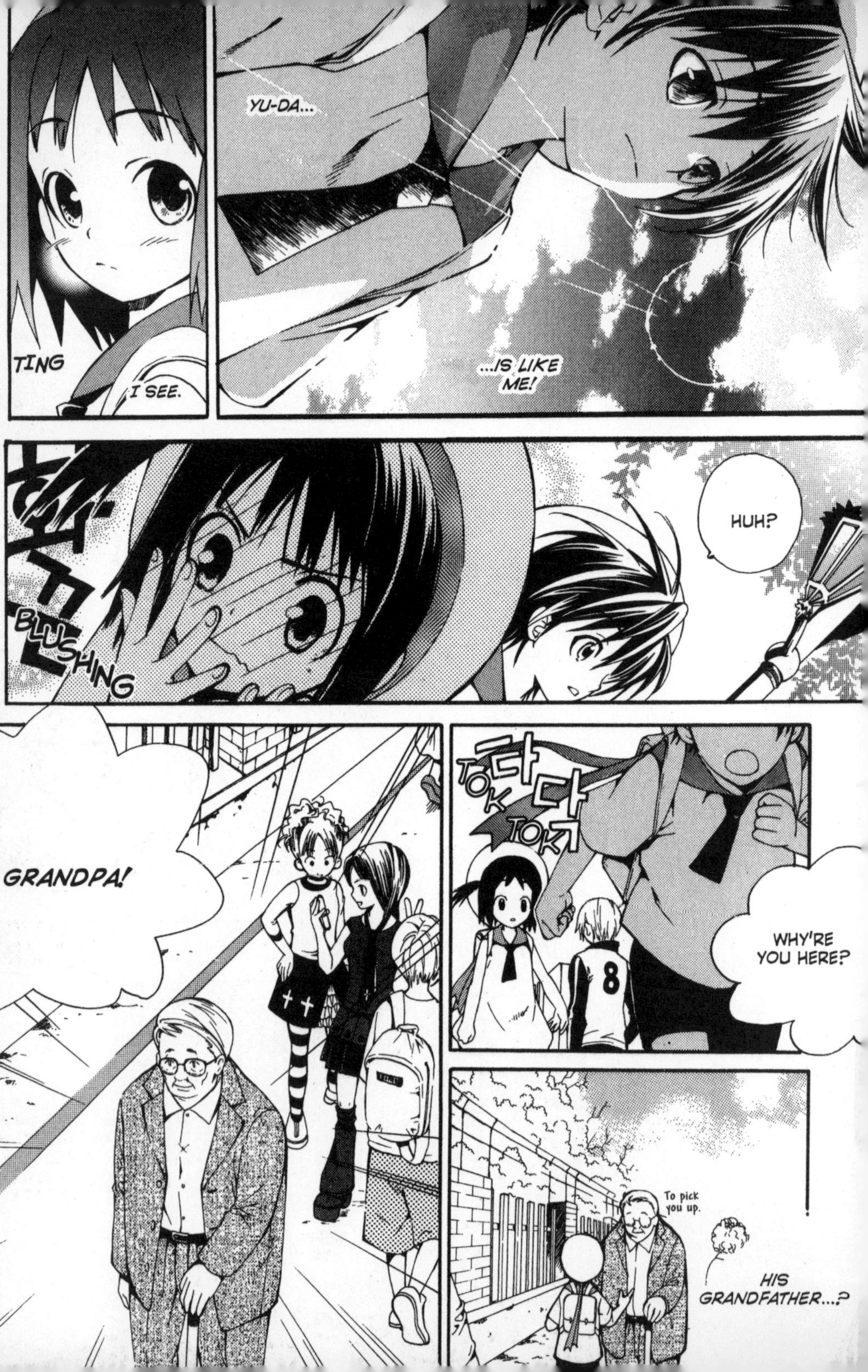
TING
I SEE.
YU-DA...
...IS LIKE ME!
BLUSHING
HUH?
GRANDPA!
TOK TOK
WHY'RE YOU HERE?
To pick you up.
HIS GRANDFATHER...?

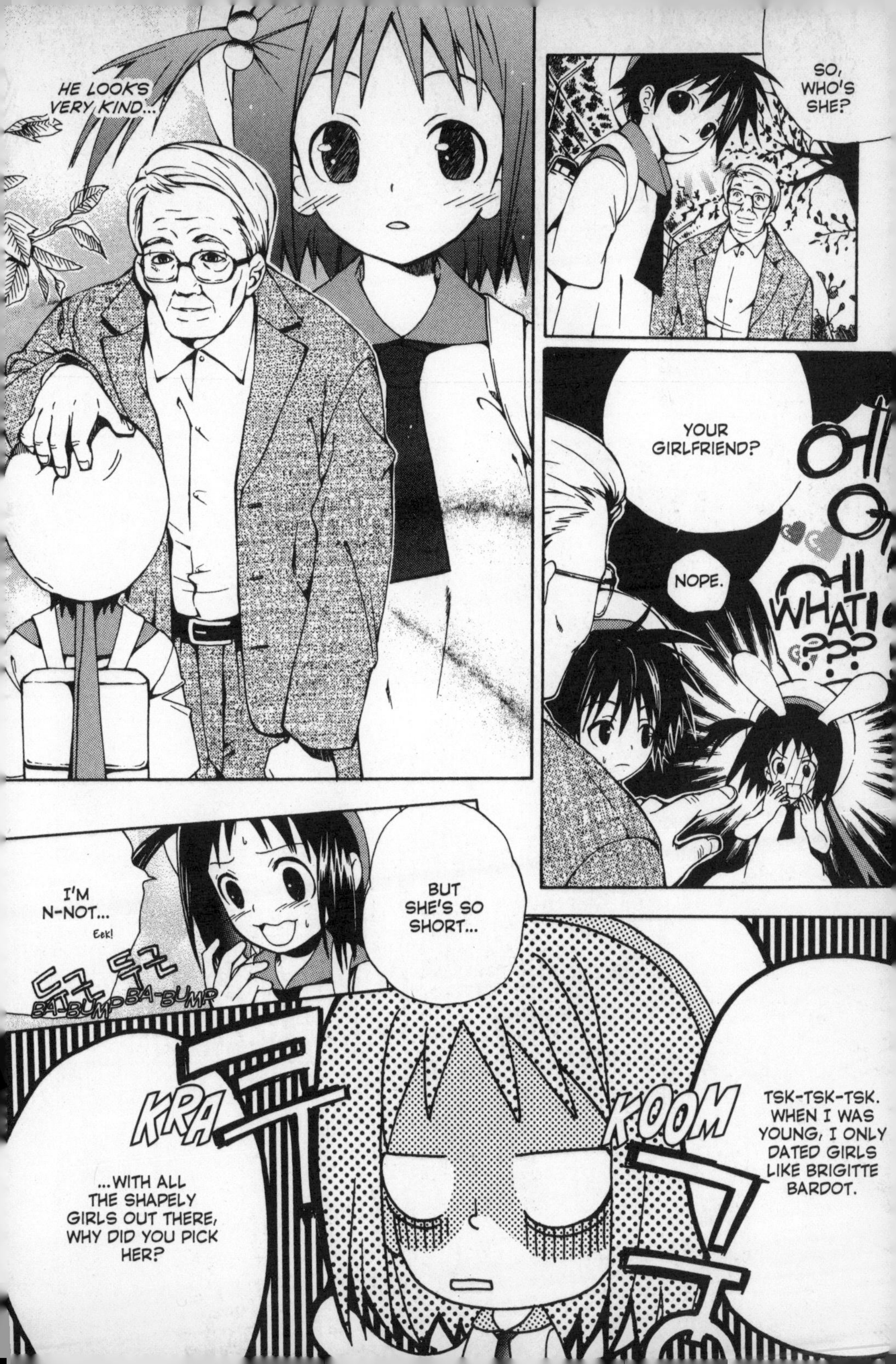
HE LOOKS VERY KIND...
SO, WHO'S SHE?
YOUR GIRLFRIEND?
NOPE.
WHAT???
I'M N-NOT...
Eek!
BA-BUMP BA-BUMP
BUT SHE'S SO SHORT...
KRA-KOOM
TSK-TSK-TSK. WHEN I WAS YOUNG, I ONLY DATED GIRLS LIKE BRIGITTE BARDOT.
...WITH ALL THE SHAPELY GIRLS OUT THERE, WHY DID YOU PICK HER?

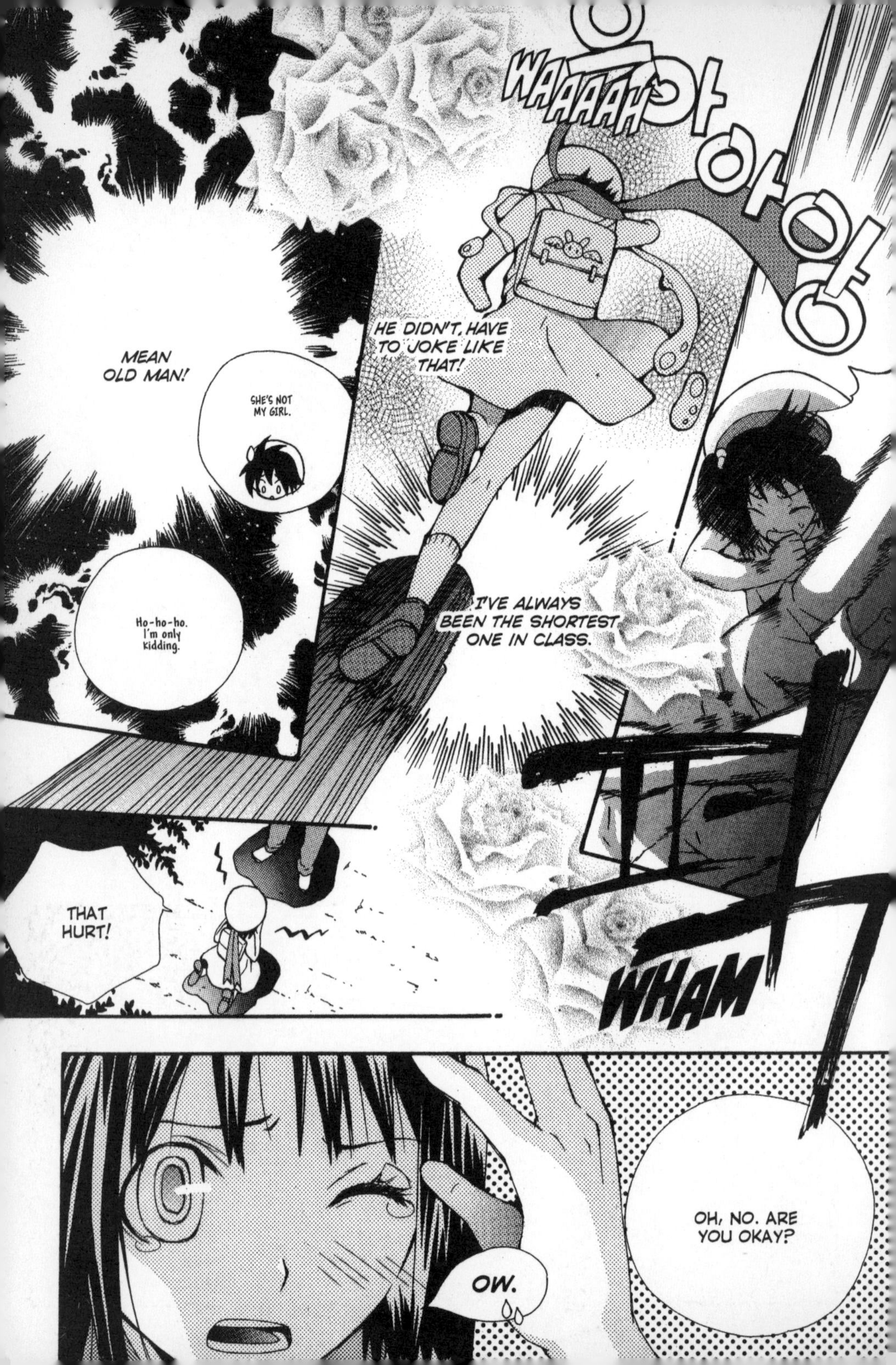
WAAAAH
HE DIDN'T HAVE TO JOKE LIKE THAT!
I'VE ALWAYS BEEN THE SHORTEST ONE IN CLASS.
WHAM
SHE'S NOT MY GIRL.
MEAN OLD MAN!
Ho-ho-ho. I'm only kidding.
THAT HURT!
OH, NO. ARE YOU OKAY?
OW.

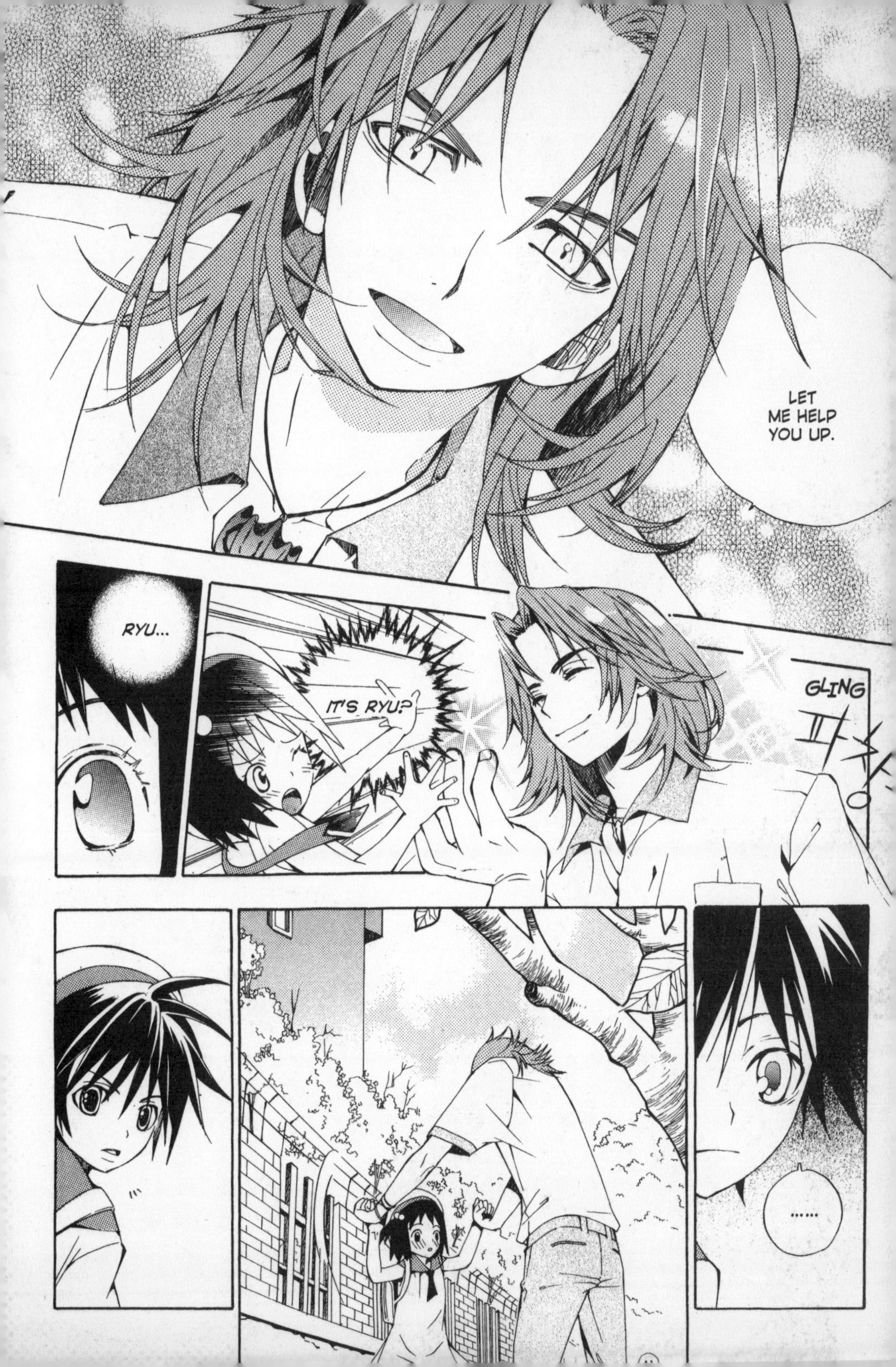
LET ME HELP YOU UP.
RYU...
IT'S RYU?
GLING
......

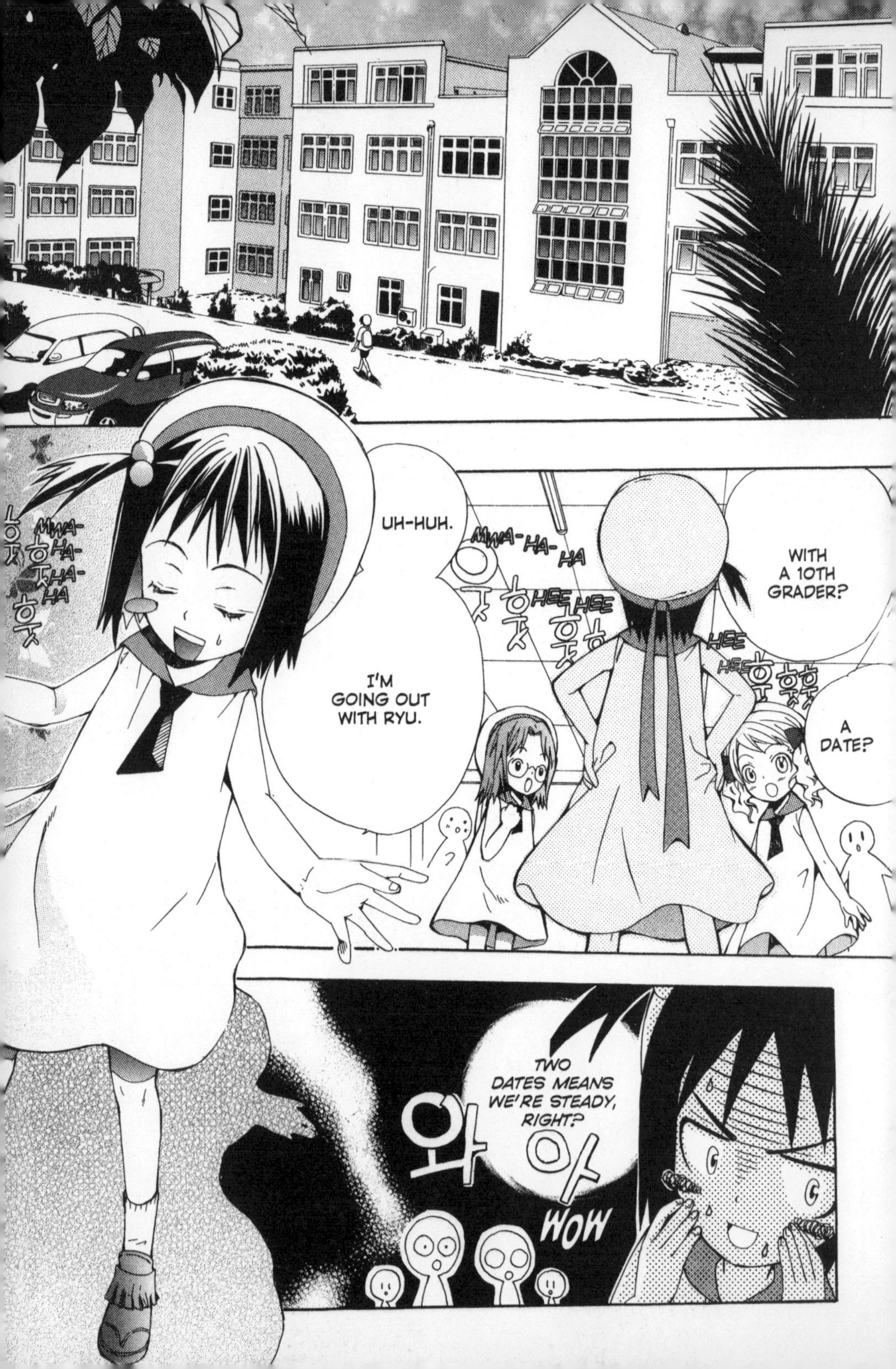

MWA-HA-HA-HA
UH-HUH.
I'M GOING OUT WITH RYU.
MWA-HA-HA
HEE HEE
WITH A 10TH GRADER?
HEE HEE
A DATE?
TWO DATES MEANS WE'RE STEADY, RIGHT?
WOW

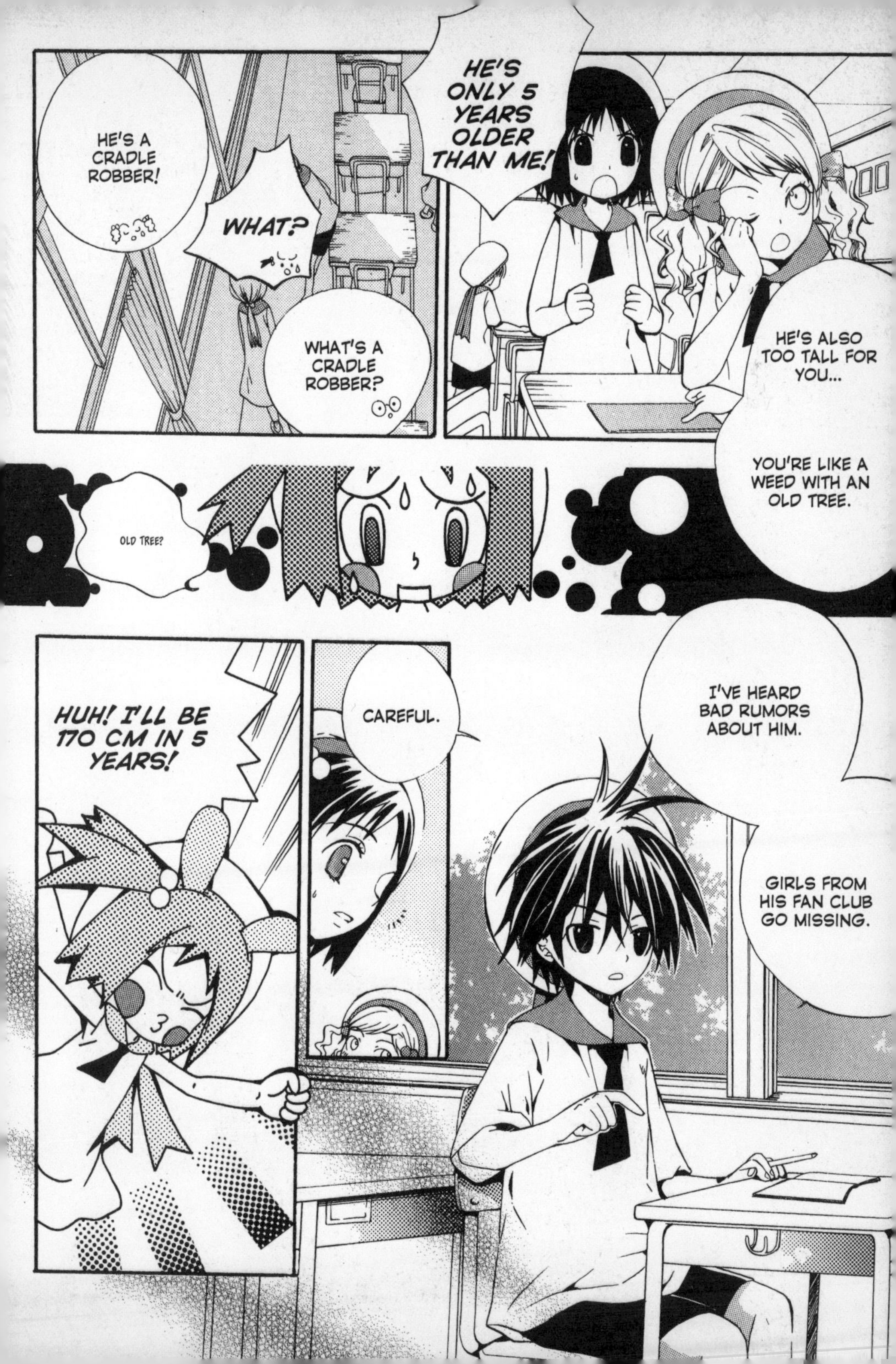

HE'S A CRADLE ROBBER!
WHAT?
WHAT'S A CRADLE ROBBER?
HE'S ONLY 5 YEARS OLDER THAN ME!
HE'S ALSO TOO TALL FOR YOU...
YOU'RE LIKE A WEED WITH AN OLD TREE.
OLD TREE?
I'VE HEARD BAD RUMORS ABOUT HIM.
GIRLS FROM HIS FAN CLUB GO MISSING.
CAREFUL.
HUH! I'LL BE 170 CM IN 5 YEARS!

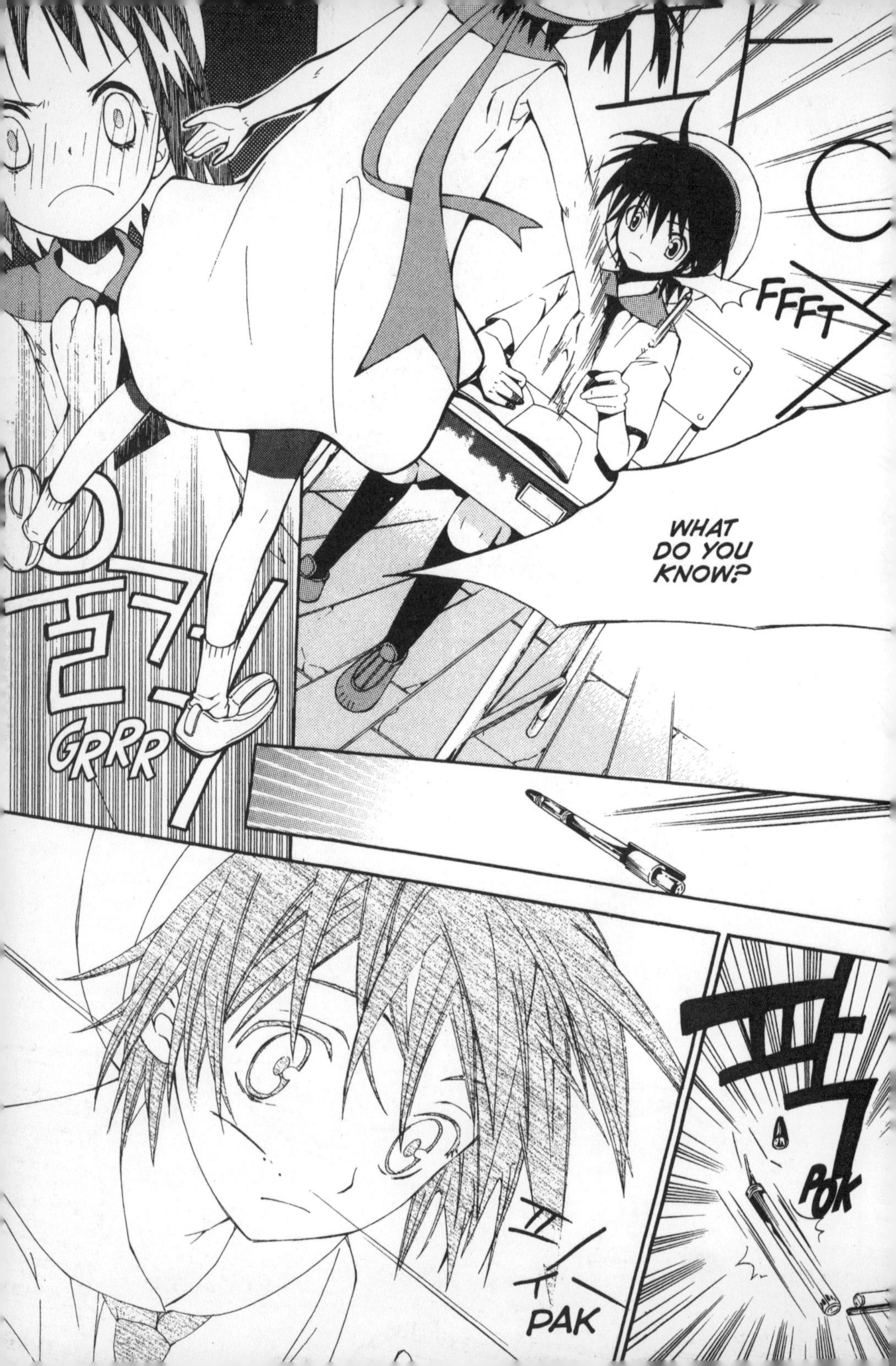
FFFT
WHAT DO YOU KNOW?
GRRR
POK
PAK

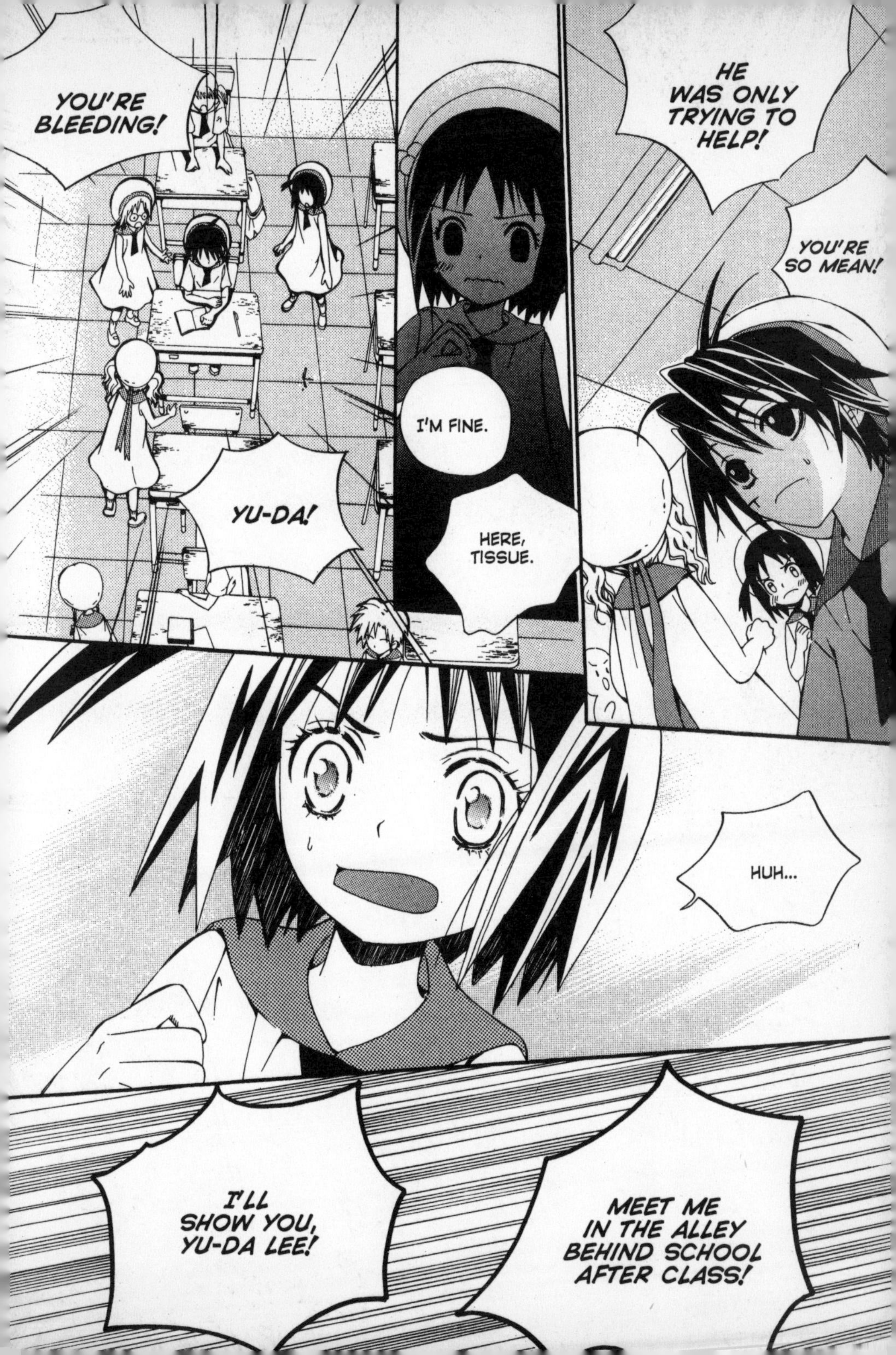
YOU'RE BLEEDING!
YU-DA!
I'M FINE.
HERE, TISSUE.
HE WAS ONLY TRYING TO HELP!
YOU'RE SO MEAN!
HUH...
I'LL SHOW YOU, YU-DA LEE!
MEET ME IN THE ALLEY BEHIND SCHOOL AFTER CLASS!

What's wrong with her?

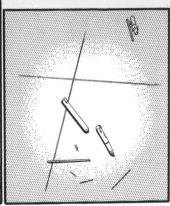

... ...

DRRRING

DRRRING

TIME
TO GO
HOME.

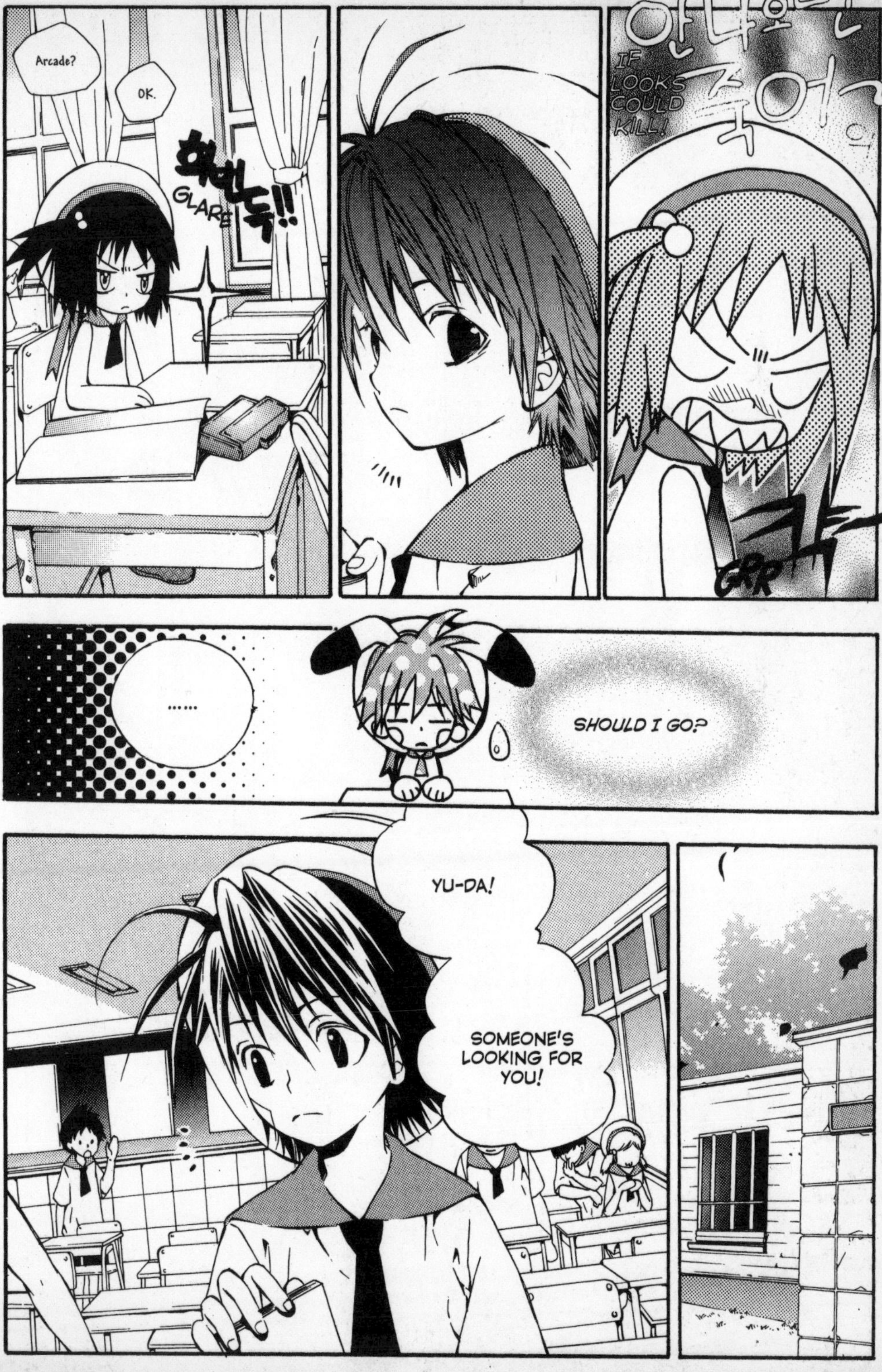

Arcade?
OK.
GLARE
IF LOOKS COULD KILL!
GRR
......
SHOULD I GO?
YU-DA!
SOMEONE'S LOOKING FOR YOU!

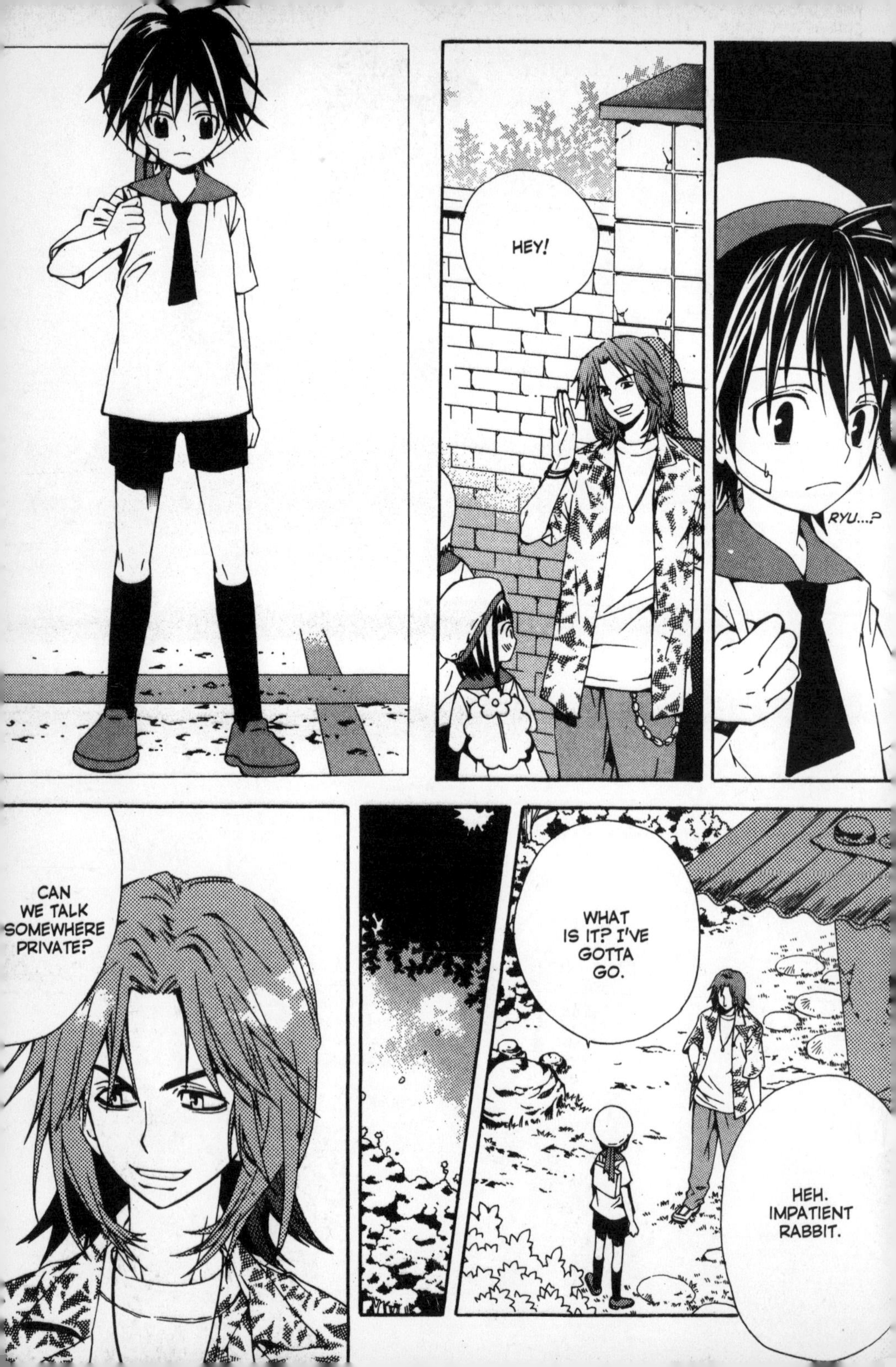
HEY!
RYU...?
CAN WE TALK SOMEWHERE PRIVATE?
WHAT IS IT? I'VE GOTTA GO.
HEH. IMPATIENT RABBIT.

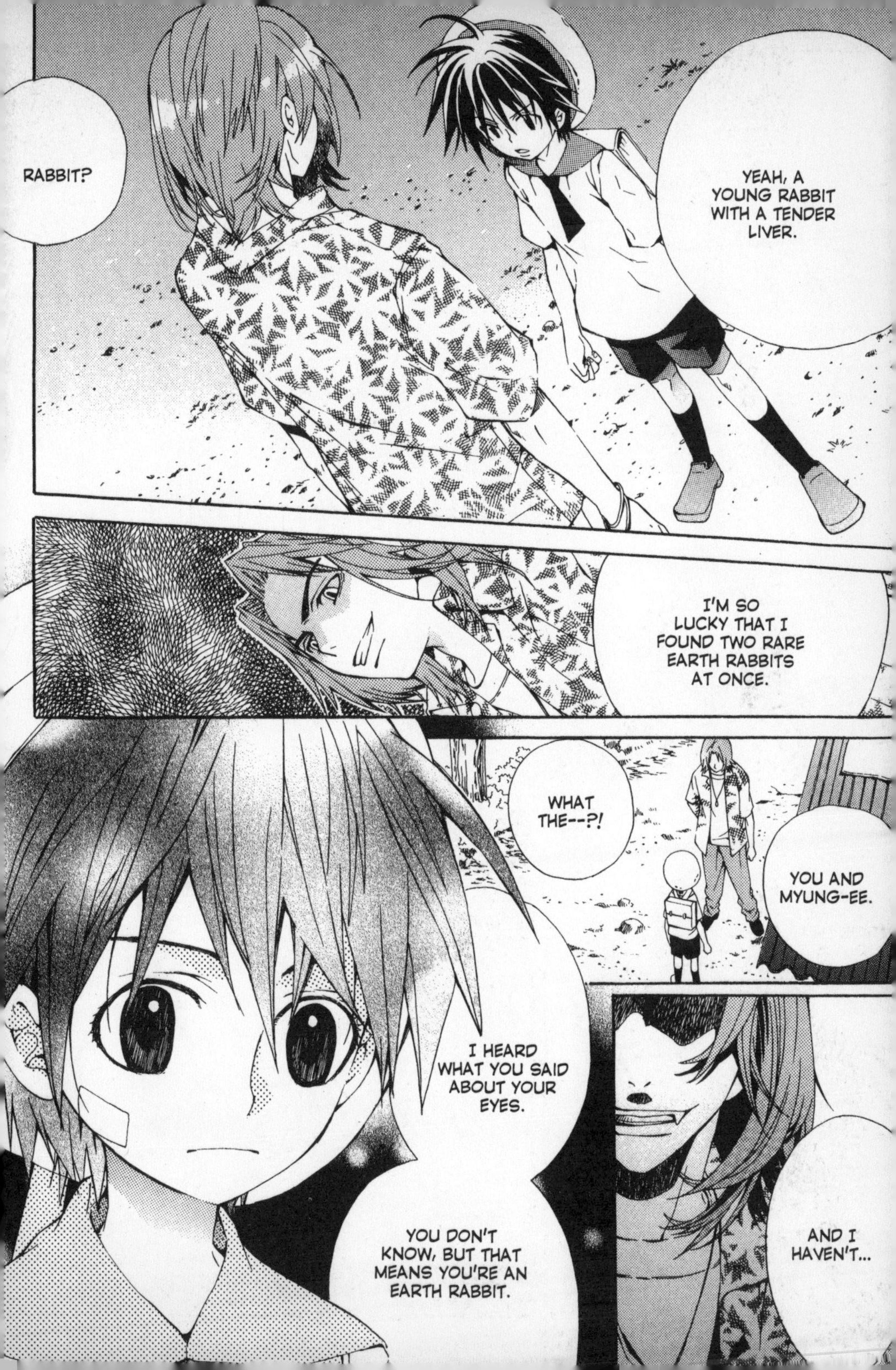
RABBIT?
YEAH, A YOUNG RABBIT WITH A TENDER LIVER.
I'M SO LUCKY THAT I FOUND TWO RARE EARTH RABBITS AT ONCE.
WHAT THE--?!
YOU AND MYUNG-EE.
I HEARD WHAT YOU SAID ABOUT YOUR EYES.
YOU DON'T KNOW, BUT THAT MEANS YOU'RE AN EARTH RABBIT.
AND I HAVEN'T...

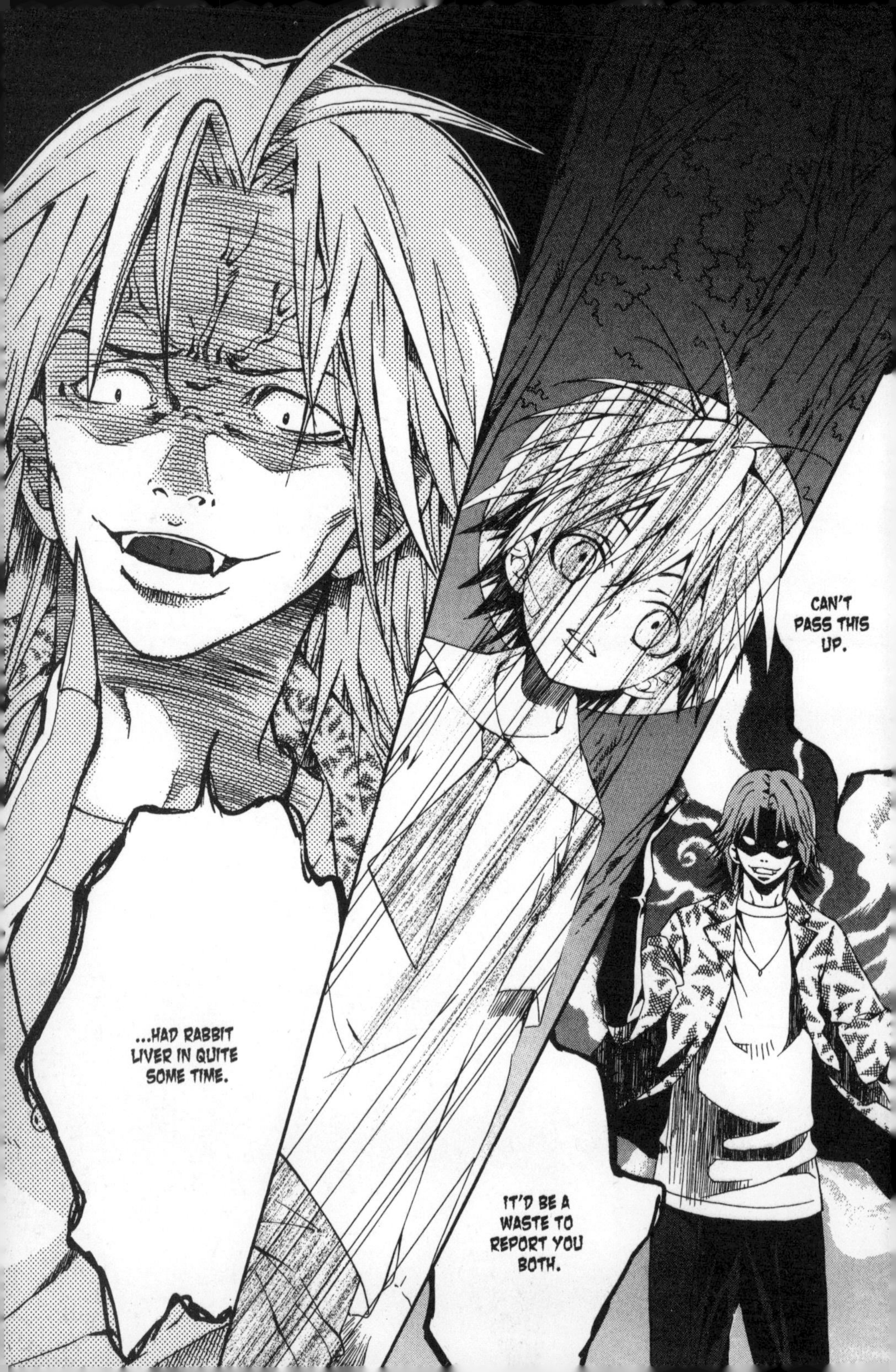
CAN'T PASS THIS UP.
IT'D BE A WASTE TO REPORT YOU BOTH.
...HAD RABBIT LIVER IN QUITE SOME TIME.

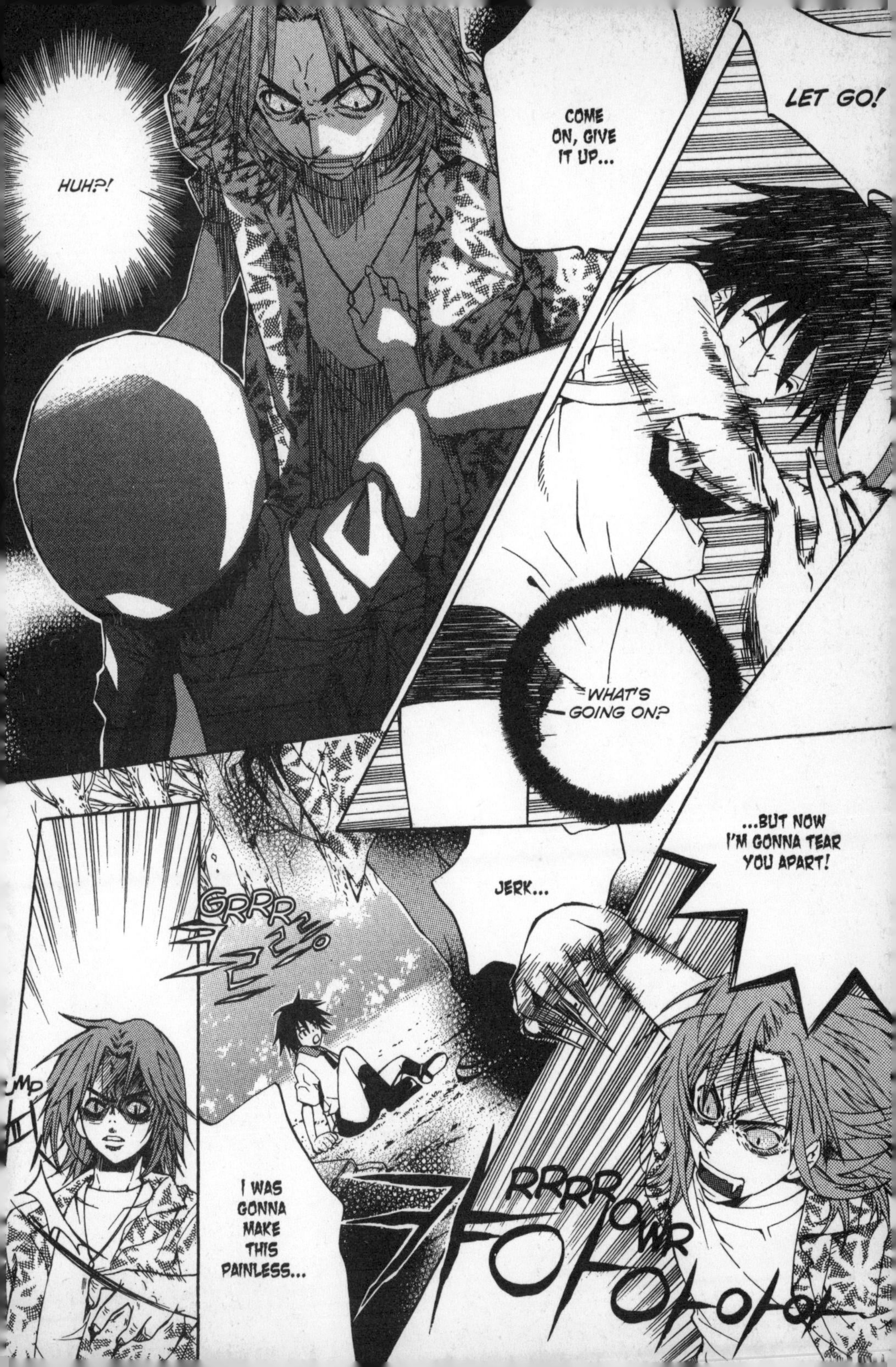
LET GO!
COME ON, GIVE IT UP...
HUH?!
WHAT'S GOING ON?
...BUT NOW I'M GONNA TEAR YOU APART!
JERK...
RRRRROWR
GRRR
I WAS GONNA MAKE THIS PAINLESS...

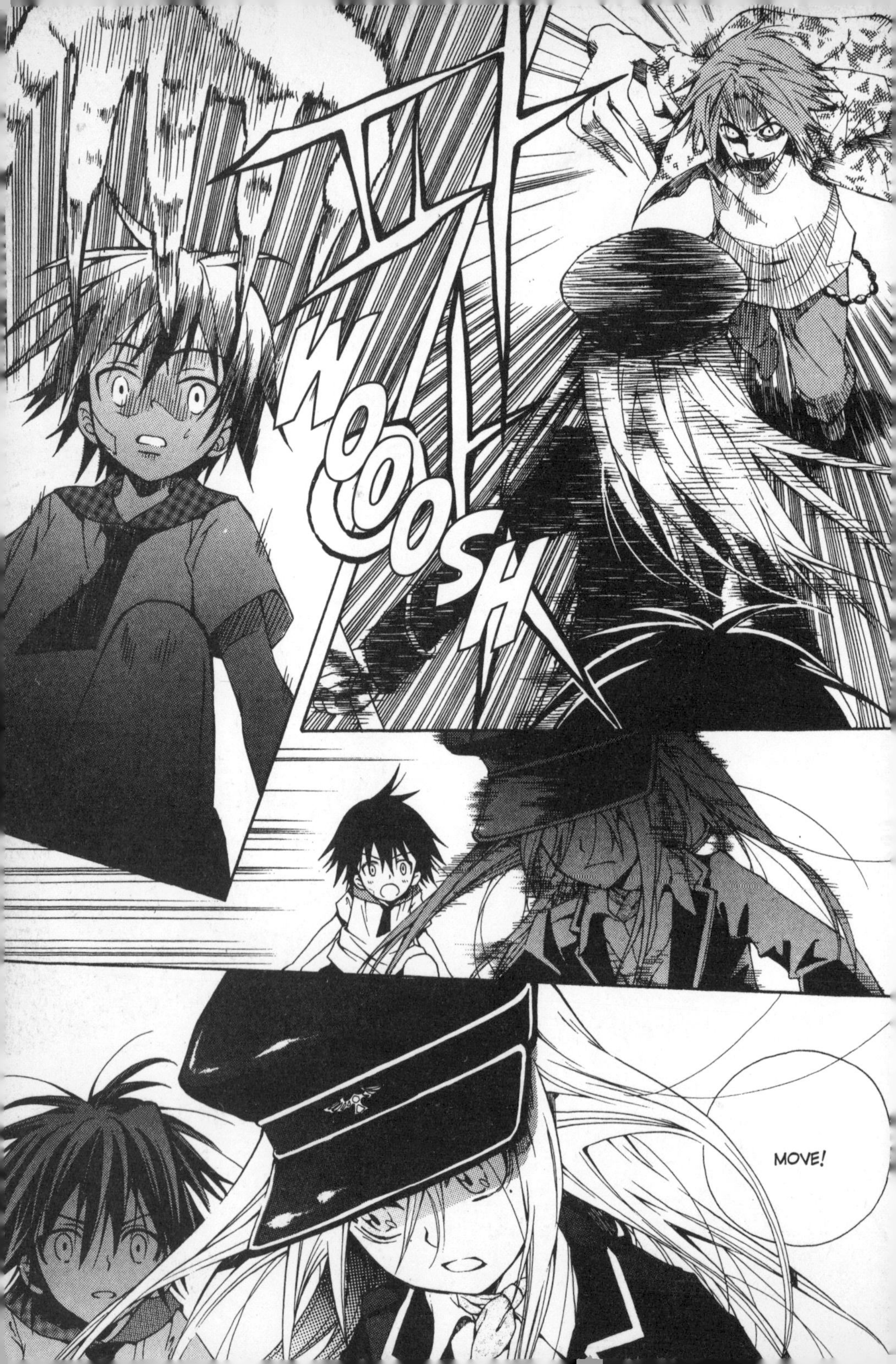
WOOOOSH
MOVE!

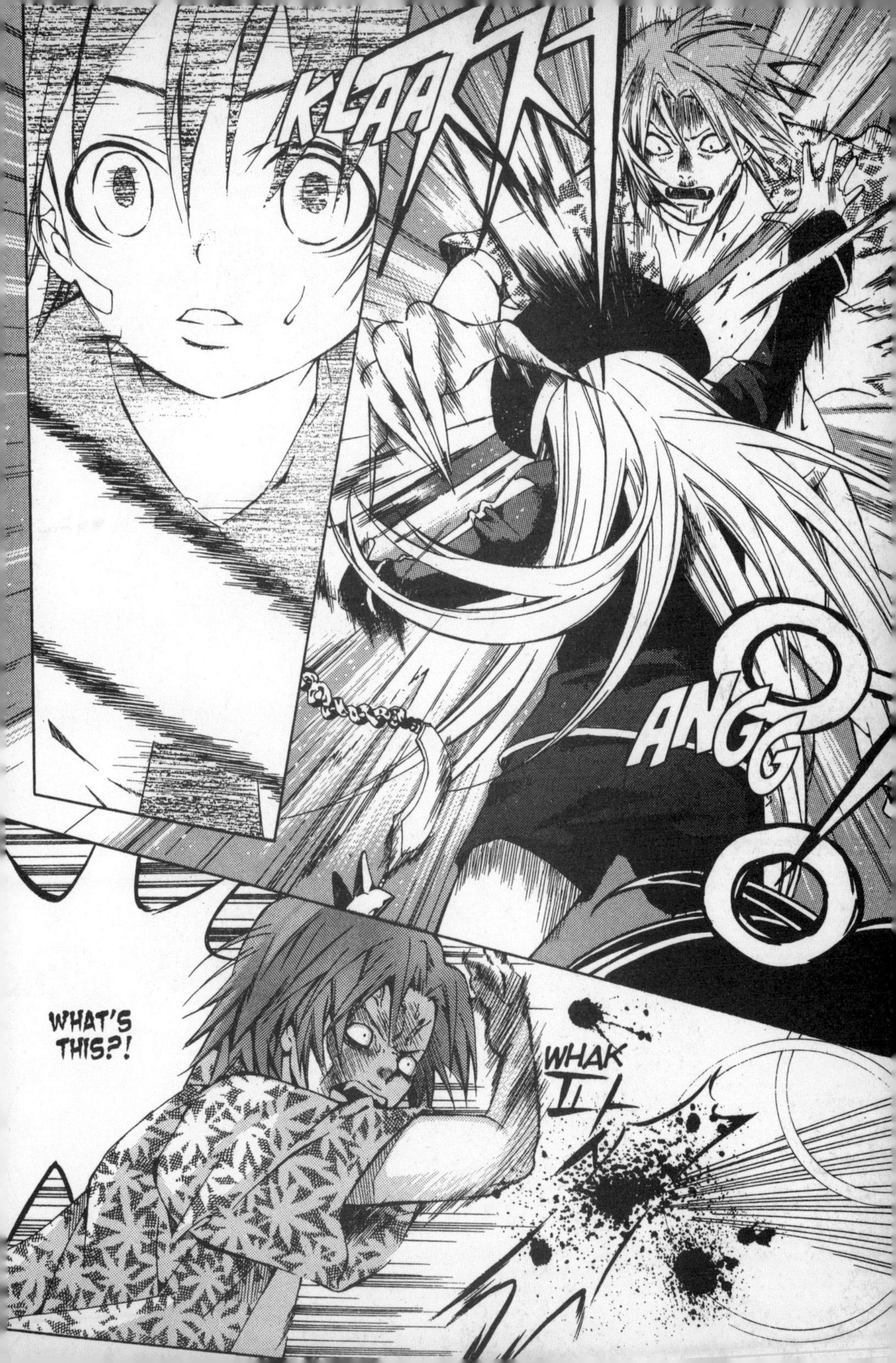
KLAAAK
ANGG
WHAT'S THIS?!
WHAK

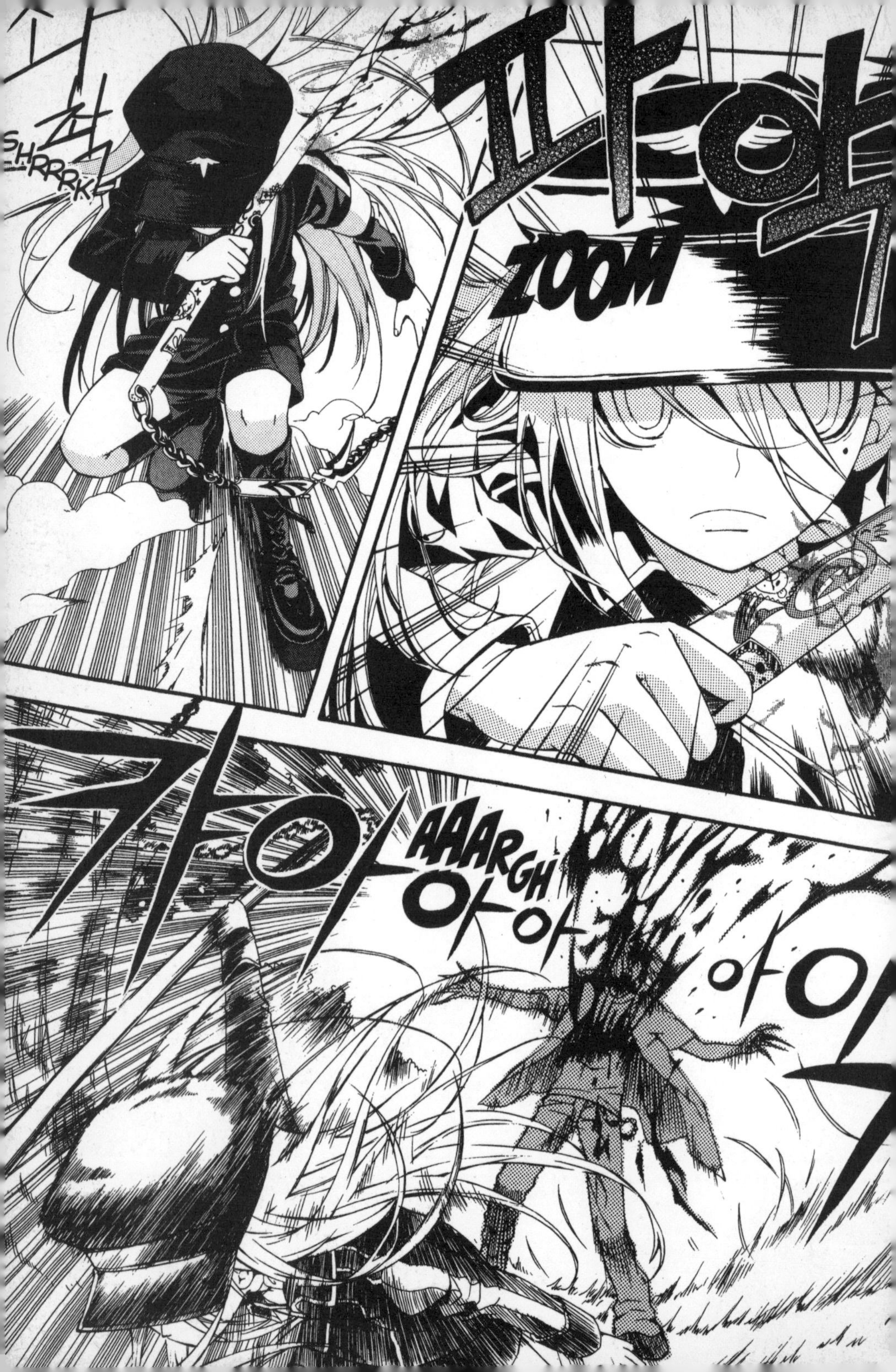
서걱
SHRRRK
파앗
ZOOM
가아아아아아아
AAARGH

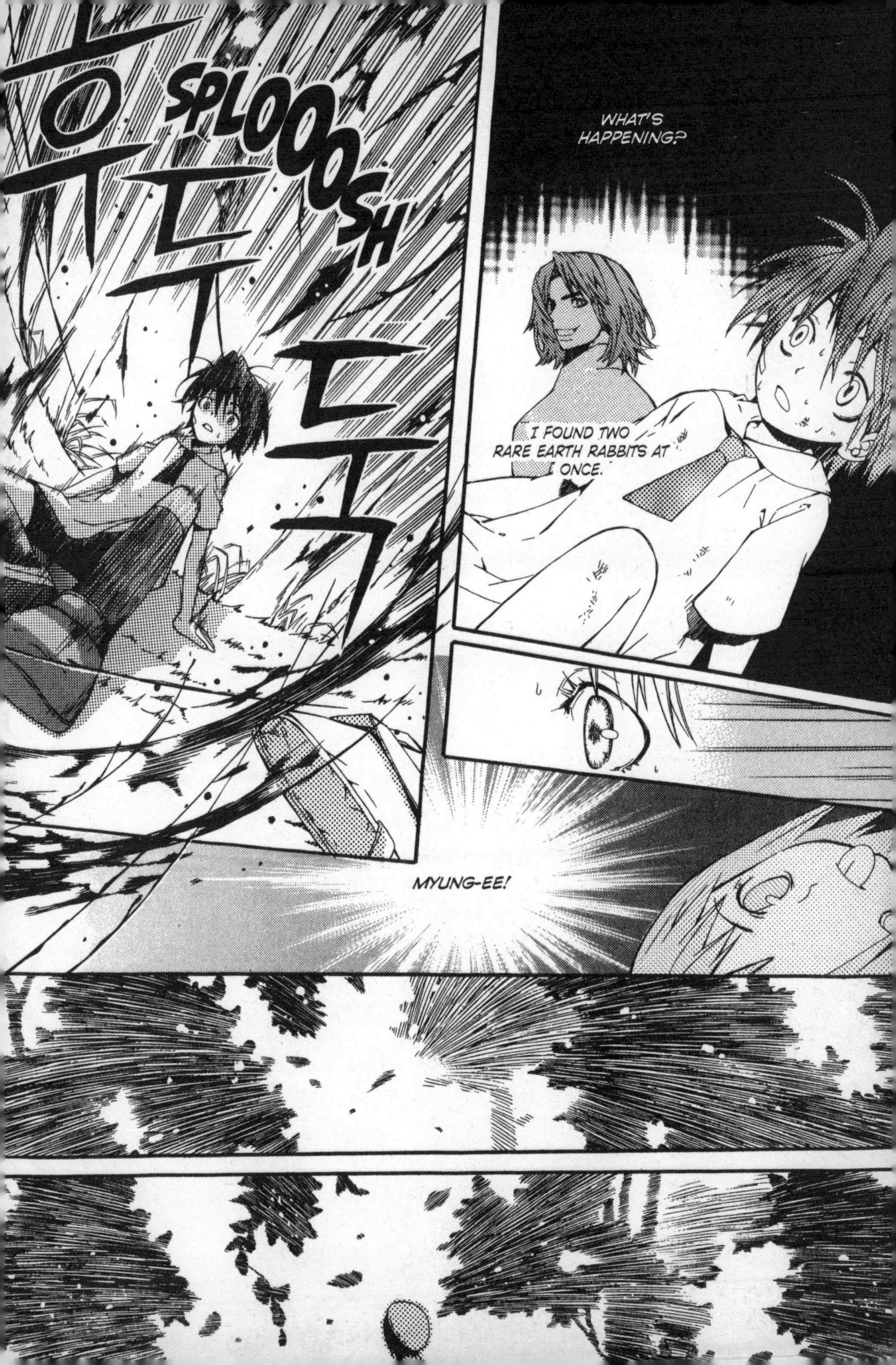
WHAT'S HAPPENING?
I FOUND TWO RARE EARTH RABBITS AT ONCE.
SPLOOOOOSH
MYUNG-EE!

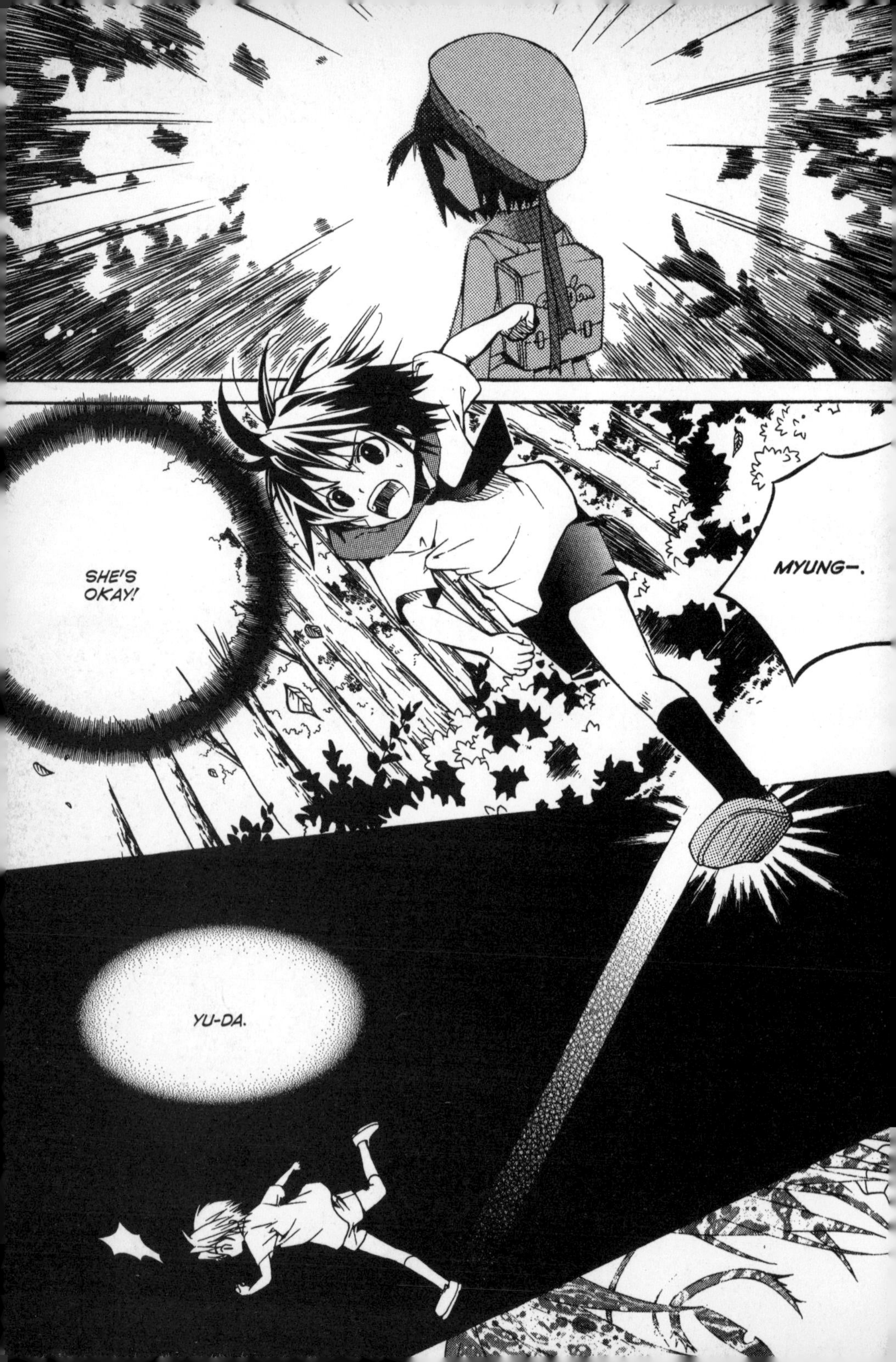
MYUNG-.
SHE'S OKAY!
YU-DA.

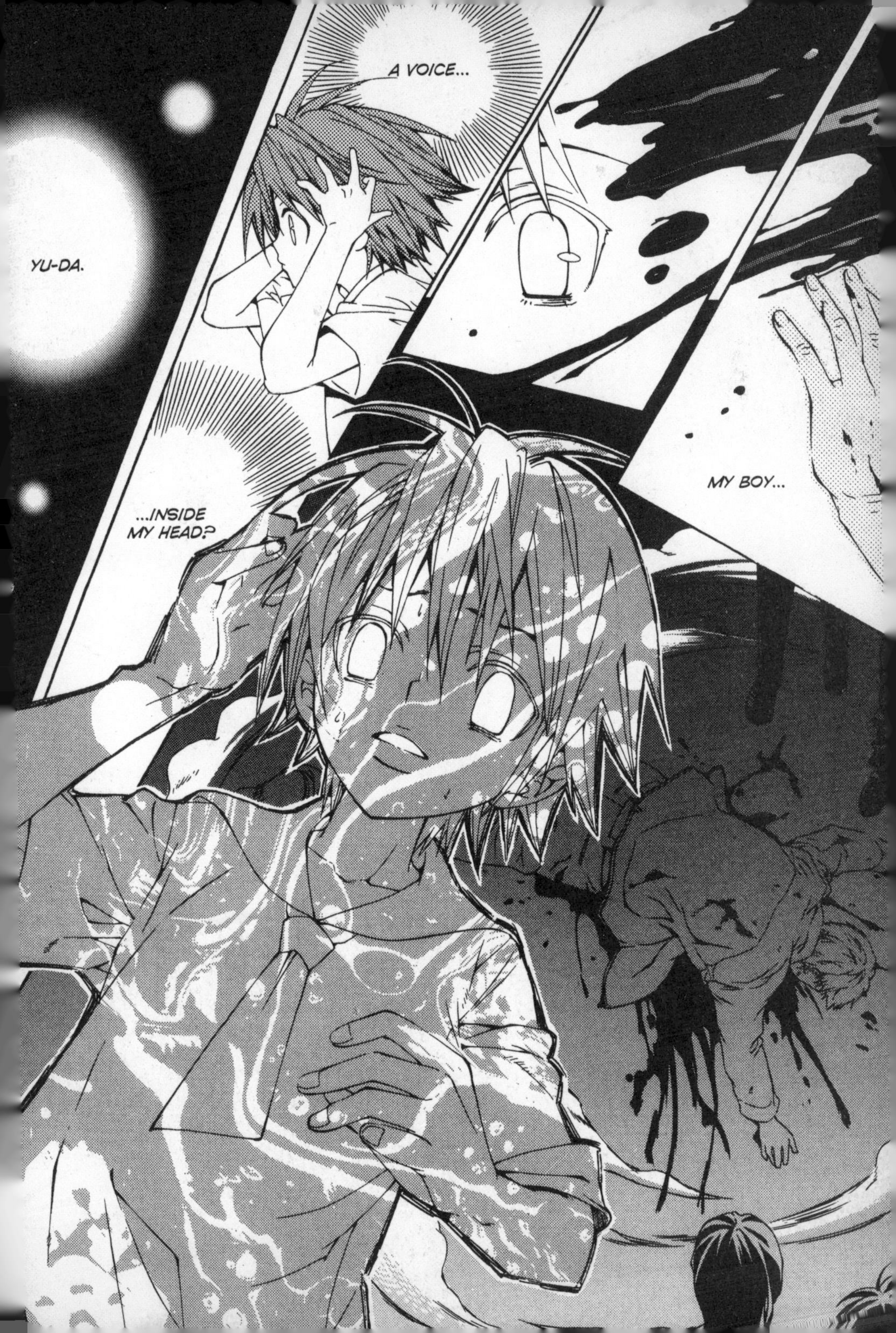
A VOICE...
MY BOY...
...INSIDE MY HEAD?
YU-DA.

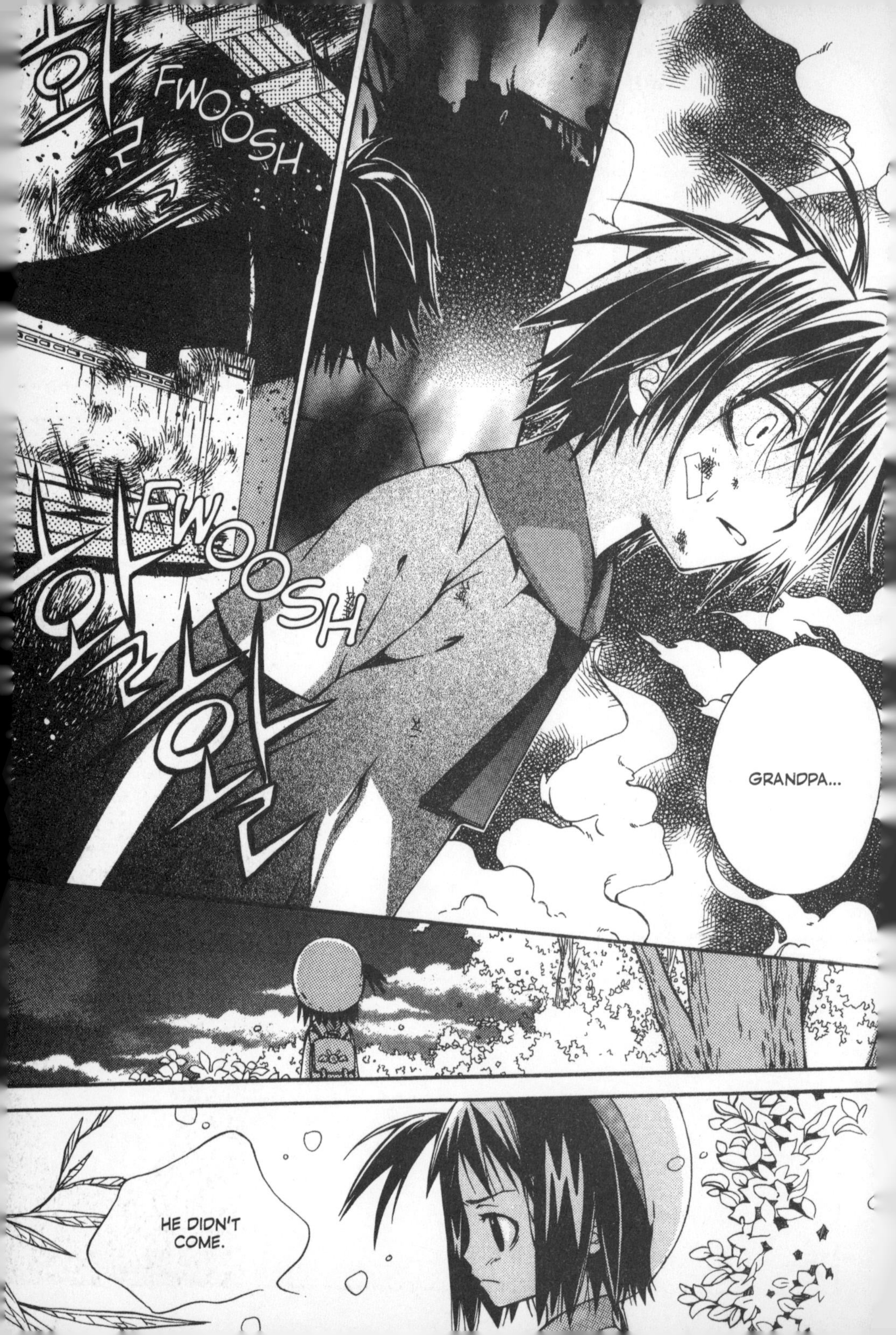
FWOOSH
FWOOSH
GRANDPA...
HE DIDN'T COME.

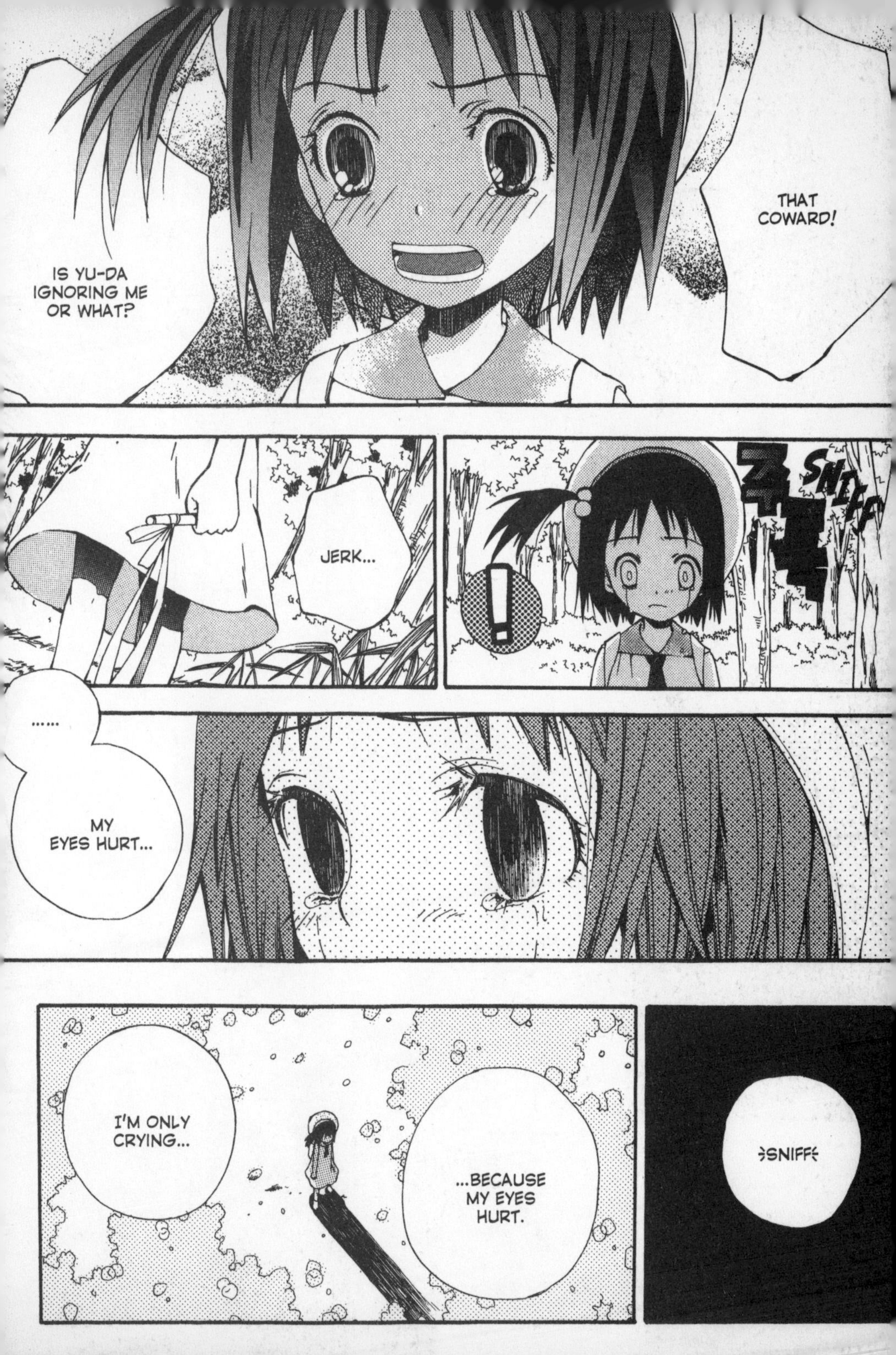

IS YU-DA IGNORING ME OR WHAT?
THAT COWARD!
JERK...
SNIFF
!
......
MY EYES HURT...
I'M ONLY CRYING...
...BECAUSE MY EYES HURT.
SNIFF

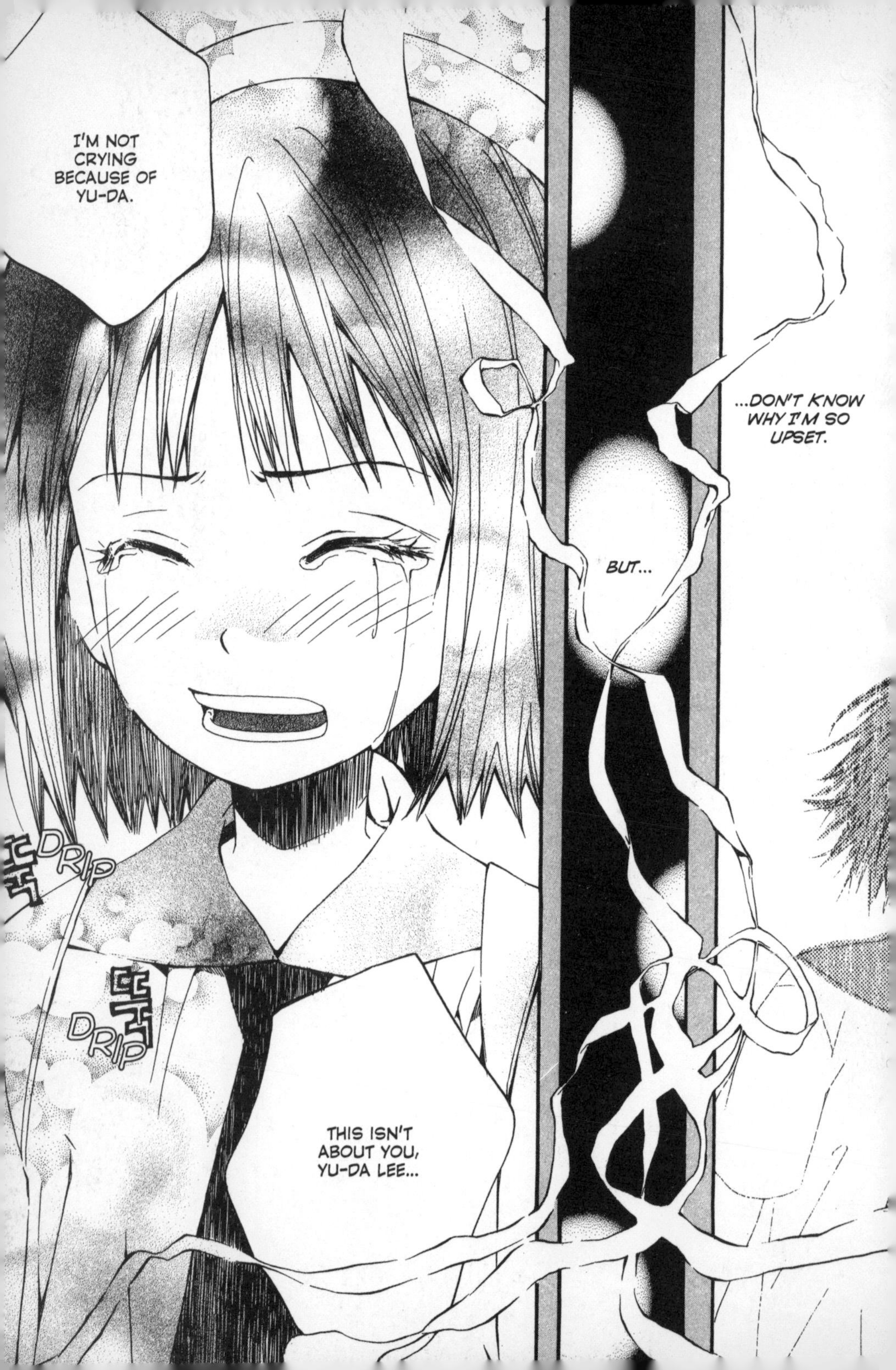
I'M NOT CRYING BECAUSE OF YU-DA.
...DON'T KNOW WHY I'M SO UPSET.
BUT...
DRIP
DRIP
THIS ISN'T ABOUT YOU, YU-DA LEE...

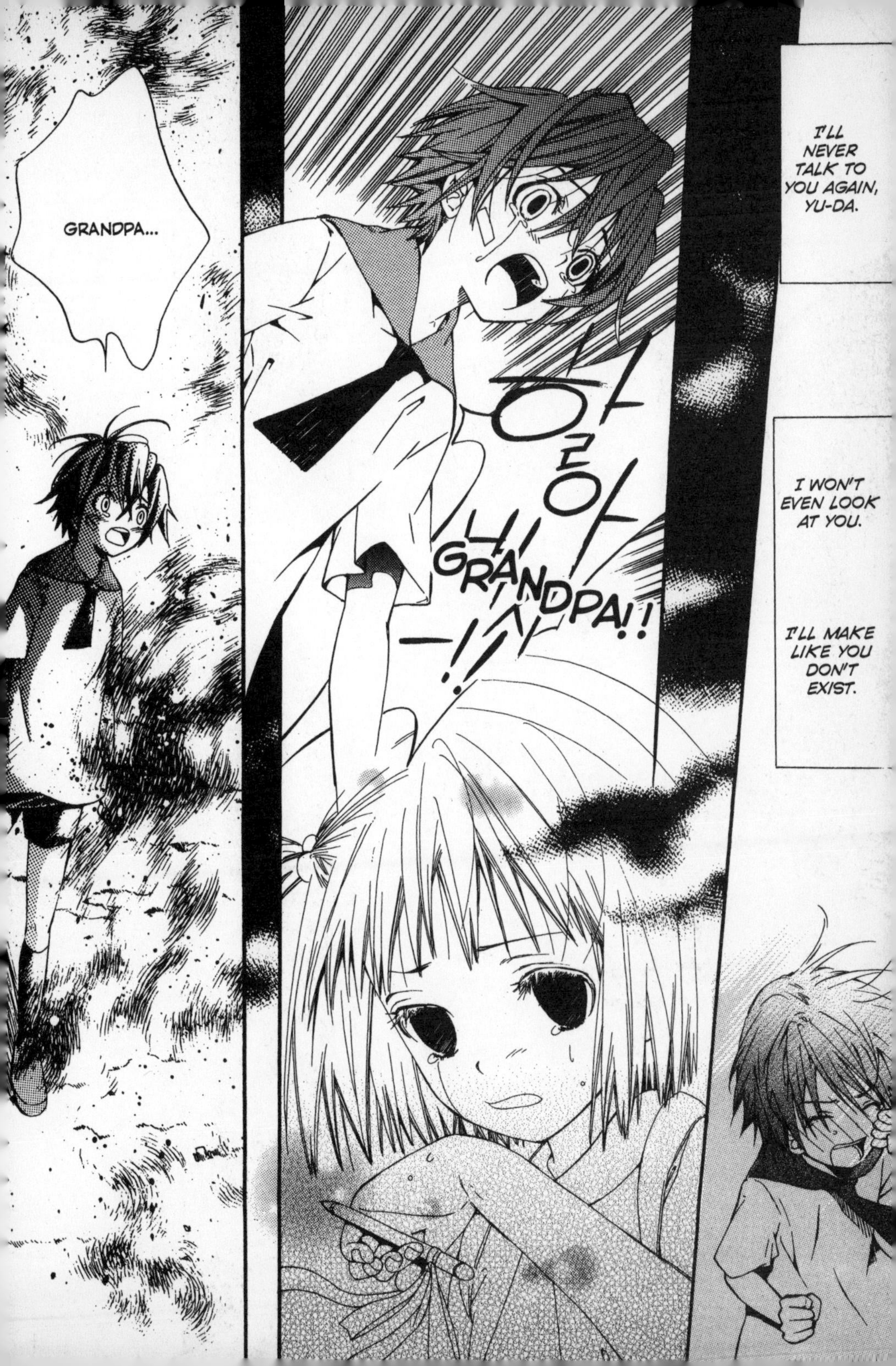
I'LL NEVER TALK TO YOU AGAIN, YU-DA.
I WON'T EVEN LOOK AT YOU.
I'LL MAKE LIKE YOU DON'T EXIST.
GRANDPA!!
GRANDPA...

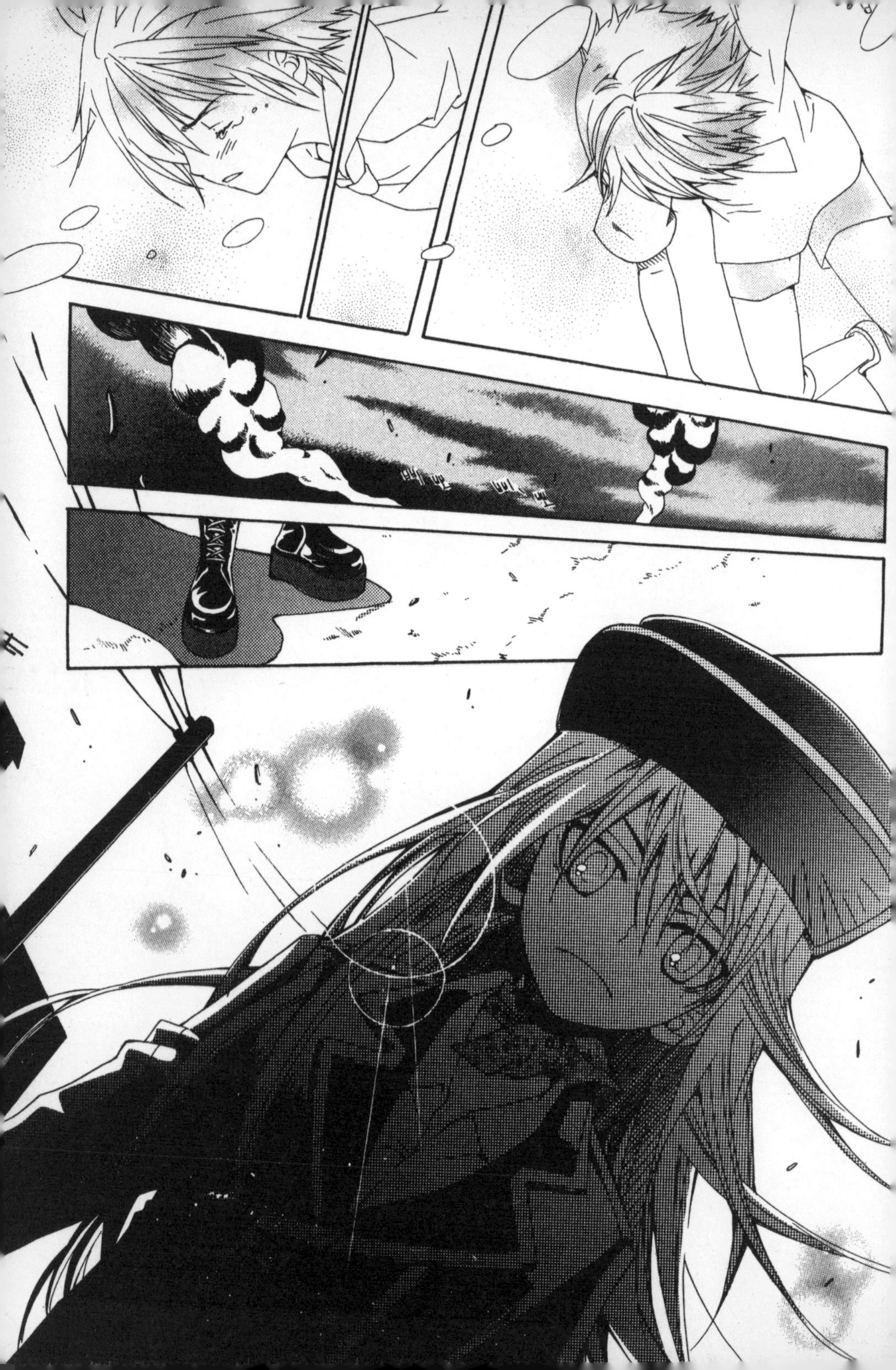

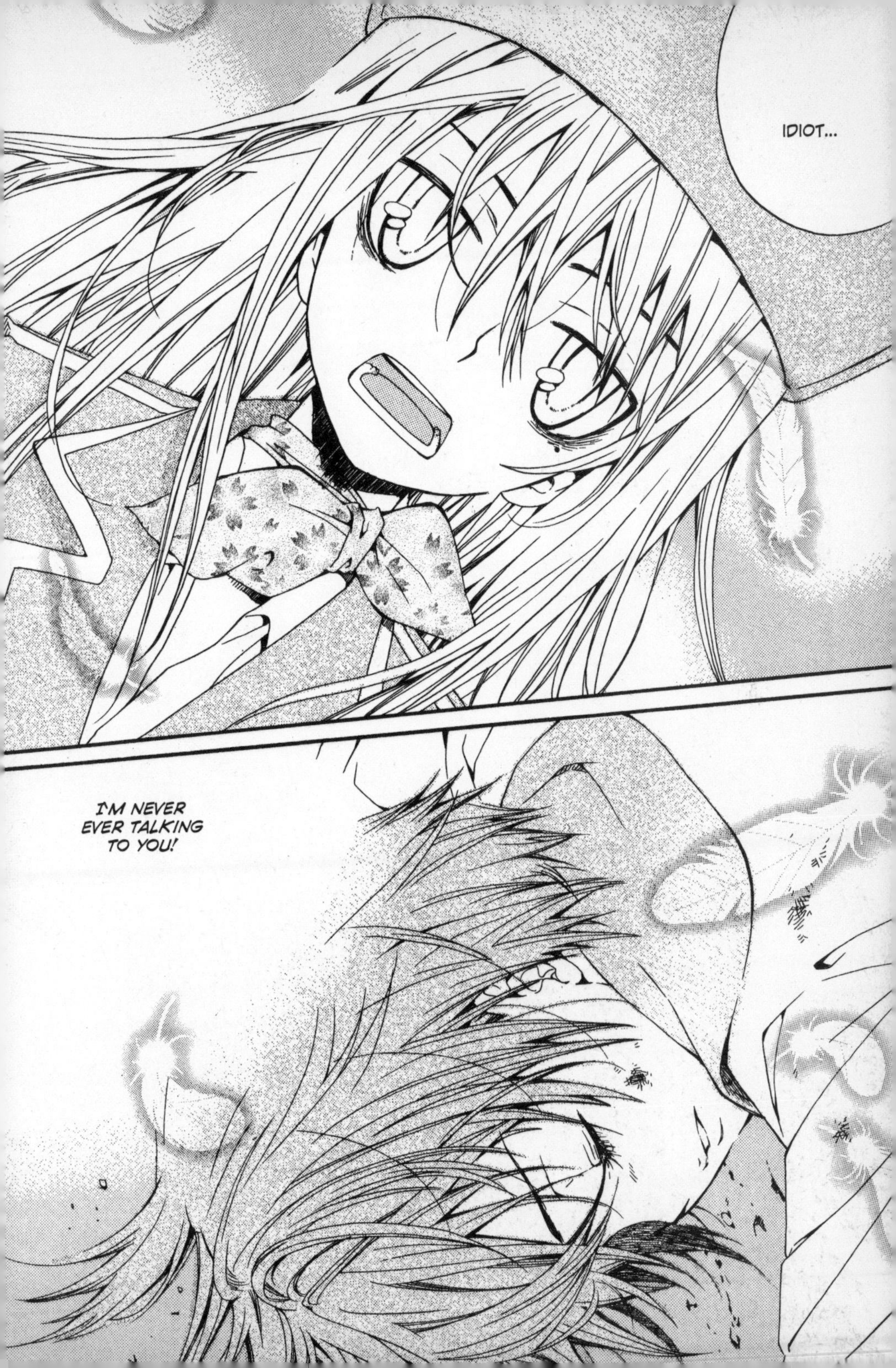
IDIOT...
I'M NEVER EVER TALKING TO YOU!

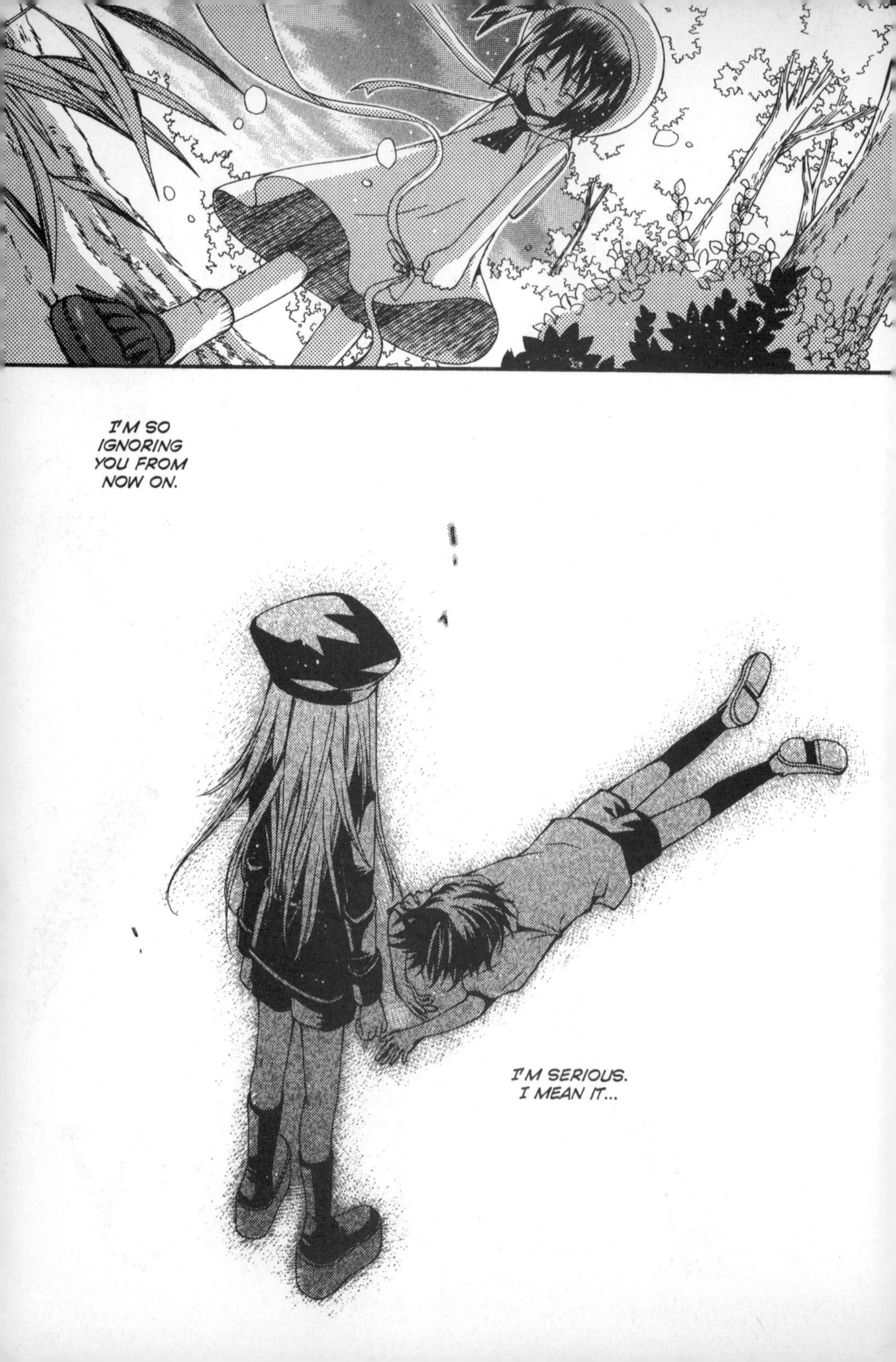
I'M SO IGNORING YOU FROM NOW ON.
I'M SERIOUS. I MEAN IT...

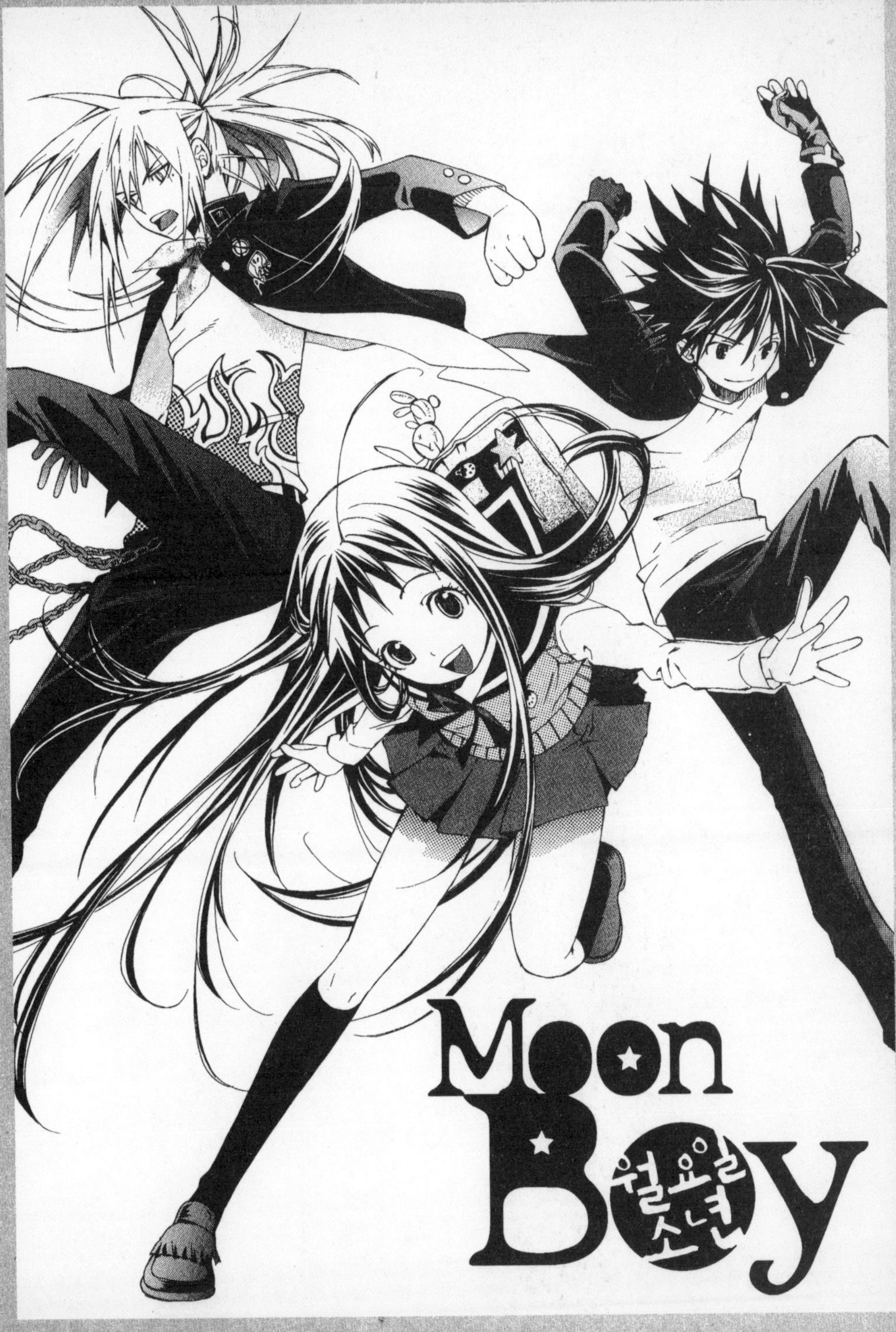
Moon Boy
월요일 소녀

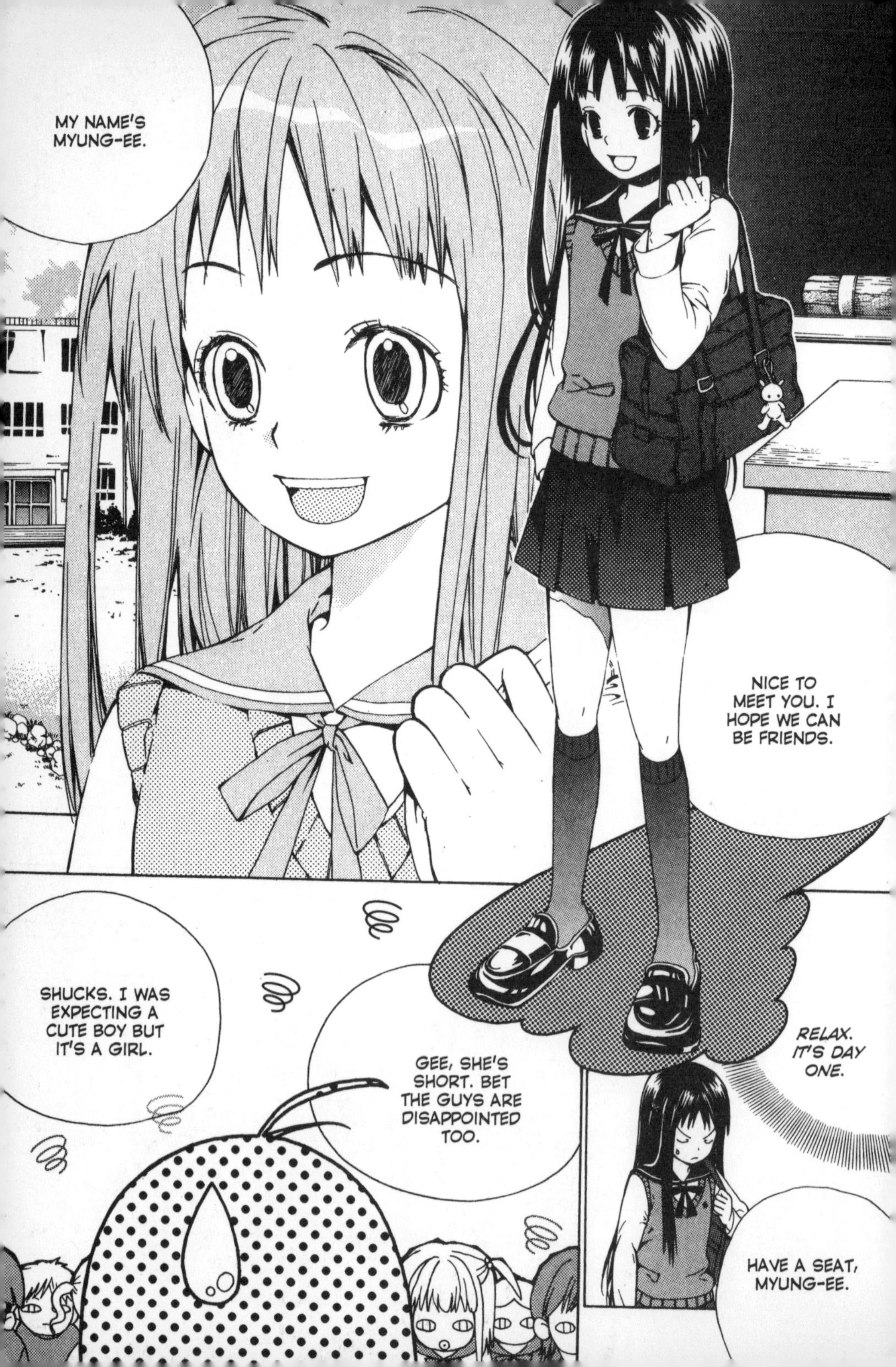
MY NAME'S MYUNG-EE.
NICE TO MEET YOU. I HOPE WE CAN BE FRIENDS.
SHUCKS. I WAS EXPECTING A CUTE BOY BUT IT'S A GIRL.
GEE, SHE'S SHORT. BET THE GUYS ARE DISAPPOINTED TOO.
RELAX. IT'S DAY ONE.
HAVE A SEAT, MYUNG-EE.

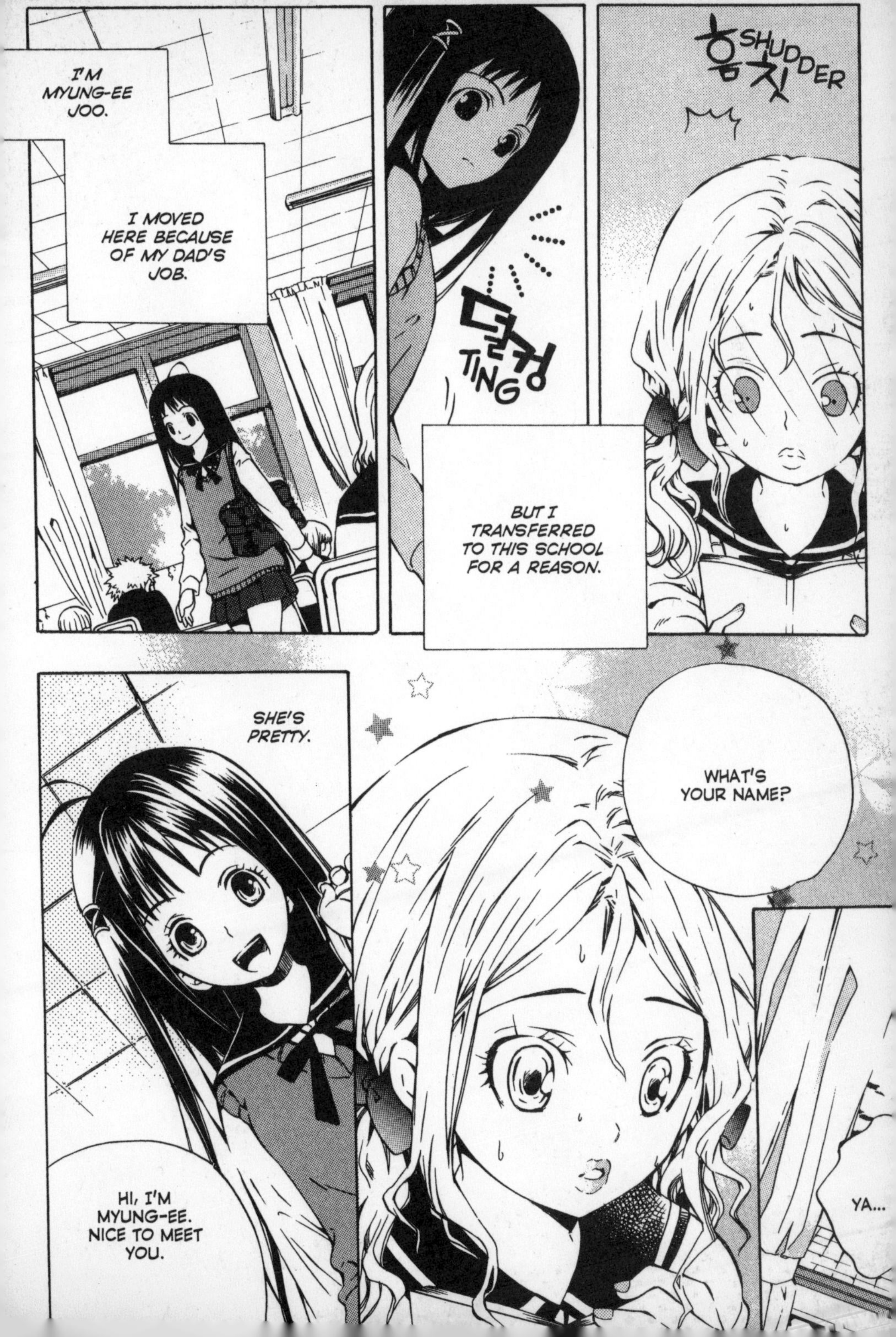

I'M MYUNG-EE JOO.
I MOVED HERE BECAUSE OF MY DAD'S JOB.
덜컹 TING
BUT I TRANSFERRED TO THIS SCHOOL FOR A REASON.
움찔 SHUDDER
SHE'S PRETTY.
HI, I'M MYUNG-EE. NICE TO MEET YOU.
WHAT'S YOUR NAME?
YA...

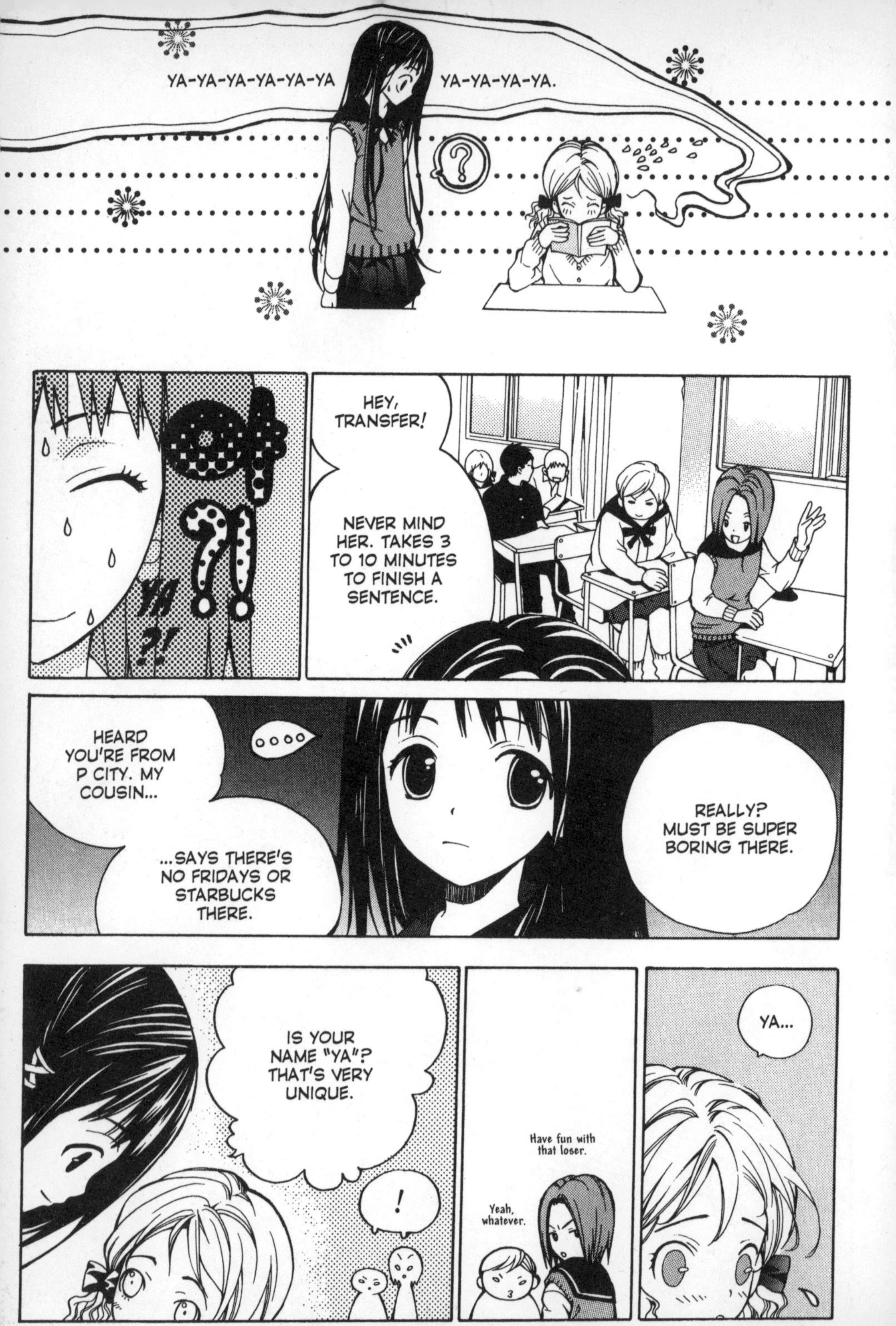
YA-YA-YA-YA-YA-YA
YA-YA-YA-YA.
?
YA ?!
?!
HEY, TRANSFER!
NEVER MIND HER. TAKES 3 TO 10 MINUTES TO FINISH A SENTENCE.
HEARD YOU'RE FROM P CITY. MY COUSIN...
...SAYS THERE'S NO FRIDAYS OR STARBUCKS THERE.
REALLY? MUST BE SUPER BORING THERE.
IS YOUR NAME "YA"? THAT'S VERY UNIQUE.
!
Have fun with that loser.
Yeah, whatever.
YA...

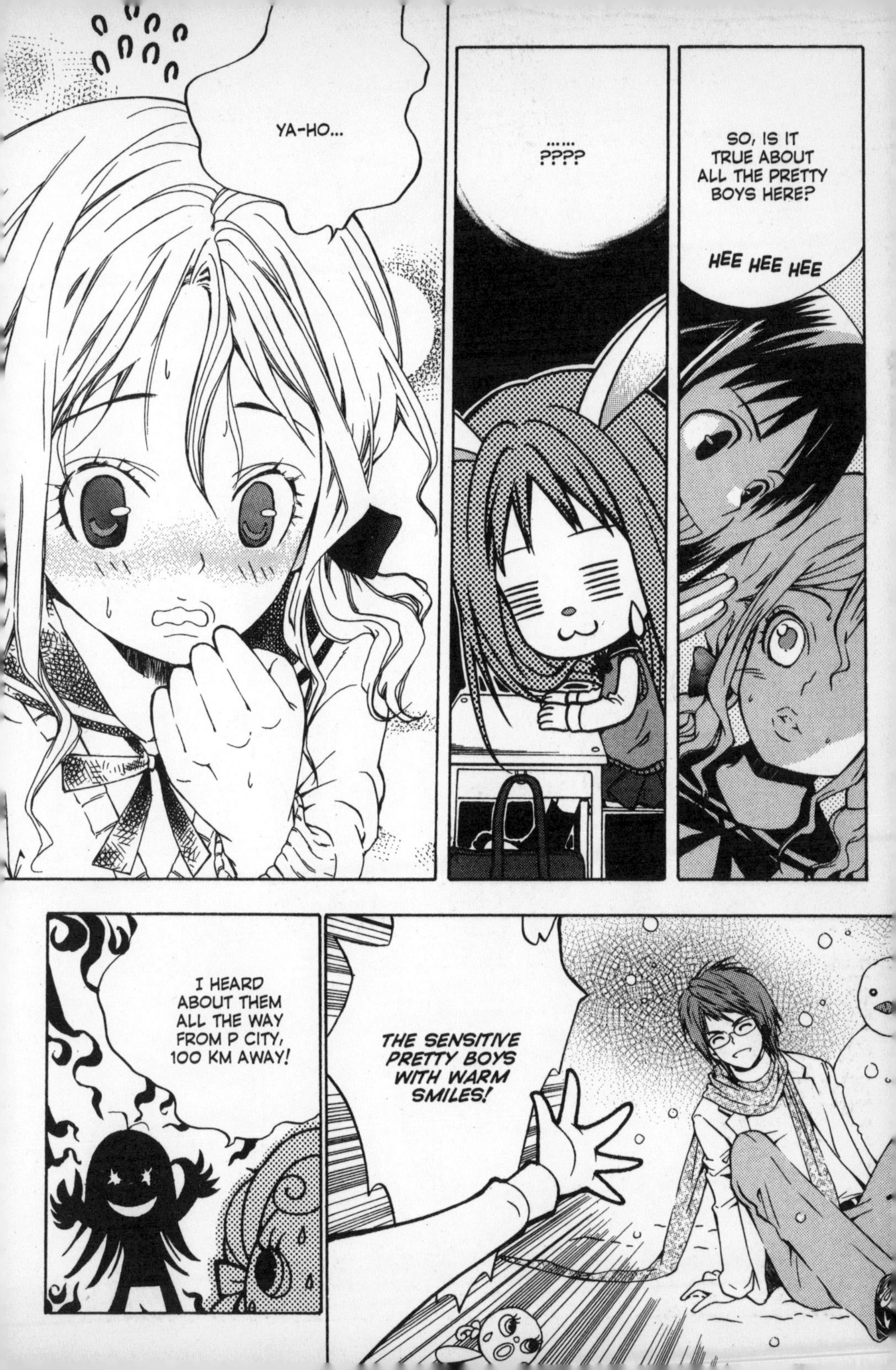

SO, IS IT TRUE ABOUT ALL THE PRETTY BOYS HERE?
HEE HEE HEE
......
????
YA-HO...
THE SENSITIVE PRETTY BOYS WITH WARM SMILES!
I HEARD ABOUT THEM ALL THE WAY FROM P CITY, 100 KM AWAY!

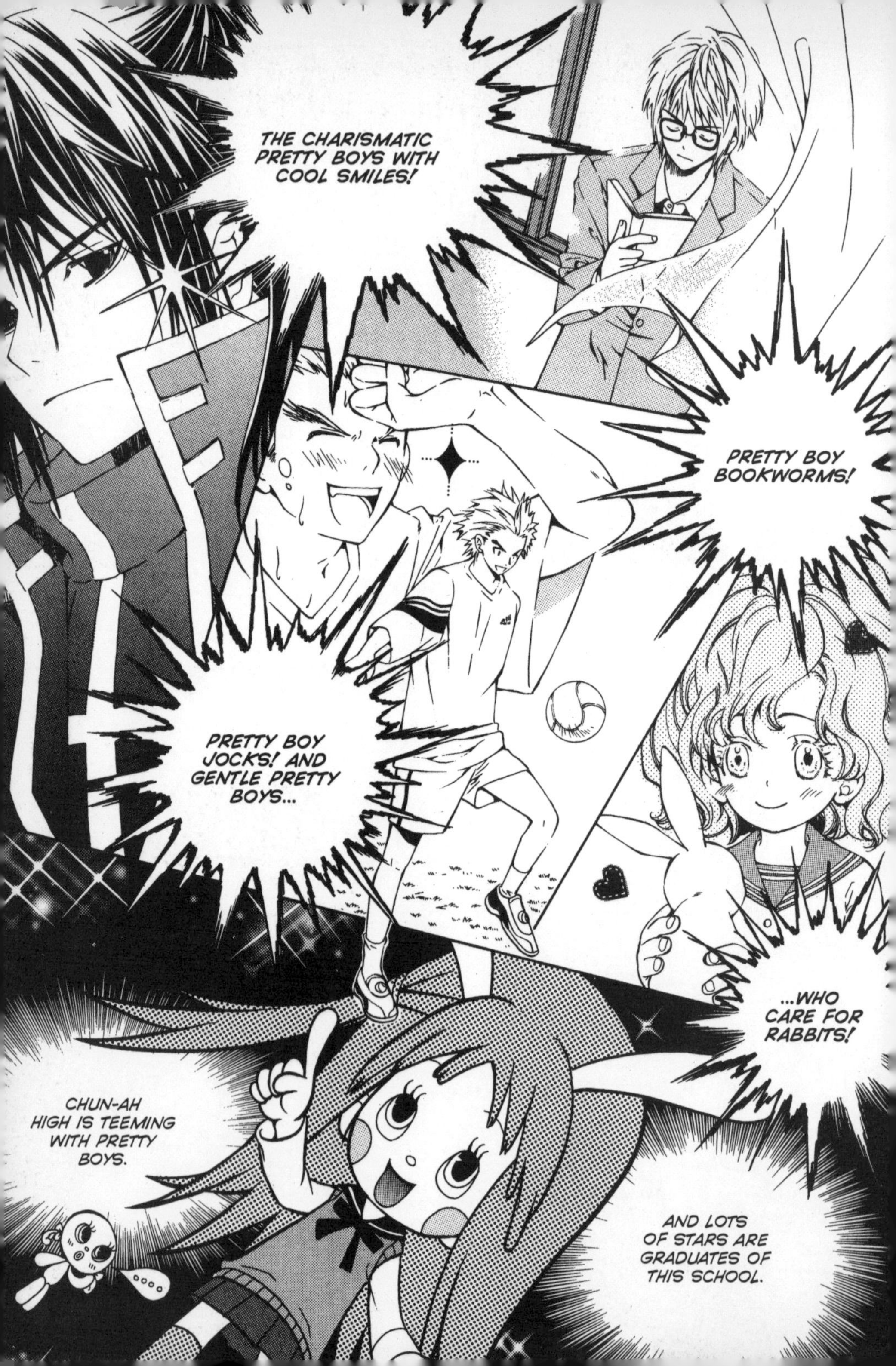
THE CHARISMATIC PRETTY BOYS WITH COOL SMILES!
PRETTY BOY BOOKWORMS!
PRETTY BOY JOCKS! AND GENTLE PRETTY BOYS...
...WHO CARE FOR RABBITS!
CHUN-AH HIGH IS TEEMING WITH PRETTY BOYS.
AND LOTS OF STARS ARE GRADUATES OF THIS SCHOOL.

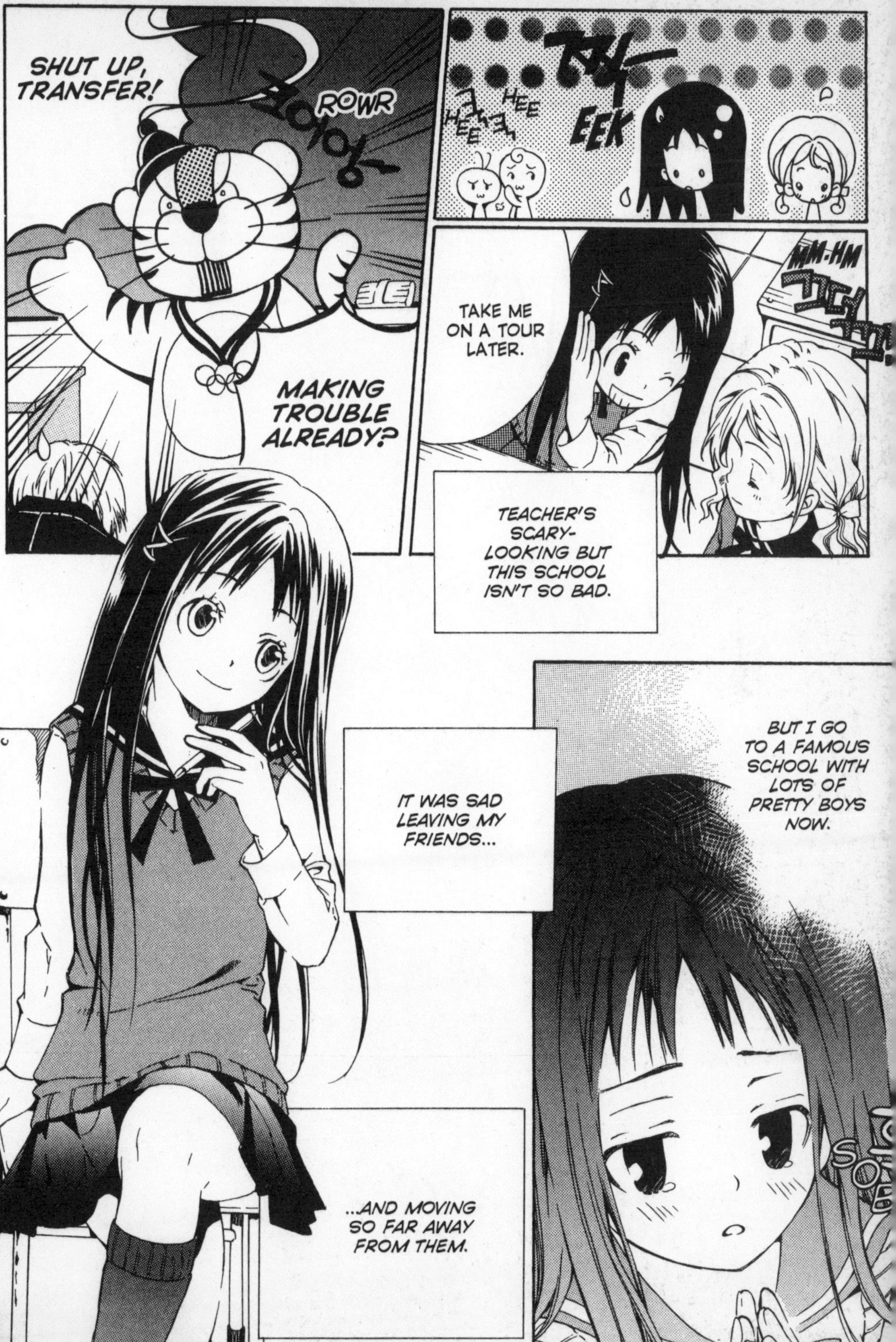
SHUT UP, TRANSFER!
ROWR
MAKING TROUBLE ALREADY?
HEE HEE
EEK
TAKE ME ON A TOUR LATER.
MM-HM
TEACHER'S SCARY-LOOKING BUT THIS SCHOOL ISN'T SO BAD.
IT WAS SAD LEAVING MY FRIENDS...
...AND MOVING SO FAR AWAY FROM THEM.
BUT I GO TO A FAMOUS SCHOOL WITH LOTS OF PRETTY BOYS NOW.
SOB

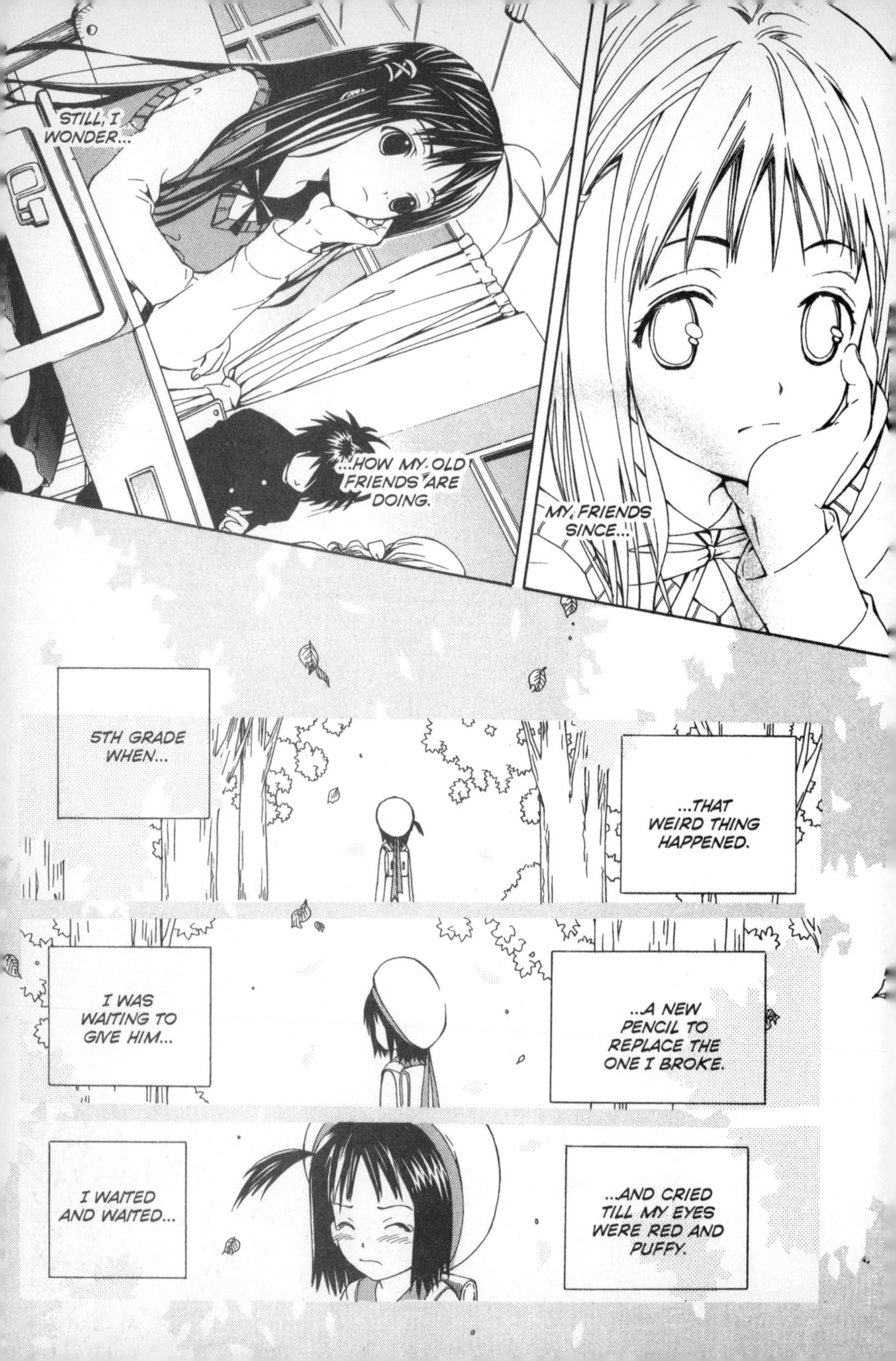
MY FRIENDS SINCE...
STILL, I WONDER...
...HOW MY OLD FRIENDS ARE DOING.
5TH GRADE WHEN...
...THAT WEIRD THING HAPPENED.
I WAS WAITING TO GIVE HIM...
...A NEW PENCIL TO REPLACE THE ONE I BROKE.
I WAITED AND WAITED...
...AND CRIED TILL MY EYES WERE RED AND PUFFY.

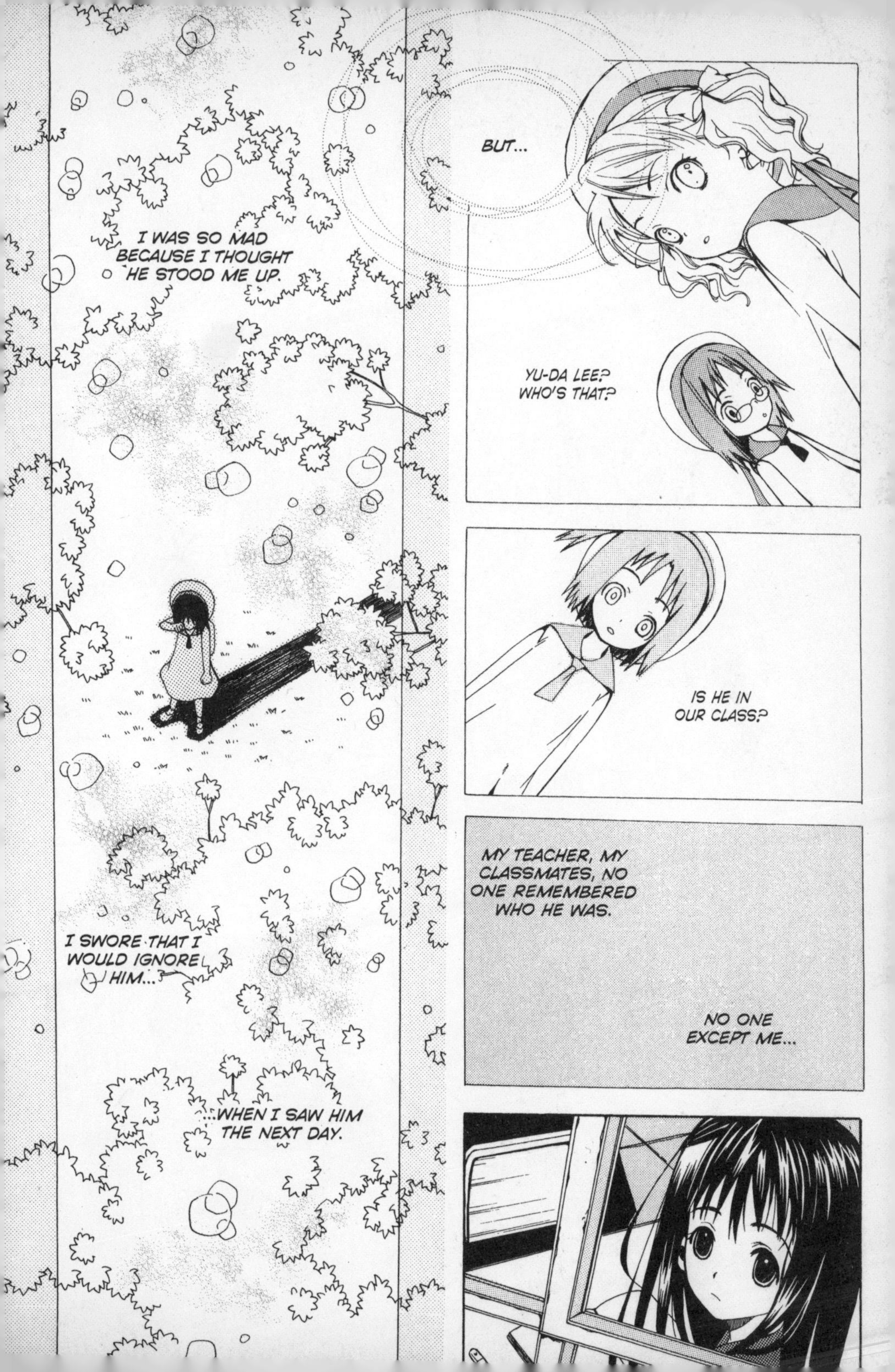
I WAS SO MAD BECAUSE I THOUGHT HE STOOD ME UP.
I SWORE THAT I WOULD IGNORE HIM...
...WHEN I SAW HIM THE NEXT DAY.
BUT...
YU-DA LEE? WHO'S THAT?
IS HE IN OUR CLASS?
MY TEACHER, MY CLASSMATES, NO ONE REMEMBERED WHO HE WAS.
NO ONE EXCEPT ME...

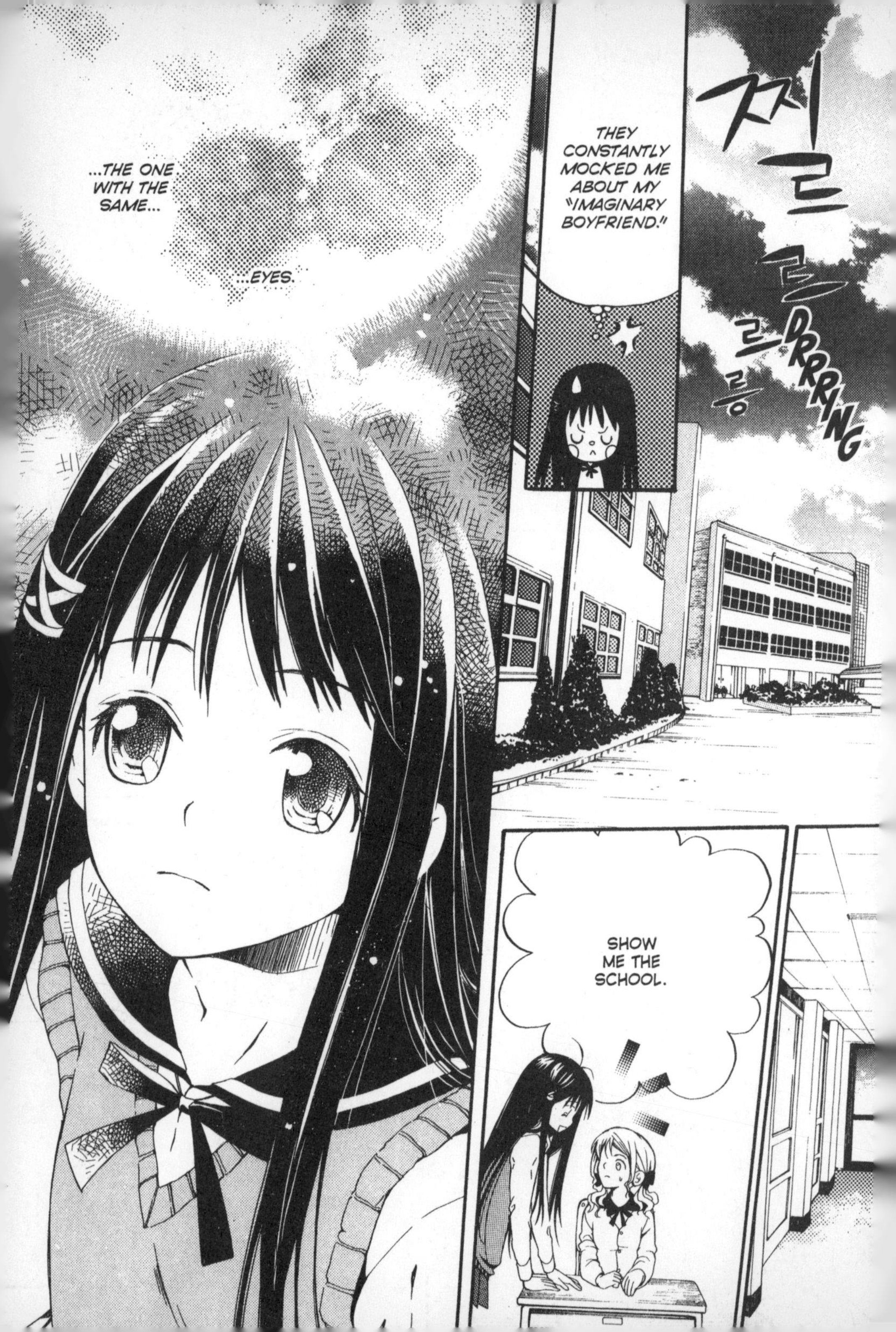
...THE ONE WITH THE SAME...
...EYES.
THEY CONSTANTLY MOCKED ME ABOUT MY "IMAGINARY BOYFRIEND."
찌르르릉
DRRRING
SHOW ME THE SCHOOL.

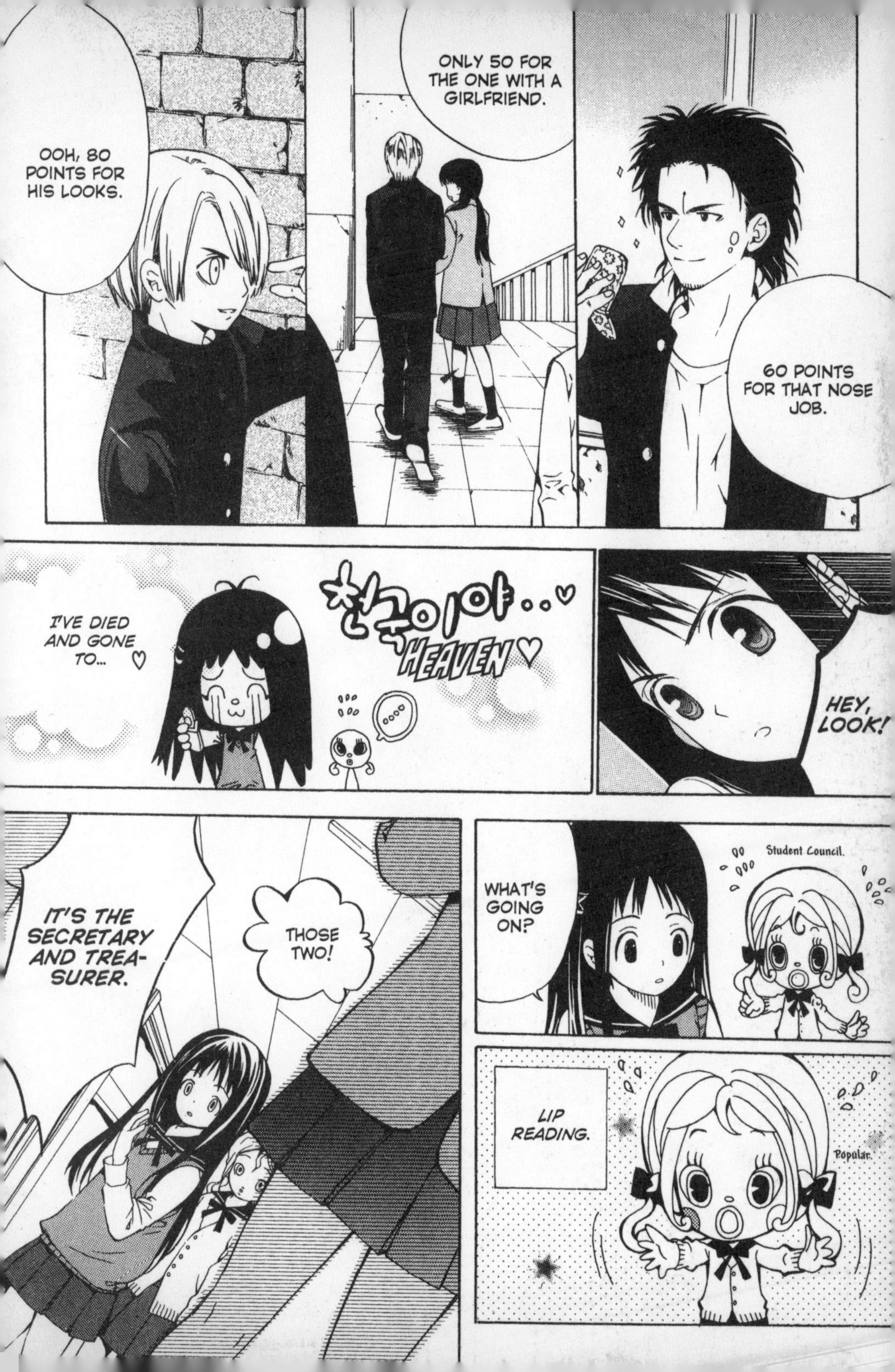
60 POINTS FOR THAT NOSE JOB.
ONLY 50 FOR THE ONE WITH A GIRLFRIEND.
OOH, 80 POINTS FOR HIS LOOKS.
HEY, LOOK!
천국이야..♥
HEAVEN♥
I'VE DIED AND GONE TO... ♡
Student Council.
WHAT'S GOING ON?
THOSE TWO!
IT'S THE SECRETARY AND TREA-SURER.
Popular.
LIP READING.

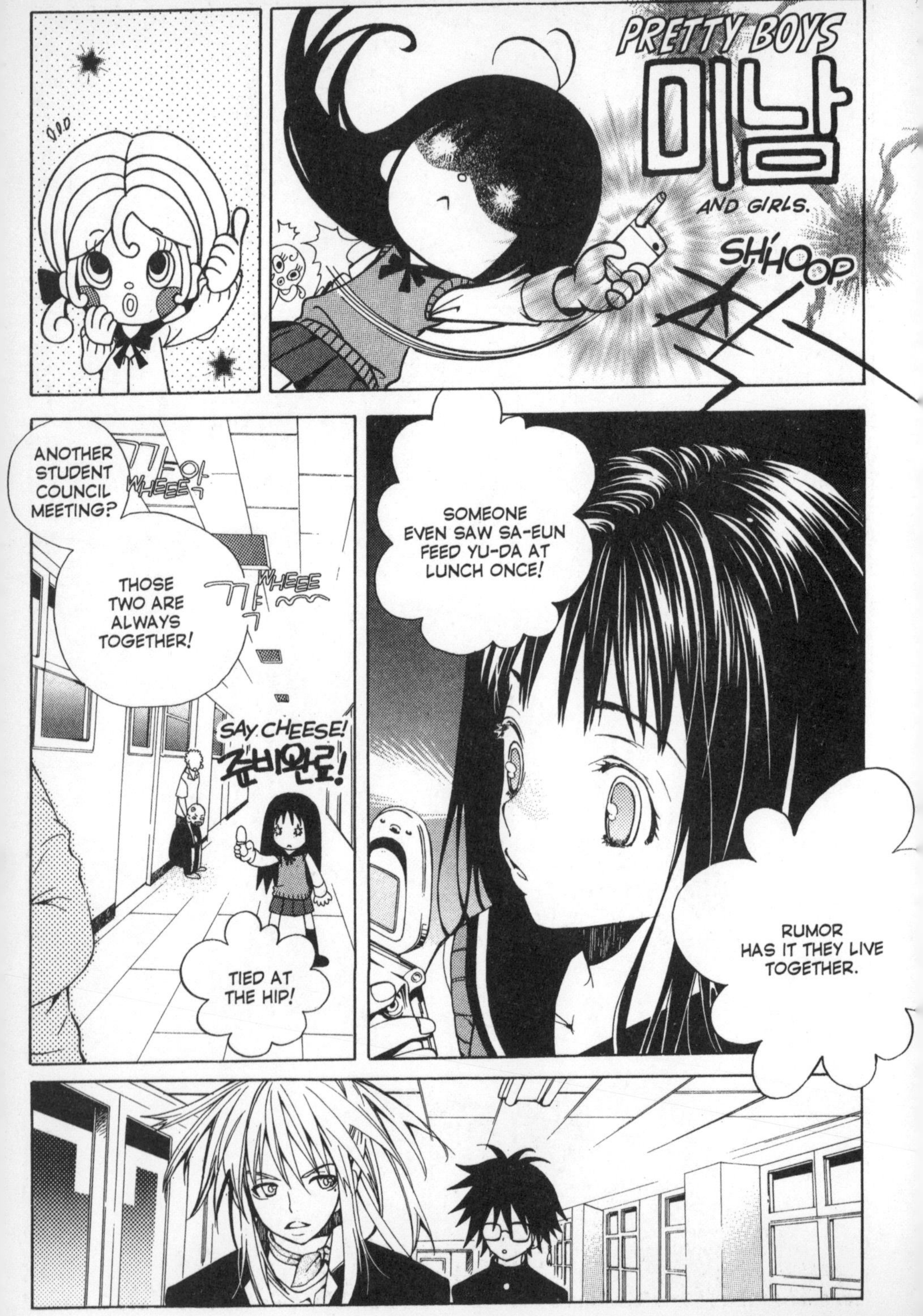

PRETTY BOYS
미남
AND GIRLS.
SH'HOOP
ANOTHER STUDENT COUNCIL MEETING?
WHEEE
THOSE TWO ARE ALWAYS TOGETHER!
WHEEE
SAY CHEESE!
준비완료!
TIED AT THE HIP!
SOMEONE EVEN SAW SA-EUN FEED YU-DA AT LUNCH ONCE!
RUMOR HAS IT THEY LIVE TOGETHER.

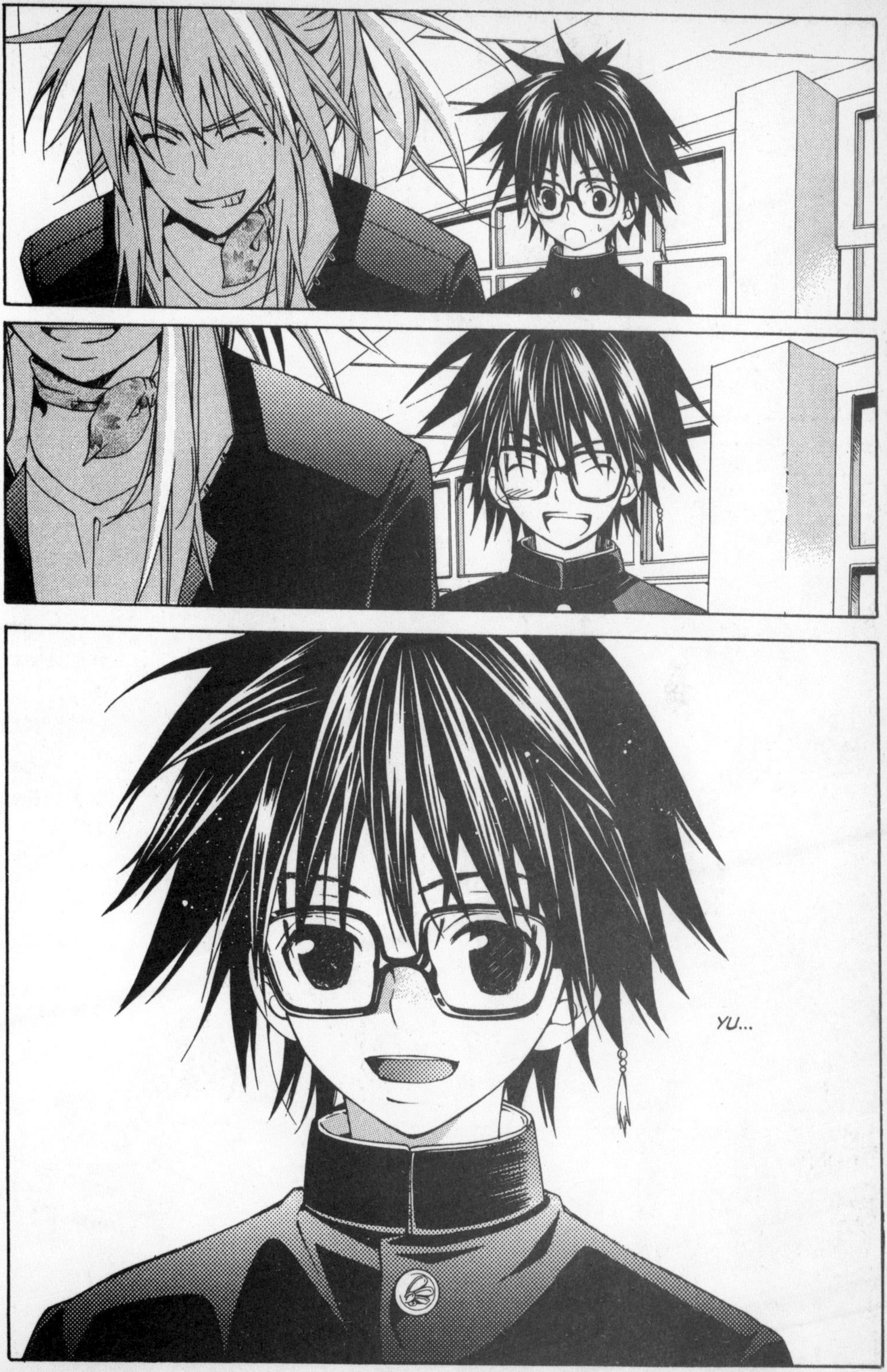
YU...

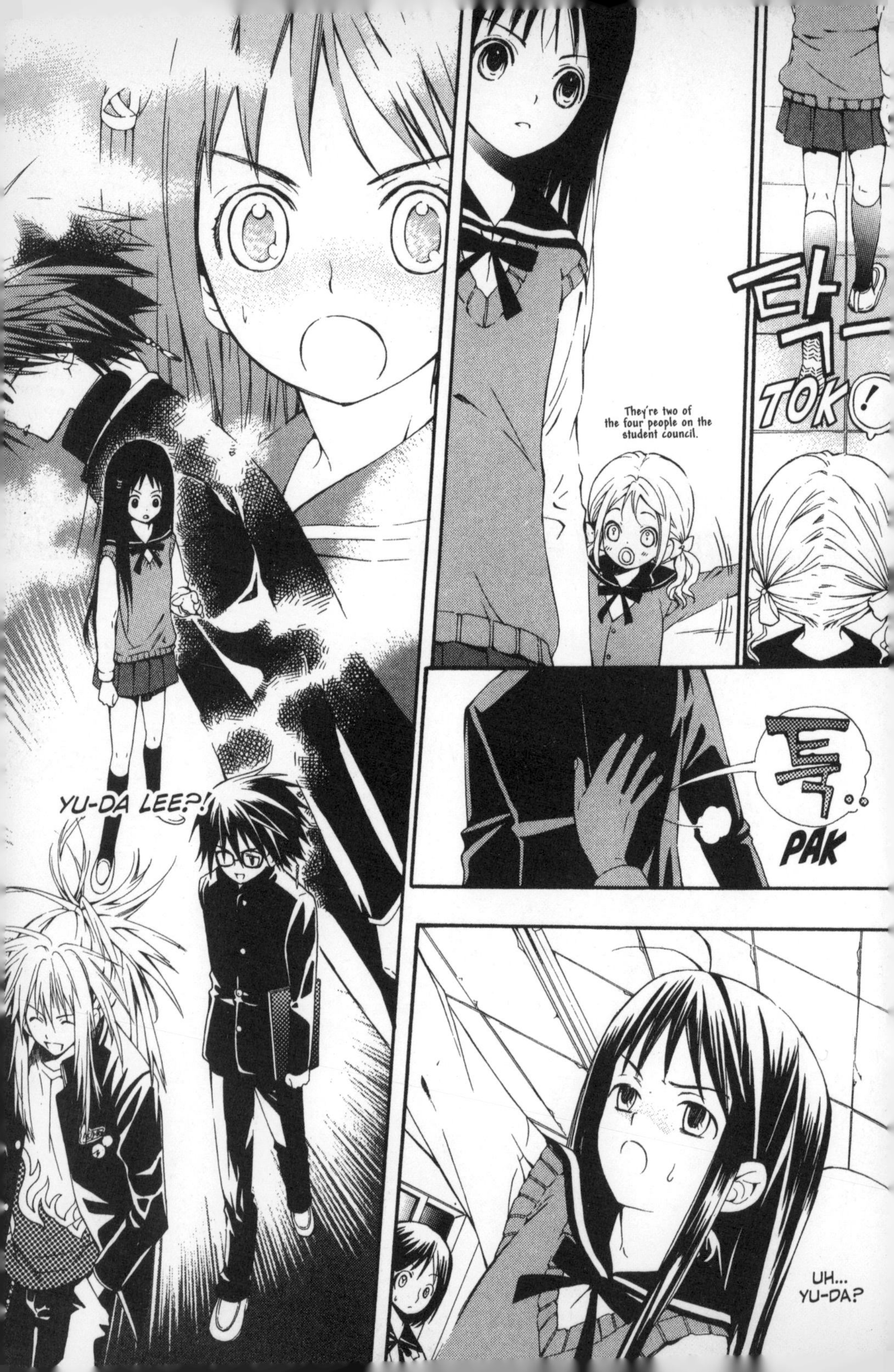
YU-DA LEE?!
They're two of the four people on the student council.
탁-
TOK!
툭
PAK
UH... YU-DA?

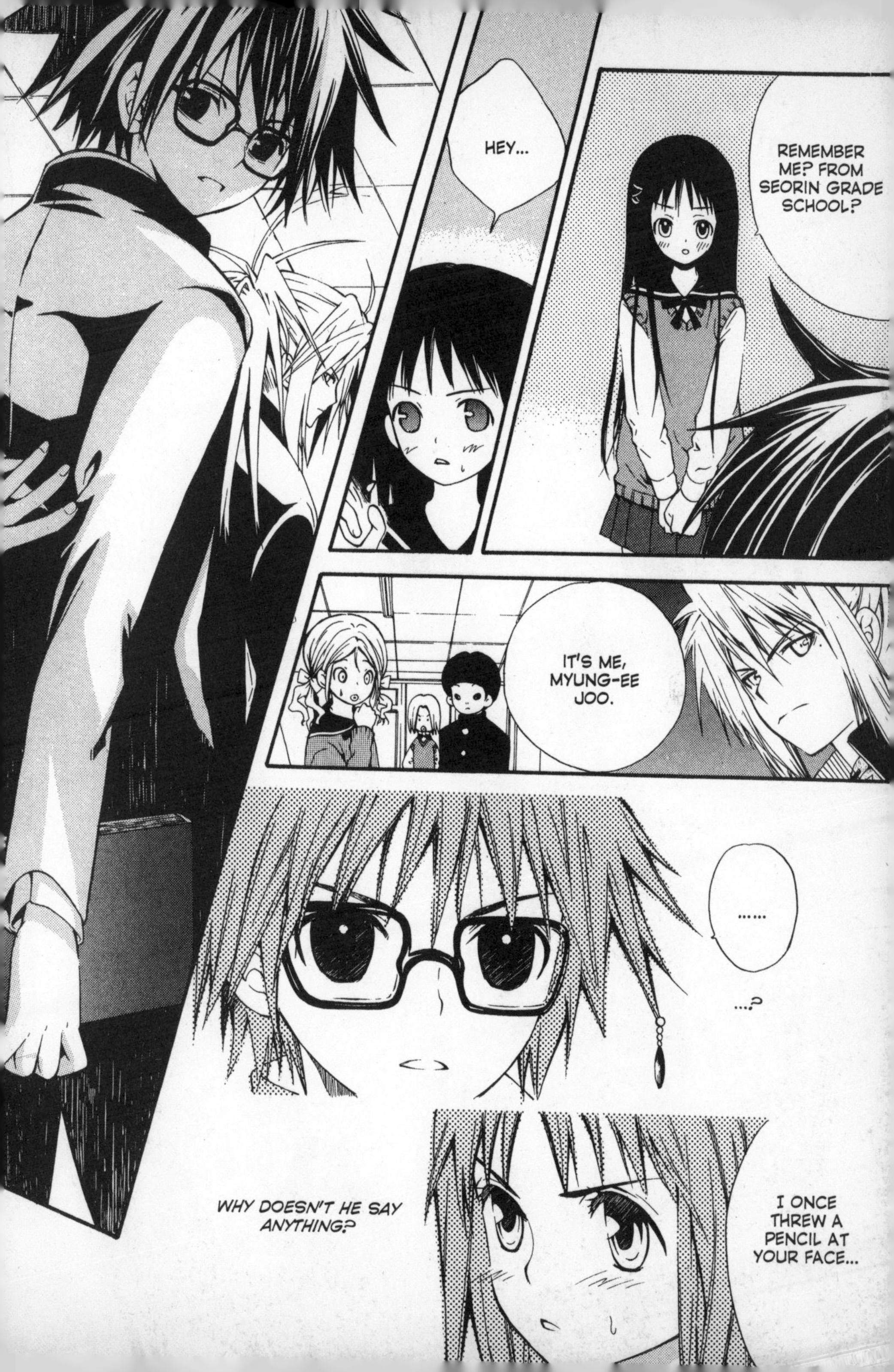
HEY...
REMEMBER ME? FROM SEORIN GRADE SCHOOL?
IT'S ME, MYUNG-EE JOO.
......
...?
WHY DOESN'T HE SAY ANYTHING?
I ONCE THREW A PENCIL AT YOUR FACE...

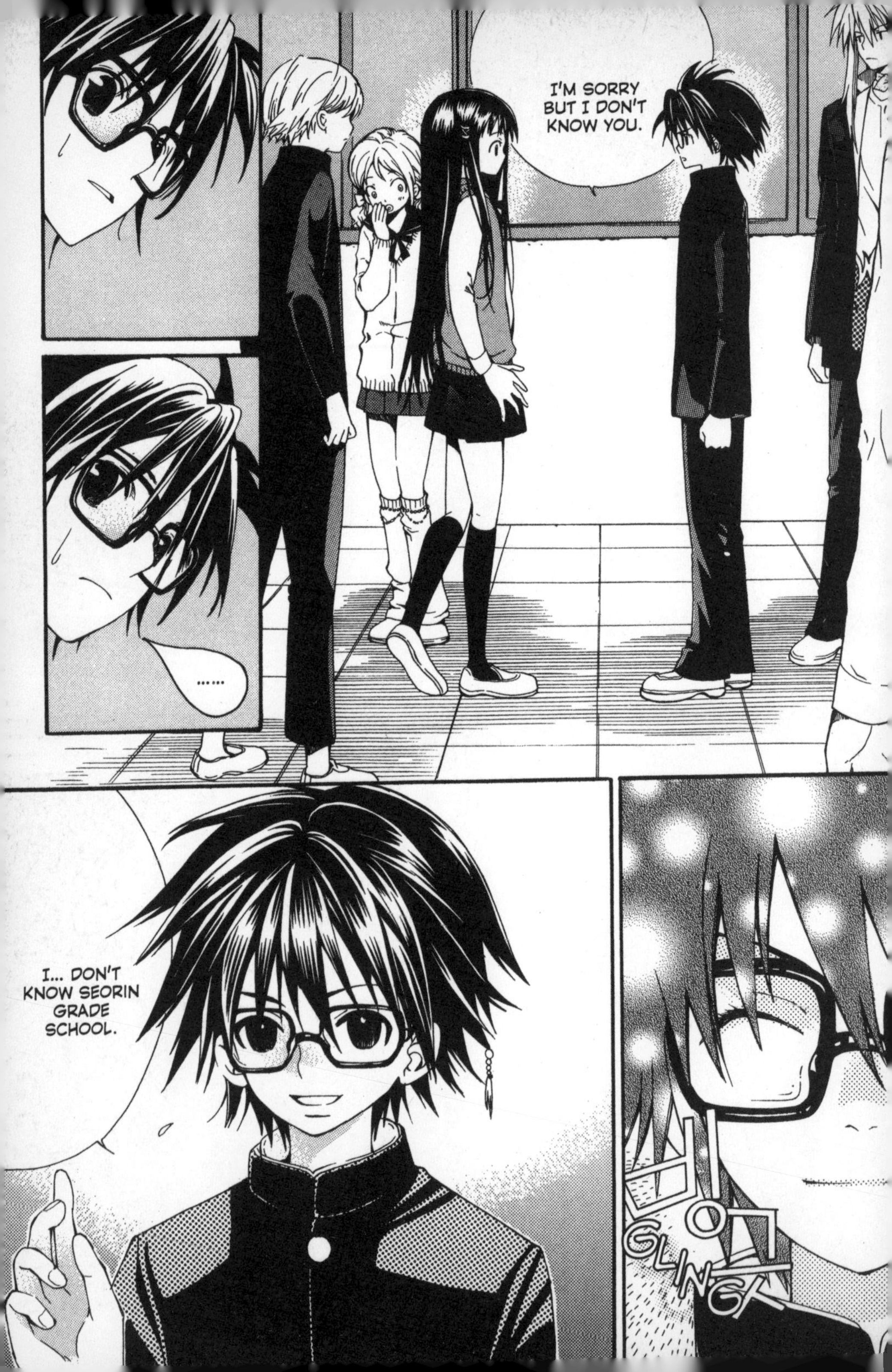
I'M SORRY BUT I DON'T KNOW YOU.
......
GLINK
I... DON'T KNOW SEORIN GRADE SCHOOL.

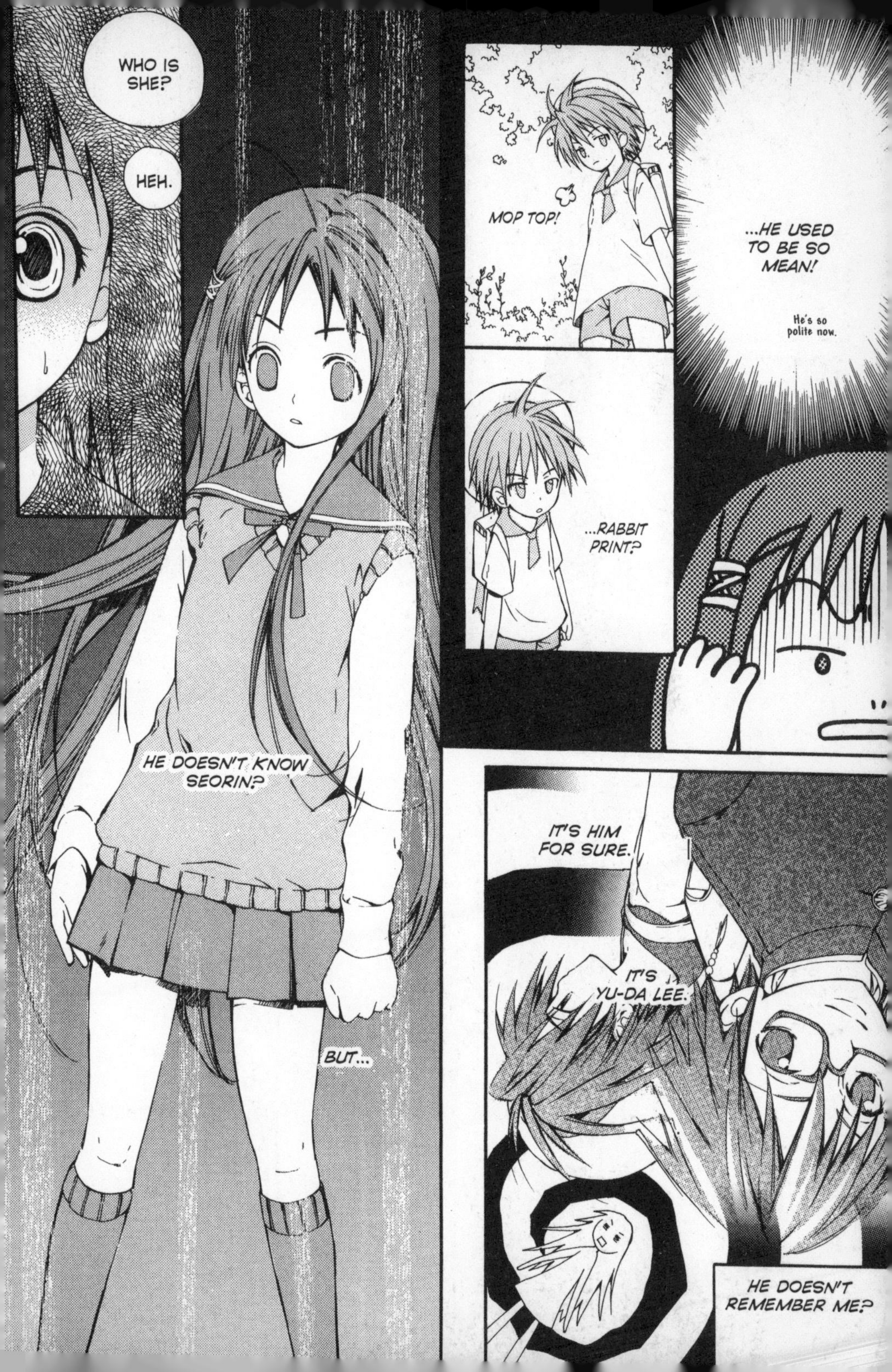

WHO IS SHE?
HEH.
HE DOESN'T KNOW SEORIN?
BUT...
MOP TOP!
...HE USED TO BE SO MEAN!
He's so polite now.
...RABBIT PRINT?
IT'S HIM FOR SURE.
IT'S YU-DA LEE.
HE DOESN'T REMEMBER ME?

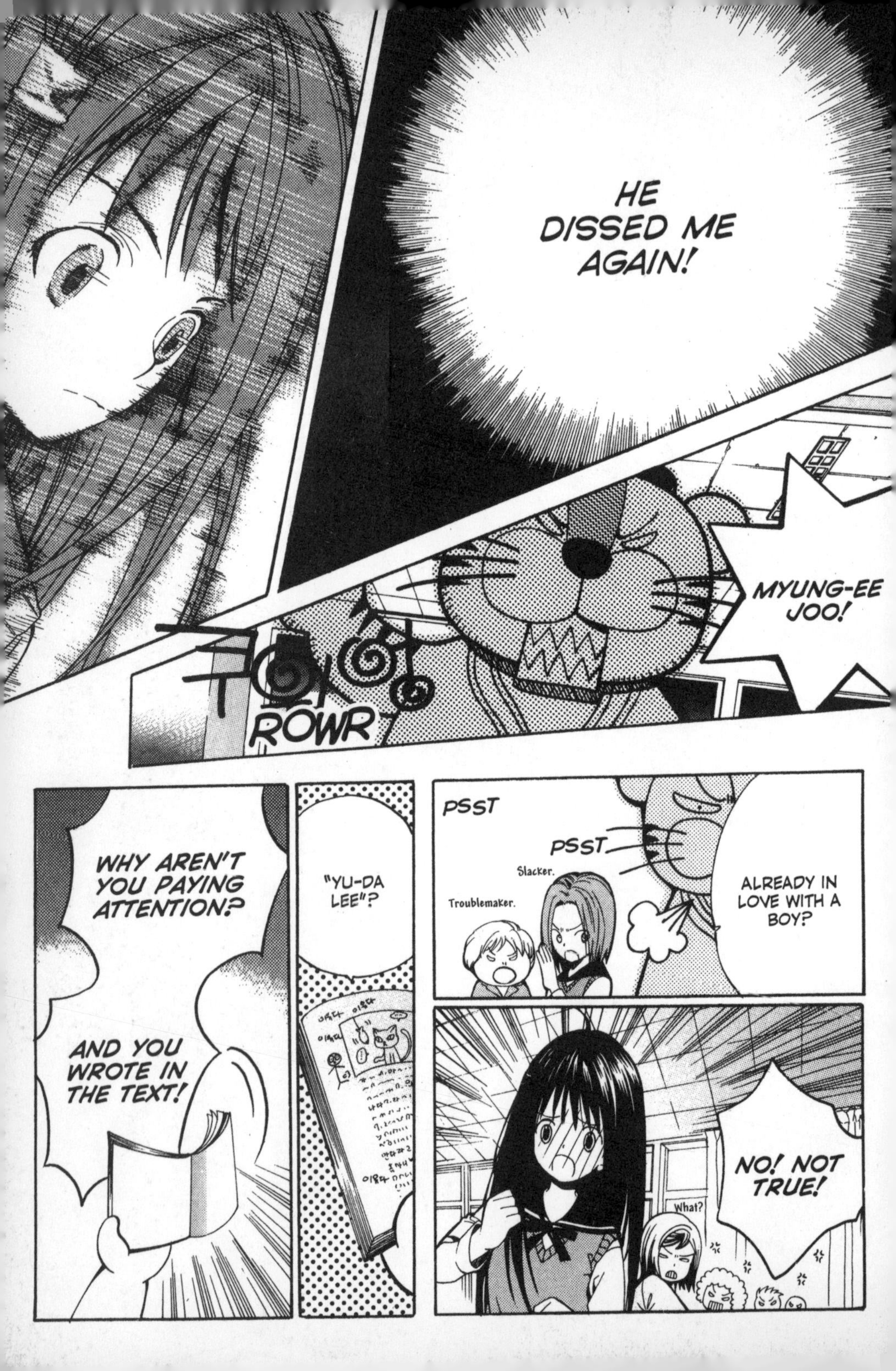

HE DISSED ME AGAIN!
MYUNG-EE JOO!
ROWR
WHY AREN'T YOU PAYING ATTENTION?
AND YOU WROTE IN THE TEXT!
"YU-DA LEE"?
PSST
PSST
Troublemaker.
Slacker.
ALREADY IN LOVE WITH A BOY?
NO! NOT TRUE!
What?

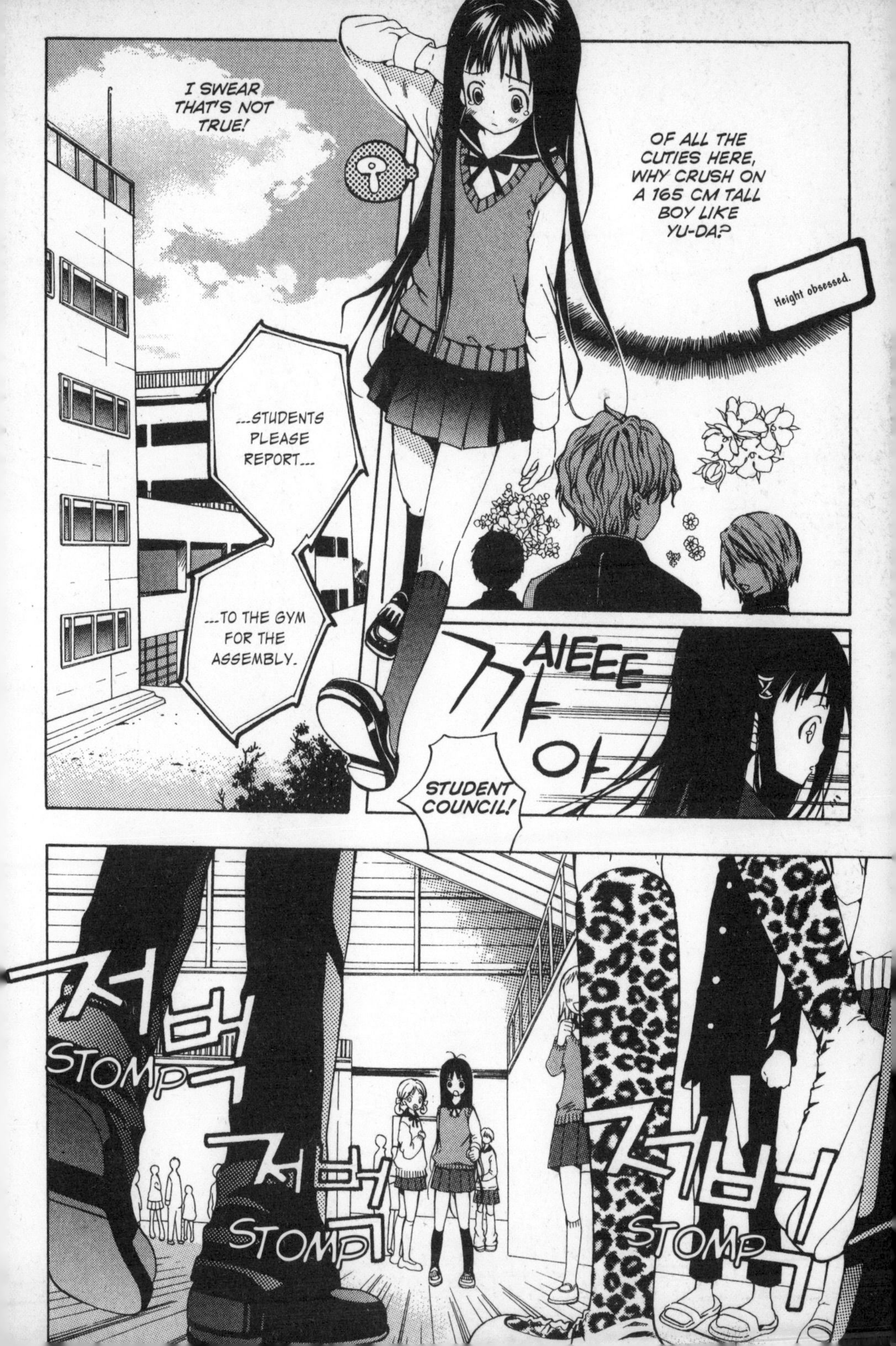
I SWEAR THAT'S NOT TRUE!
OF ALL THE CUTIES HERE, WHY CRUSH ON A 165 CM TALL BOY LIKE YU-DA?
Height obsessed.
...STUDENTS PLEASE REPORT...
...TO THE GYM FOR THE ASSEMBLY.
AIEEEE
까아
STUDENT COUNCIL!
저벅
STOMP
저벅
STOMP
저벅
STOMP

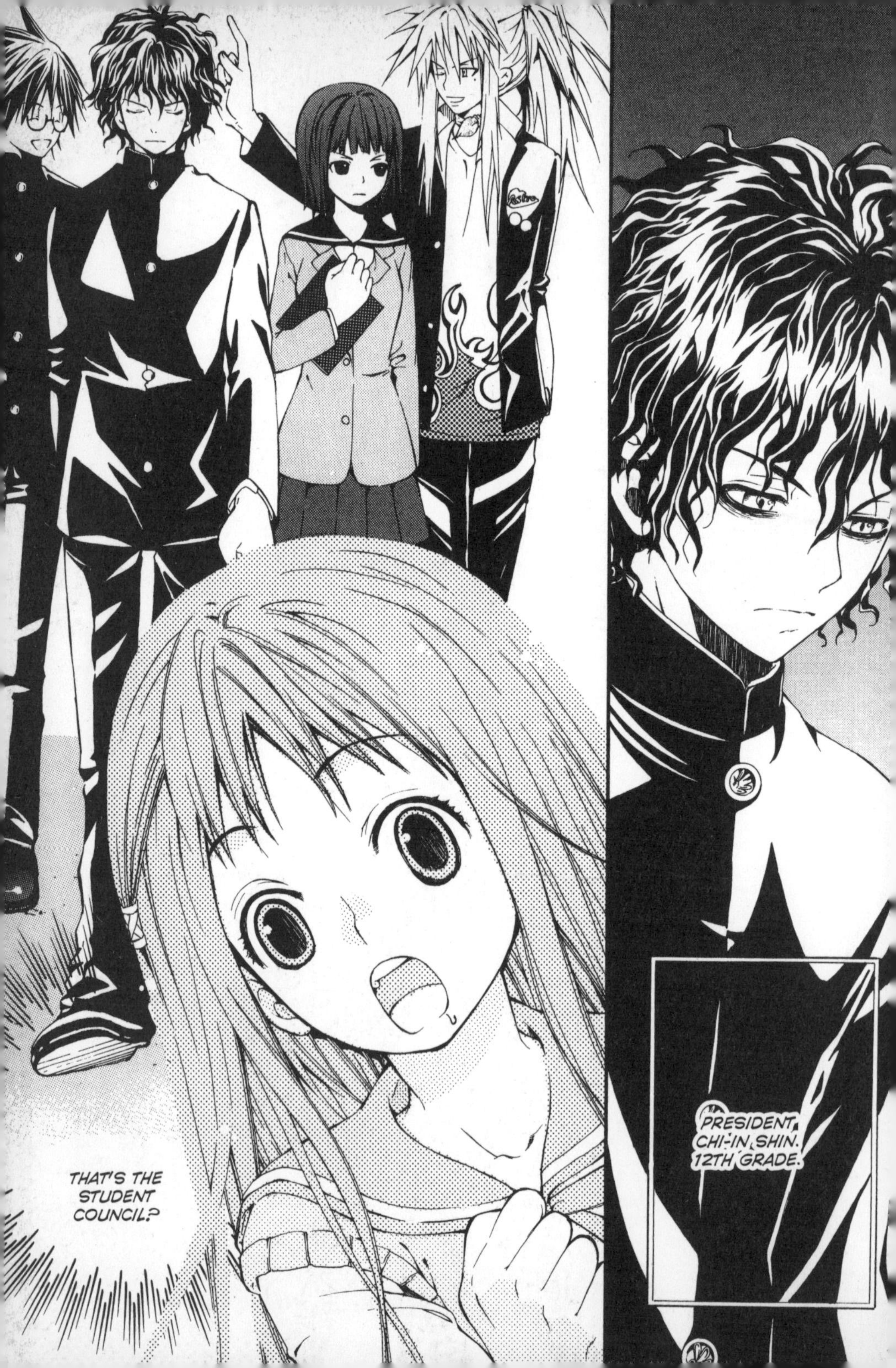
THAT'S THE STUDENT COUNCIL?
PRESIDENT, CHI-IN SHIN. 12TH GRADE.

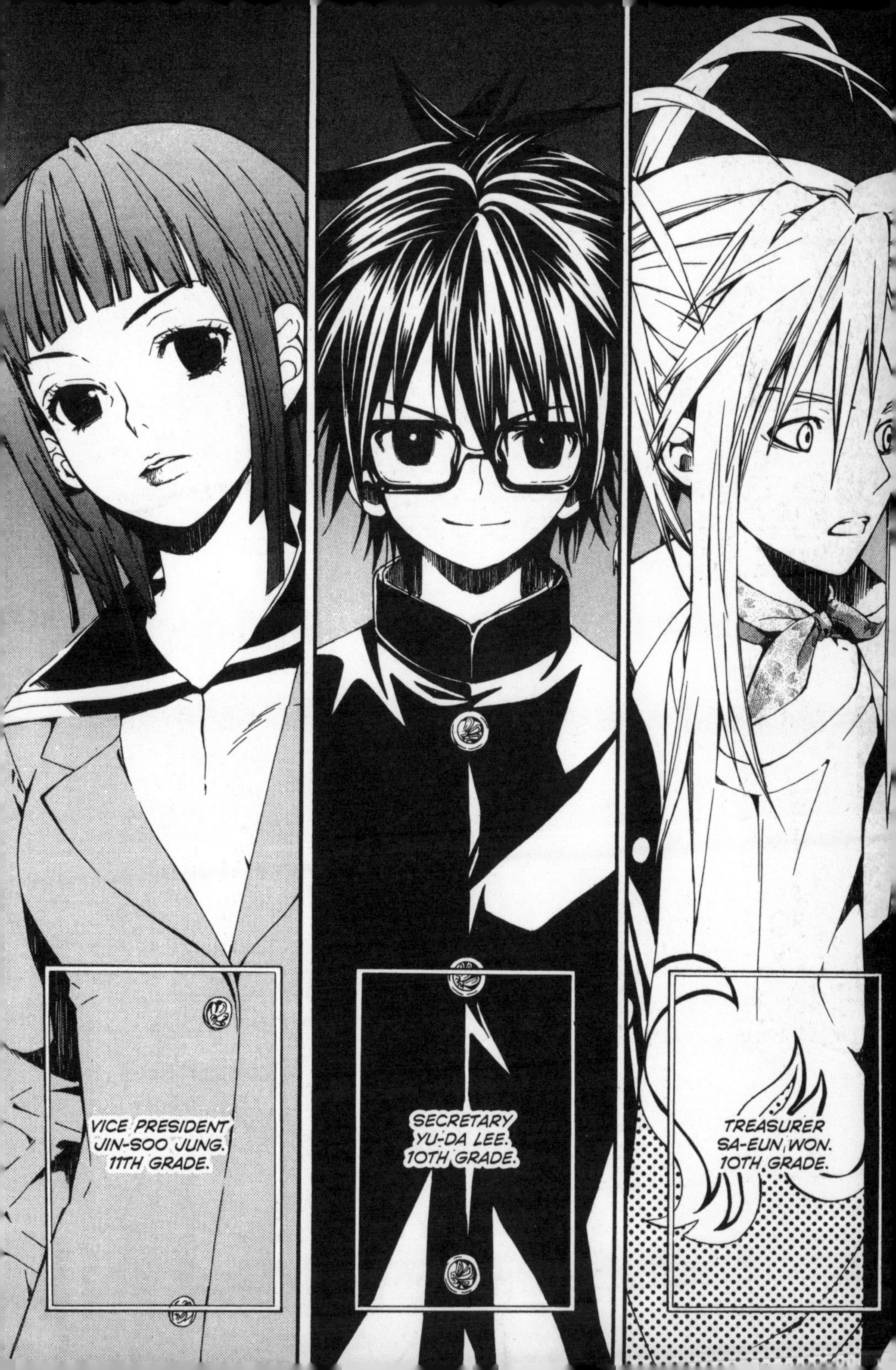
VICE PRESIDENT JIN-SOO JUNG. 11TH GRADE.
SECRETARY YU-DA LEE. 10TH GRADE.
TREASURER SA-EUN WON. 10TH GRADE.

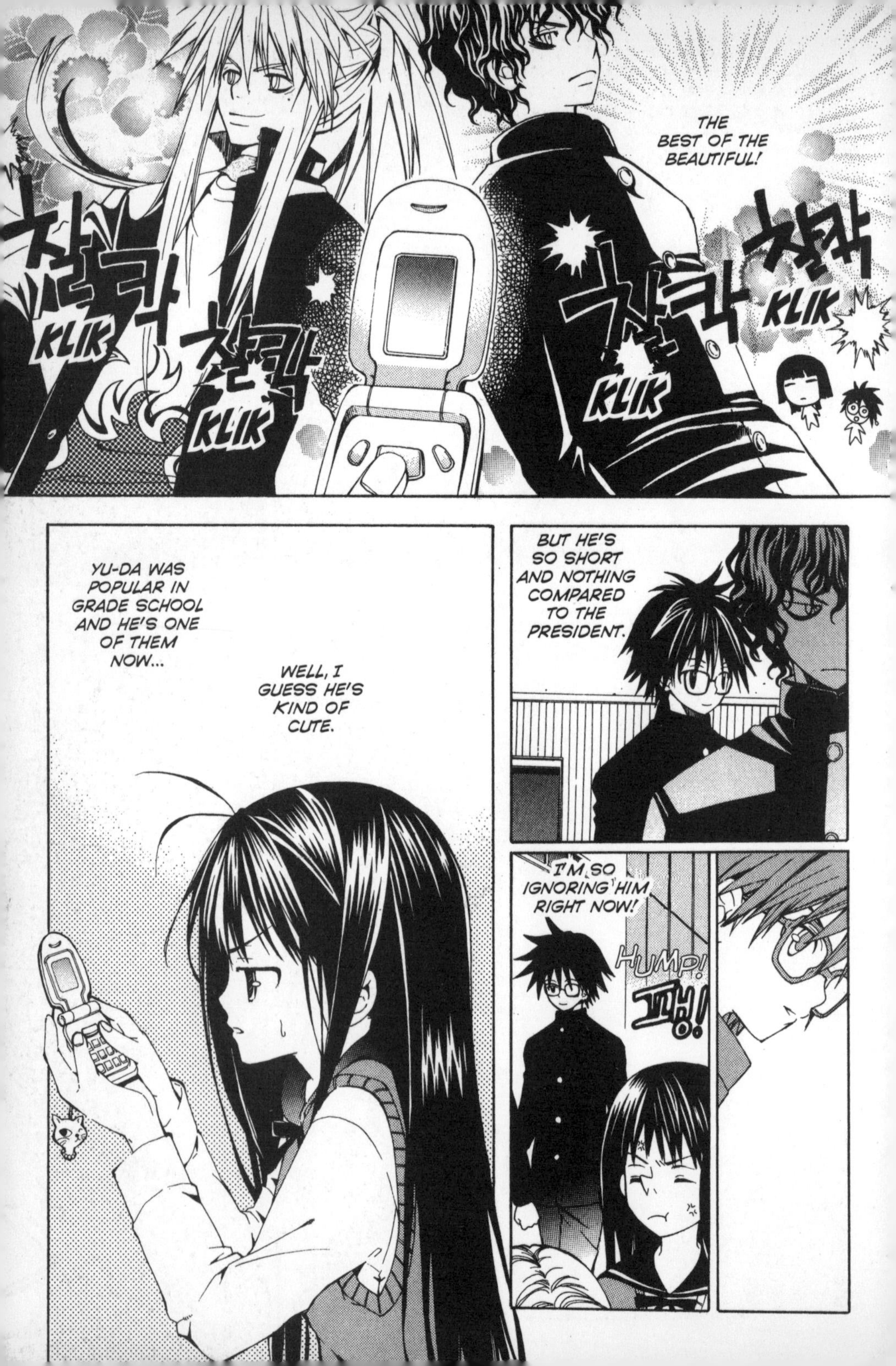
THE BEST OF THE BEAUTIFUL!
찰칵
KLIK
찰칵
KLIK
찰칵
KLIK
찰칵
KLIK
YU-DA WAS POPULAR IN GRADE SCHOOL AND HE'S ONE OF THEM NOW...
WELL, I GUESS HE'S KIND OF CUTE.
BUT HE'S SO SHORT AND NOTHING COMPARED TO THE PRESIDENT.
I'M SO IGNORING HIM RIGHT NOW!
HUMP!
흥!

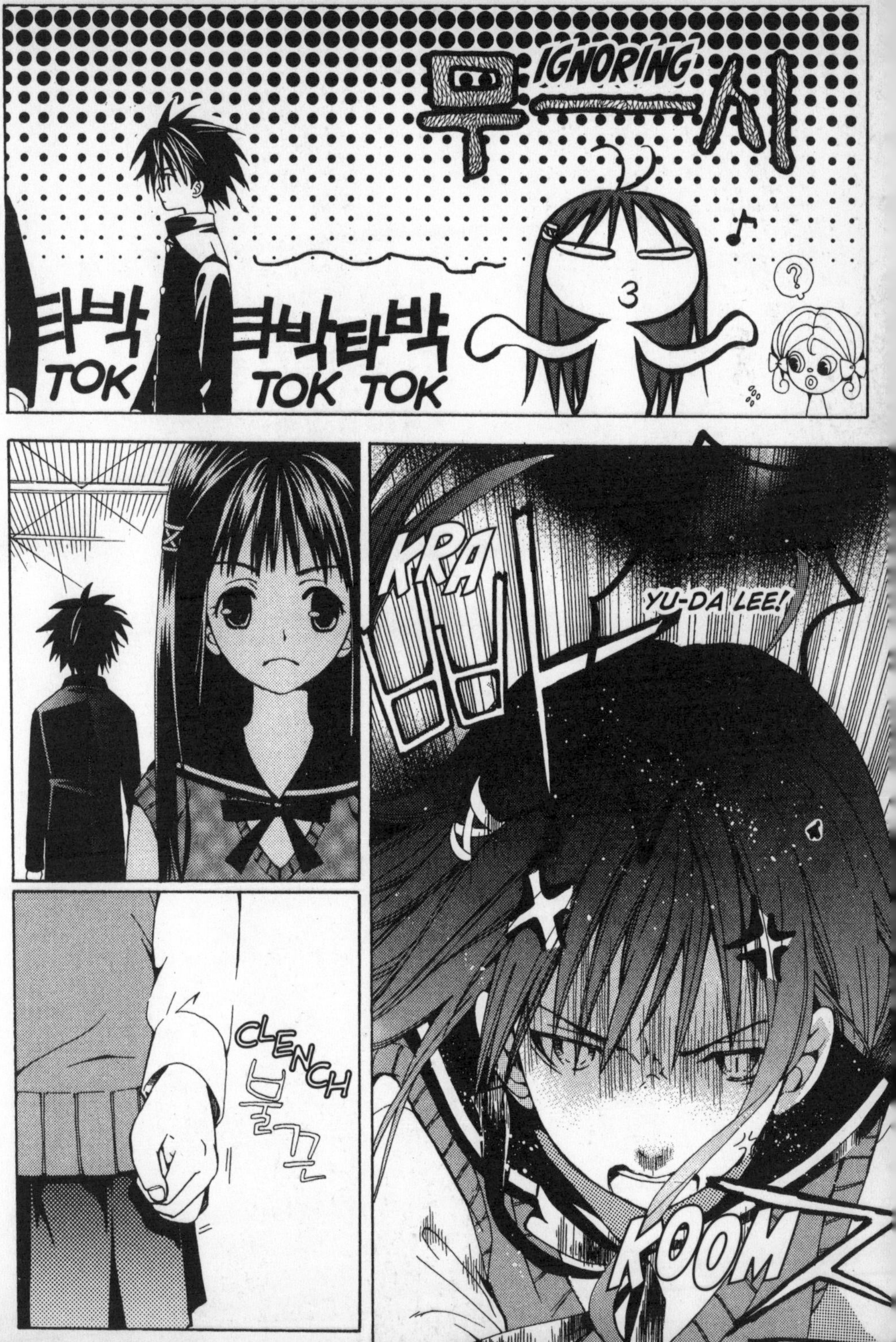

IGNORING
무-시
타박
TOK
타박타박
TOK TOK
KRA
YU-DA LEE!
CLENCH
불끈
KOOM

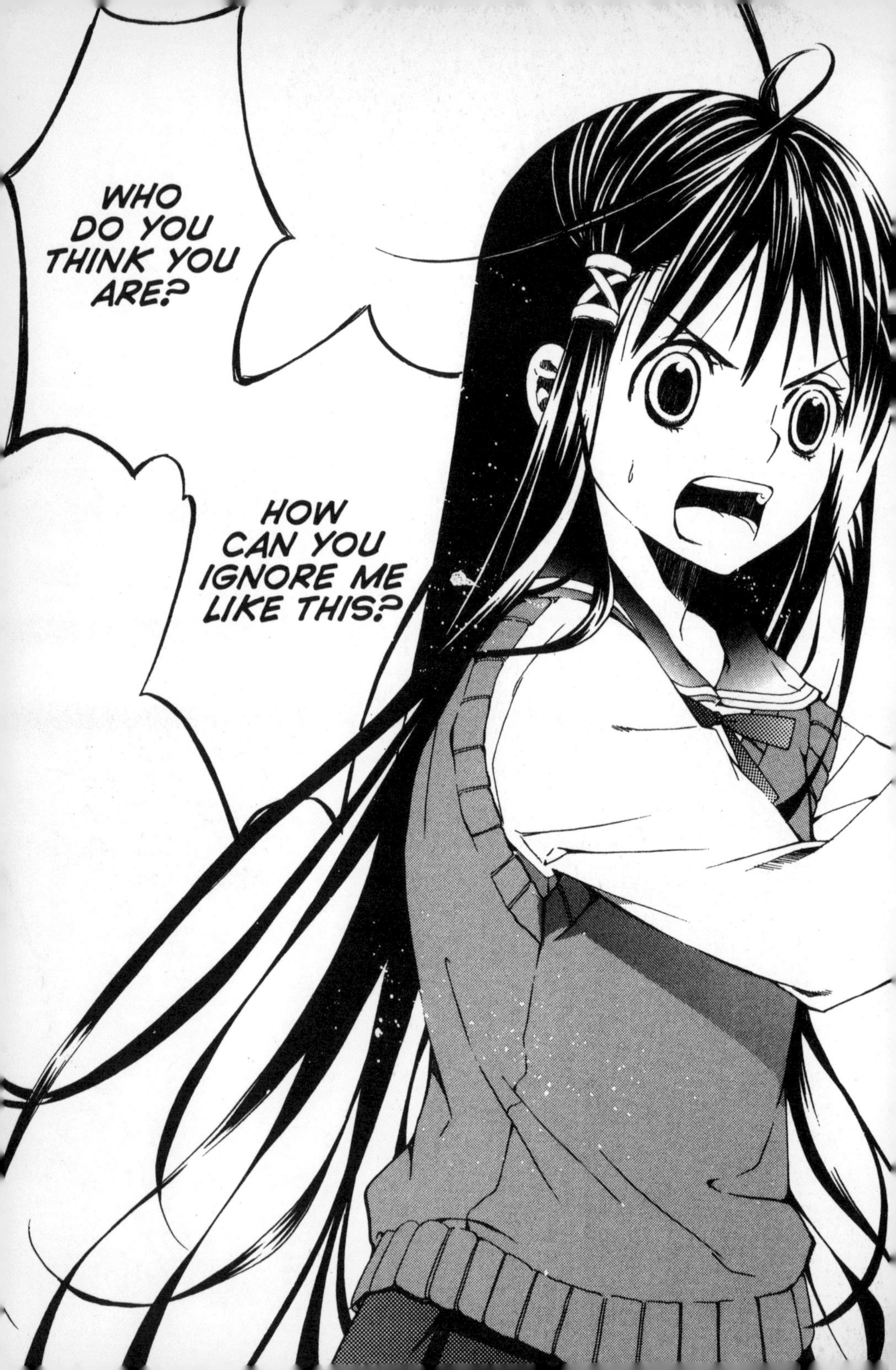
WHO DO YOU THINK YOU ARE?
HOW CAN YOU IGNORE ME LIKE THIS?

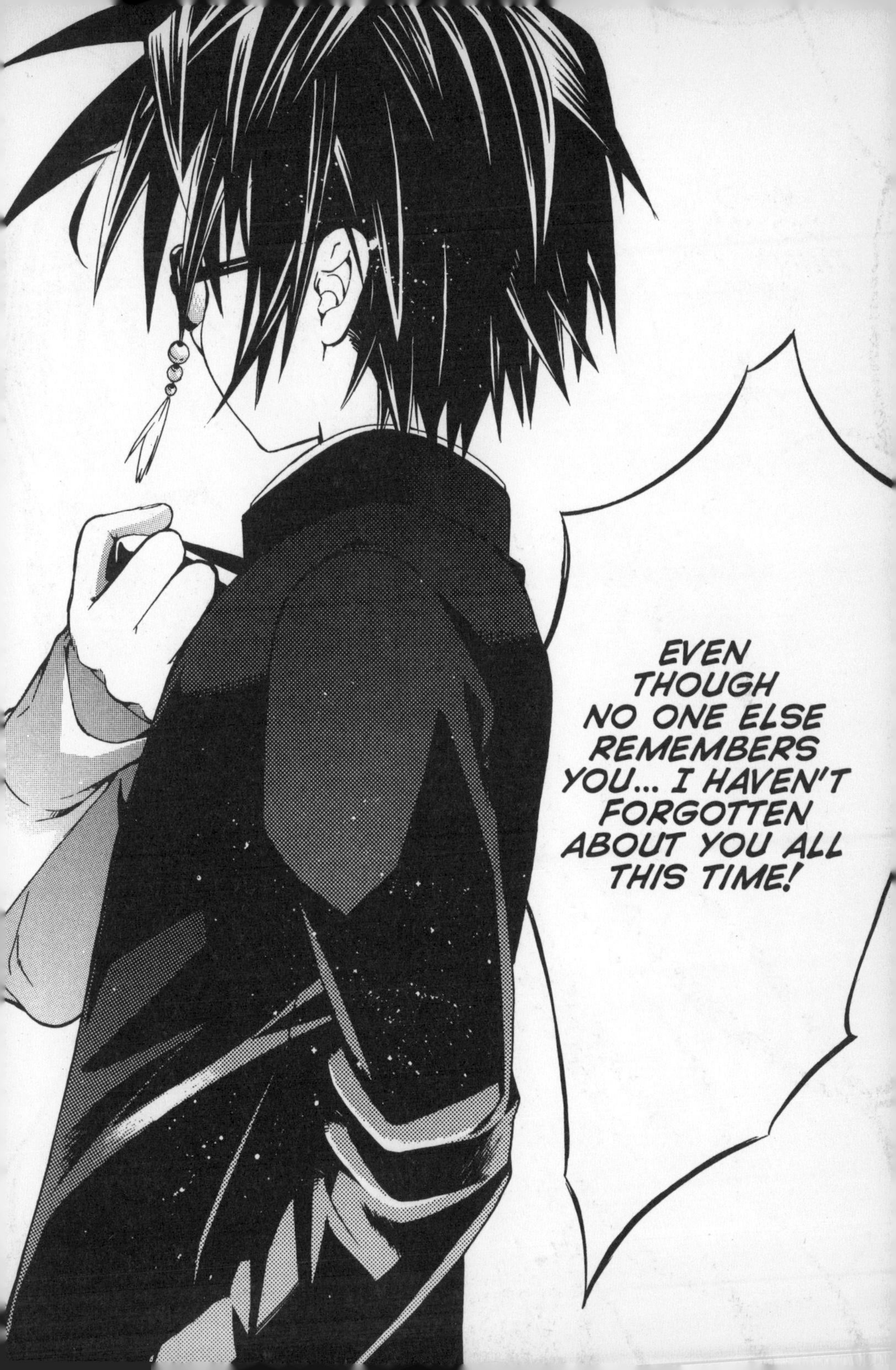
EVEN THOUGH NO ONE ELSE REMEMBERS YOU... I HAVEN'T FORGOTTEN ABOUT YOU ALL THIS TIME!

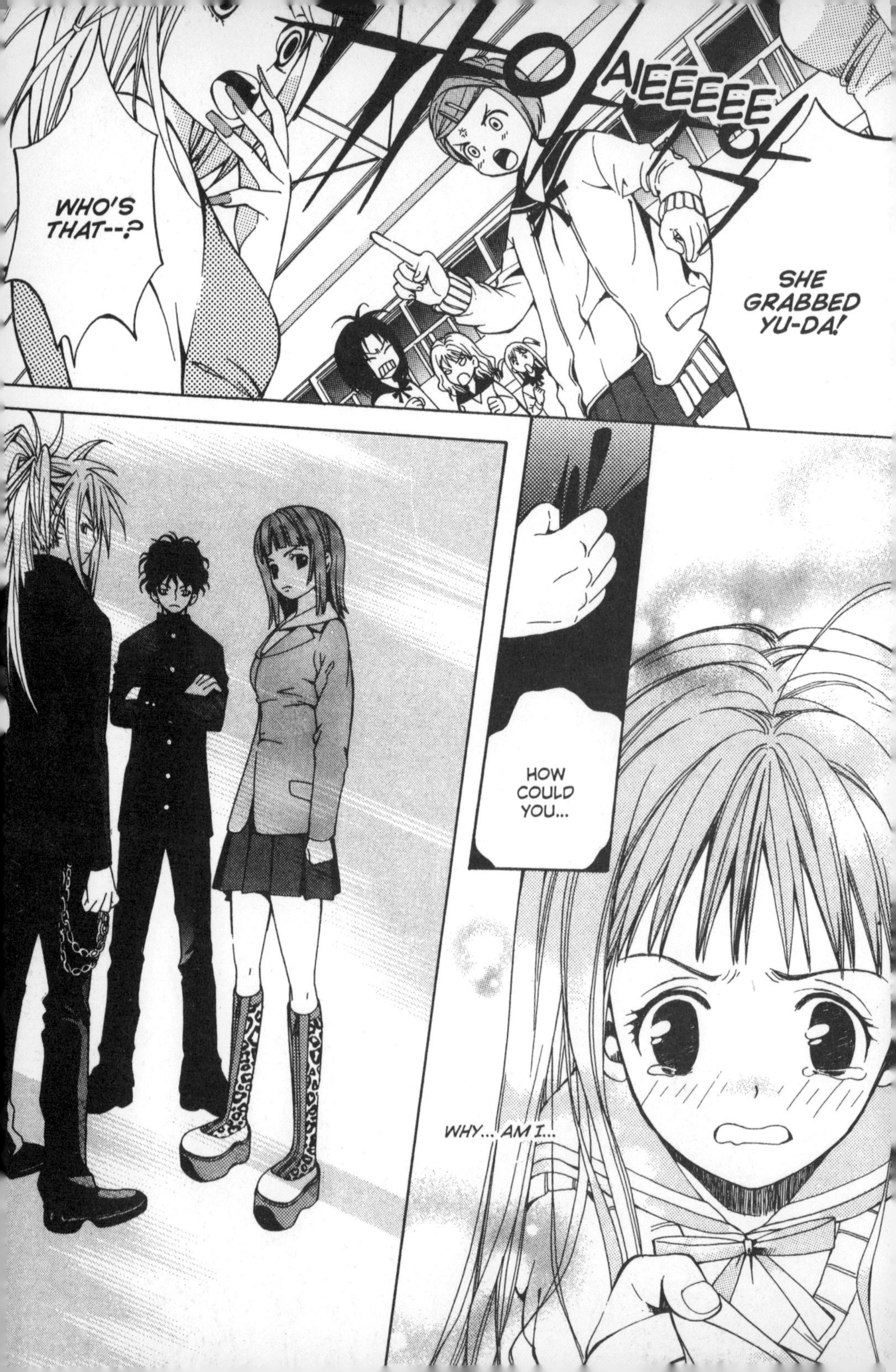
AIEEEEEE
WHO'S THAT--?
SHE GRABBED YU-DA!
HOW COULD YOU...
WHY... AM I...

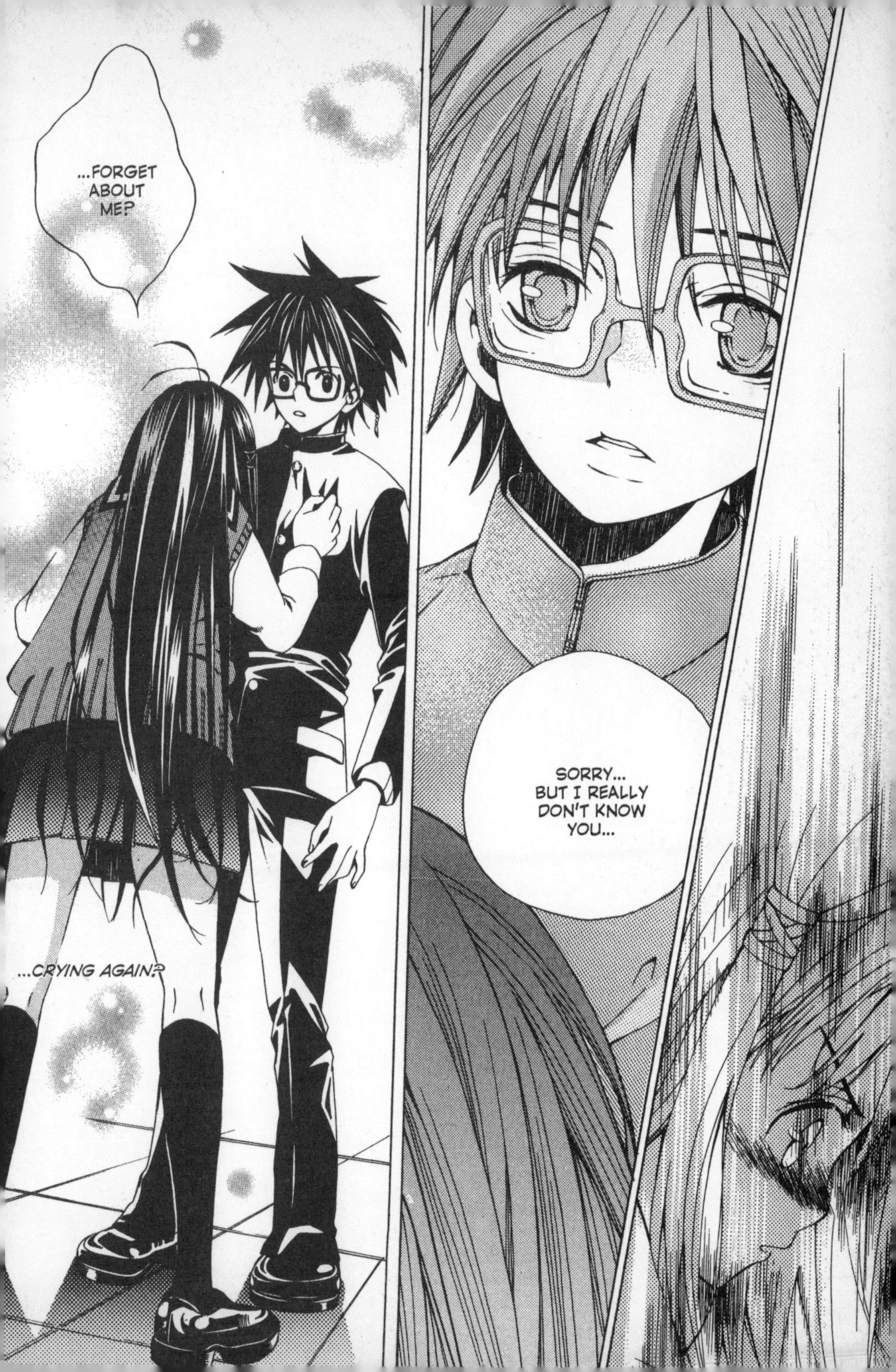
SORRY... BUT I REALLY DON'T KNOW YOU...
...FORGET ABOUT ME?
...CRYING AGAIN?

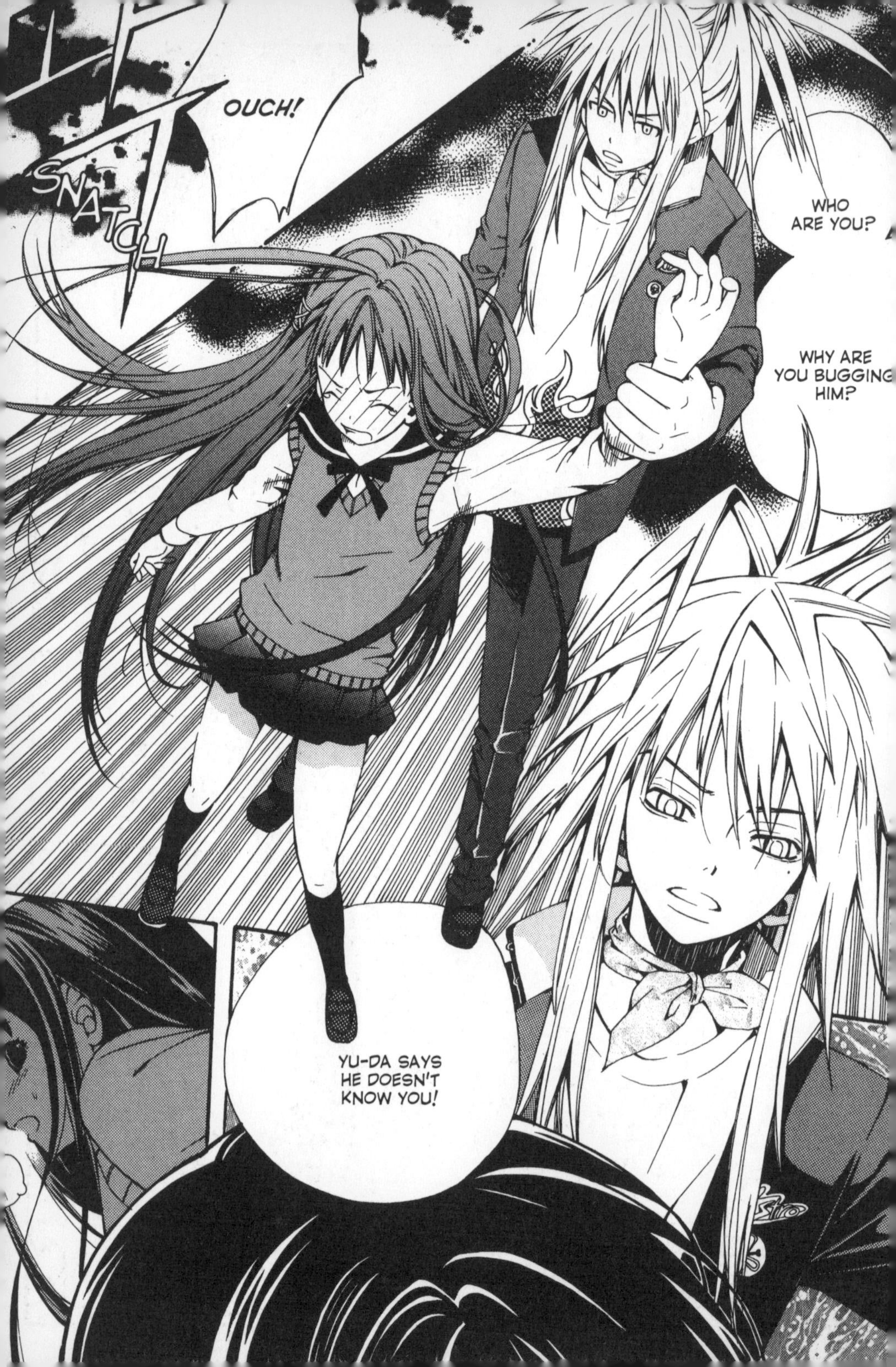
SNATCH
OUCH!
WHO ARE YOU?
WHY ARE YOU BUGGING HIM?
YU-DA SAYS HE DOESN'T KNOW YOU!

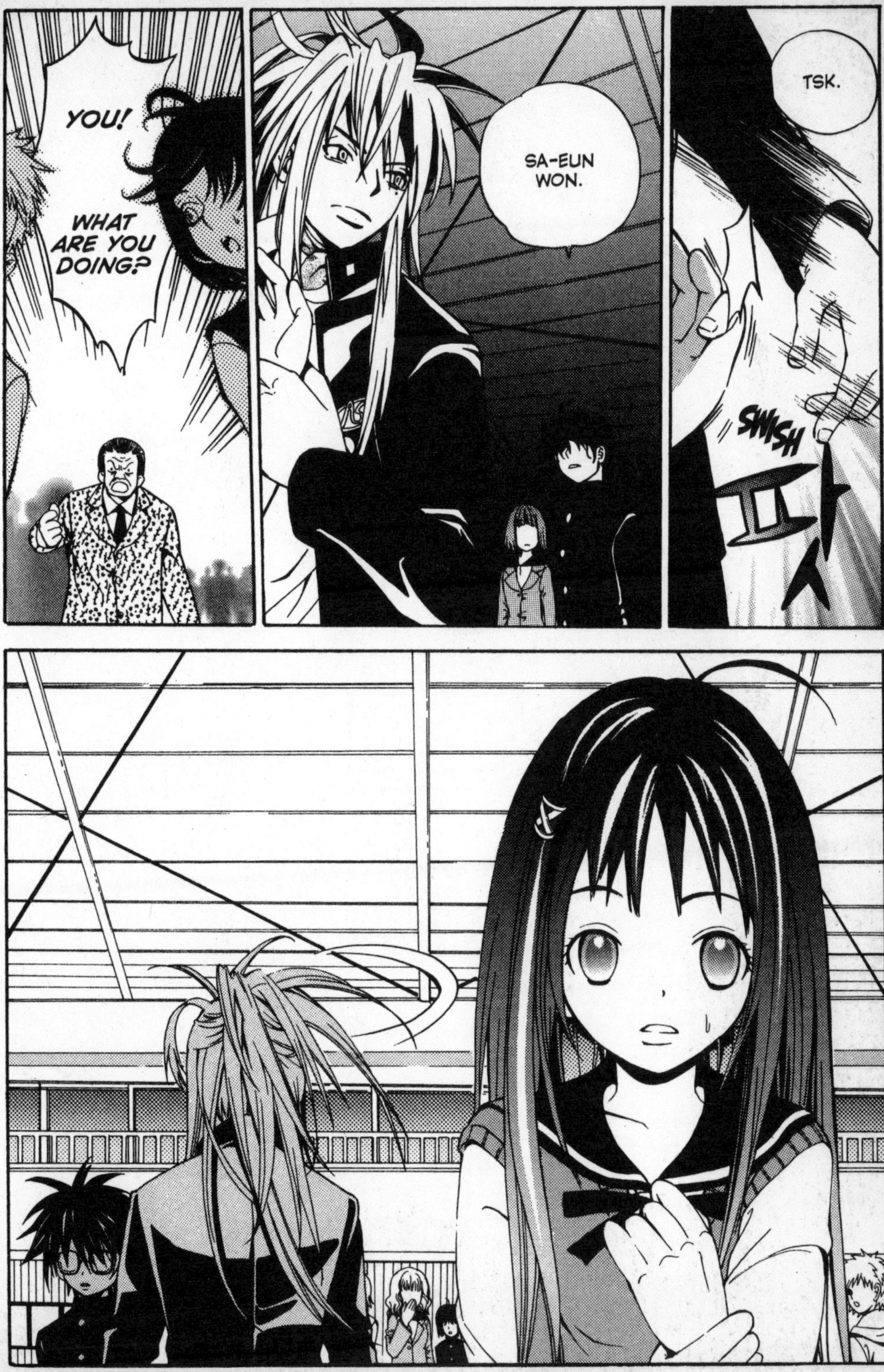
YOU!
WHAT ARE YOU DOING?
SA-EUN WON.
TSK.
SWISH

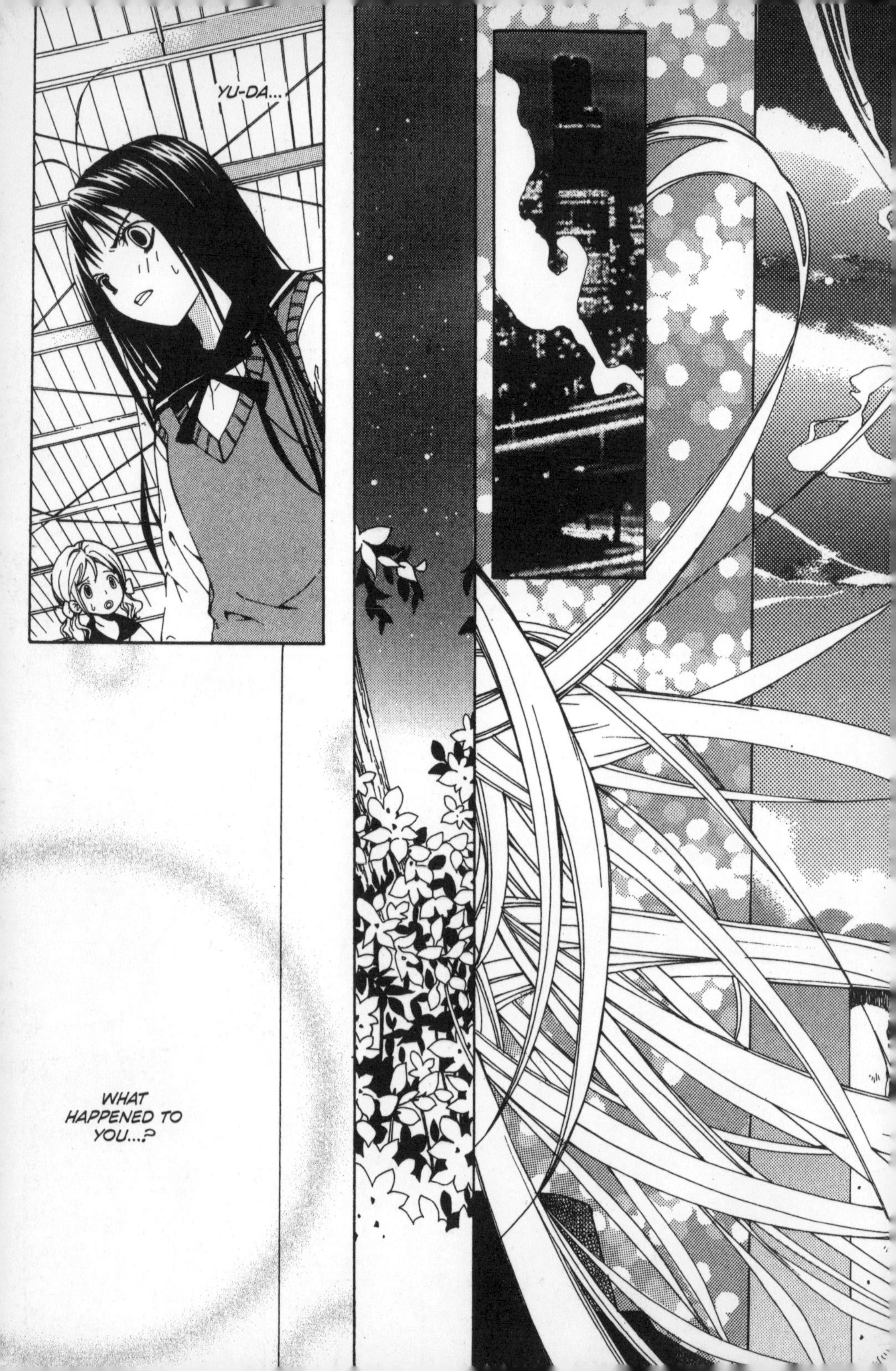
YU-DA...
WHAT HAPPENED TO YOU...?

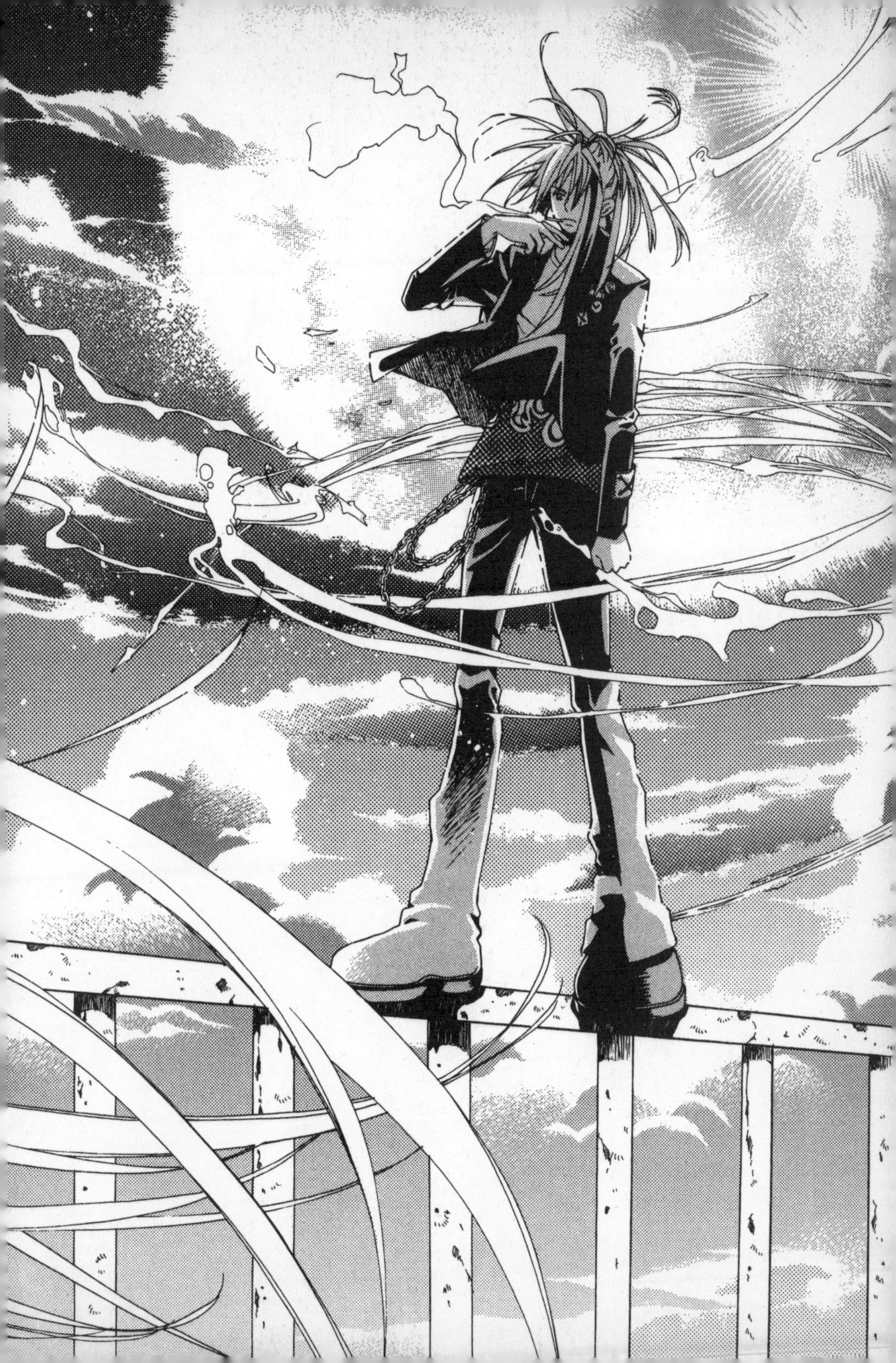

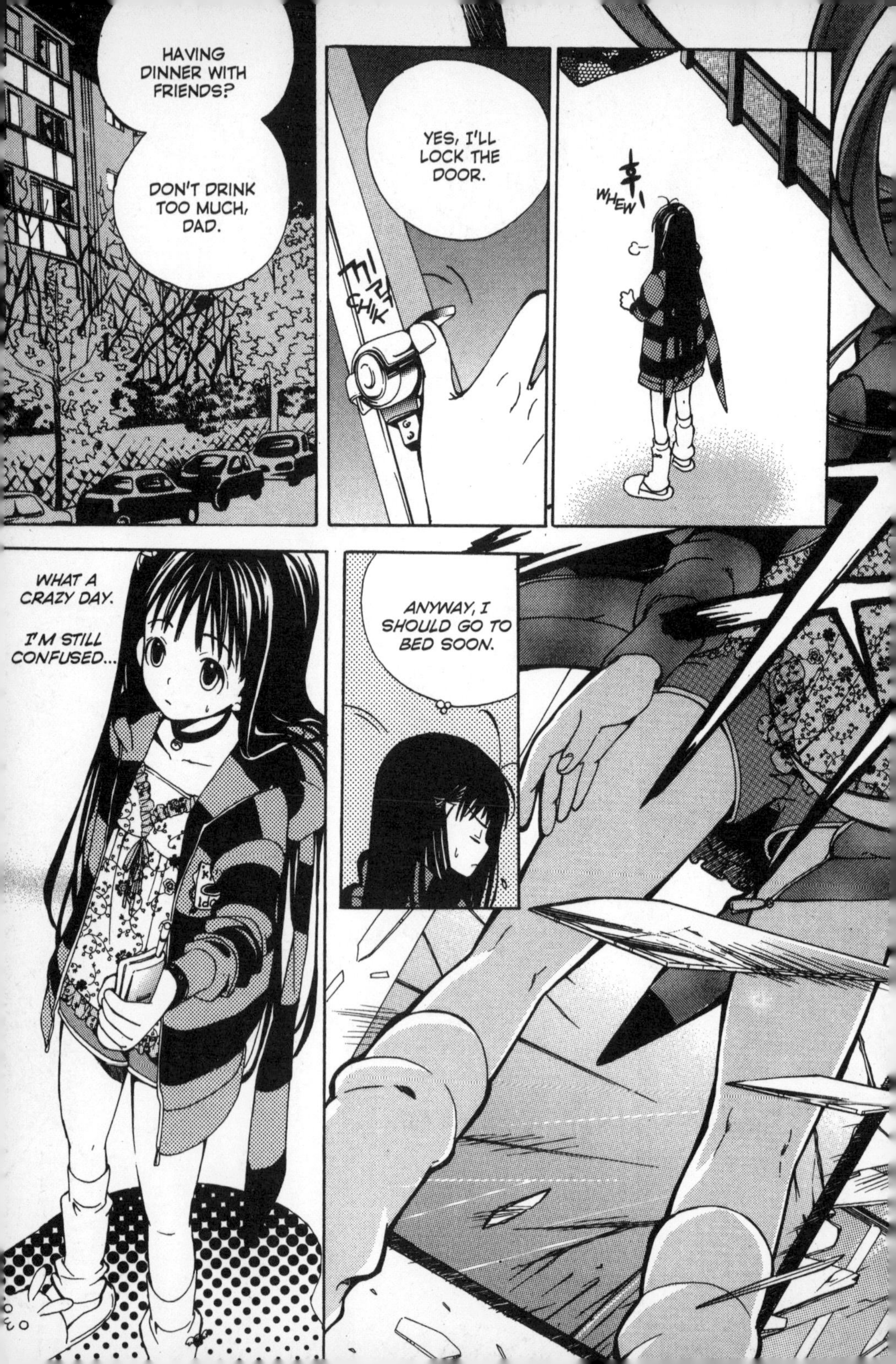

HAVING DINNER WITH FRIENDS?
DON'T DRINK TOO MUCH, DAD.
YES, I'LL LOCK THE DOOR.
CHIK
WHEW
WHAT A CRAZY DAY.
I'M STILL CONFUSED...
ANYWAY, I SHOULD GO TO BED SOON.

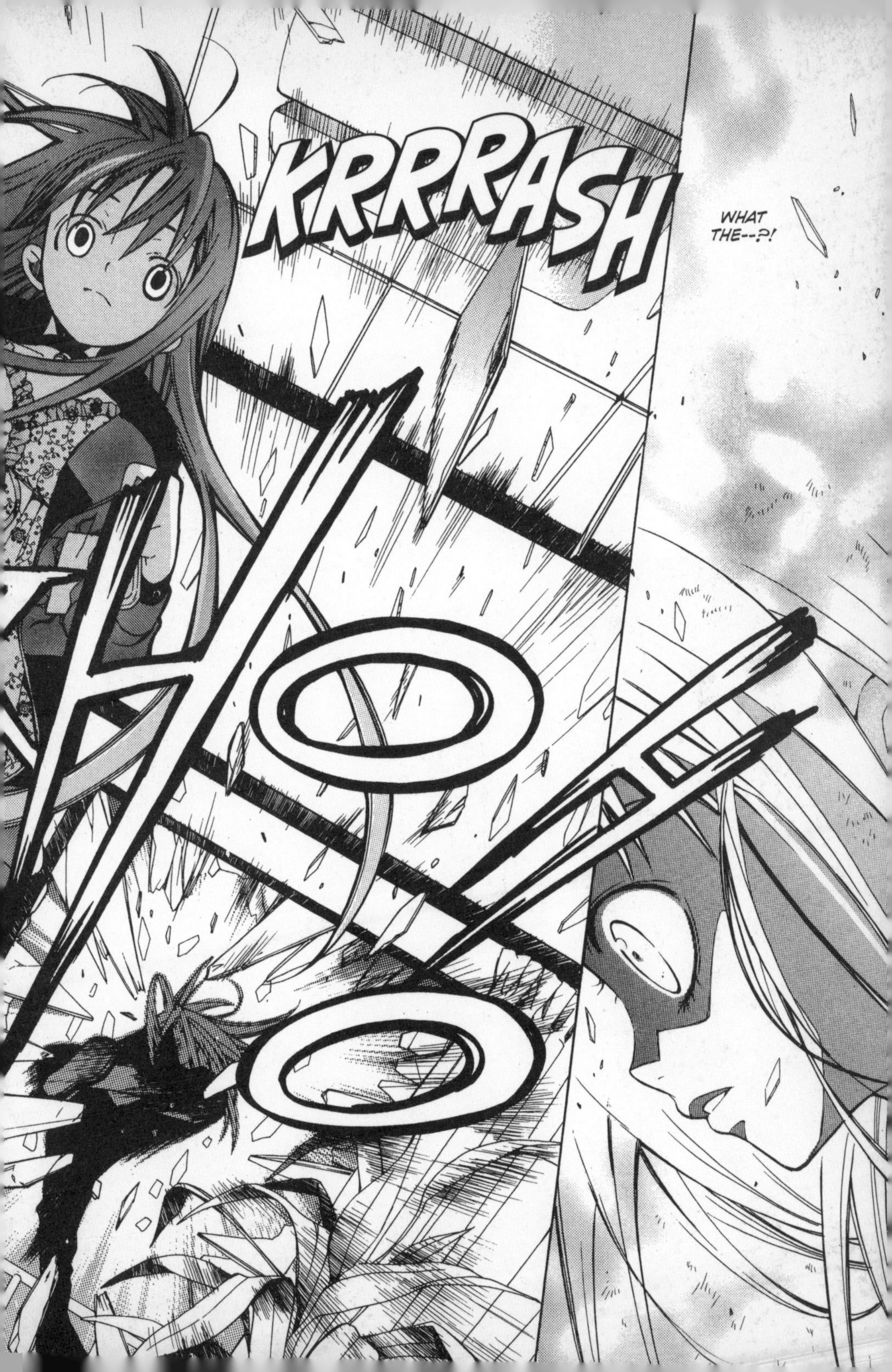
WHAT THE--?!
KRRRASH

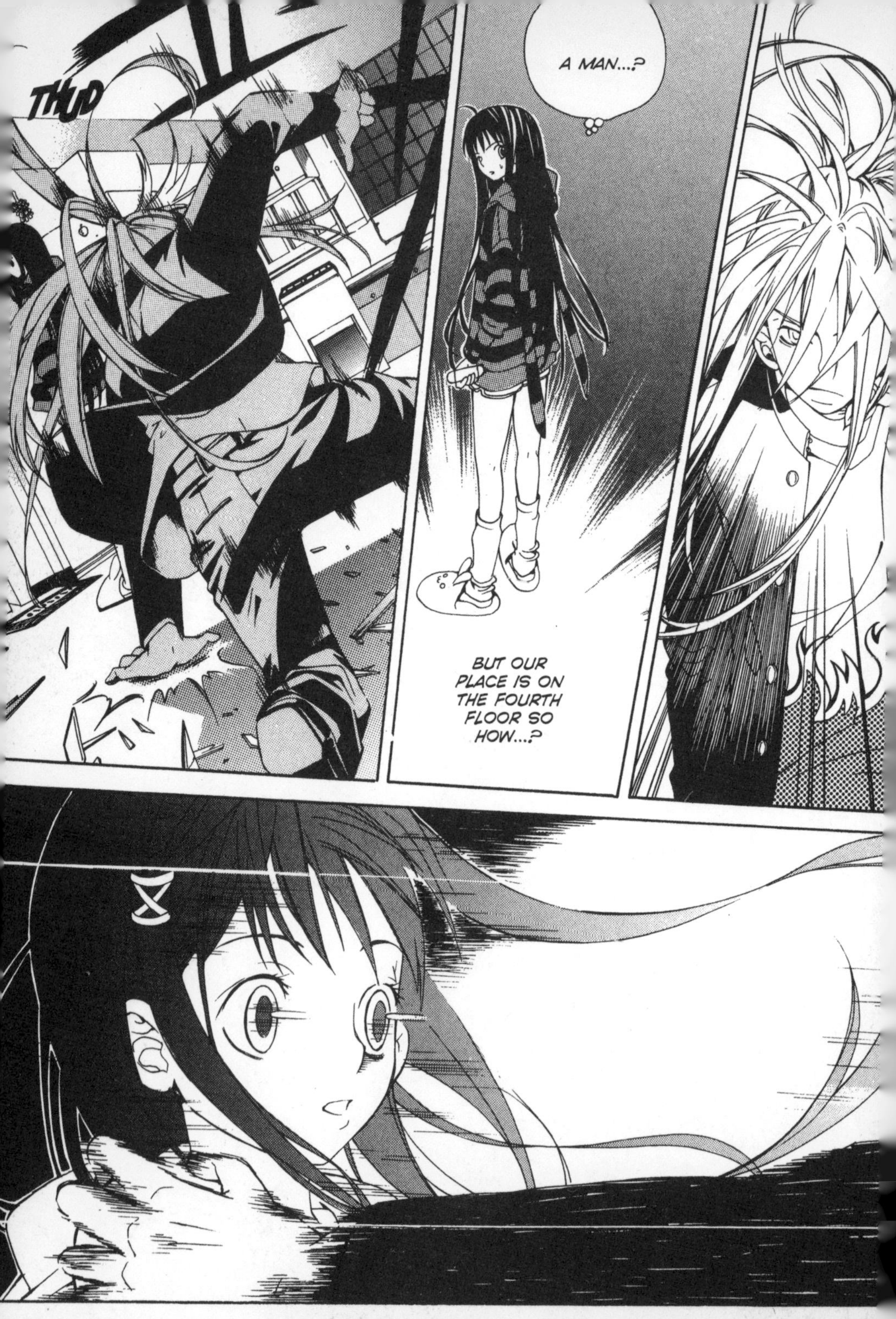
A MAN...?
BUT OUR PLACE IS ON THE FOURTH FLOOR SO HOW...?
THUD

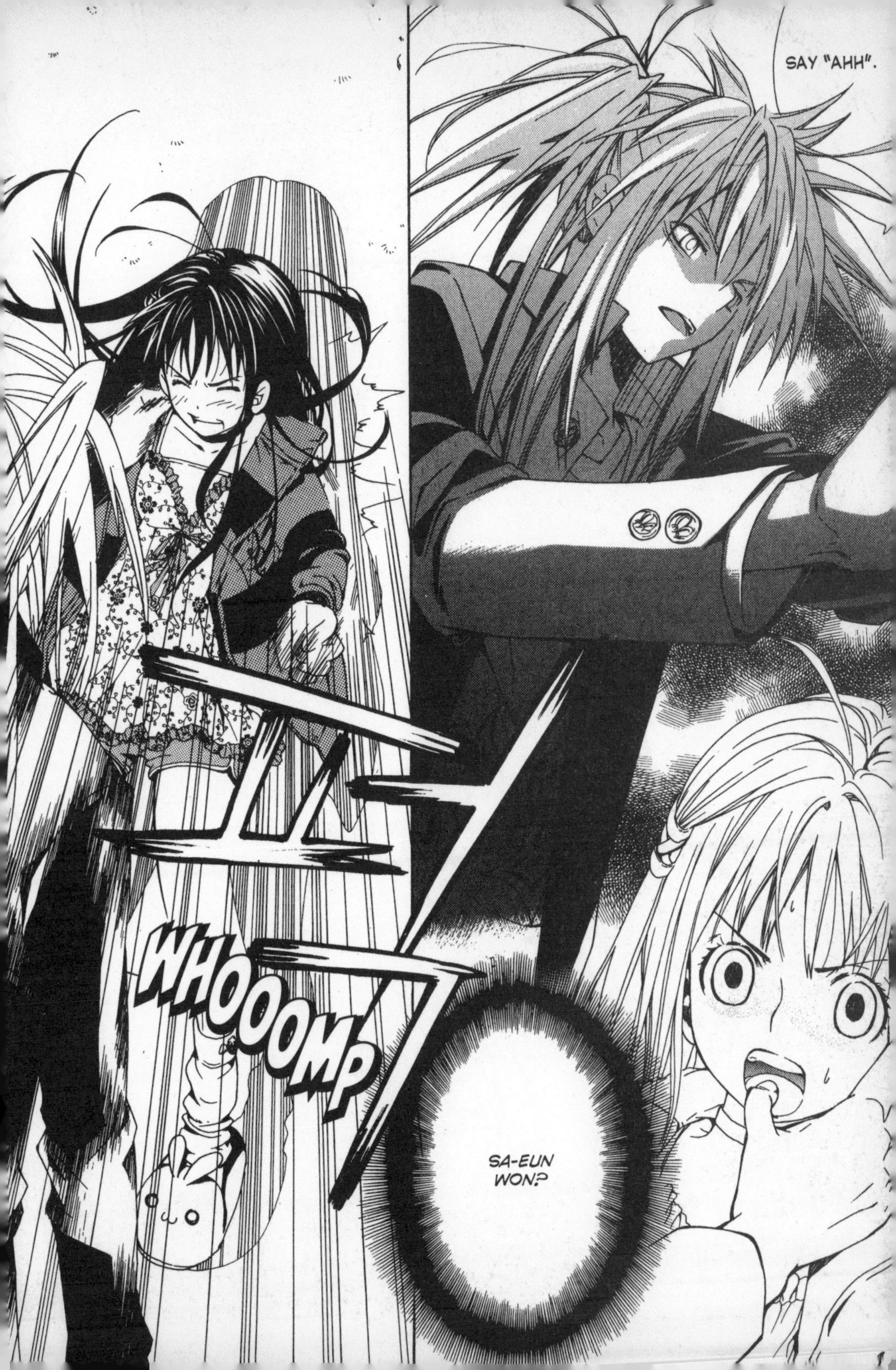
SAY "AHH".
WHOOOMP
SA-EUN WON?

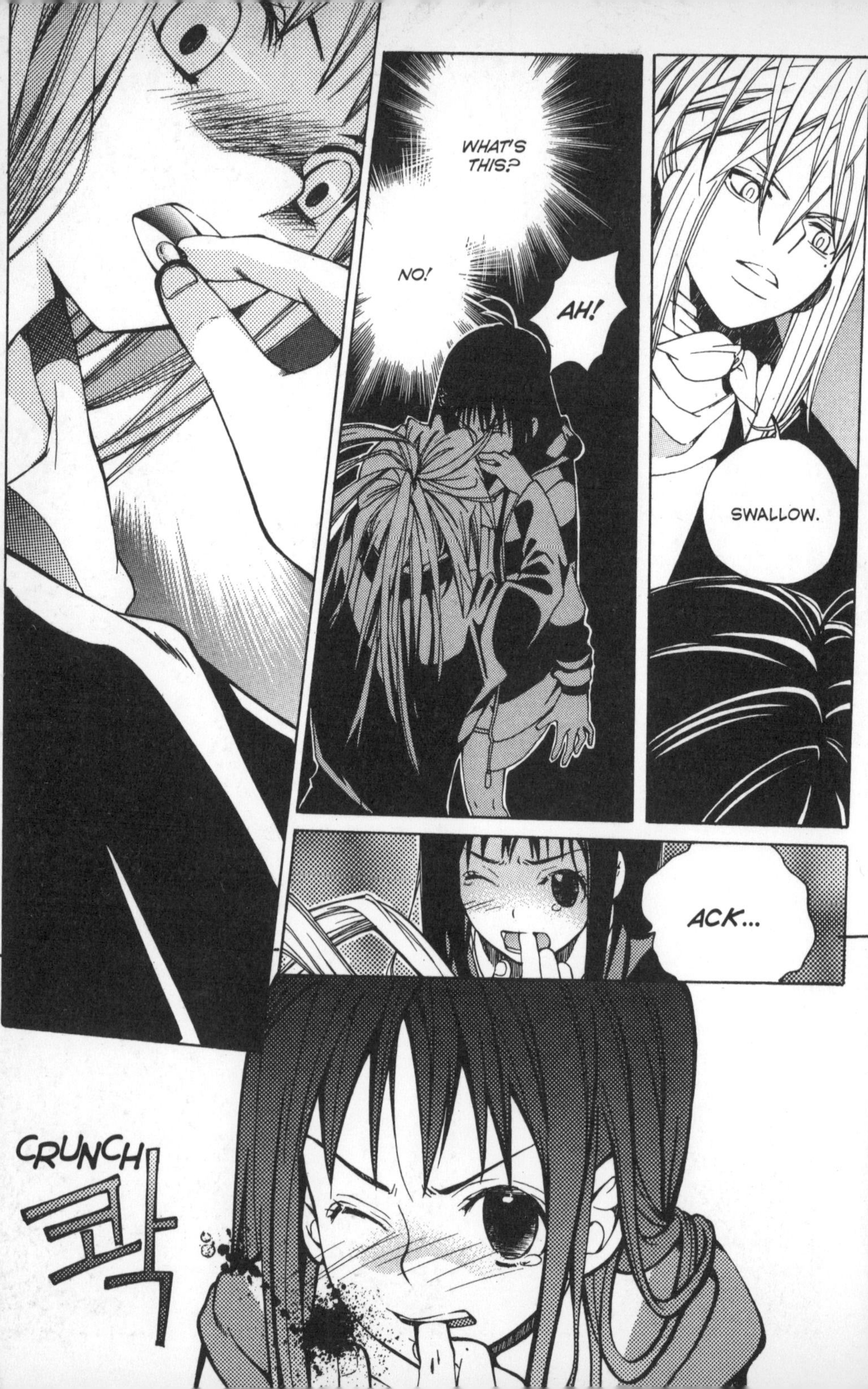
WHAT'S THIS?
NO!
AH!
SWALLOW.
ACK...
CRUNCH

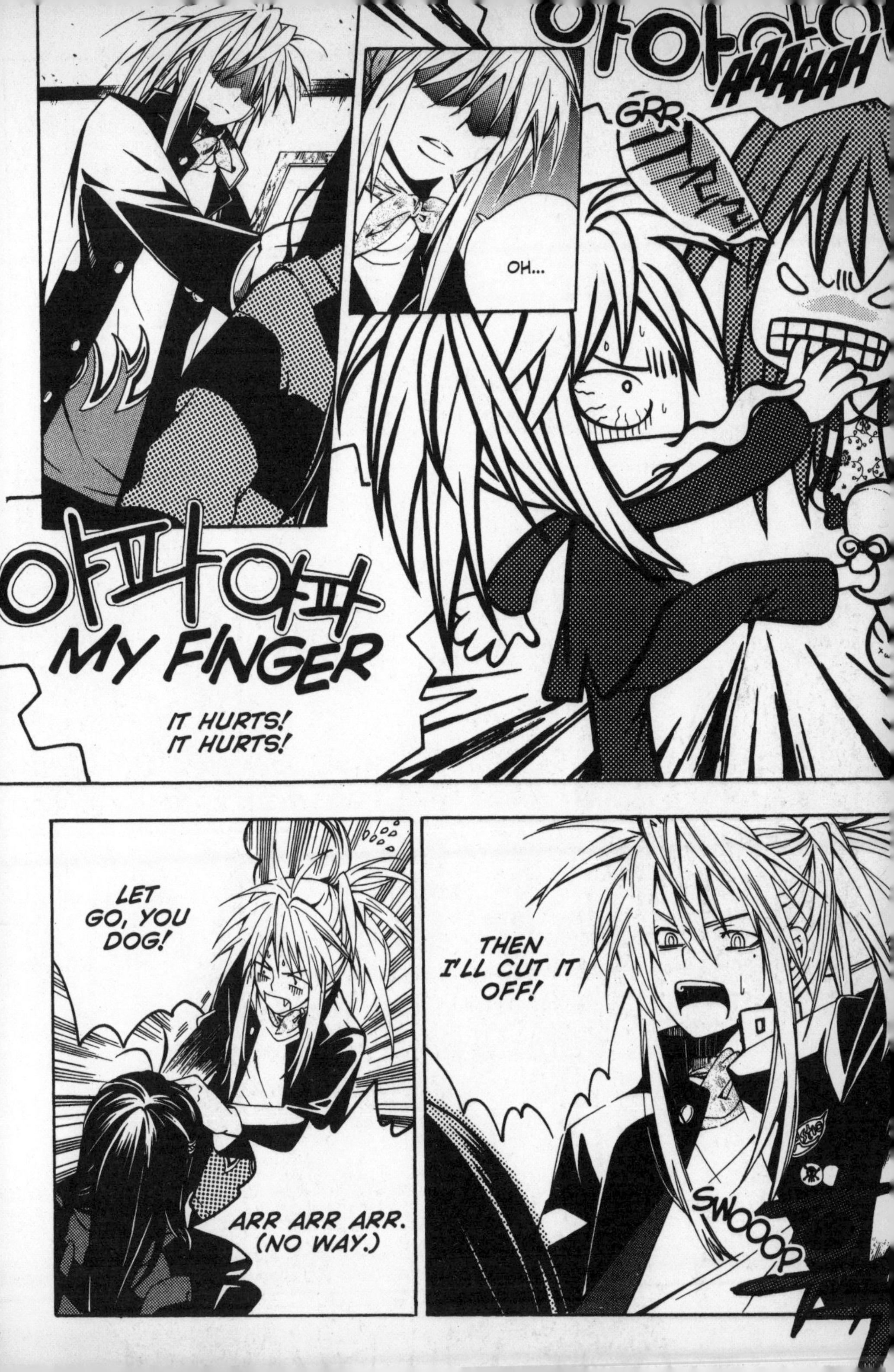

OH...
AAAAAH
GRR
MY FINGER
IT HURTS! IT HURTS!
LET GO, YOU DOG!
ARR ARR ARR. (NO WAY.)
THEN I'LL CUT IT OFF!
SWOOOOP

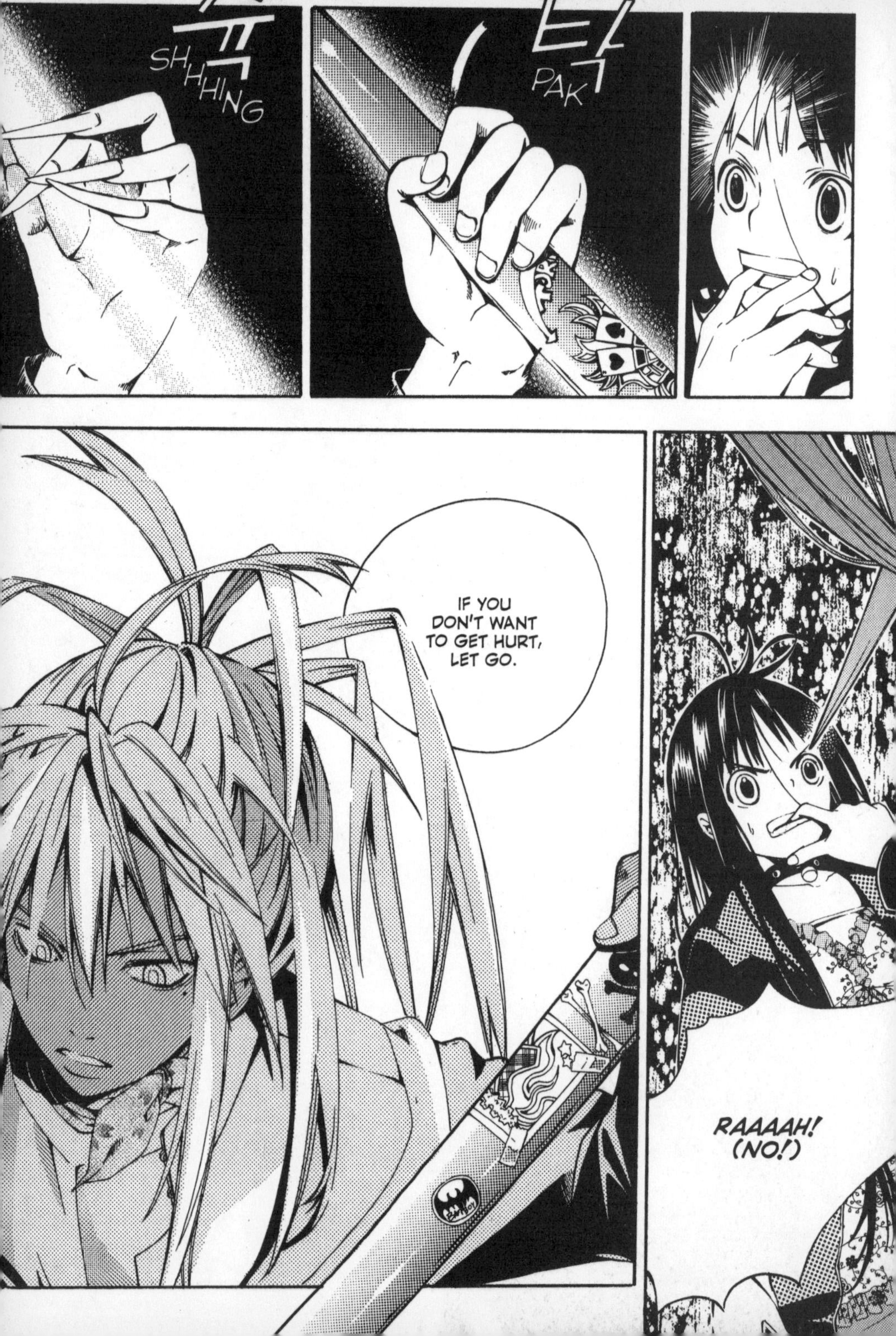
SHHHING
탁
PAK
IF YOU DON'T WANT TO GET HURT, LET GO.
RAAAAH! (NO!)

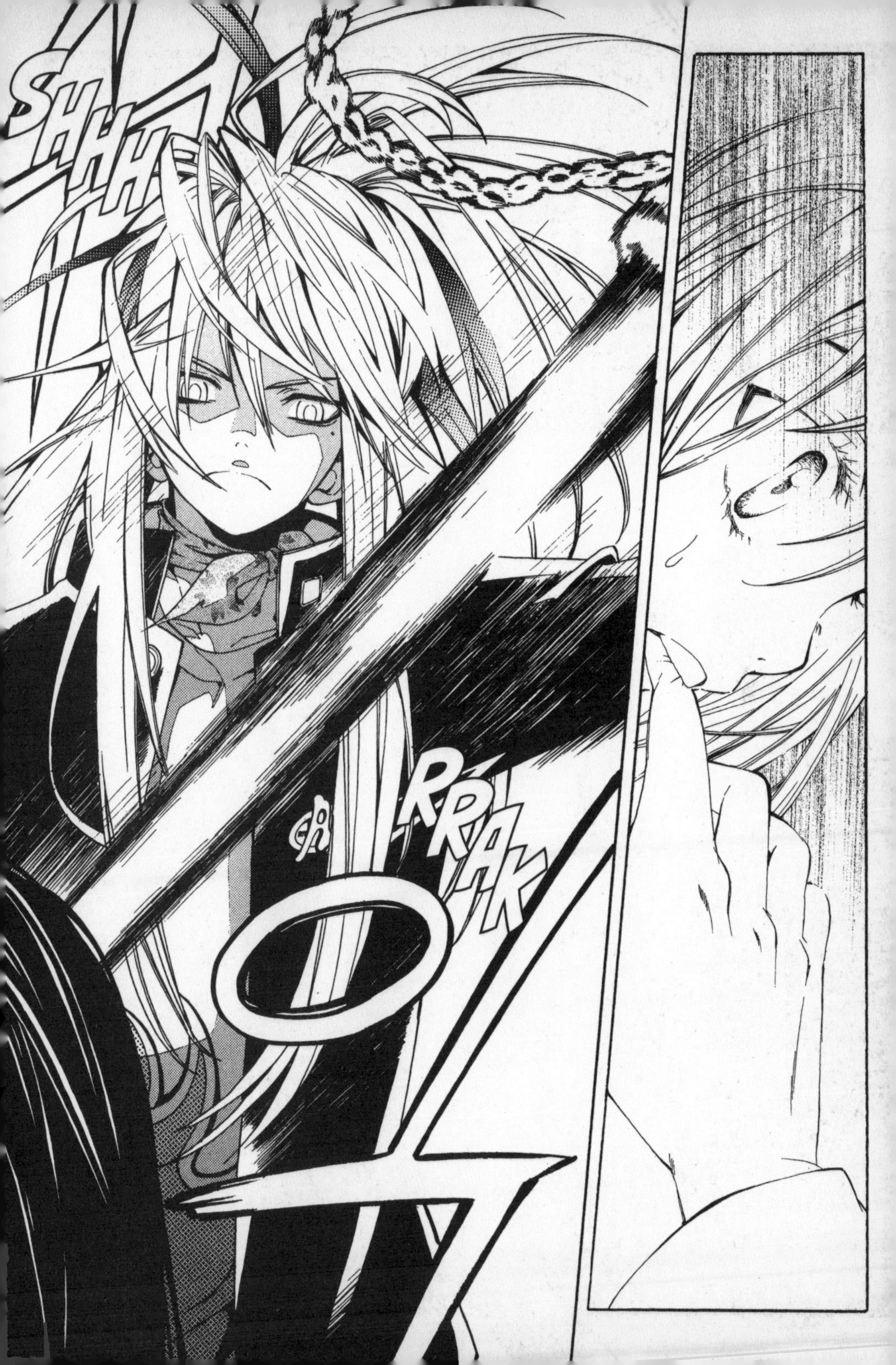
SHHH
RRAK

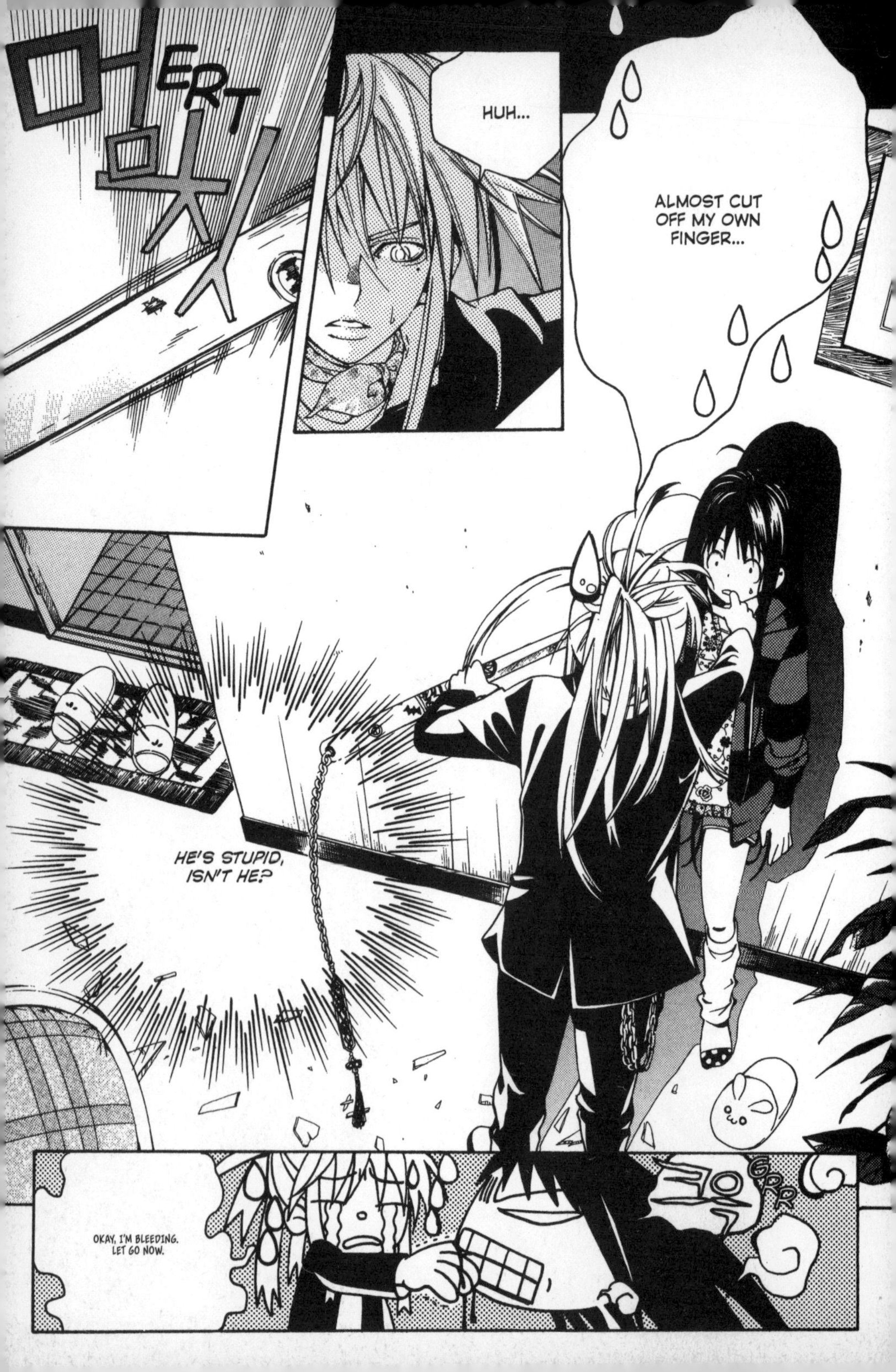
HUH...
ALMOST CUT OFF MY OWN FINGER...
HE'S STUPID, ISN'T HE?
OKAY, I'M BLEEDING. LET GO NOW.
GRR

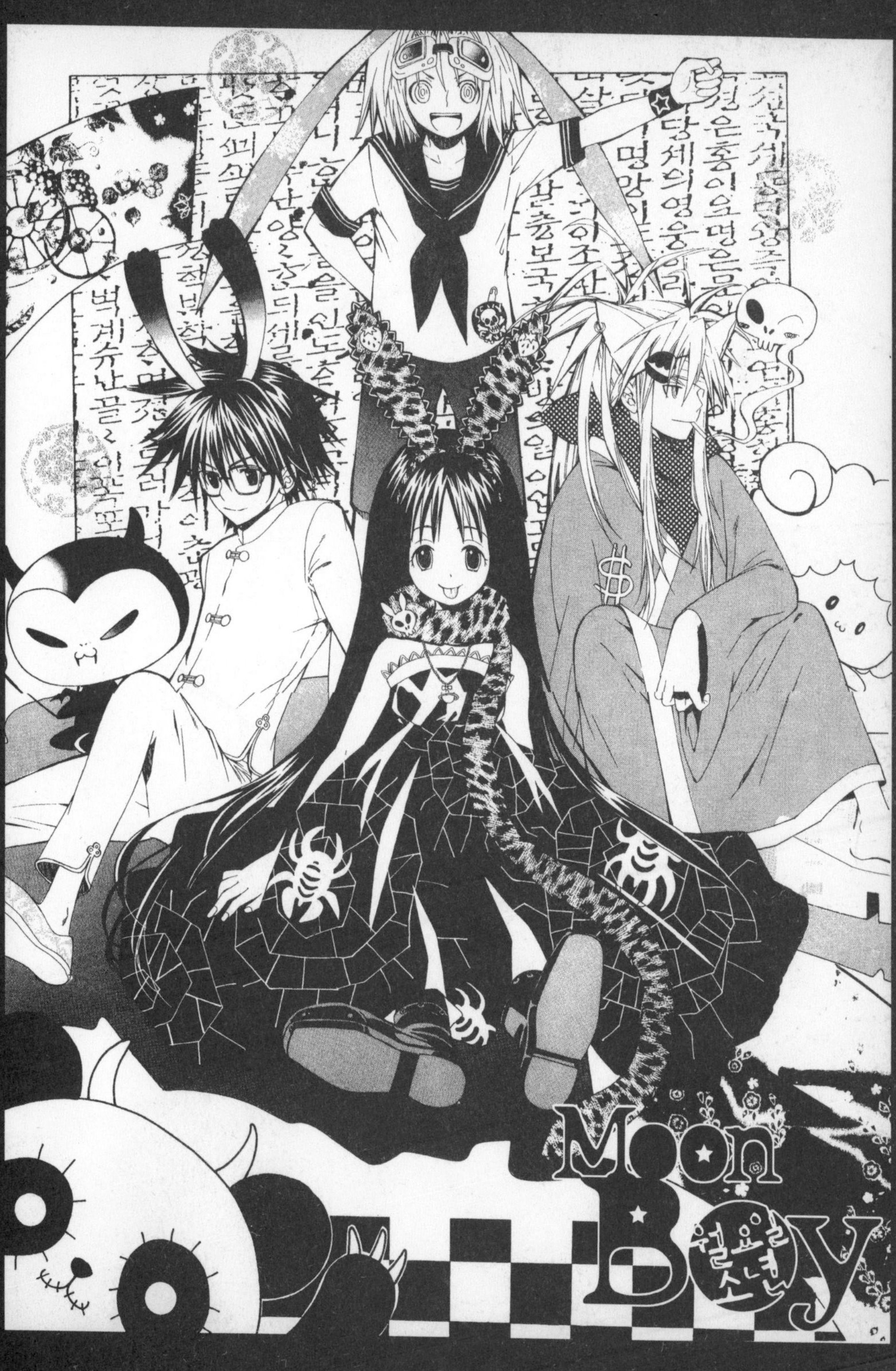
Moon
Boy
월요일 소년

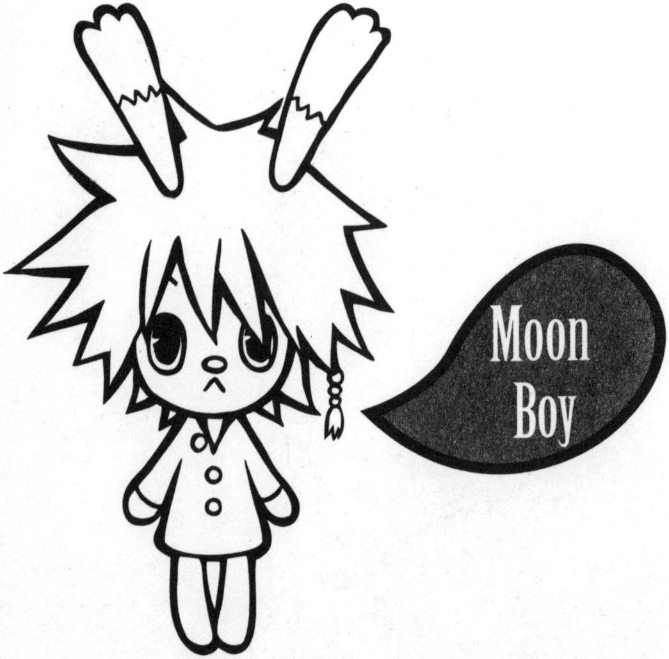
Moon Boy

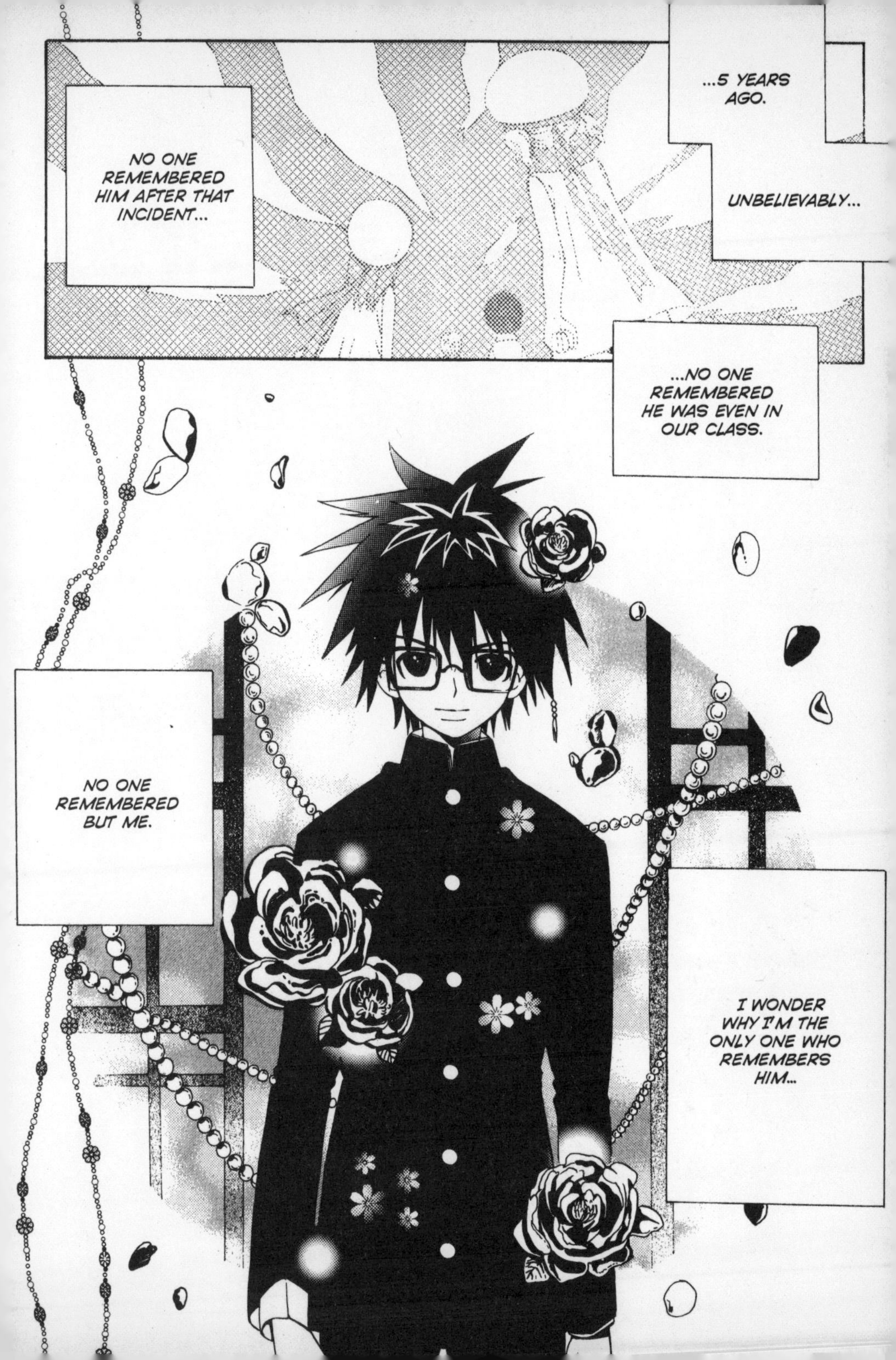
...5 YEARS AGO.
UNBELIEVABLY...
NO ONE REMEMBERED HIM AFTER THAT INCIDENT...
...NO ONE REMEMBERED HE WAS EVEN IN OUR CLASS.
NO ONE REMEMBERED BUT ME.
I WONDER WHY I'M THE ONLY ONE WHO REMEMBERS HIM...

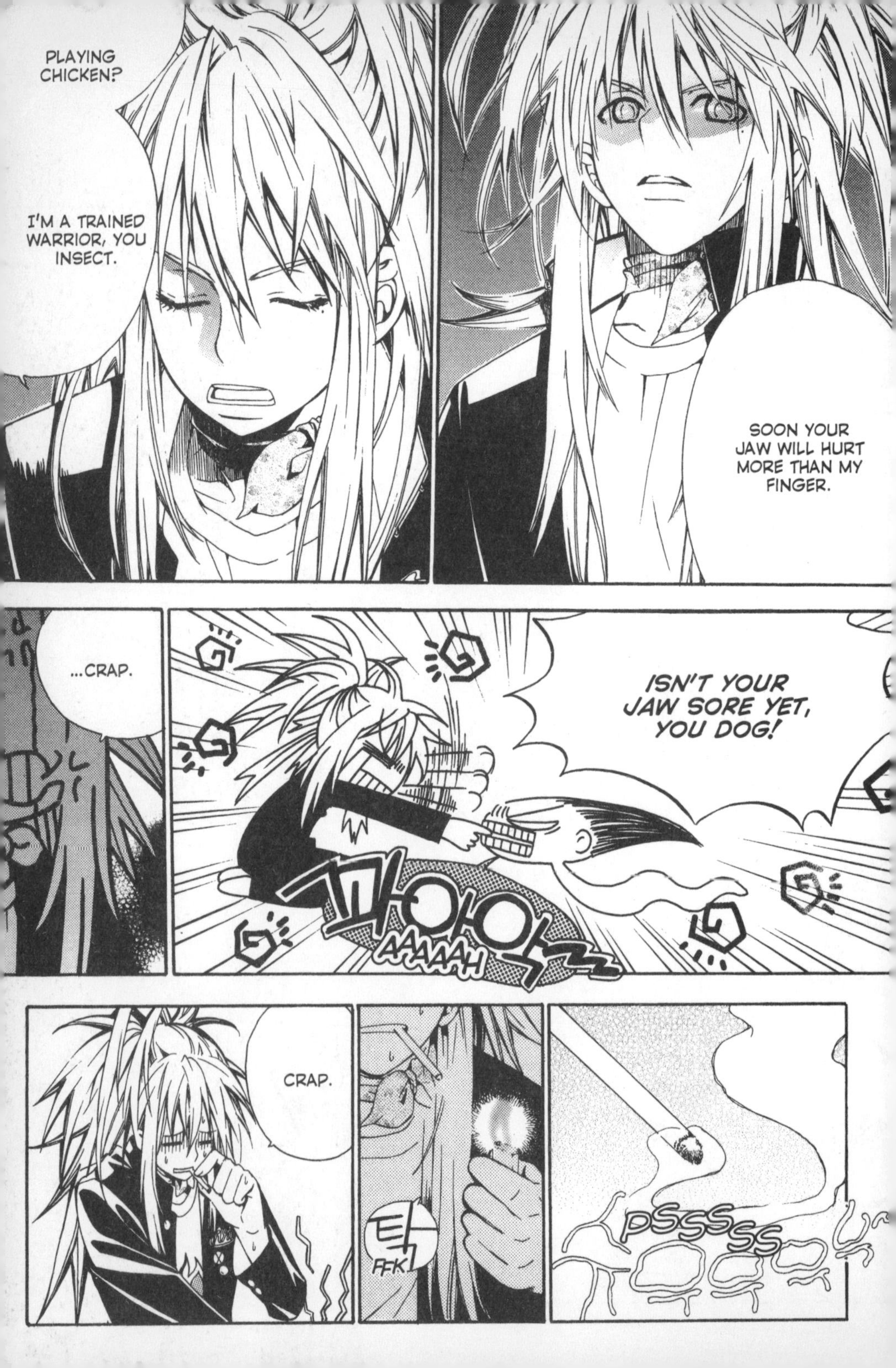
SOON YOUR JAW WILL HURT MORE THAN MY FINGER.
PLAYING CHICKEN?
I'M A TRAINED WARRIOR, YOU INSECT.
ISN'T YOUR JAW SORE YET, YOU DOG!
AAAAAH
...CRAP.
PSSSSSS
FFK
CRAP.

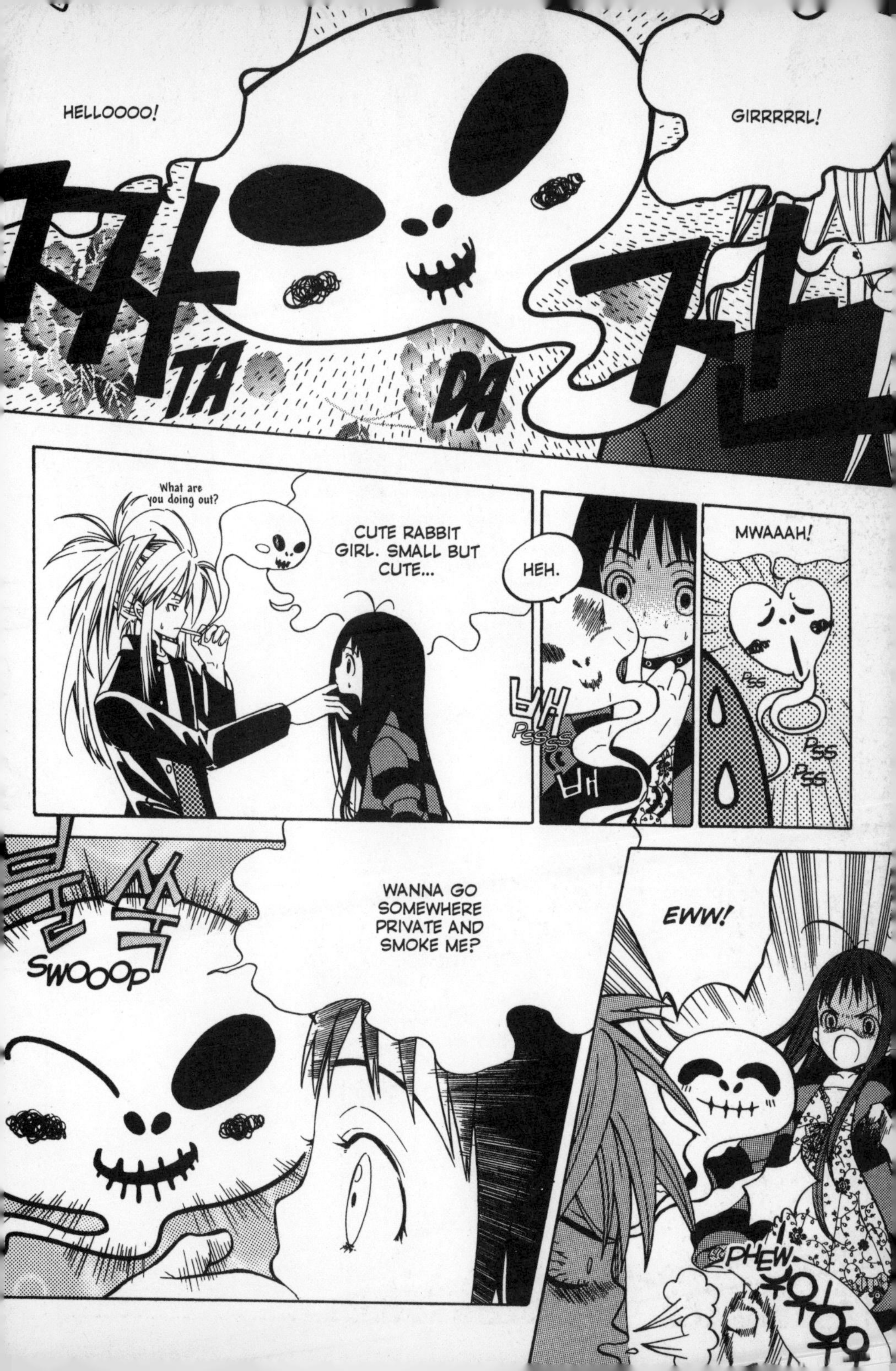
HELLOOOO!
GIRRRRRL!
TA
DA
What are you doing out?
CUTE RABBIT GIRL. SMALL BUT CUTE...
HEH.
PSSSS
MWAAAH!
PSS
PSS
PSS
SWOOOP
WANNA GO SOMEWHERE PRIVATE AND SMOKE ME?
EWW!
PHEW

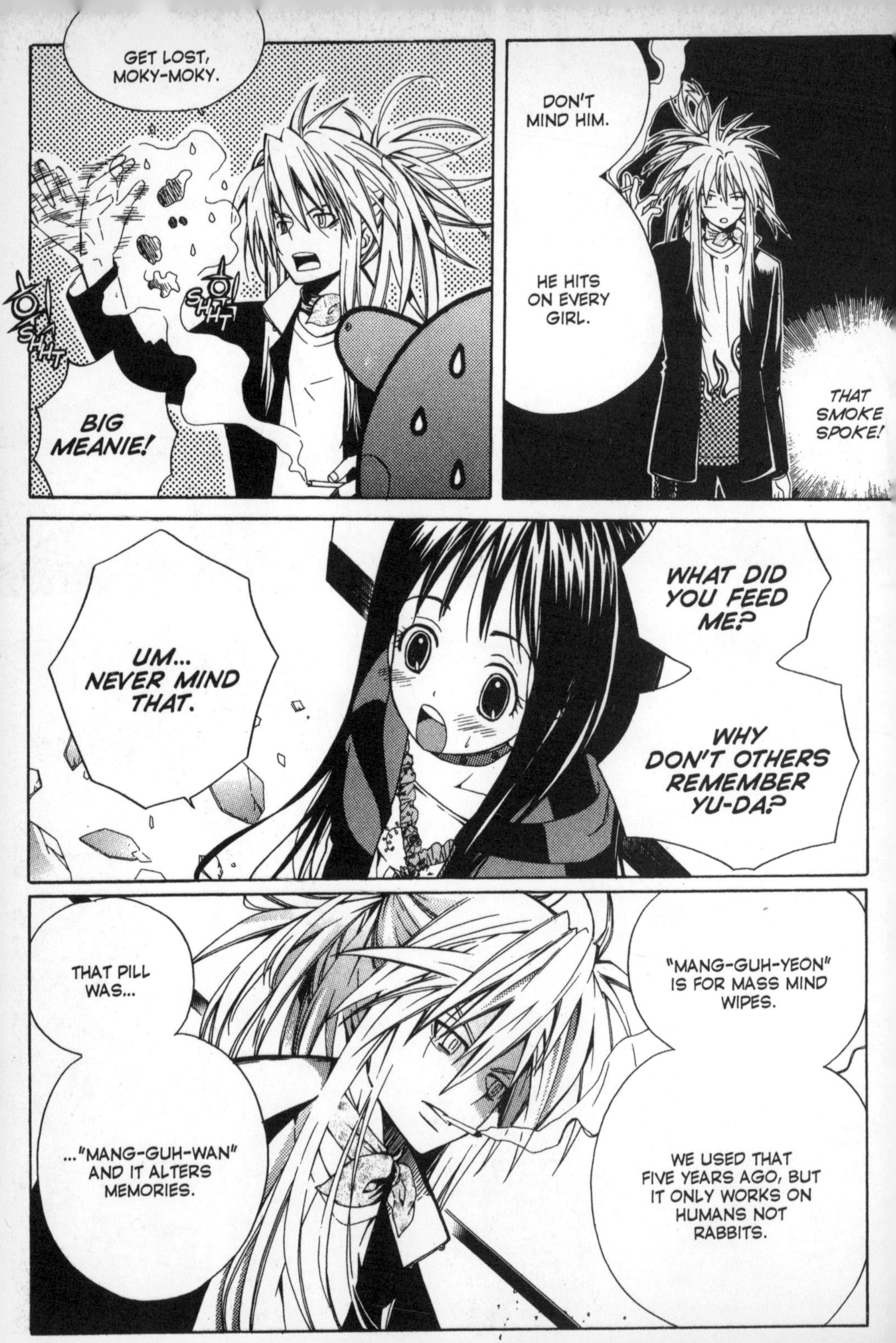
GET LOST, MOKY-MOKY.
BIG MEANIE!
DON'T MIND HIM.
HE HITS ON EVERY GIRL.
THAT SMOKE SPOKE!
WHAT DID YOU FEED ME?
WHY DON'T OTHERS REMEMBER YU-DA?
UM... NEVER MIND THAT.
THAT PILL WAS...
..."MANG-GUH-WAN" AND IT ALTERS MEMORIES.
"MANG-GUH-YEON" IS FOR MASS MIND WIPES.
WE USED THAT FIVE YEARS AGO, BUT IT ONLY WORKS ON HUMANS NOT RABBITS.

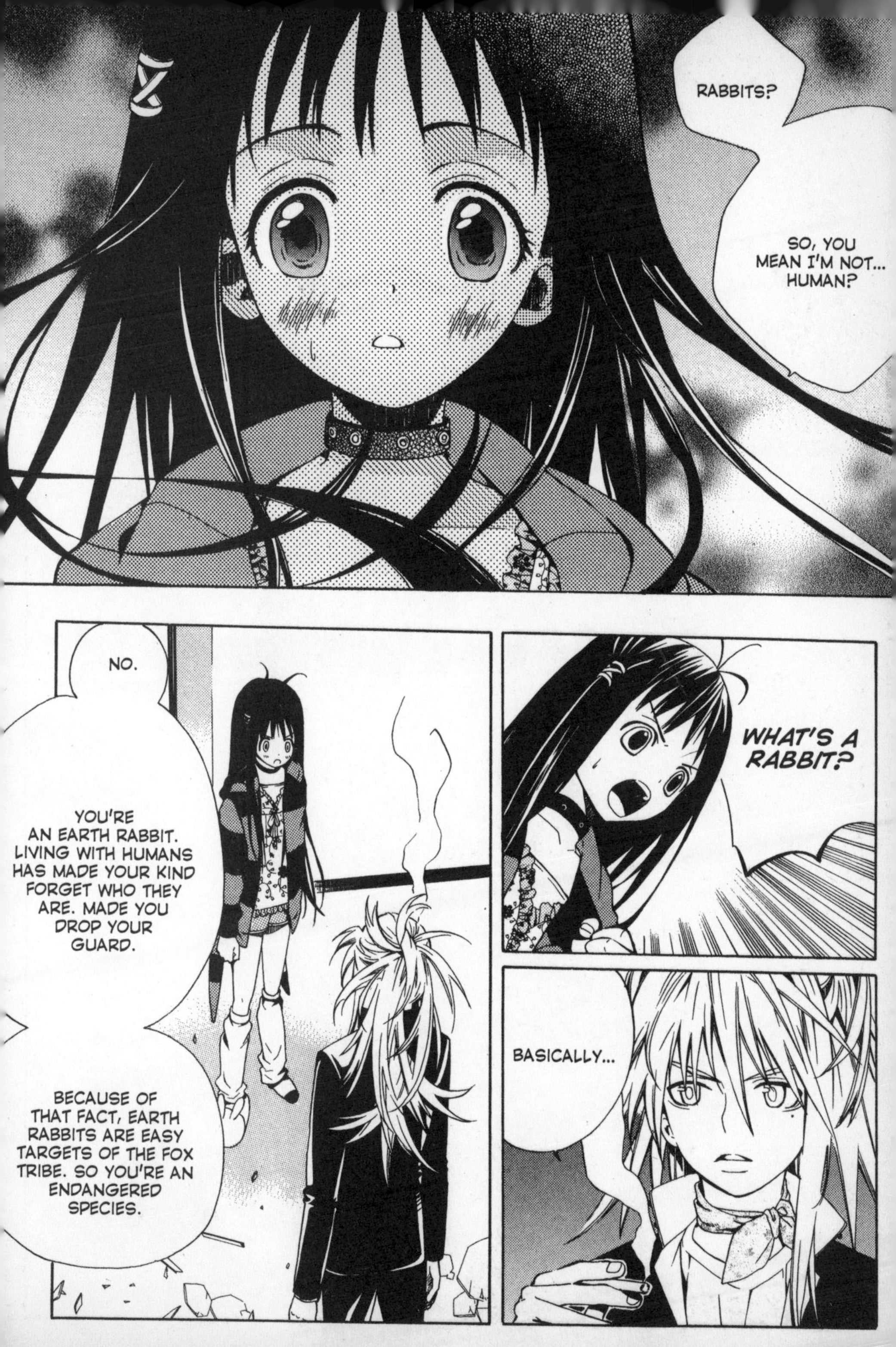
RABBITS?
SO, YOU MEAN I'M NOT... HUMAN?
WHAT'S A RABBIT?
BASICALLY...
NO.
YOU'RE AN EARTH RABBIT. LIVING WITH HUMANS HAS MADE YOUR KIND FORGET WHO THEY ARE. MADE YOU DROP YOUR GUARD.
BECAUSE OF THAT FACT, EARTH RABBITS ARE EASY TARGETS OF THE FOX TRIBE. SO YOU'RE AN ENDANGERED SPECIES.

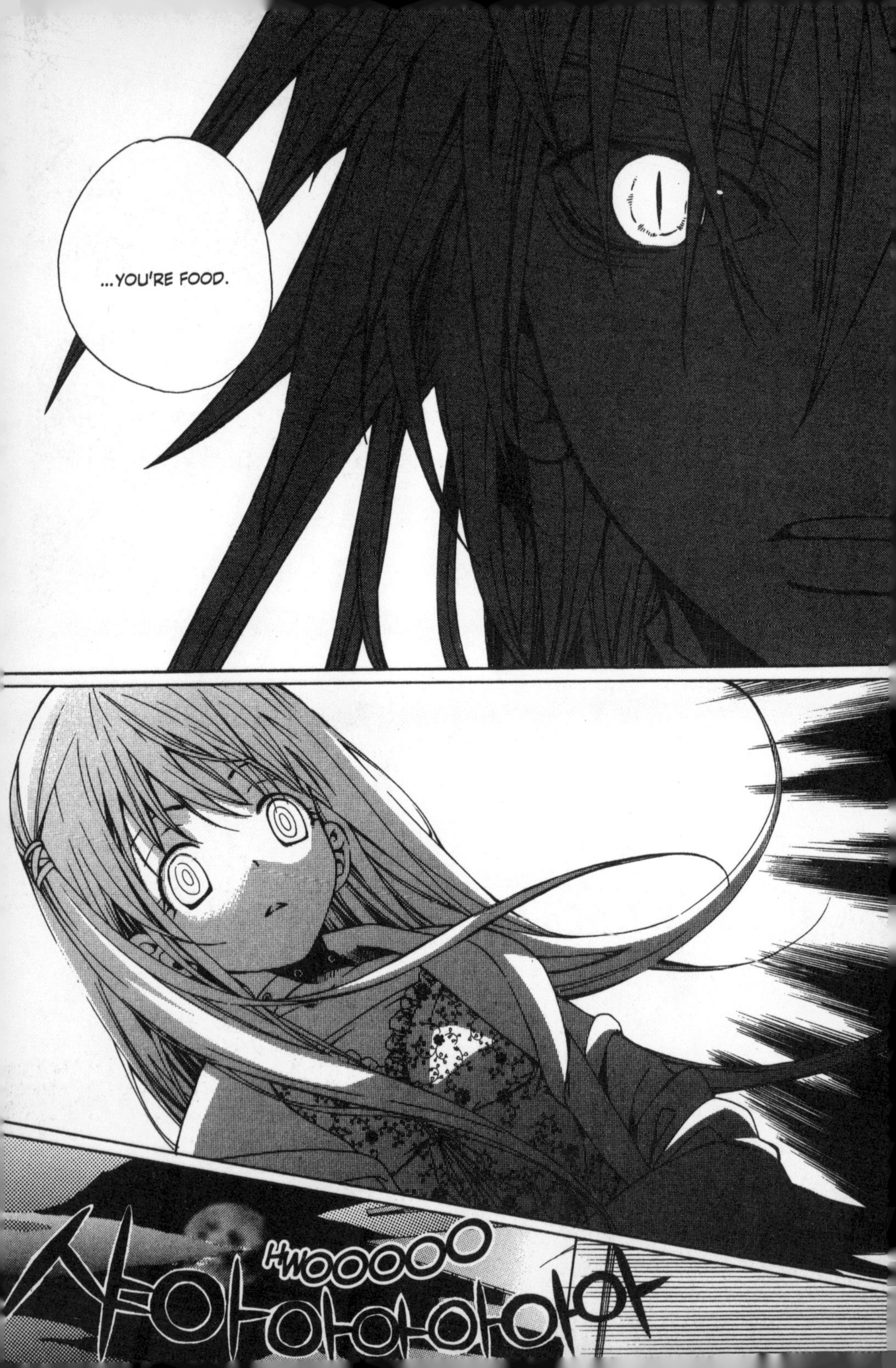
...YOU'RE FOOD.
HWOOOOO

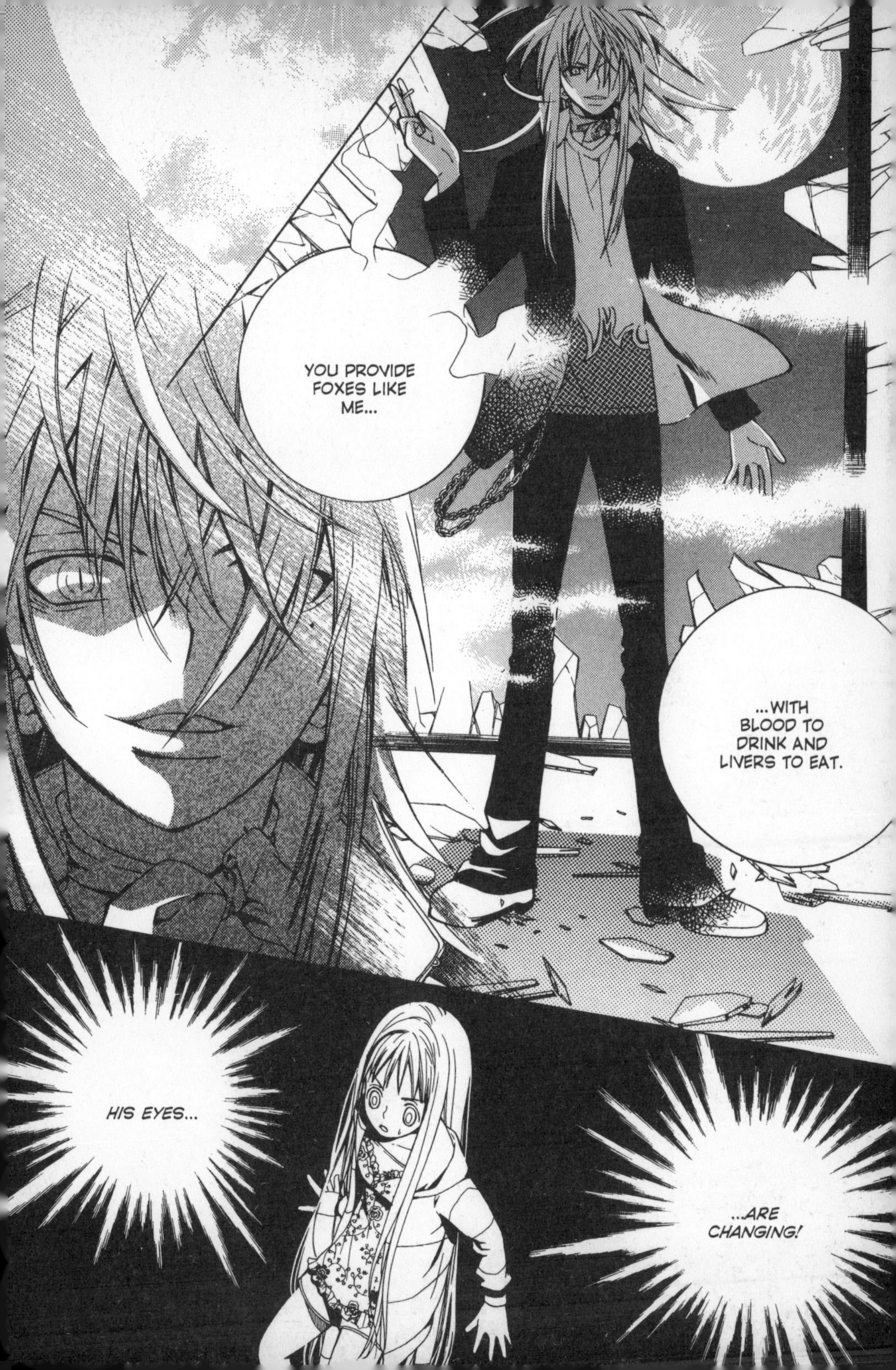
YOU PROVIDE FOXES LIKE ME...
...WITH BLOOD TO DRINK AND LIVERS TO EAT.
HIS EYES...
...ARE CHANGING!

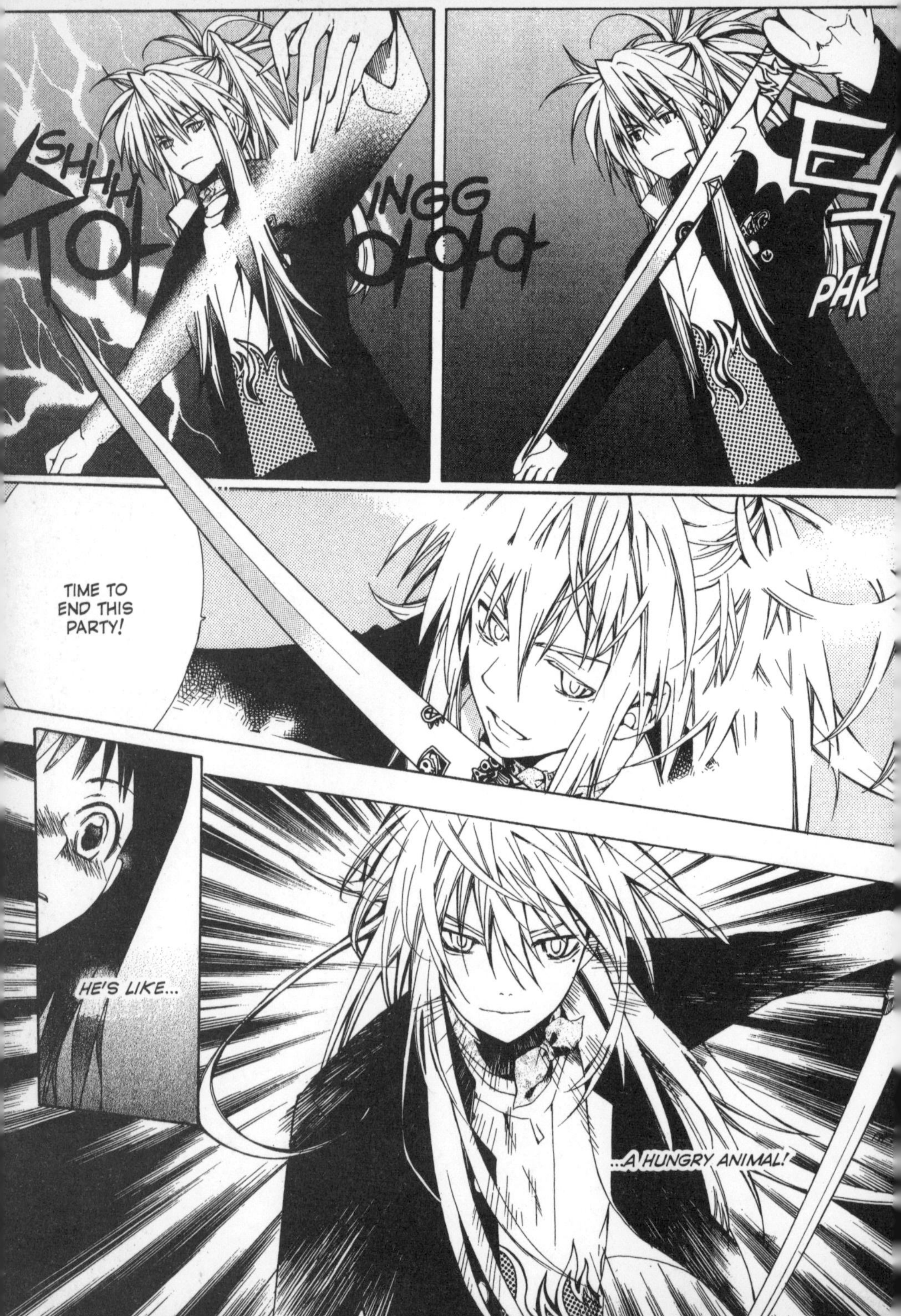
PAK
SHHH
INGG
TIME TO END THIS PARTY!
HE'S LIKE...
...A HUNGRY ANIMAL!

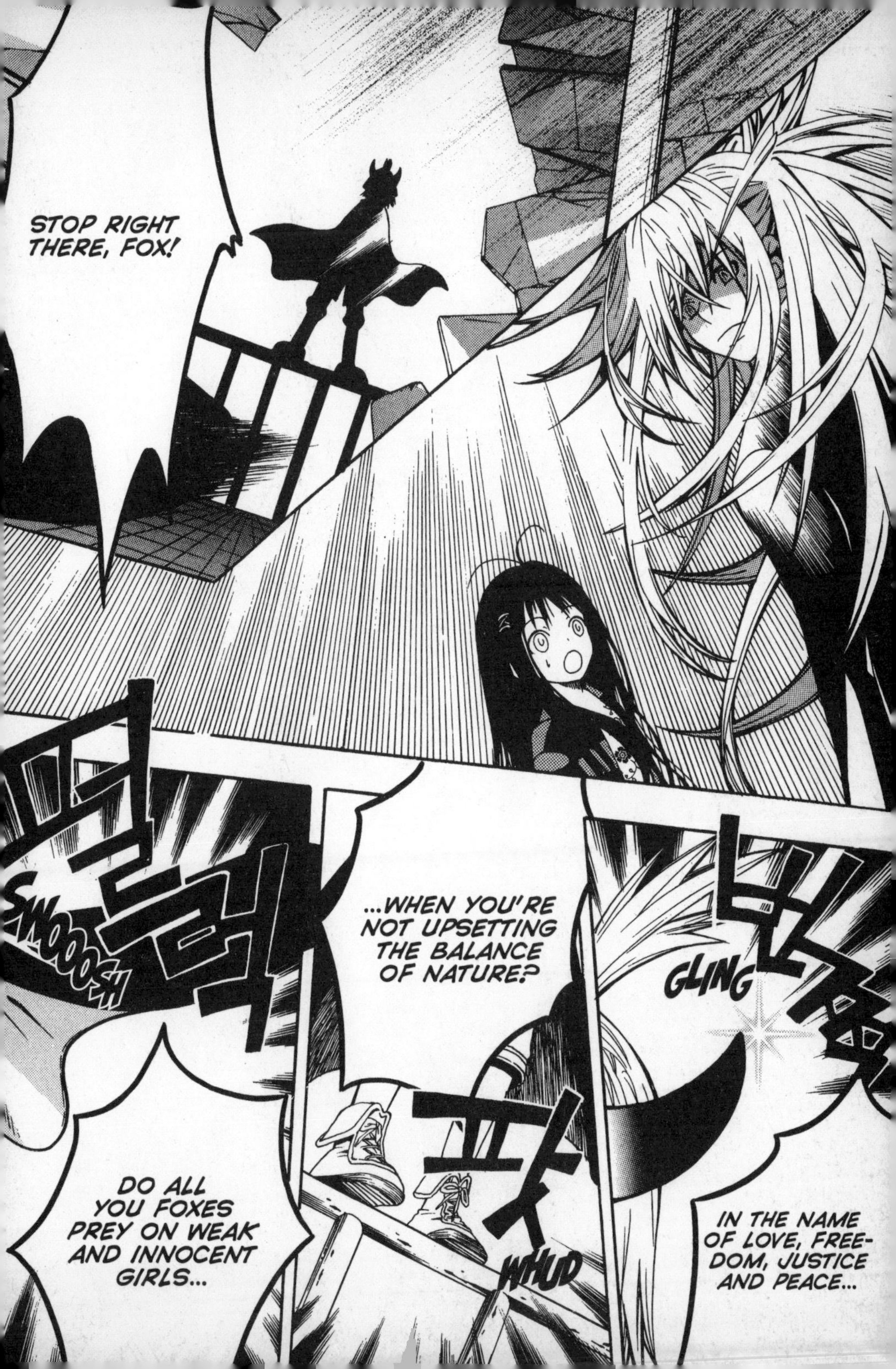

STOP RIGHT THERE, FOX!
IN THE NAME OF LOVE, FREE-DOM, JUSTICE AND PEACE...
GLING
WHUD
DO ALL YOU FOXES PREY ON WEAK AND INNOCENT GIRLS...
...WHEN YOU'RE NOT UPSETTING THE BALANCE OF NATURE?
SWOOOSH

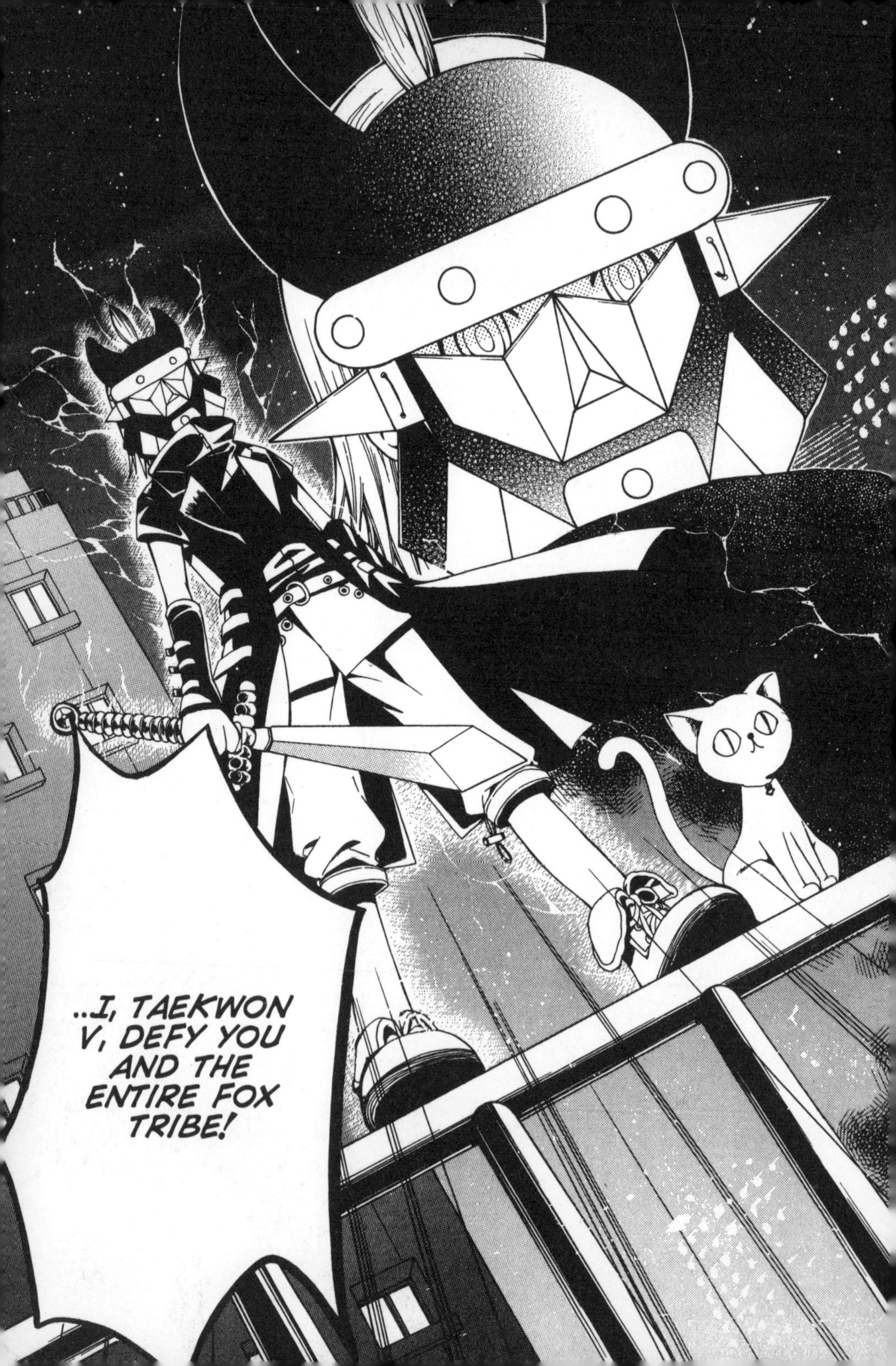
..I, TAEKWON V, DEFY YOU AND THE ENTIRE FOX TRIBE!

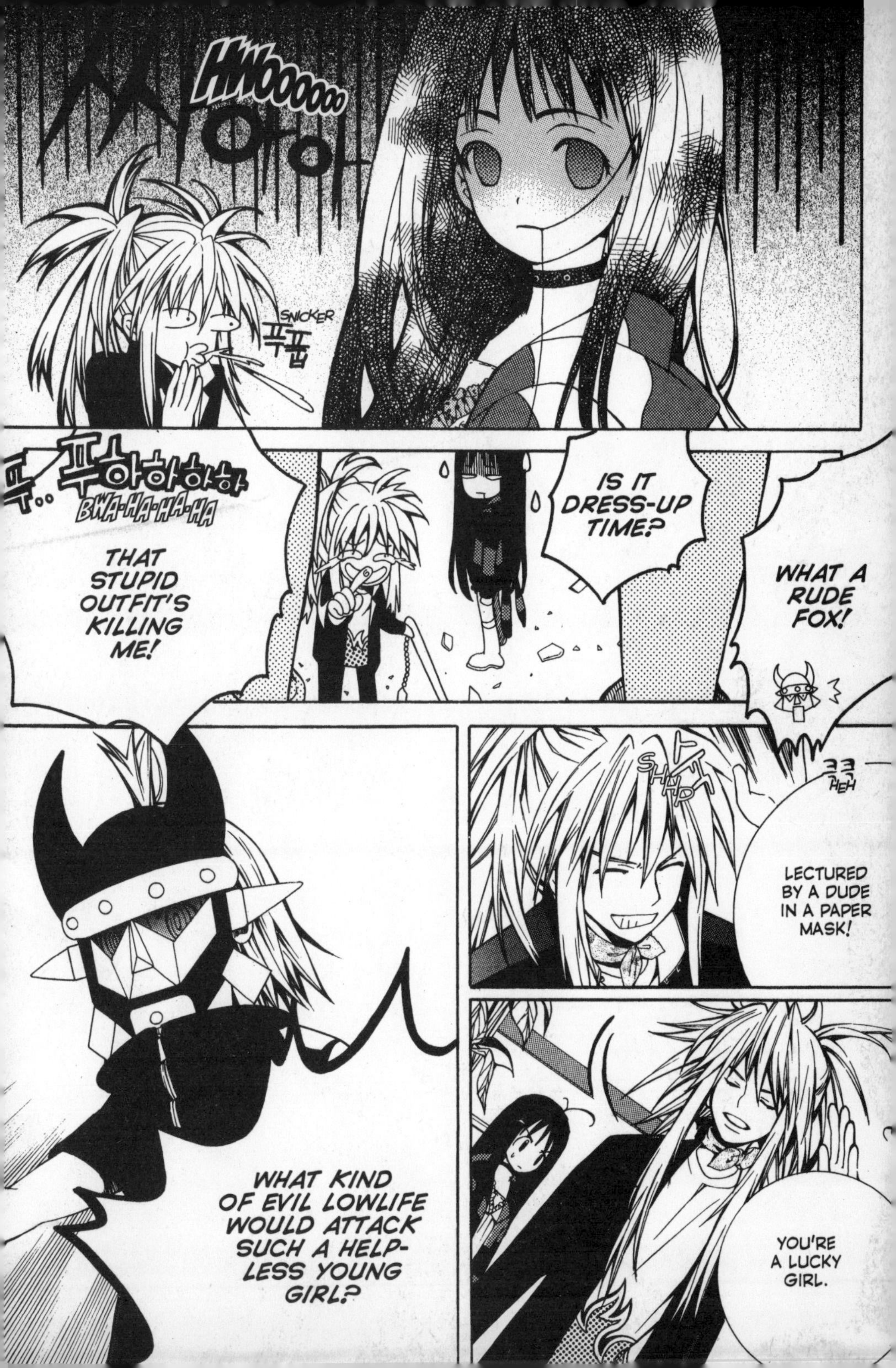

HWOOOOOO
SNICKER
BWA-HA-HA-HA
THAT STUPID OUTFIT'S KILLING ME!
IS IT DRESS-UP TIME?
WHAT A RUDE FOX!
WHAT KIND OF EVIL LOWLIFE WOULD ATTACK SUCH A HELP-LESS YOUNG GIRL?
SHHHP
HEH
LECTURED BY A DUDE IN A PAPER MASK!
YOU'RE A LUCKY GIRL.

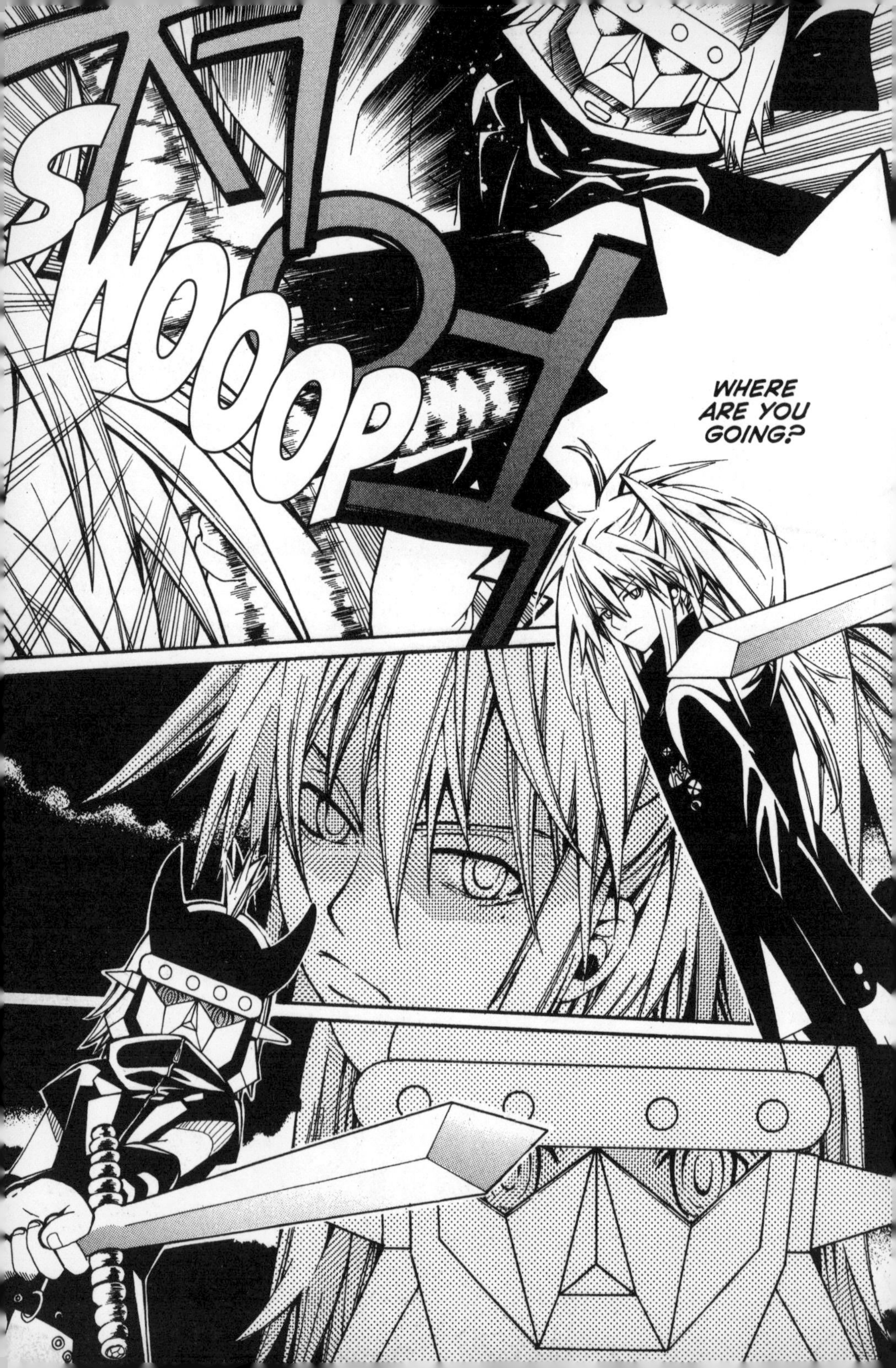
SWOOOP
WHERE ARE YOU GOING?

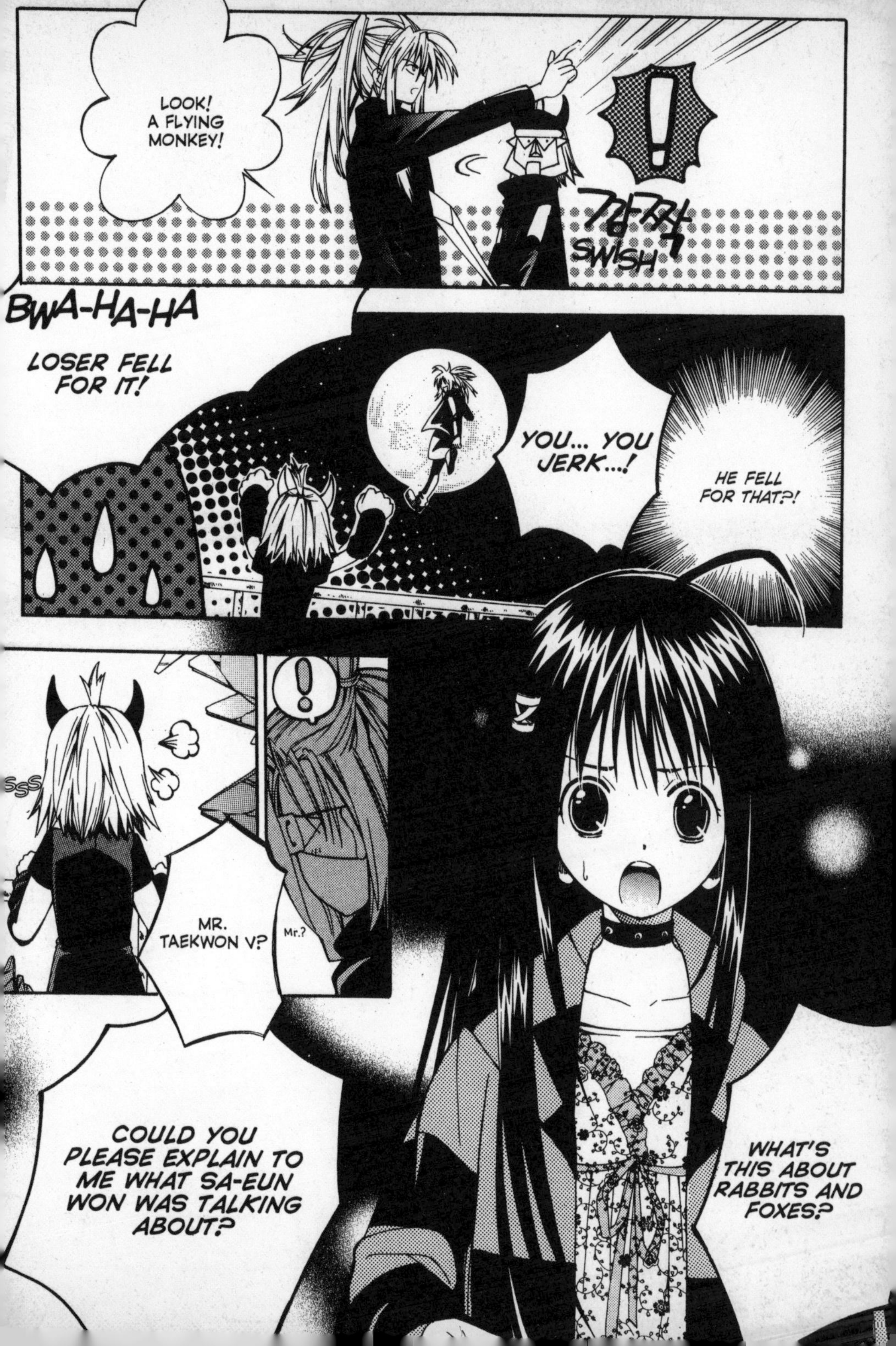
LOOK! A FLYING MONKEY!
!
갑작
SWISH
BWA-HA-HA
LOSER FELL FOR IT!
YOU... YOU JERK...!
HE FELL FOR THAT?!
!
SSS
MR. TAEKWON V?
Mr.?
COULD YOU PLEASE EXPLAIN TO ME WHAT SA-EUN WON WAS TALKING ABOUT?
WHAT'S THIS ABOUT RABBITS AND FOXES?

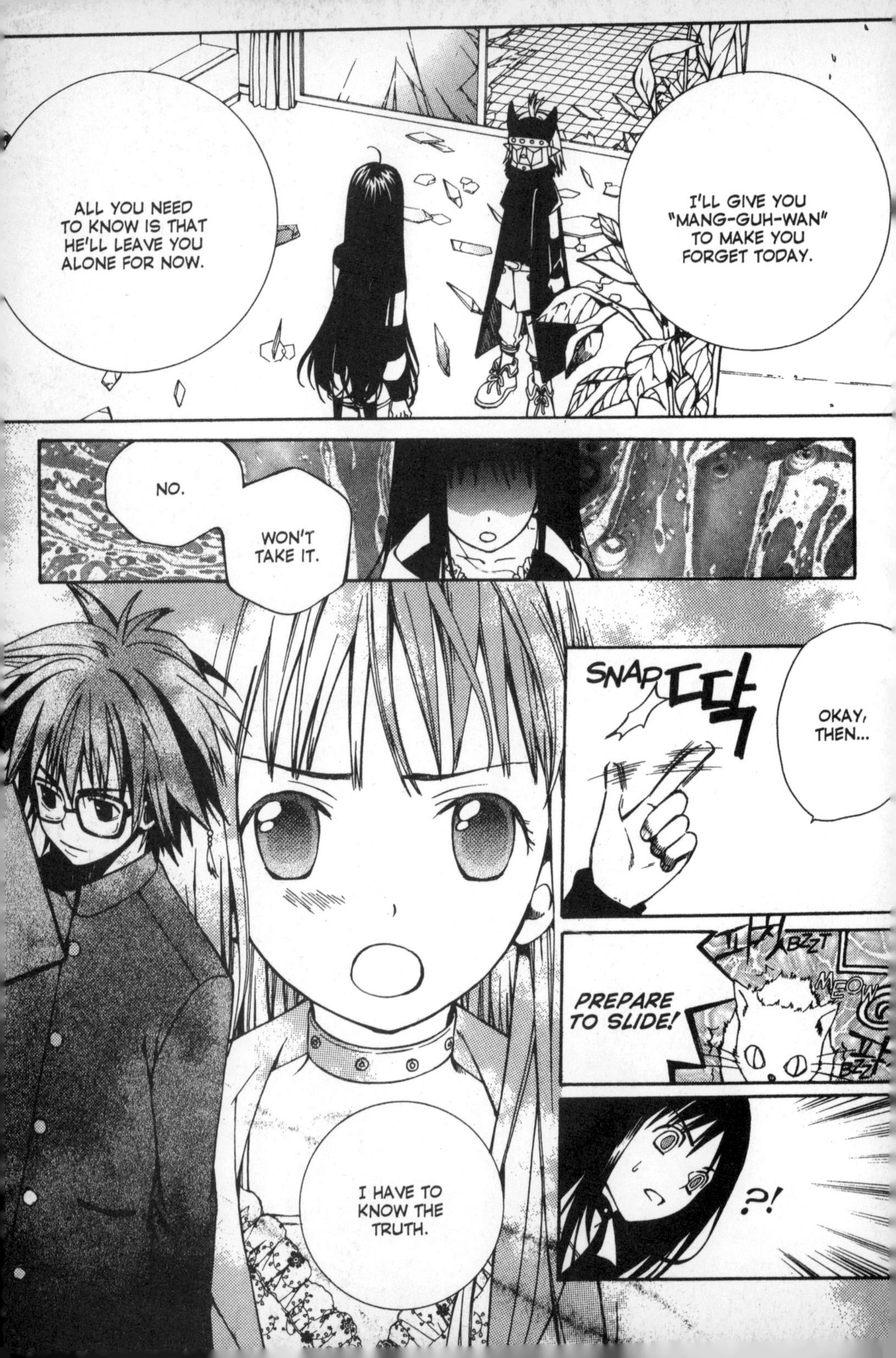
I'LL GIVE YOU "MANG-GUH-WAN" TO MAKE YOU FORGET TODAY.
ALL YOU NEED TO KNOW IS THAT HE'LL LEAVE YOU ALONE FOR NOW.
NO.
WON'T TAKE IT.
I HAVE TO KNOW THE TRUTH.
OKAY, THEN...
SNAP
BZZT
PREPARE TO SLIDE!
MEOW
BZZT
?!

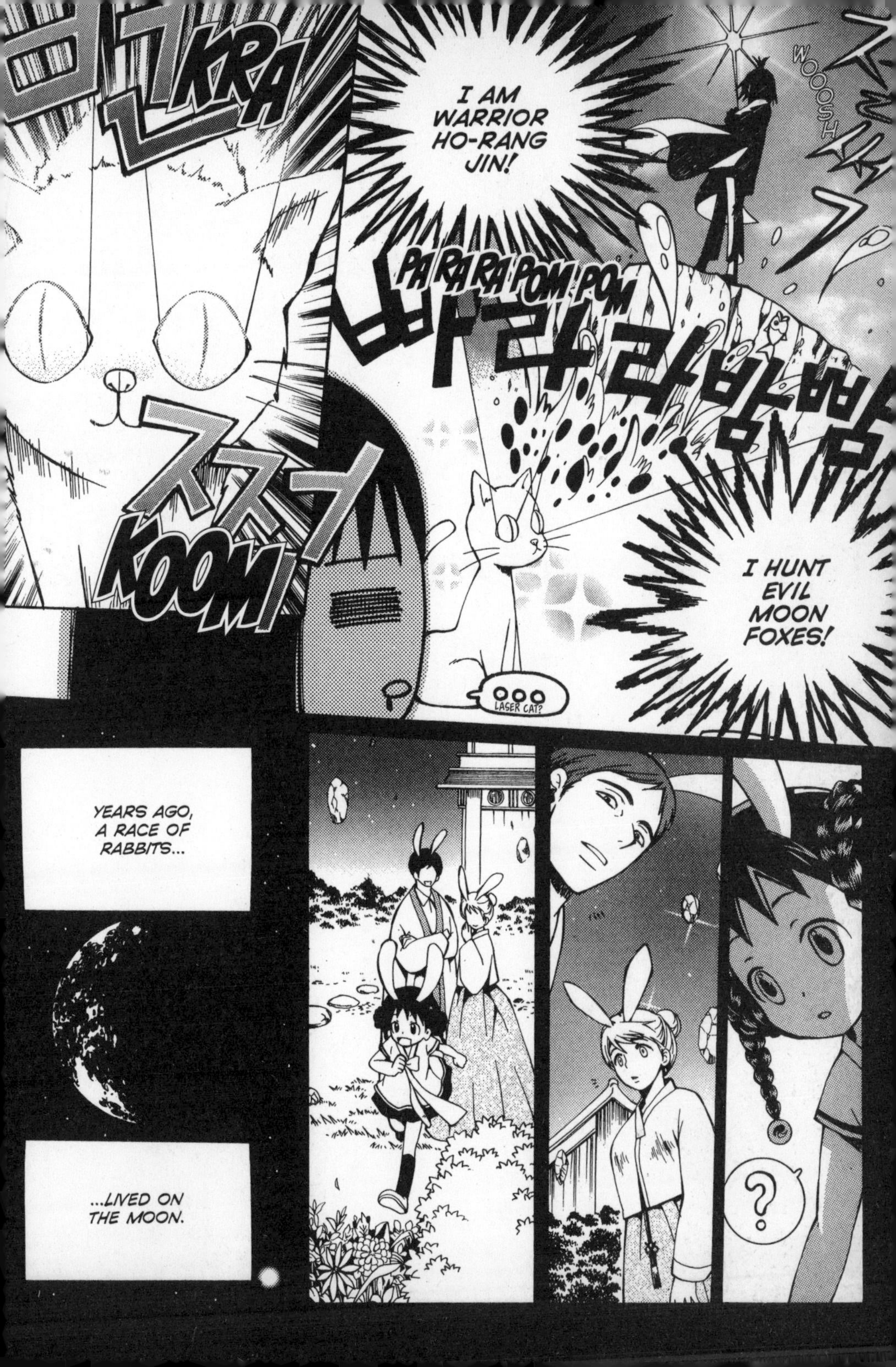
I AM WARRIOR HO-RANG JIN!
WOOOSH
KRA
PA RA RA POM POM
KOOM
I HUNT EVIL MOON FOXES!
LASER CAT?
YEARS AGO, A RACE OF RABBITS...
...LIVED ON THE MOON.
?

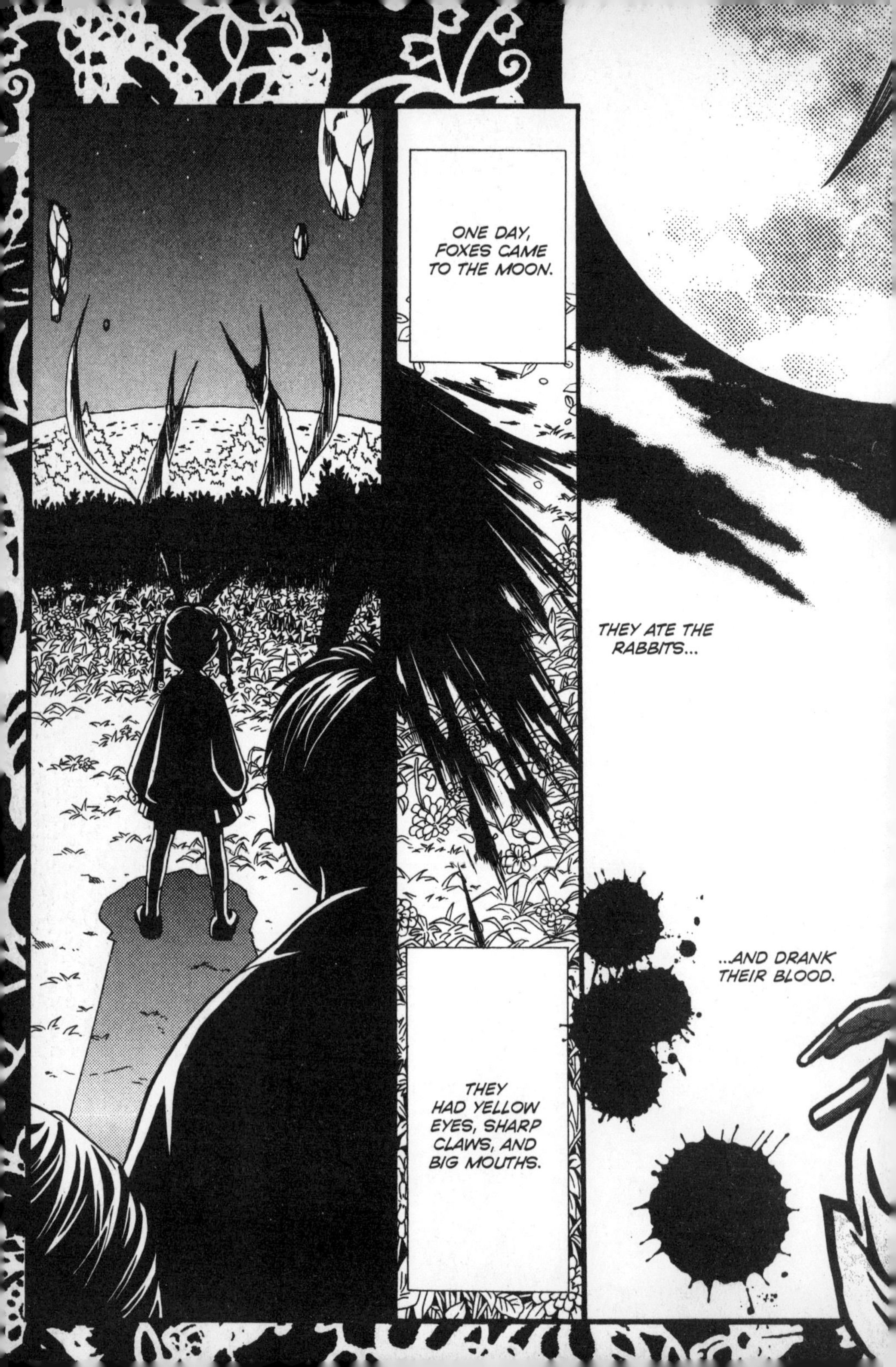
ONE DAY, FOXES CAME TO THE MOON.
THEY ATE THE RABBITS...
...AND DRANK THEIR BLOOD.
THEY HAD YELLOW EYES, SHARP CLAWS, AND BIG MOUTHS.

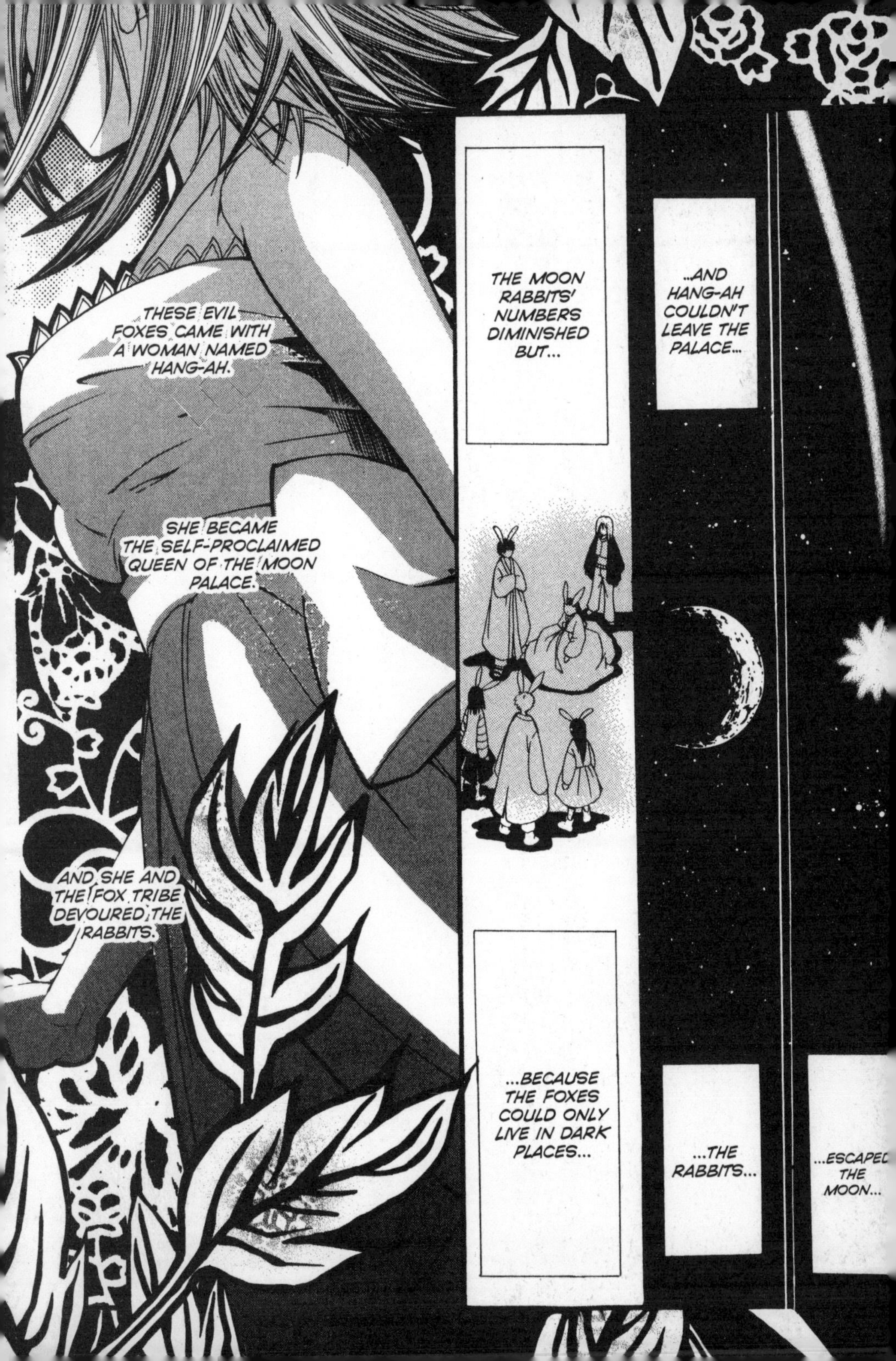
THESE EVIL FOXES CAME WITH A WOMAN NAMED HANG-AH.
SHE BECAME THE SELF-PROCLAIMED QUEEN OF THE MOON PALACE.
AND SHE AND THE FOX TRIBE DEVOURED THE RABBITS.
THE MOON RABBITS' NUMBERS DIMINISHED BUT...
...AND HANG-AH COULDN'T LEAVE THE PALACE...
...BECAUSE THE FOXES COULD ONLY LIVE IN DARK PLACES...
...THE RABBITS...
...ESCAPED THE MOON...

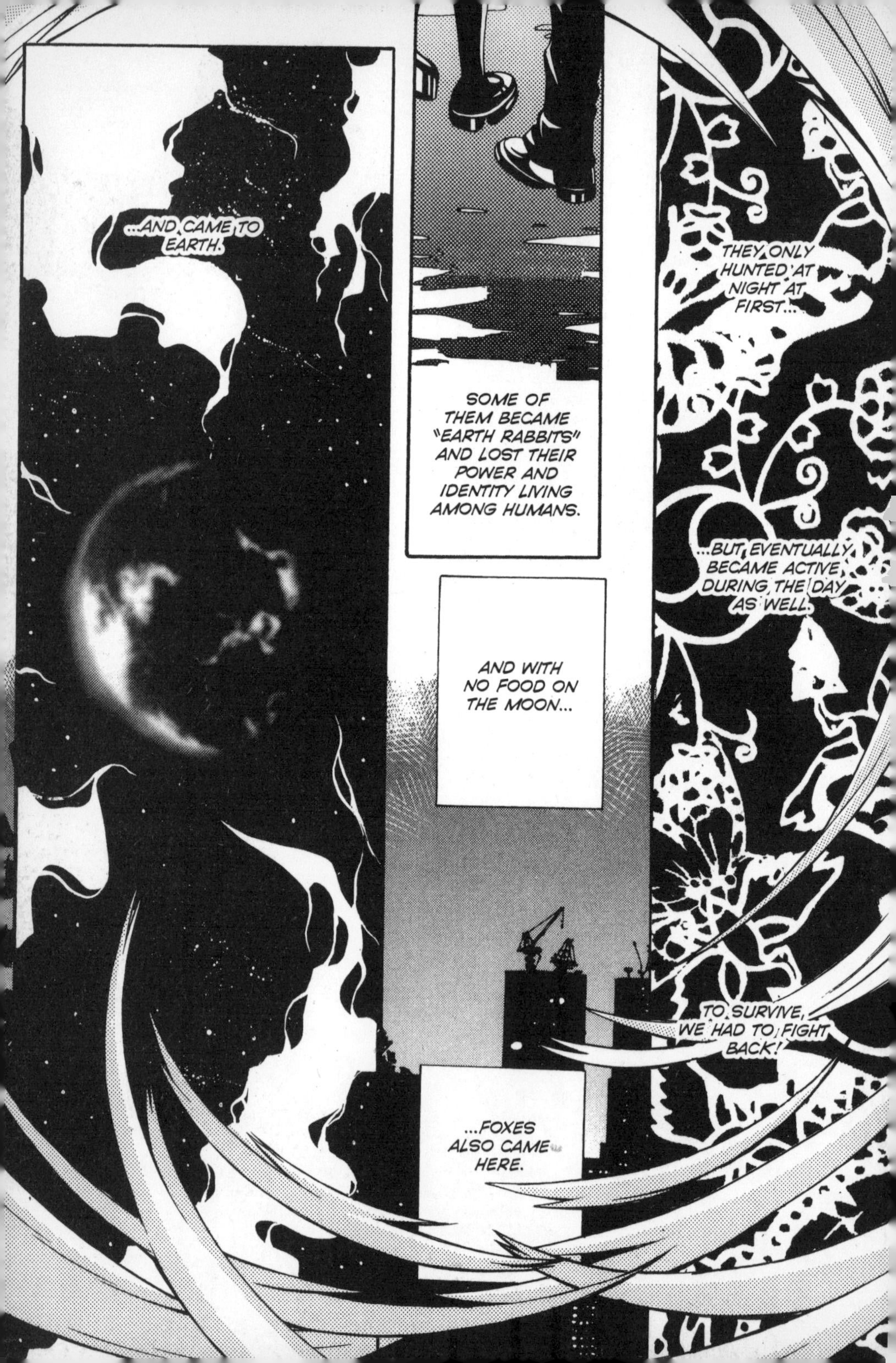
...AND CAME TO EARTH.
SOME OF THEM BECAME "EARTH RABBITS" AND LOST THEIR POWER AND IDENTITY LIVING AMONG HUMANS.
AND WITH NO FOOD ON THE MOON...
...FOXES ALSO CAME HERE.
THEY ONLY HUNTED AT NIGHT AT FIRST...
...BUT EVENTUALLY BECAME ACTIVE DURING THE DAY AS WELL.
TO SURVIVE, WE HAD TO FIGHT BACK!

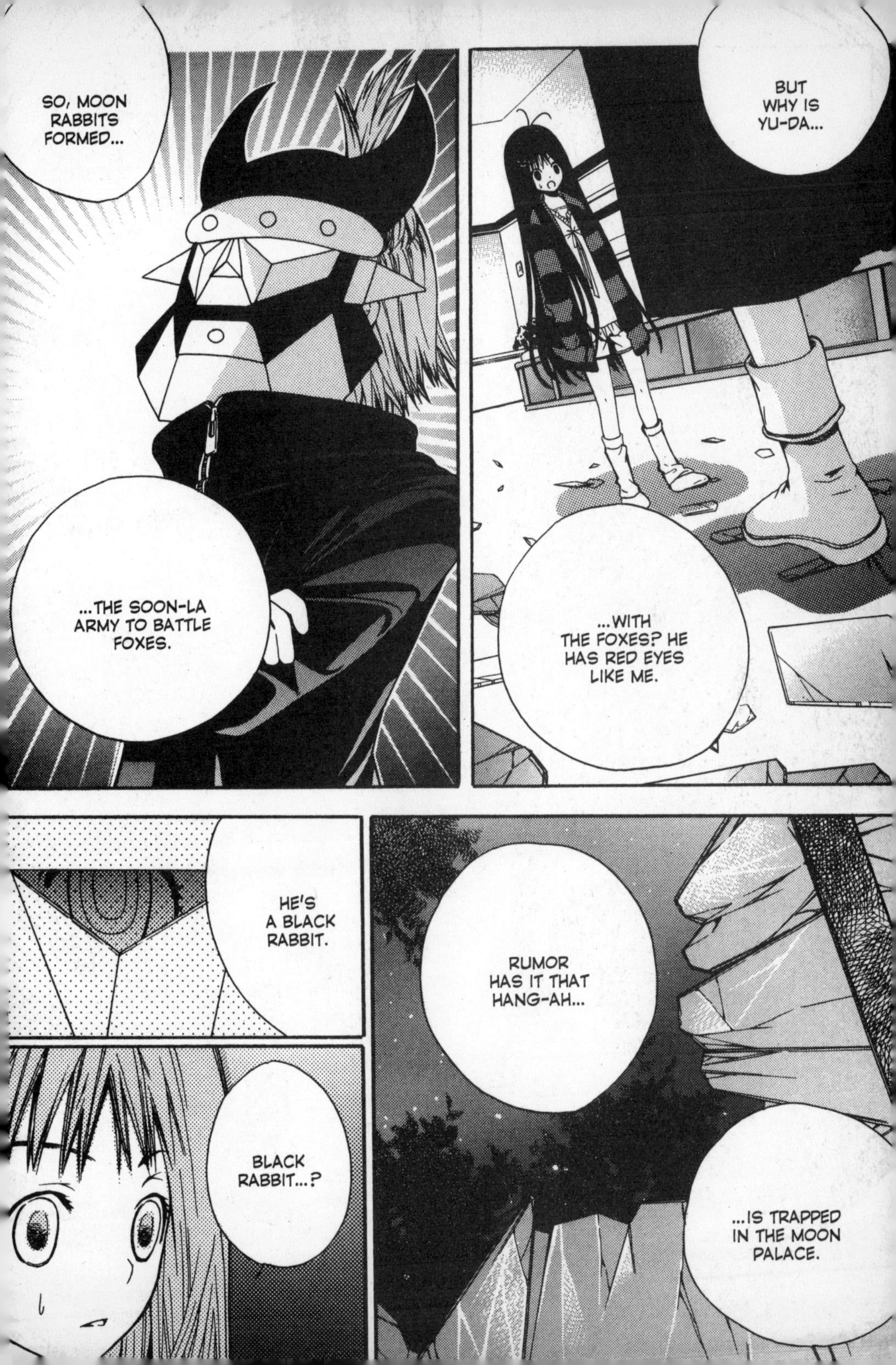
SO, MOON RABBITS FORMED...
...THE SOON-LA ARMY TO BATTLE FOXES.
BUT WHY IS YU-DA...
...WITH THE FOXES? HE HAS RED EYES LIKE ME.
HE'S A BLACK RABBIT.
BLACK RABBIT...?
RUMOR HAS IT THAT HANG-AH...
...IS TRAPPED IN THE MOON PALACE.

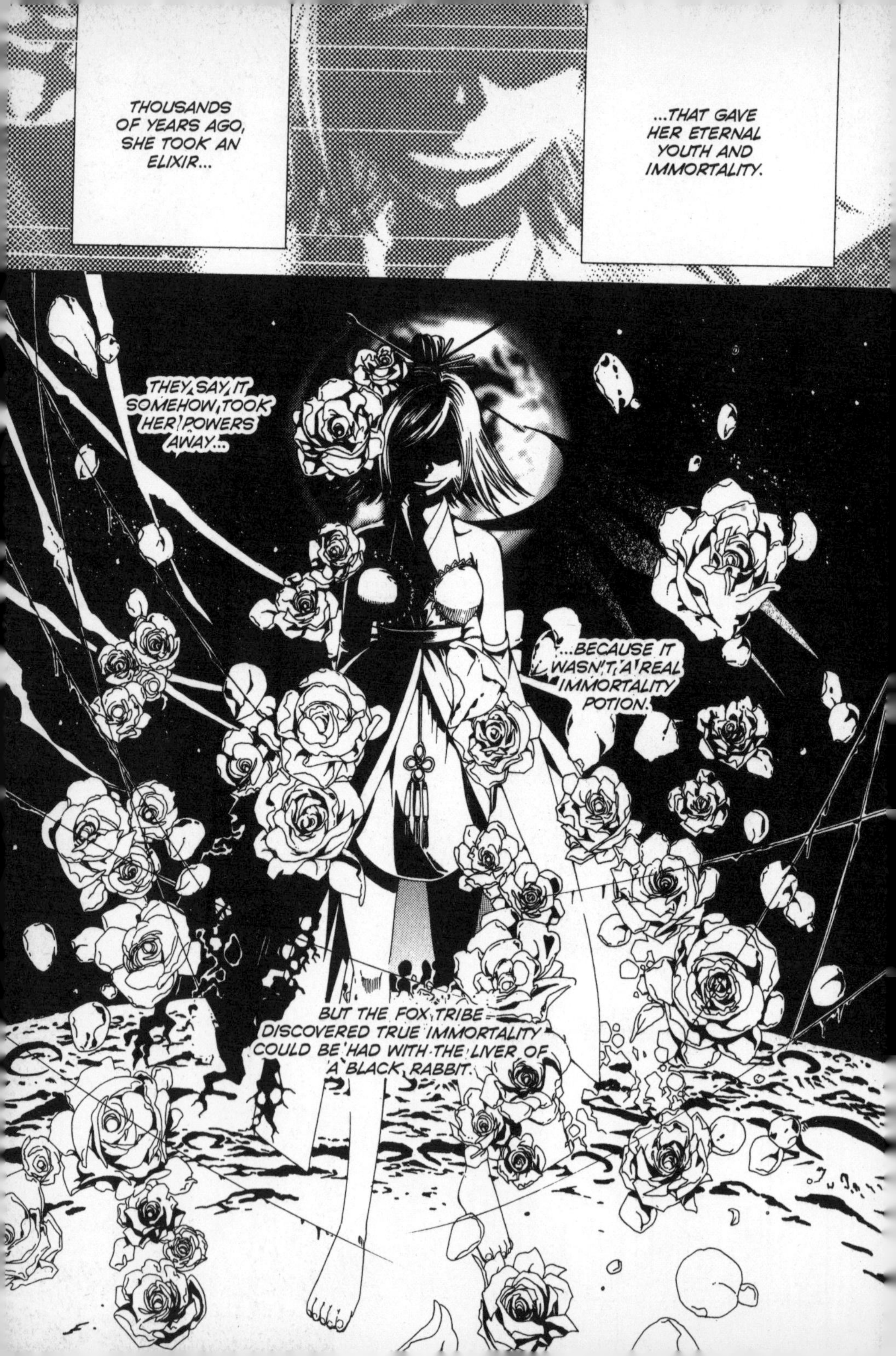

...THAT GAVE HER ETERNAL YOUTH AND IMMORTALITY.
THOUSANDS OF YEARS AGO, SHE TOOK AN ELIXIR...
...BECAUSE IT WASN'T A REAL IMMORTALITY POTION.
THEY SAY IT SOMEHOW TOOK HER POWERS AWAY...
BUT THE FOX TRIBE DISCOVERED TRUE IMMORTALITY COULD BE HAD WITH THE LIVER OF A BLACK RABBIT.

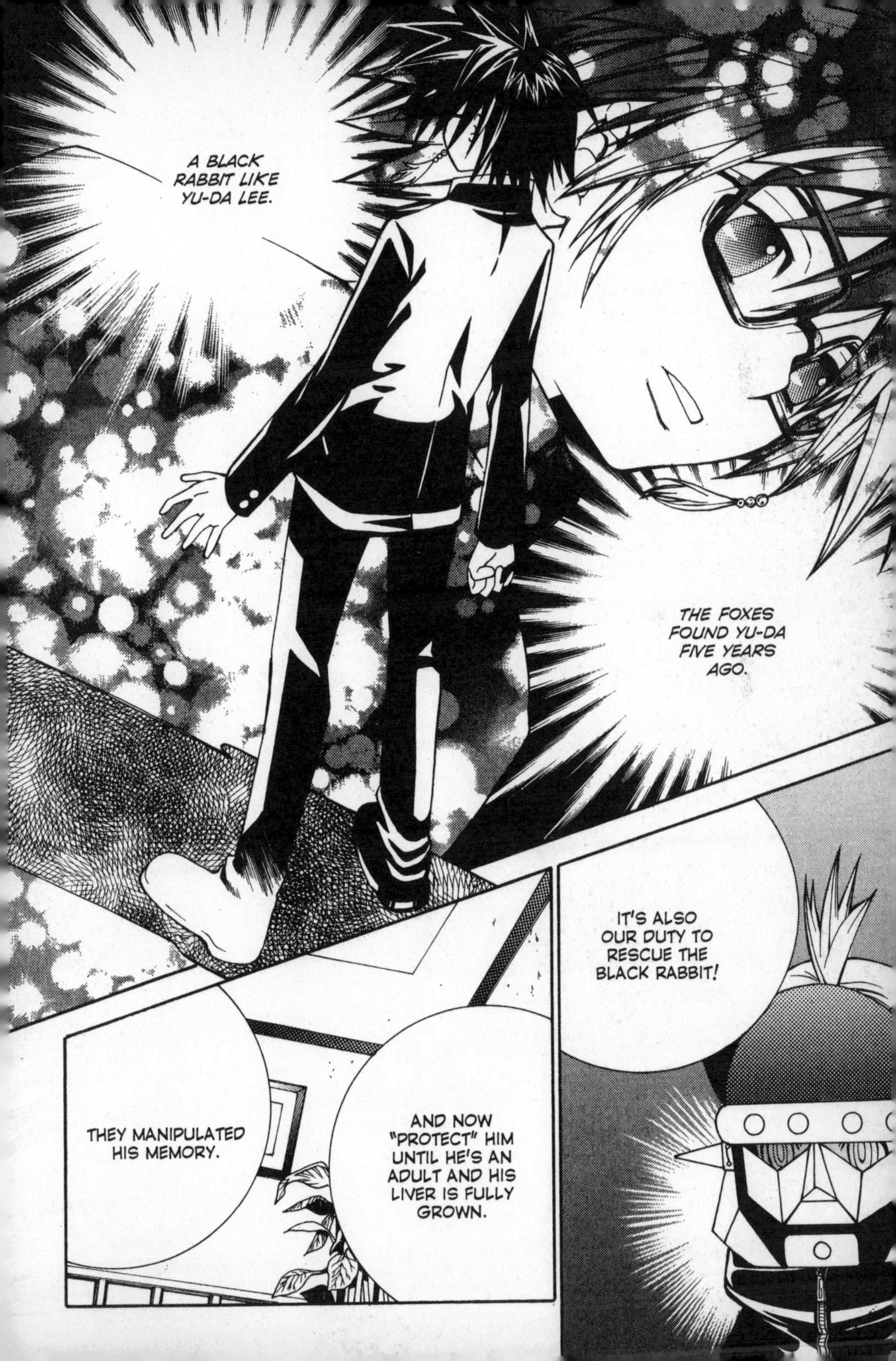
A BLACK RABBIT LIKE YU-DA LEE.
THE FOXES FOUND YU-DA FIVE YEARS AGO.
IT'S ALSO OUR DUTY TO RESCUE THE BLACK RABBIT!
AND NOW "PROTECT" HIM UNTIL HE'S AN ADULT AND HIS LIVER IS FULLY GROWN.
THEY MANIPULATED HIS MEMORY.

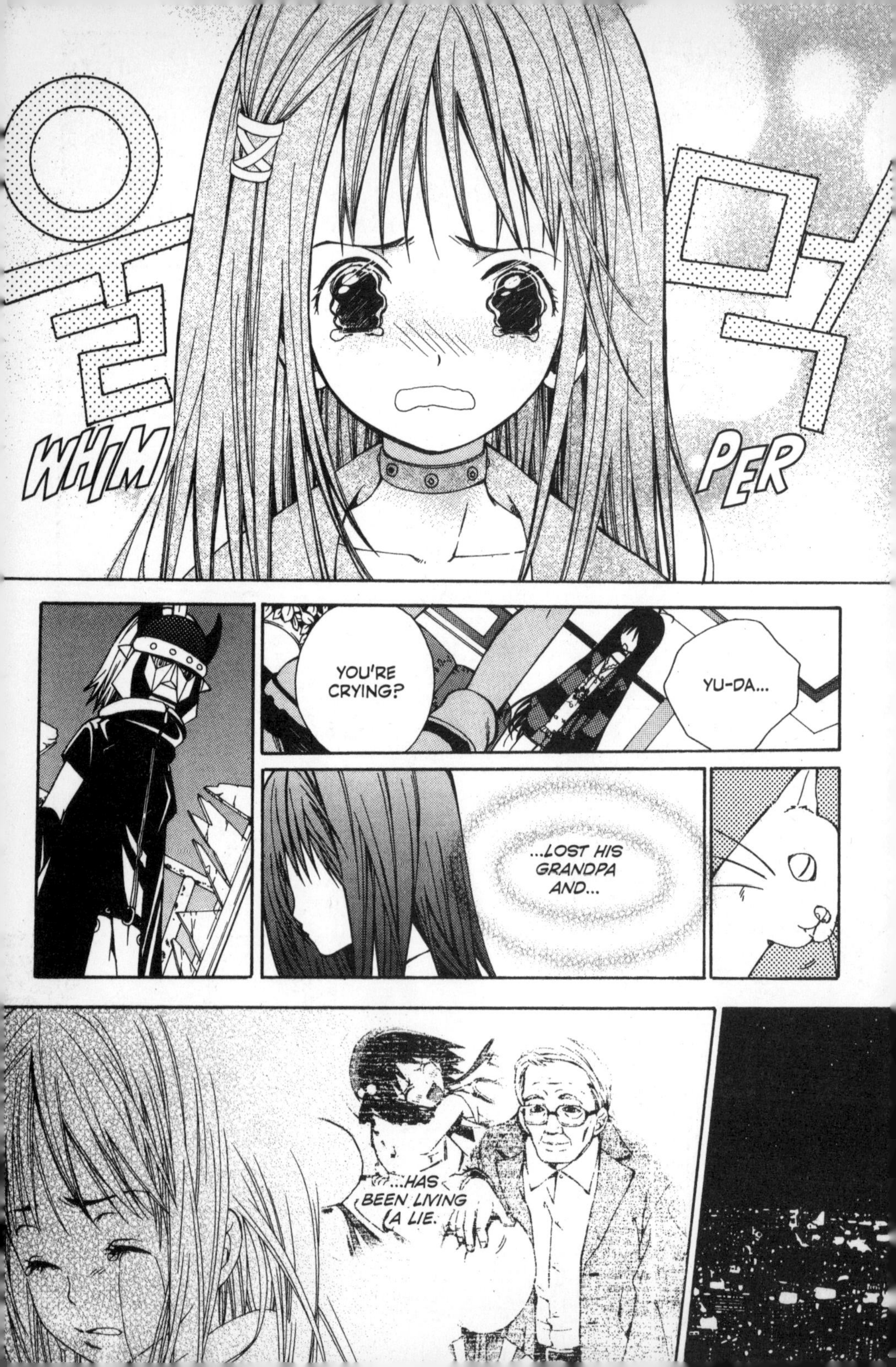
울먹
WHIMPER
YU-DA...
YOU'RE CRYING?
...LOST HIS GRANDPA AND...
...HAS BEEN LIVING A LIE.

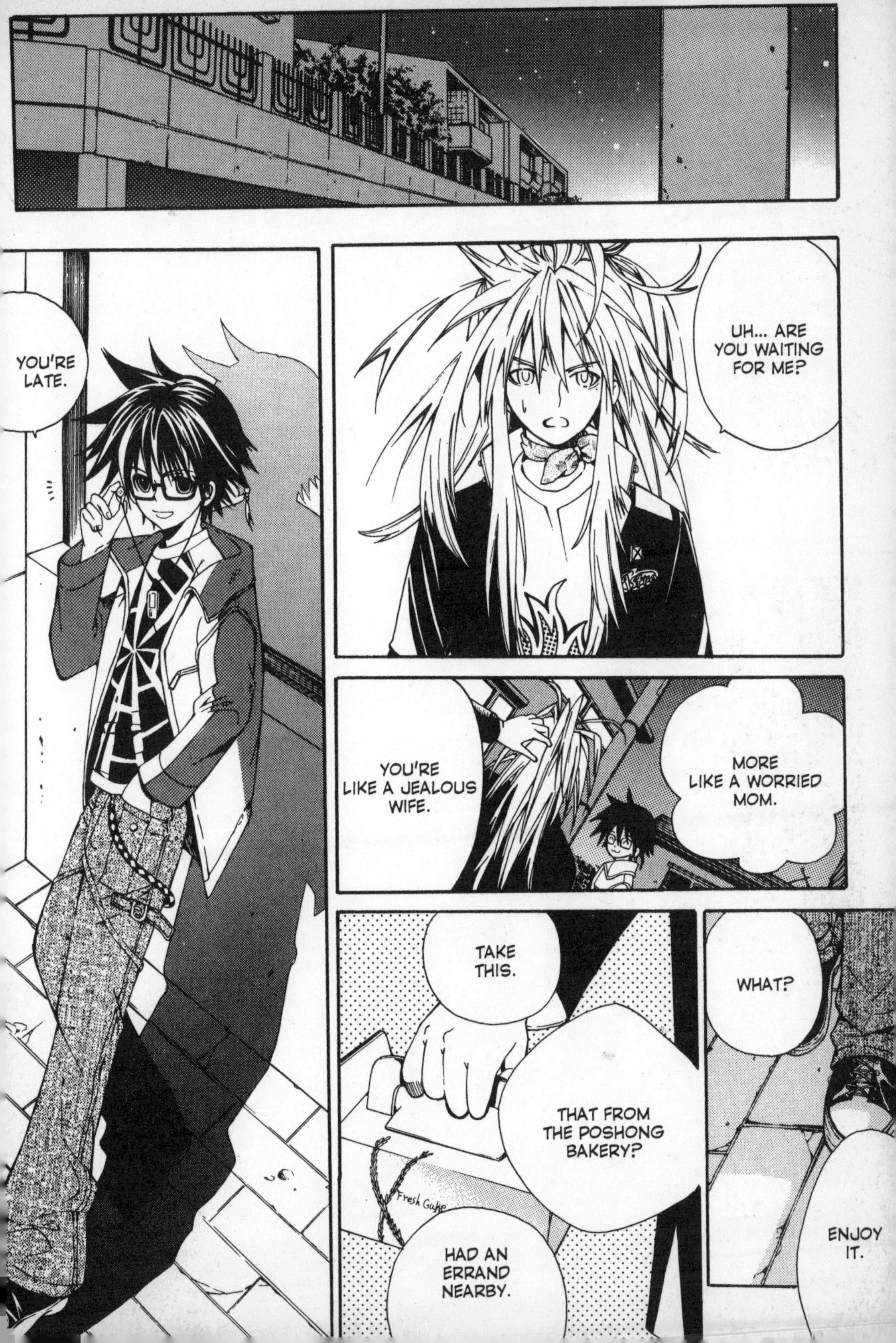
YOU'RE LATE.
UH... ARE YOU WAITING FOR ME?
YOU'RE LIKE A JEALOUS WIFE.
MORE LIKE A WORRIED MOM.
TAKE THIS.
THAT FROM THE POSHONG BAKERY?
HAD AN ERRAND NEARBY.
WHAT?
ENJOY IT.

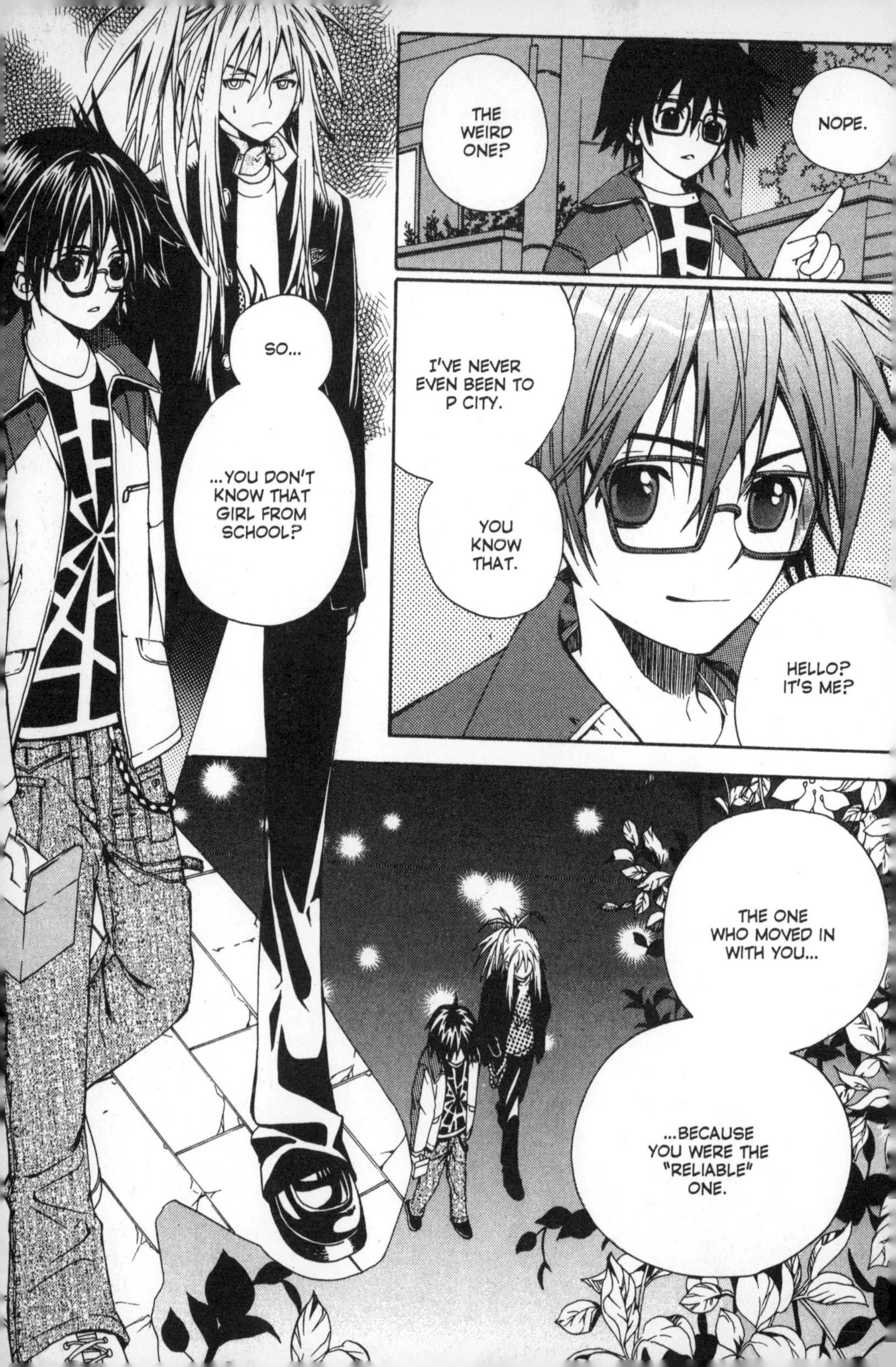
SO...
...YOU DON'T KNOW THAT GIRL FROM SCHOOL?
THE WEIRD ONE?
NOPE.
I'VE NEVER EVEN BEEN TO P CITY.
YOU KNOW THAT.
HELLO? IT'S ME?
THE ONE WHO MOVED IN WITH YOU...
...BECAUSE YOU WERE THE "RELIABLE" ONE.

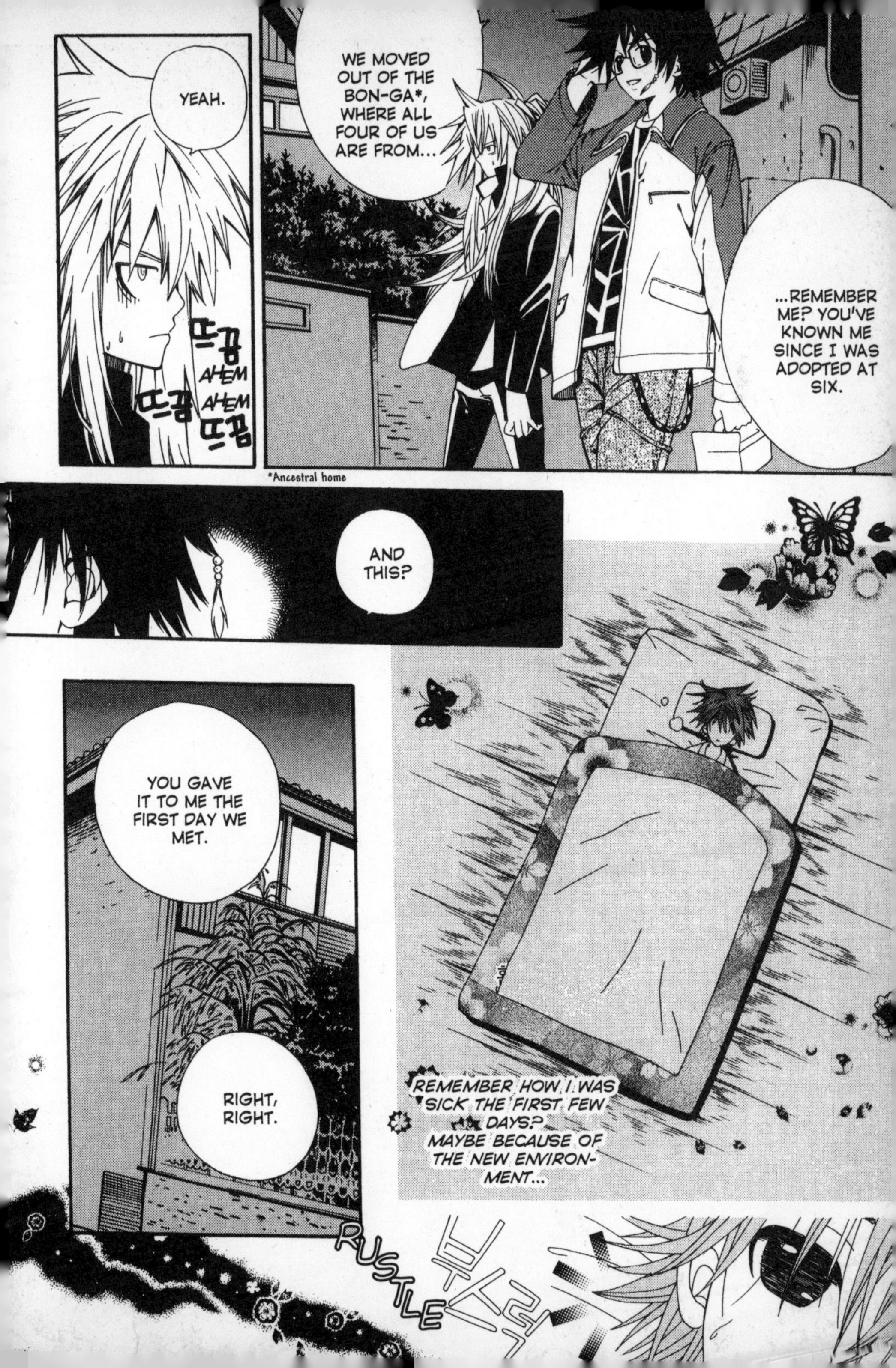
YEAH.
WE MOVED OUT OF THE BON-GA*, WHERE ALL FOUR OF US ARE FROM...
...REMEMBER ME? YOU'VE KNOWN ME SINCE I WAS ADOPTED AT SIX.
뜨끔 AHEM 뜨끔 AHEM 뜨끔
AND THIS?
YOU GAVE IT TO ME THE FIRST DAY WE MET.
RIGHT, RIGHT.
REMEMBER HOW I WAS SICK THE FIRST FEW DAYS? MAYBE BECAUSE OF THE NEW ENVIRONMENT...
RUSTLE 부스럭

*Ancestral home

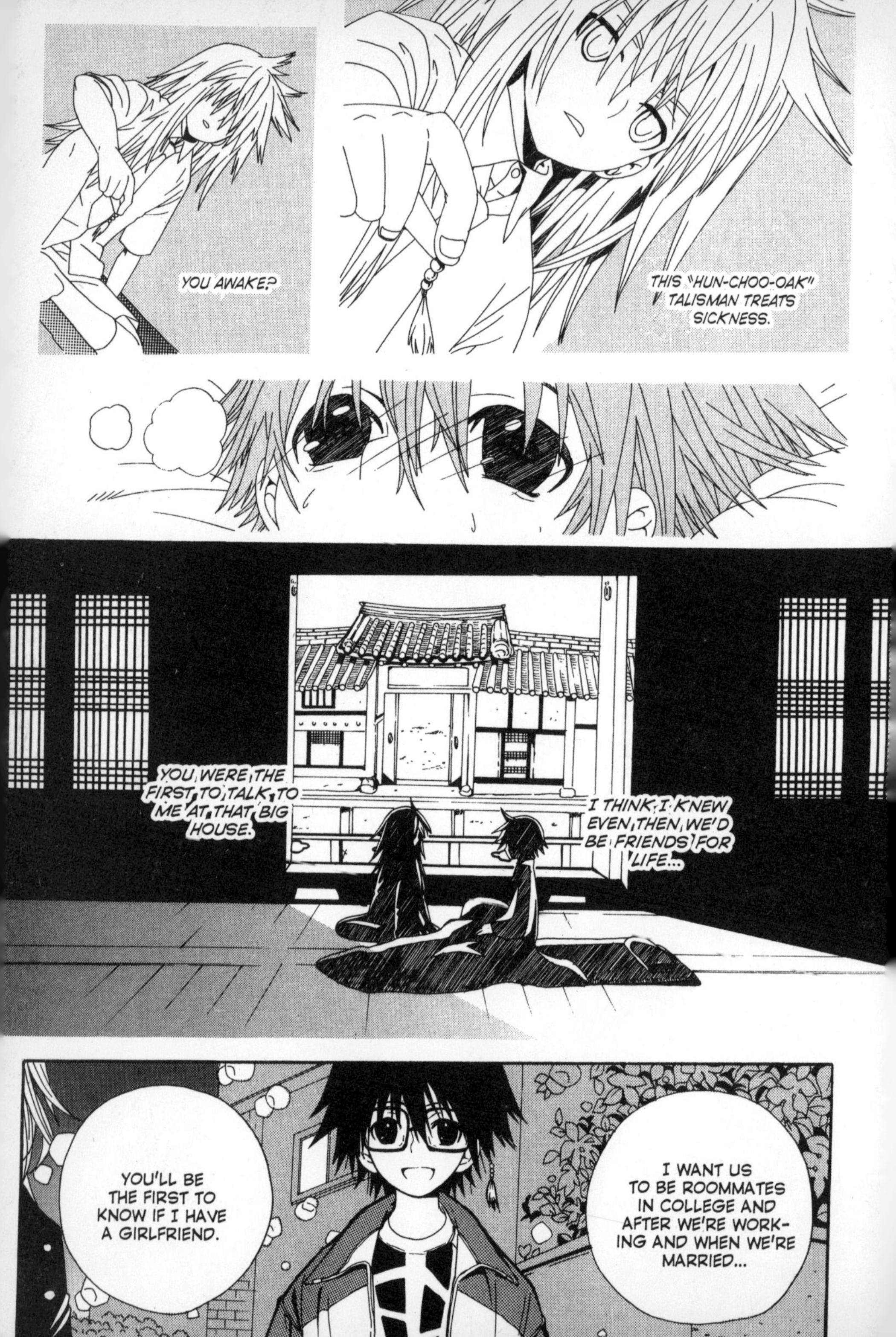
YOU AWAKE?
THIS "HUN-CHOO-OAK" TALISMAN TREATS SICKNESS.
YOU WERE THE FIRST TO TALK TO ME AT THAT BIG HOUSE.
I THINK I KNEW EVEN THEN WE'D BE FRIENDS FOR LIFE...
YOU'LL BE THE FIRST TO KNOW IF I HAVE A GIRLFRIEND.
I WANT US TO BE ROOMMATES IN COLLEGE AND AFTER WE'RE WORKING AND WHEN WE'RE MARRIED...

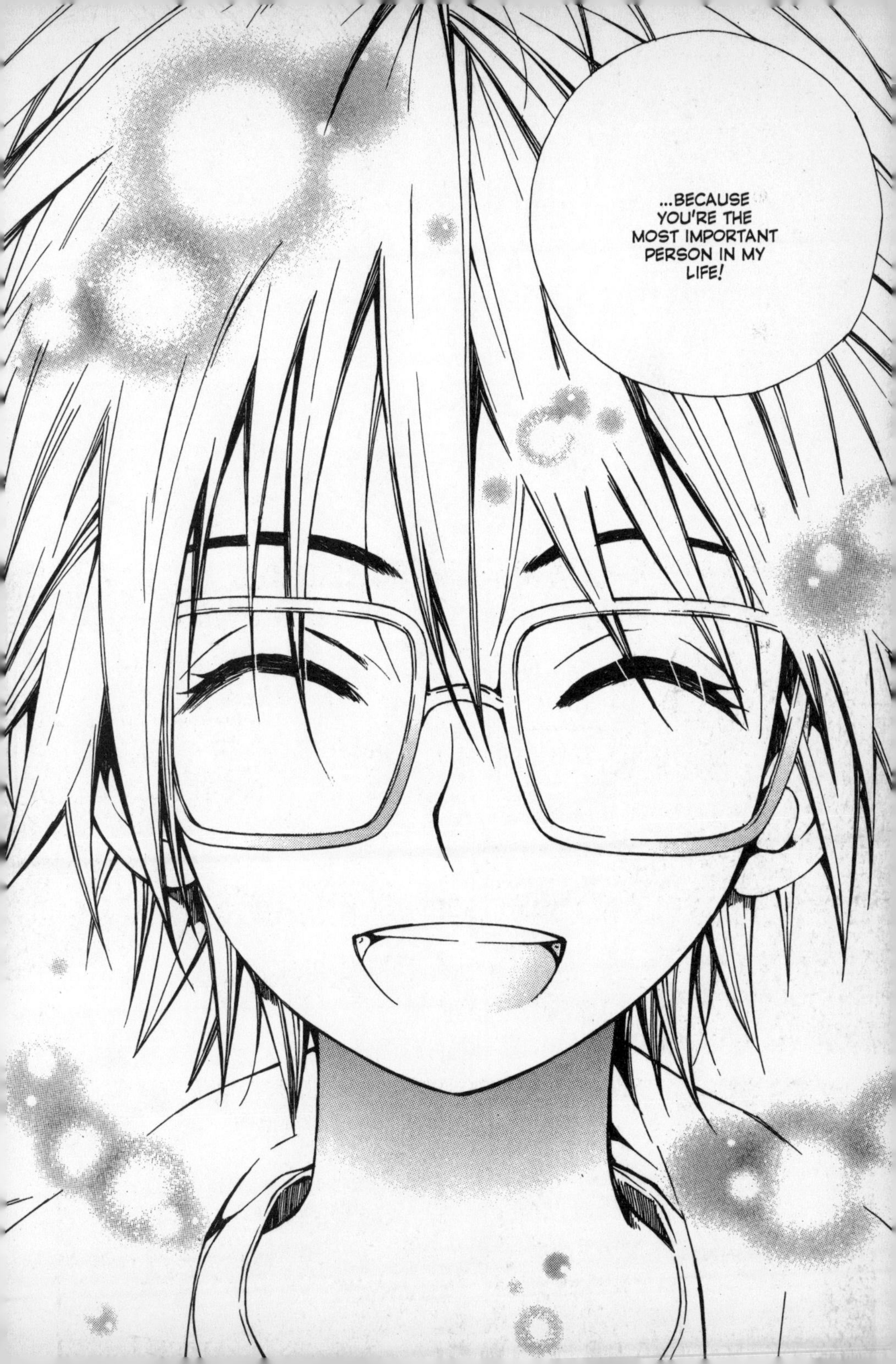
...BECAUSE YOU'RE THE MOST IMPORTANT PERSON IN MY LIFE!

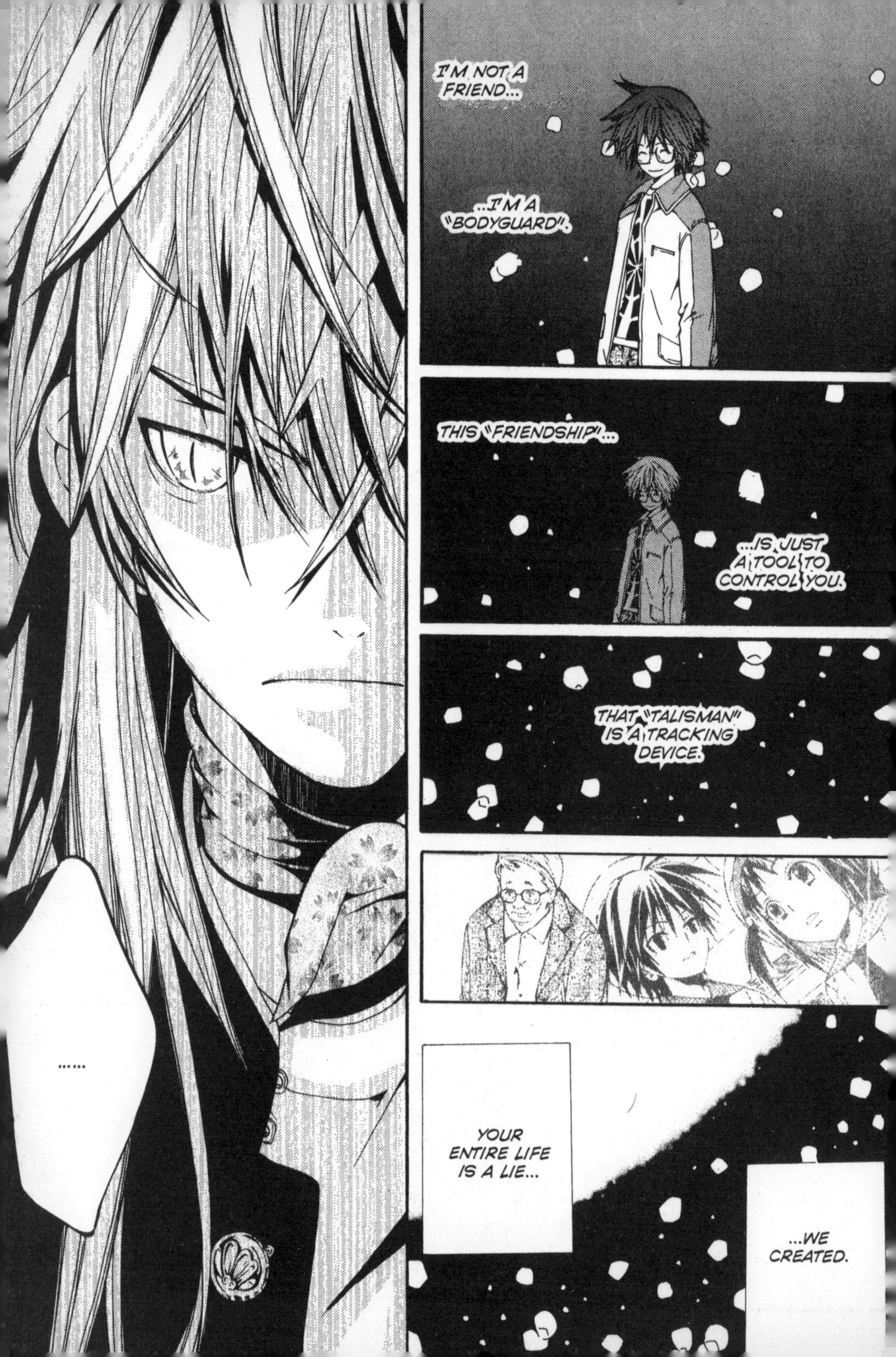
I'M NOT A FRIEND...
...I'M A "BODYGUARD".
THIS "FRIENDSHIP"...
...IS JUST A TOOL TO CONTROL YOU.
THAT "TALISMAN" IS A TRACKING DEVICE.
YOUR ENTIRE LIFE IS A LIE...
...WE CREATED.
……

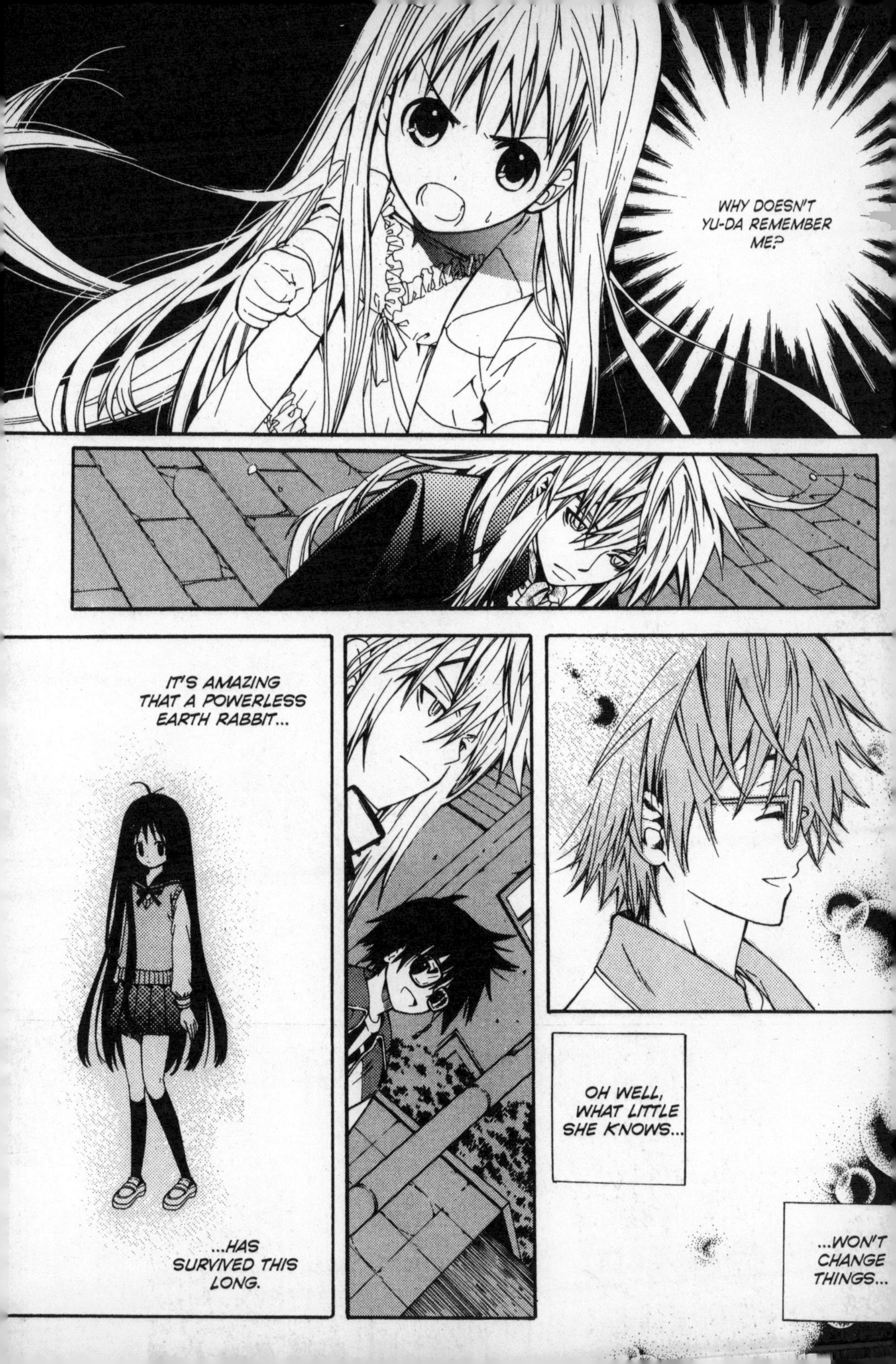
WHY DOESN'T YU-DA REMEMBER ME?
IT'S AMAZING THAT A POWERLESS EARTH RABBIT...
...HAS SURVIVED THIS LONG.
OH WELL, WHAT LITTLE SHE KNOWS...
...WON'T CHANGE THINGS...

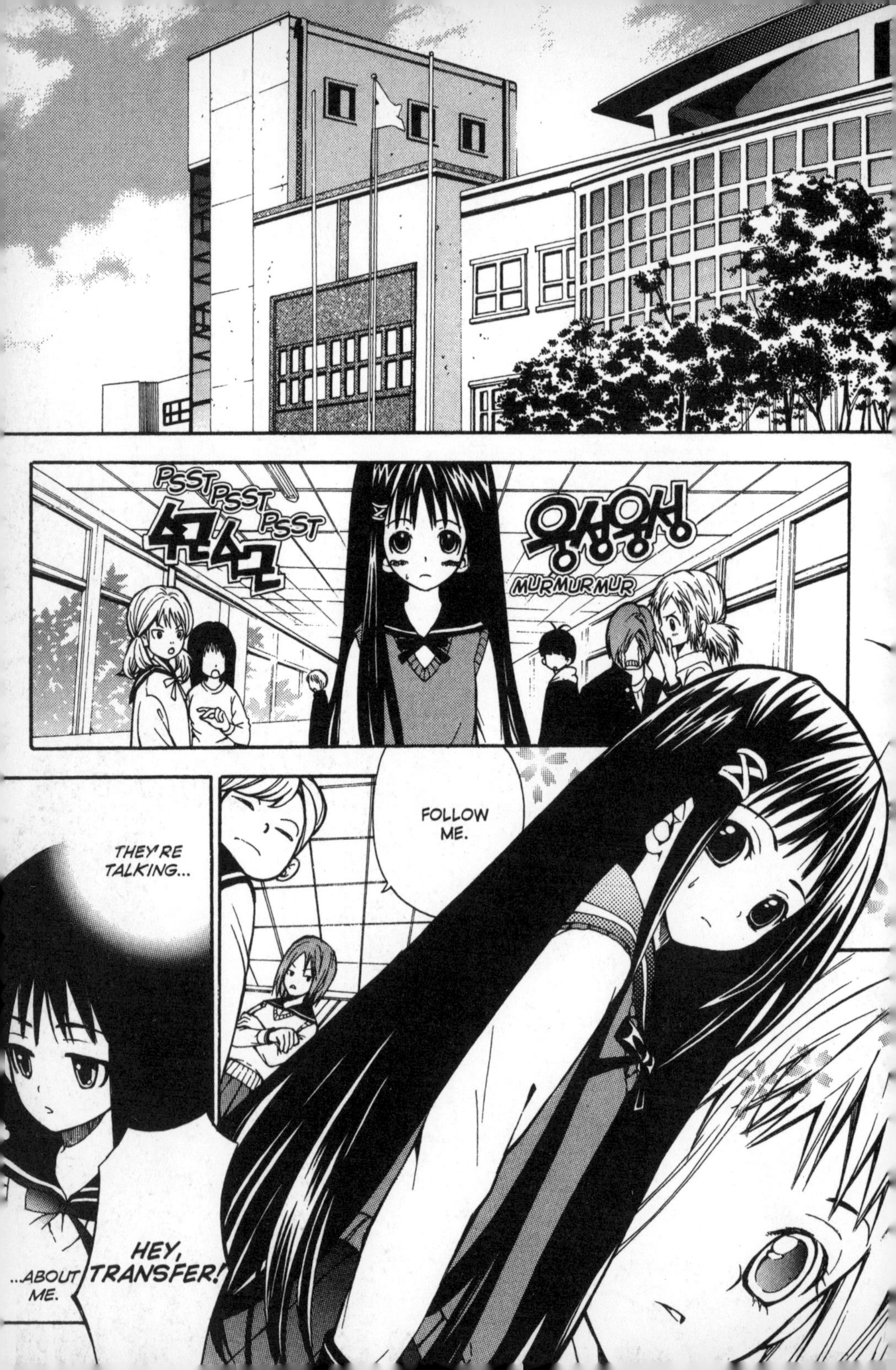

웅성웅성
MURMURMUR
PSST PSST PSST
FOLLOW ME.
THEY'RE TALKING...
HEY, TRANSFER!
...ABOUT ME.

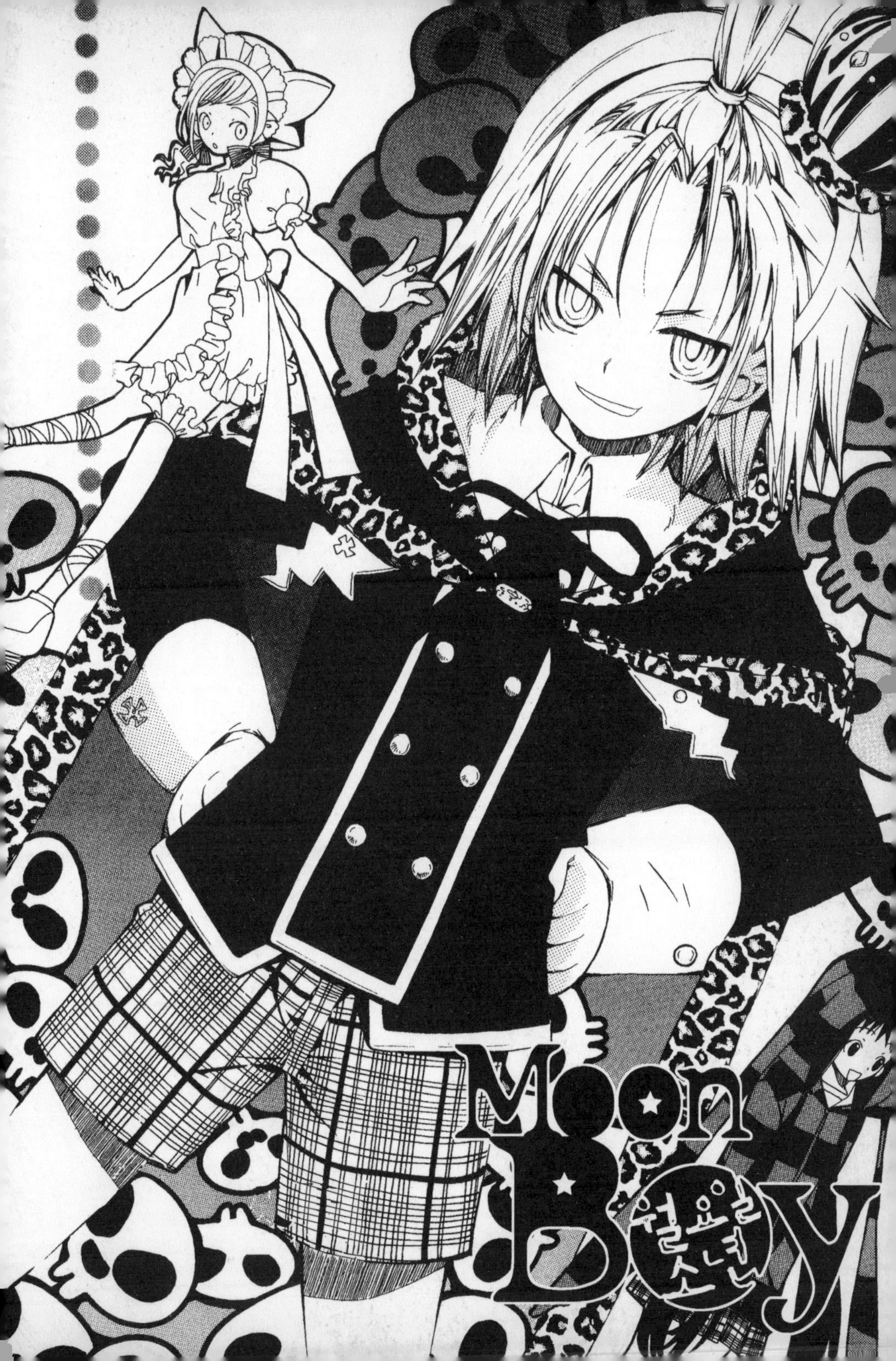
Moon Boy
월요일 소년

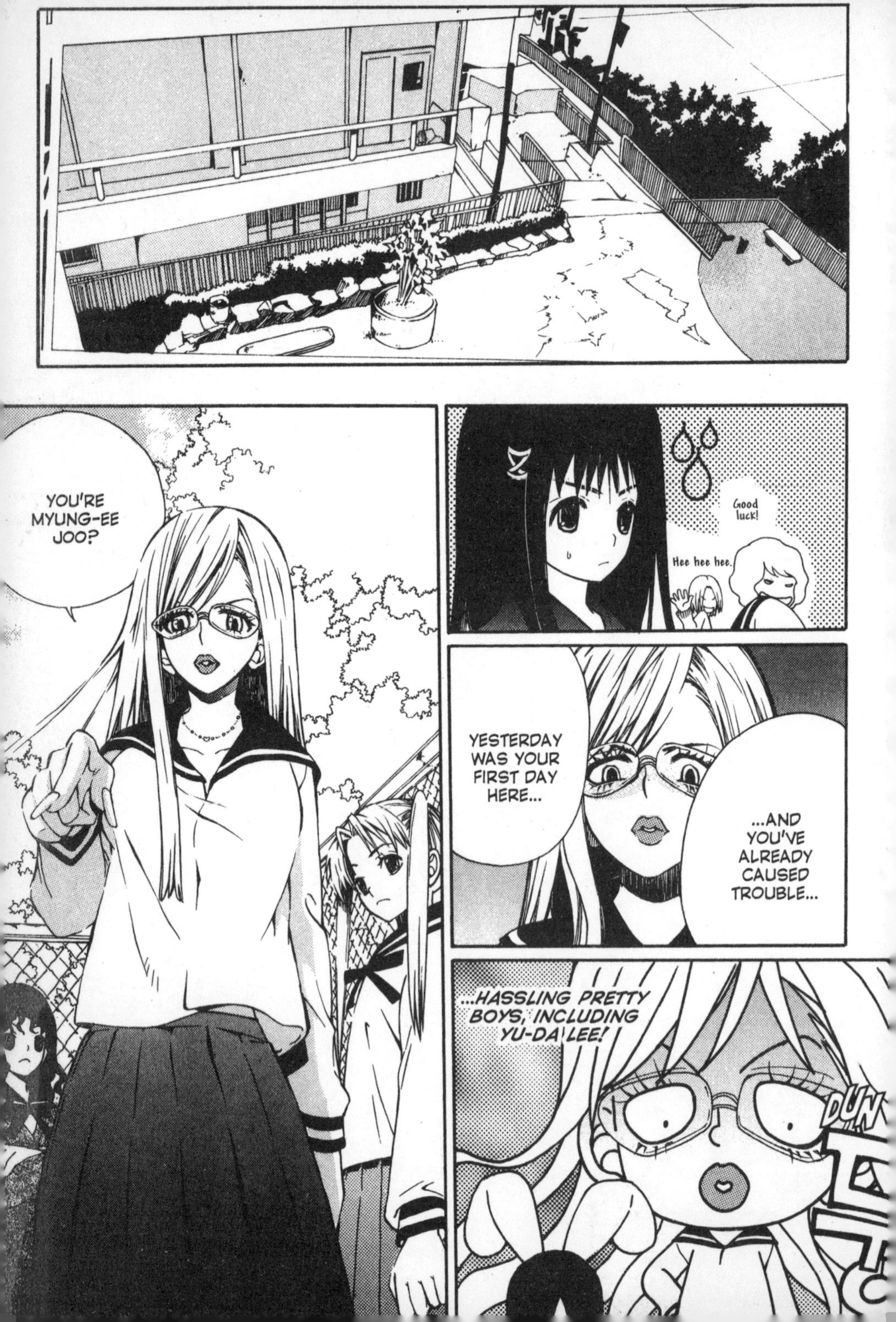
YOU'RE MYUNG-EE JOO?
Good luck!
Hee hee hee.
YESTERDAY WAS YOUR FIRST DAY HERE...
...AND YOU'VE ALREADY CAUSED TROUBLE...
...HASSLING PRETTY BOYS, INCLUDING YU-DA LEE!
DUN

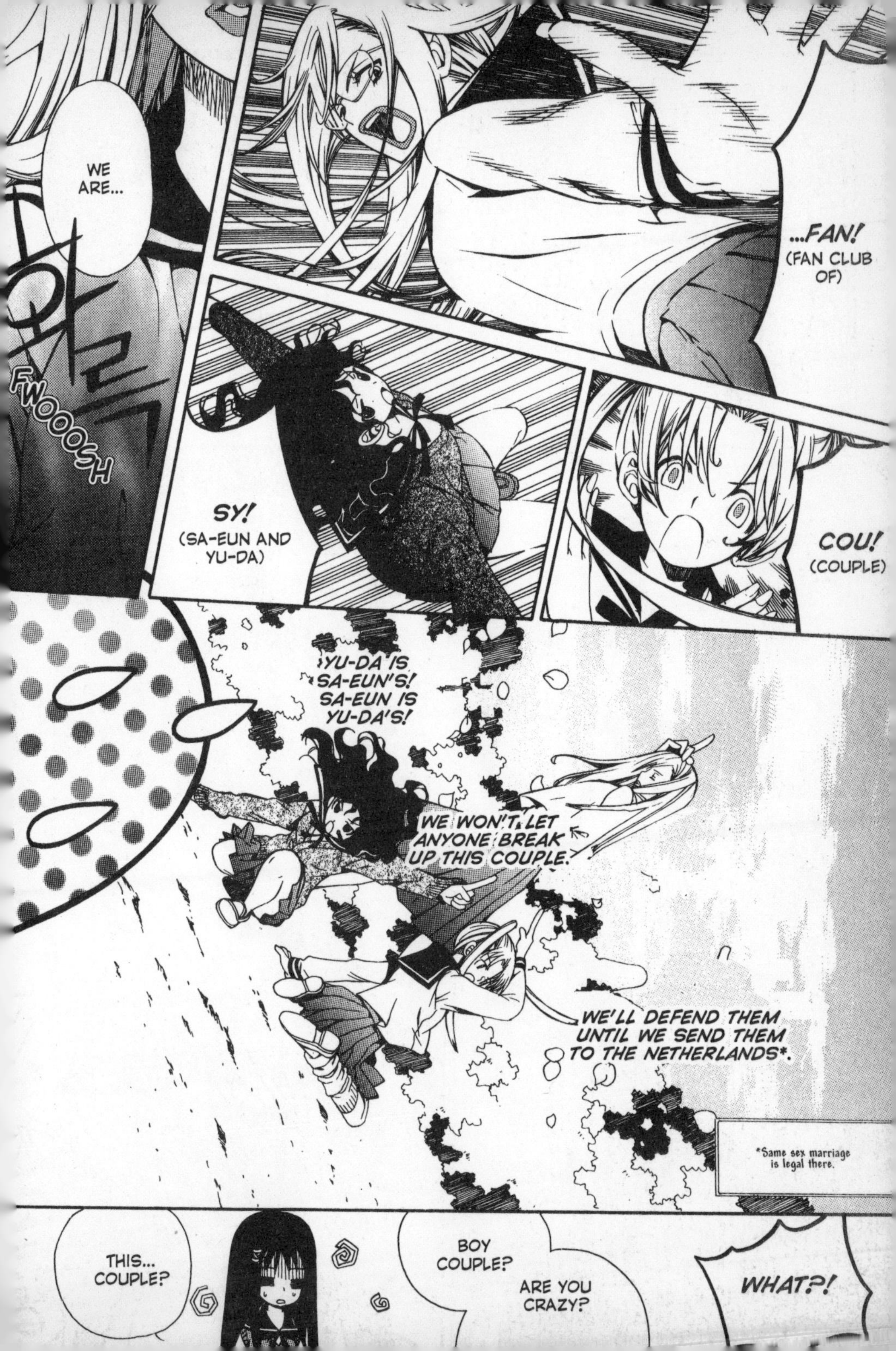
WE ARE...
FWOOOSH
...FAN!
(FAN CLUB OF)
SY!
(SA-EUN AND YU-DA)
COU!
(COUPLE)
YU-DA IS SA-EUN'S! SA-EUN IS YU-DA'S!
WE WON'T LET ANYONE BREAK UP THIS COUPLE.
WE'LL DEFEND THEM UNTIL WE SEND THEM TO THE NETHERLANDS*.
*Same sex marriage is legal there.
THIS... COUPLE?
BOY COUPLE?
ARE YOU CRAZY?
WHAT?!

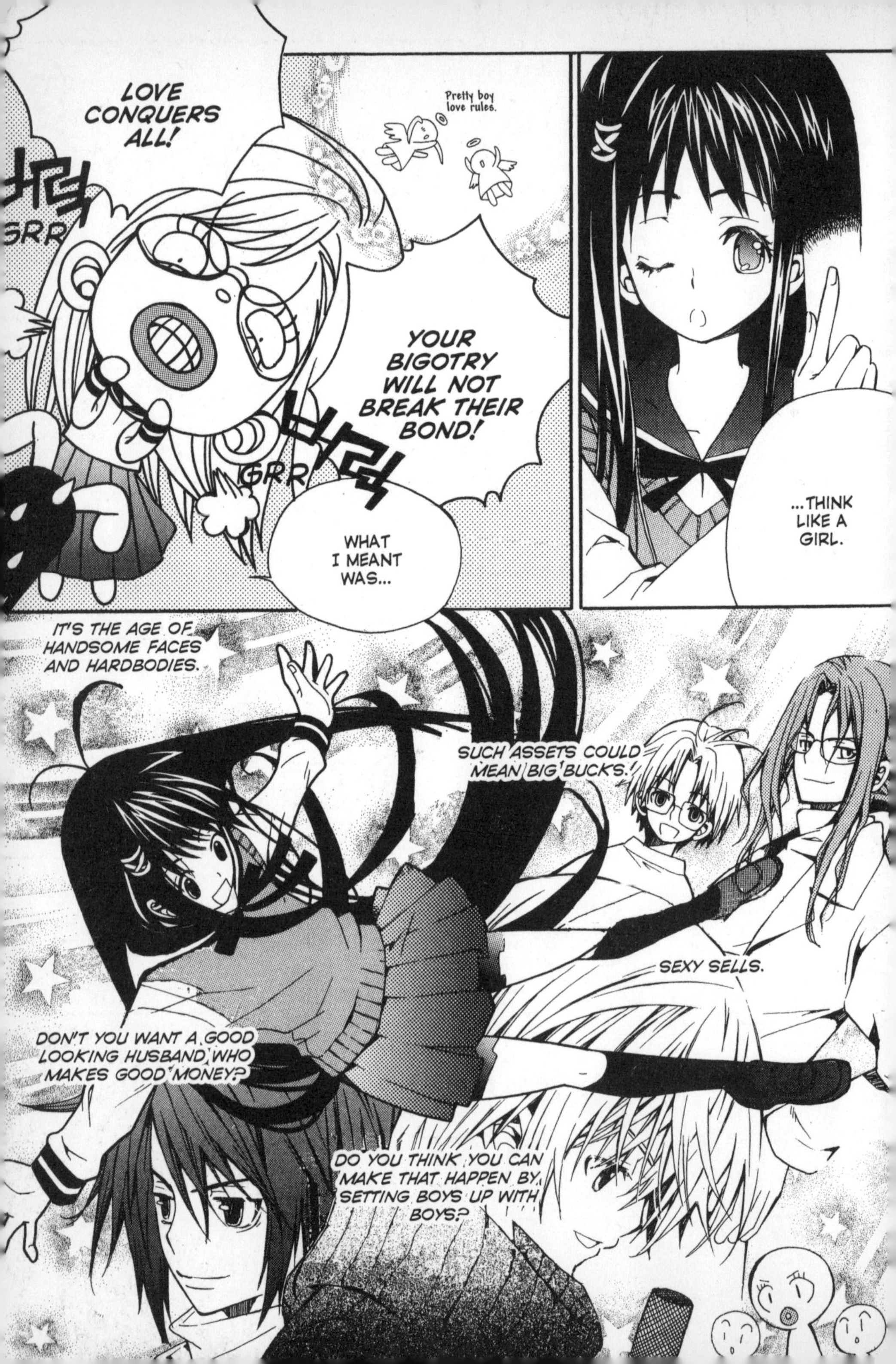
LOVE CONQUERS ALL!
GRR
Pretty boy love rules.
YOUR BIGOTRY WILL NOT BREAK THEIR BOND!
GRR
WHAT I MEANT WAS...
...THINK LIKE A GIRL.
IT'S THE AGE OF HANDSOME FACES AND HARDBODIES.
SUCH ASSETS COULD MEAN BIG BUCKS.
SEXY SELLS.
DON'T YOU WANT A GOOD LOOKING HUSBAND WHO MAKES GOOD MONEY?
DO YOU THINK YOU CAN MAKE THAT HAPPEN BY SETTING BOYS UP WITH BOYS?

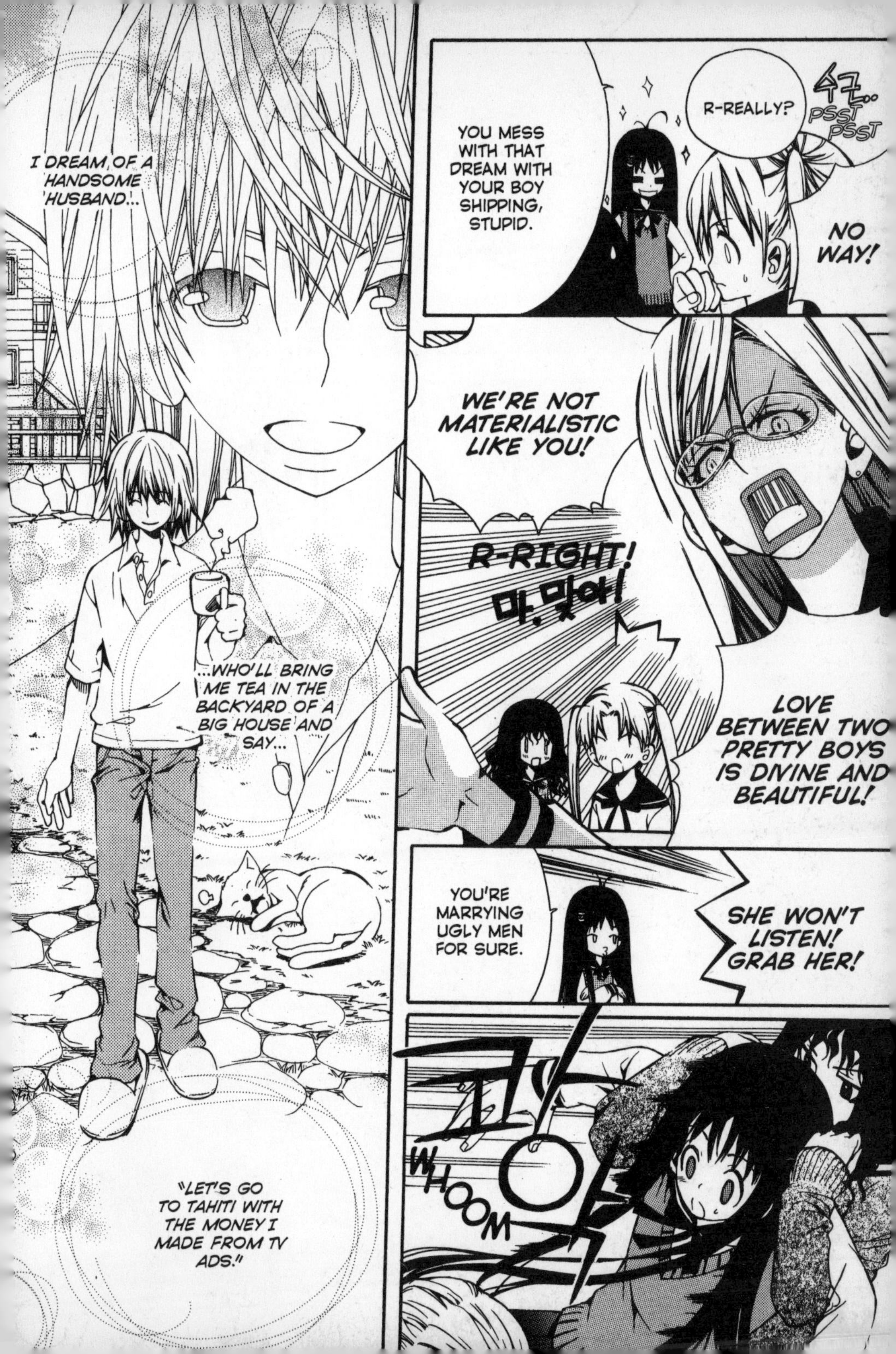
I DREAM OF A HANDSOME HUSBAND...
...WHO'LL BRING ME TEA IN THE BACKYARD OF A BIG HOUSE AND SAY...
"LET'S GO TO TAHITI WITH THE MONEY I MADE FROM TV ADS."
R-REALLY?
PSST PSST
YOU MESS WITH THAT DREAM WITH YOUR BOY SHIPPING, STUPID.
NO WAY!
WE'RE NOT MATERIALISTIC LIKE YOU!
LOVE BETWEEN TWO PRETTY BOYS IS DIVINE AND BEAUTIFUL!
R-RIGHT!
마, 맞아!
YOU'RE MARRYING UGLY MEN FOR SURE.
SHE WON'T LISTEN! GRAB HER!
WHOOM

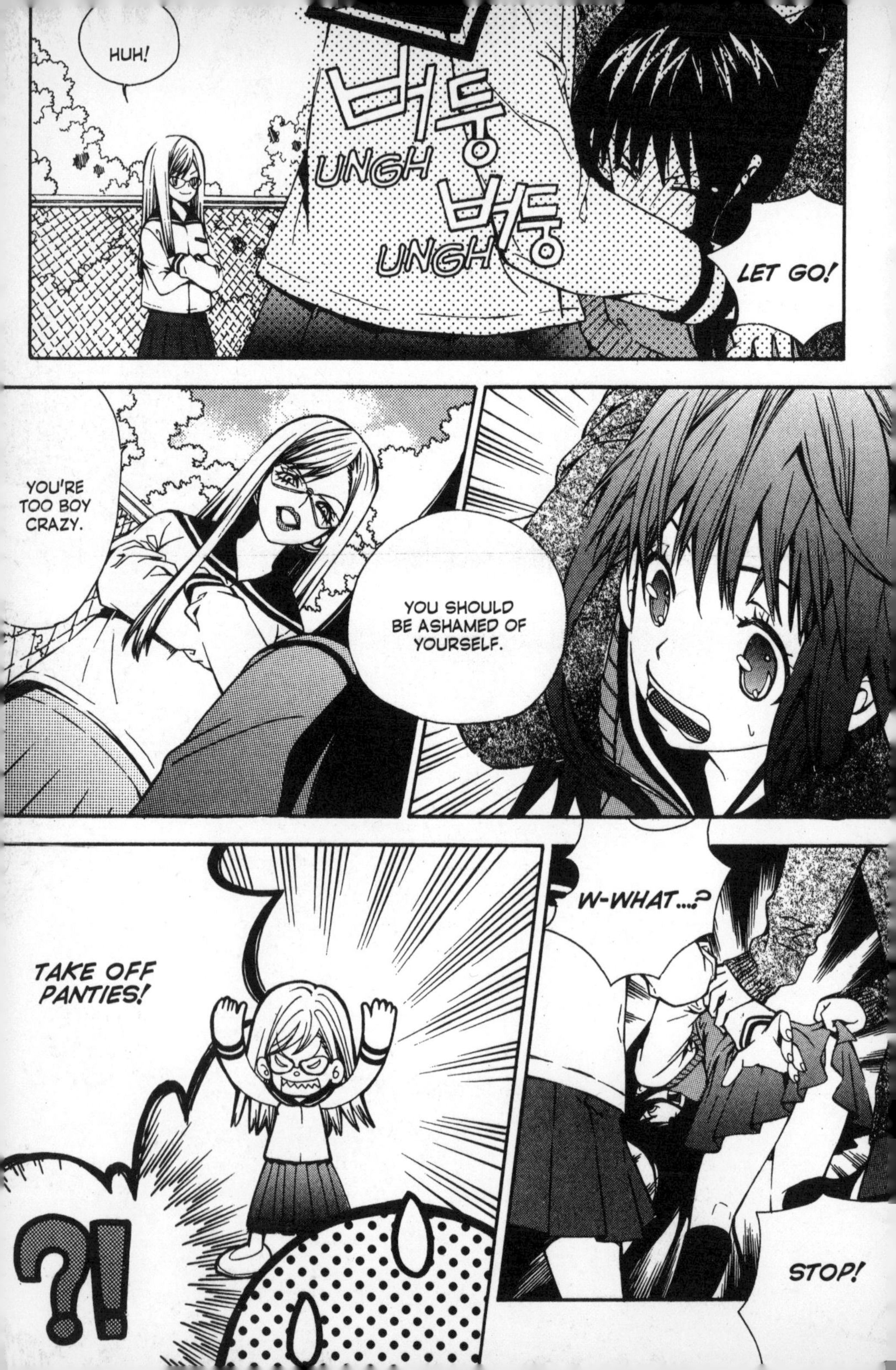
HUH!
버둥
UNGH
버둥
UNGH
LET GO!
YOU'RE TOO BOY CRAZY.
YOU SHOULD BE ASHAMED OF YOURSELF.
TAKE OFF PANTIES!
?!
W-WHAT...?
STOP!

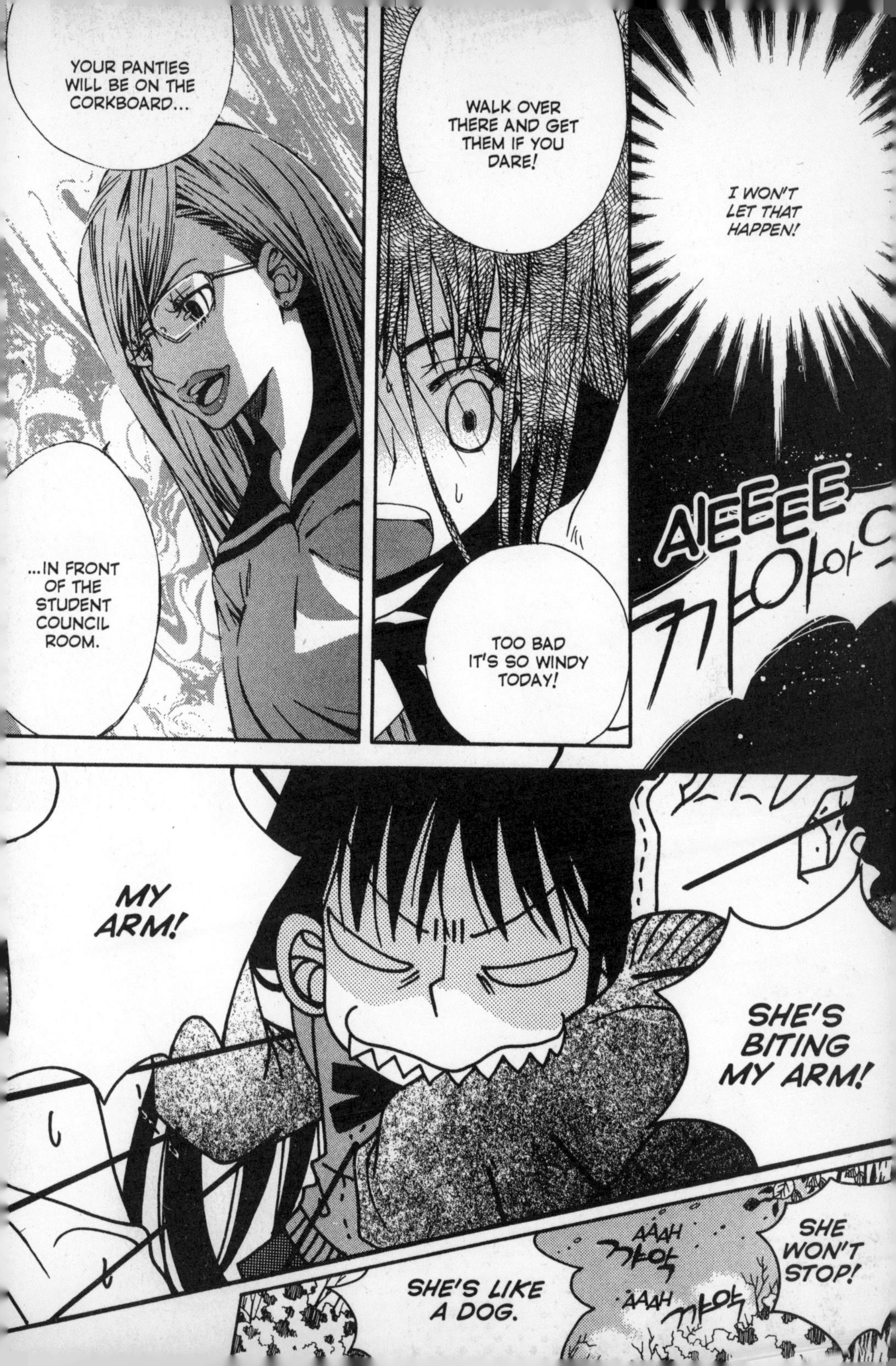
YOUR PANTIES WILL BE ON THE CORKBOARD...
...IN FRONT OF THE STUDENT COUNCIL ROOM.
WALK OVER THERE AND GET THEM IF YOU DARE!
TOO BAD IT'S SO WINDY TODAY!
I WON'T LET THAT HAPPEN!
AIEEEEE
MY ARM!
SHE'S BITING MY ARM!
SHE'S LIKE A DOG.
AAAH
AAAH
SHE WON'T STOP!

WHOSE SEAT IS THAT? WHO'S SKIPPING MY CLASS!

THE TRANSFER.

WHAT?!

SKIPPING CLASS ON HER SECOND DAY?

WHY DIDN'T YOU WATCH HER?

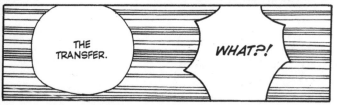

ROWR! I PUNISH YOU WITH A POP QUIZ!

BOOO

Crap.

Nice going.

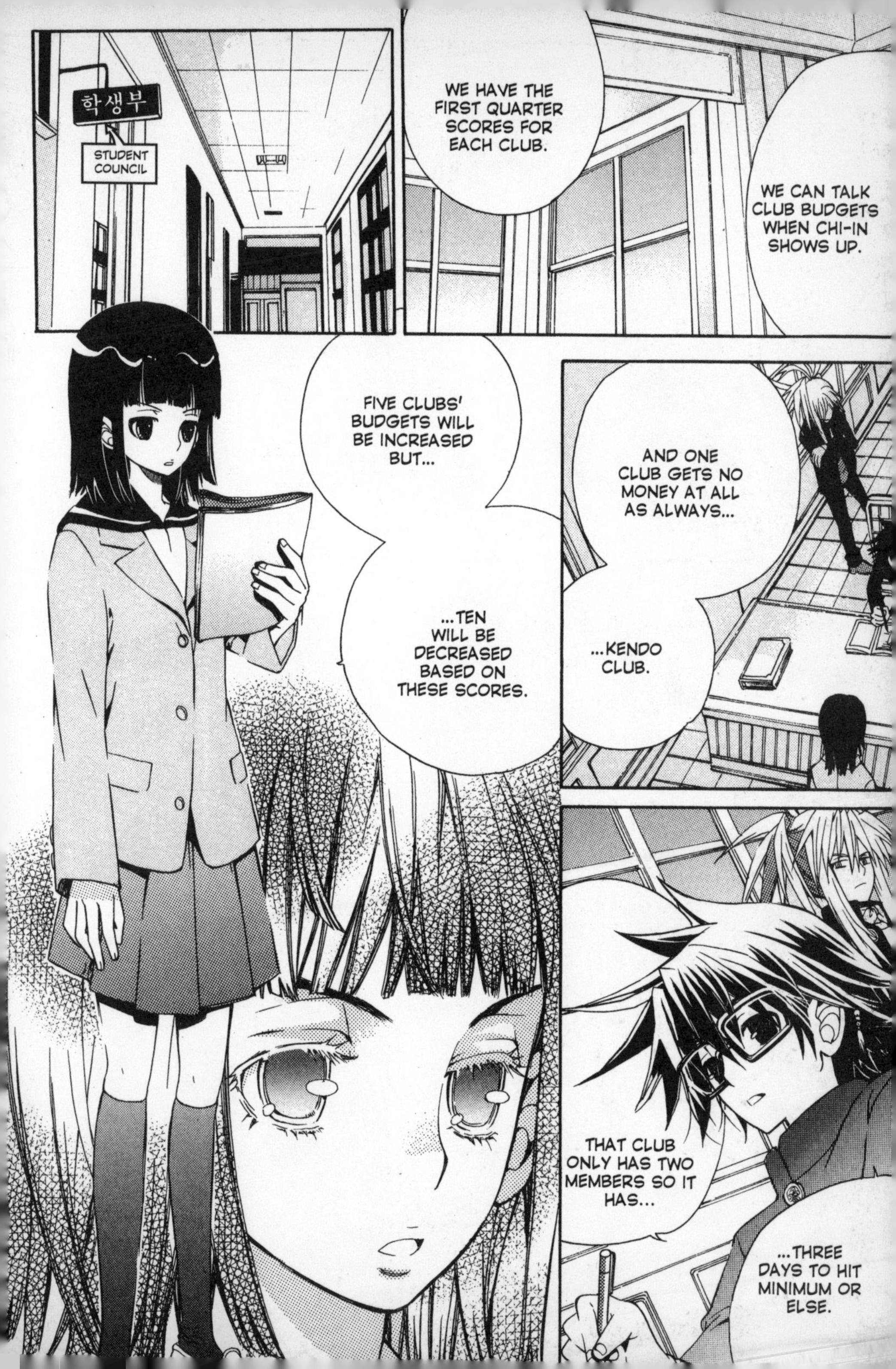
학생부
STUDENT COUNCIL
WE CAN TALK CLUB BUDGETS WHEN CHI-IN SHOWS UP.
WE HAVE THE FIRST QUARTER SCORES FOR EACH CLUB.
FIVE CLUBS' BUDGETS WILL BE INCREASED BUT...
...TEN WILL BE DECREASED BASED ON THESE SCORES.
AND ONE CLUB GETS NO MONEY AT ALL AS ALWAYS...
...KENDO CLUB.
THAT CLUB ONLY HAS TWO MEMBERS SO IT HAS...
...THREE DAYS TO HIT MINIMUM OR ELSE.

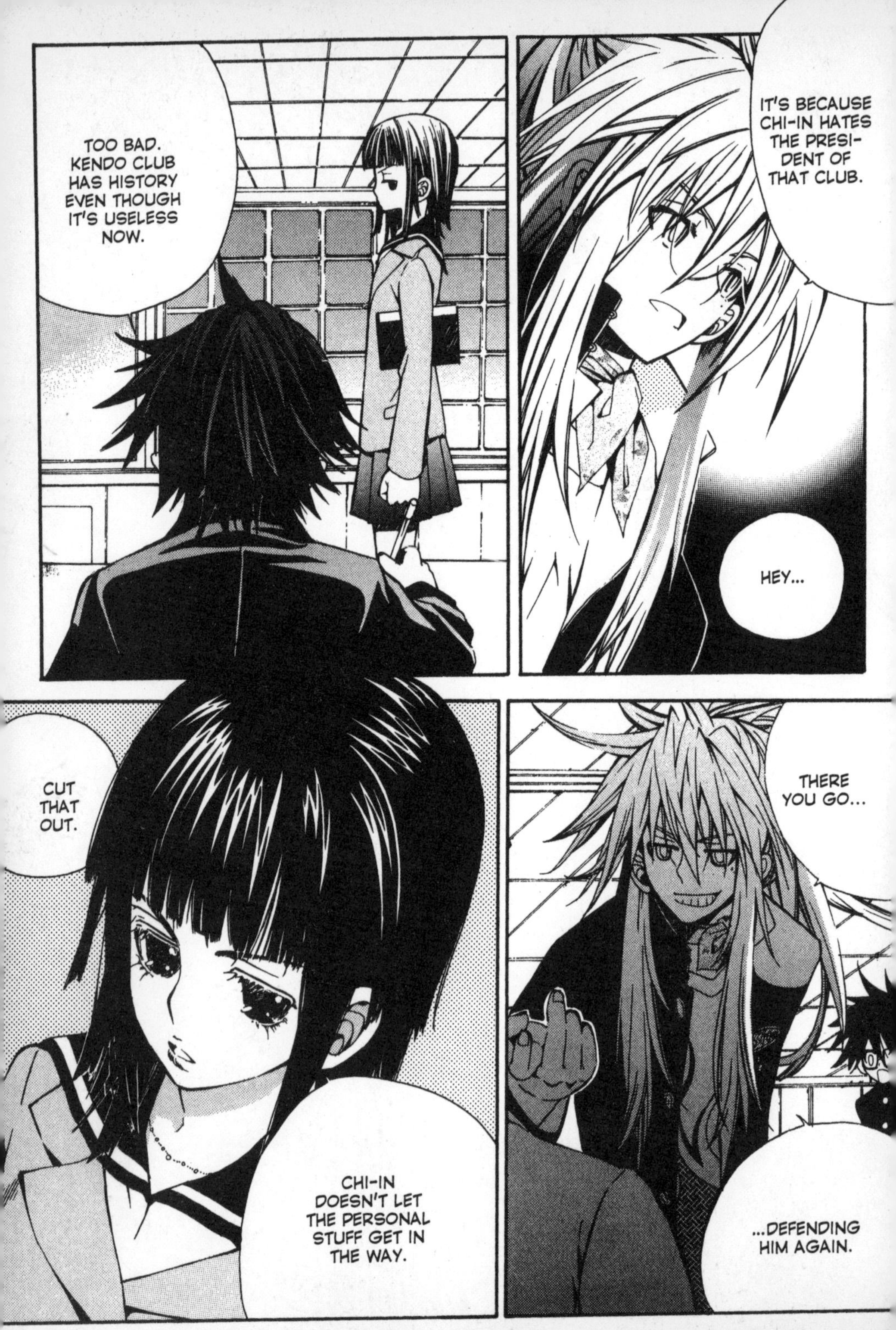
TOO BAD. KENDO CLUB HAS HISTORY EVEN THOUGH IT'S USELESS NOW.
IT'S BECAUSE CHI-IN HATES THE PRESI-DENT OF THAT CLUB.
HEY...
CUT THAT OUT.
CHI-IN DOESN'T LET THE PERSONAL STUFF GET IN THE WAY.
THERE YOU GO...
...DEFENDING HIM AGAIN.

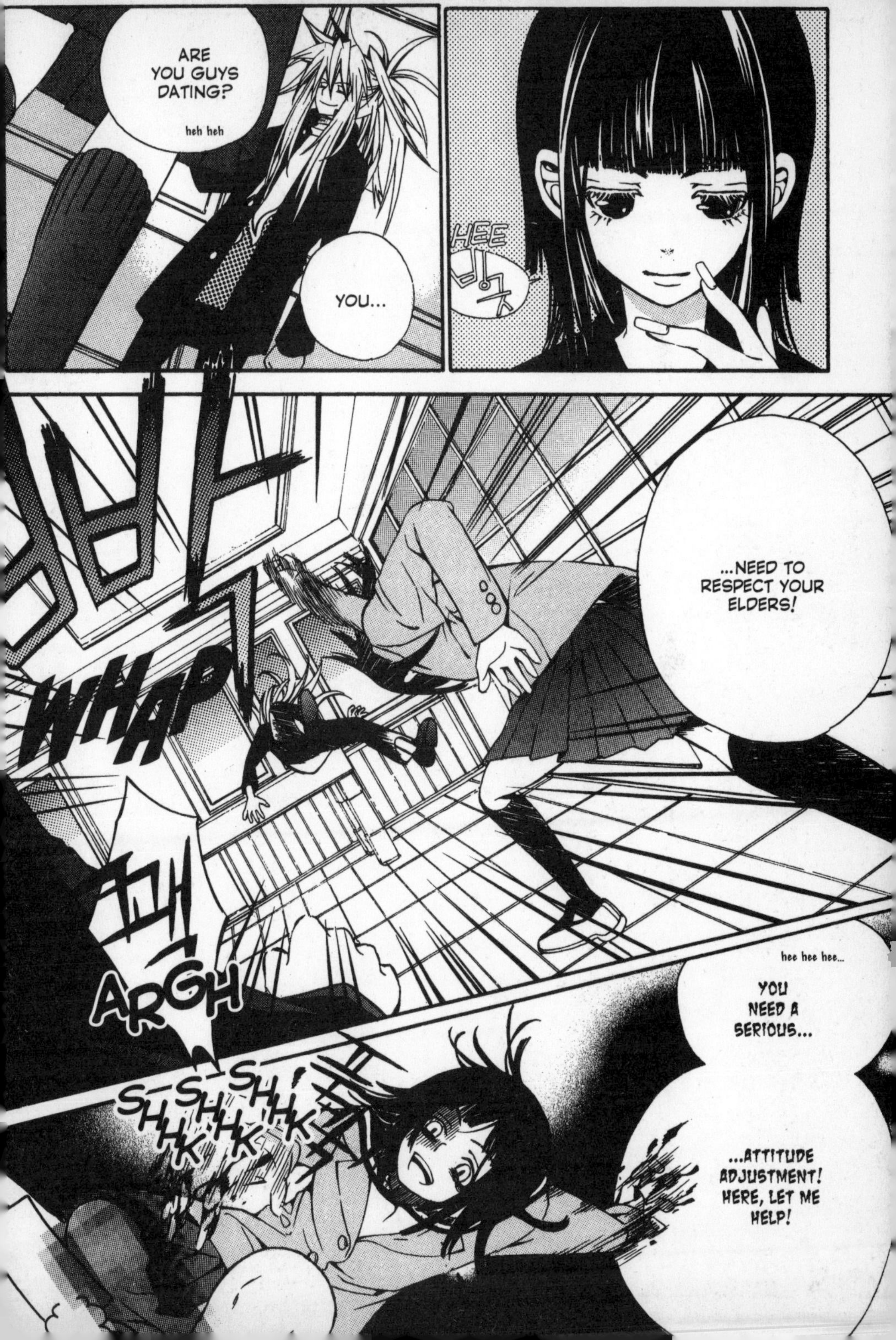
ARE YOU GUYS DATING?
heh heh
YOU...
HEE
...NEED TO RESPECT YOUR ELDERS!
WHAP
ARGH
hee hee hee...
YOU NEED A SERIOUS...
S-S-SHHK
SHHK
...ATTITUDE ADJUSTMENT! HERE, LET ME HELP!

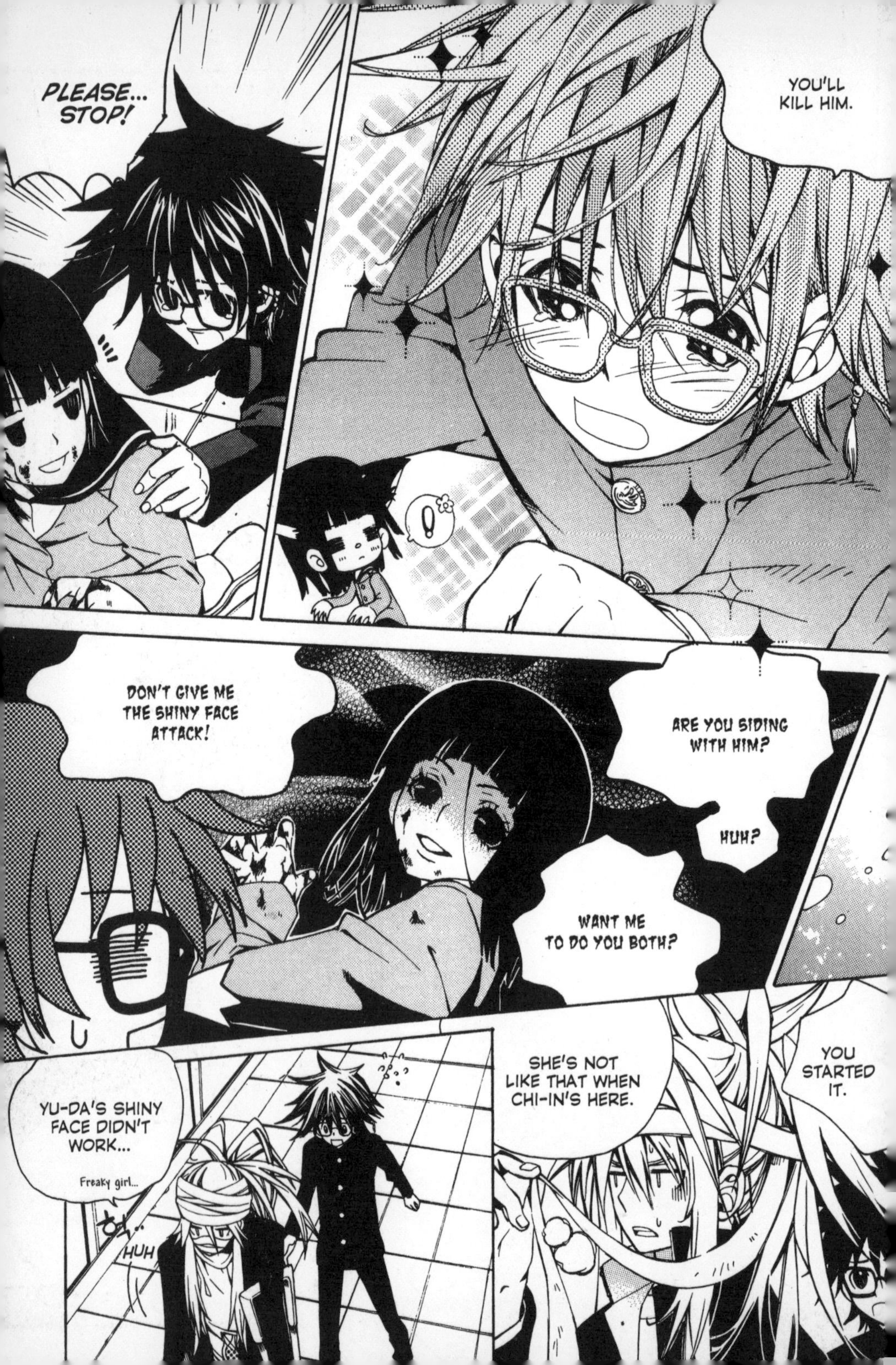
YOU'LL KILL HIM.
PLEASE... STOP!
ARE YOU SIDING WITH HIM?
HUH?
WANT ME TO DO YOU BOTH?
DON'T GIVE ME THE SHINY FACE ATTACK!
YOU STARTED IT.
SHE'S NOT LIKE THAT WHEN CHI-IN'S HERE.
YU-DA'S SHINY FACE DIDN'T WORK...
Freaky girl...
HUH

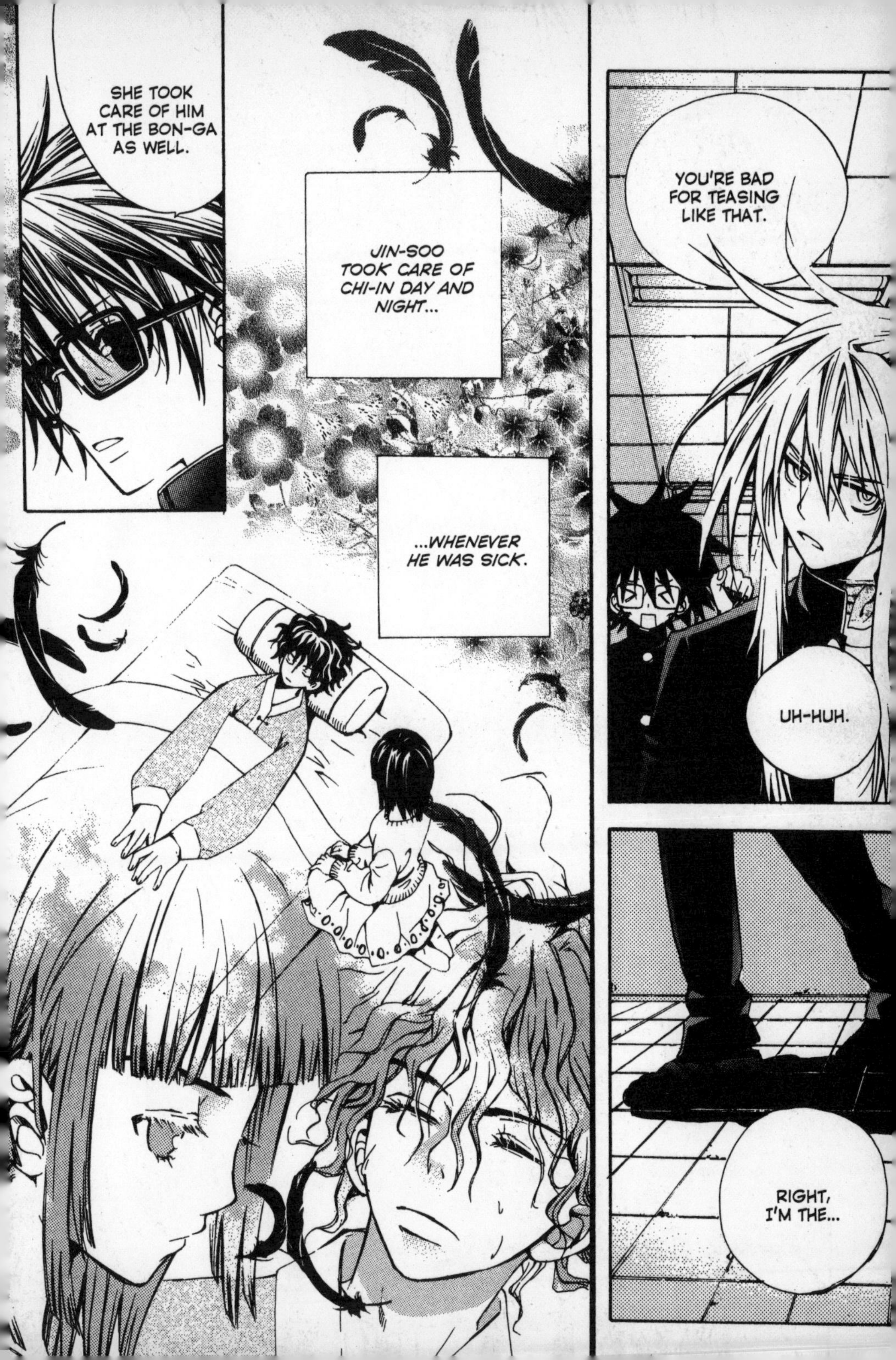
SHE TOOK CARE OF HIM AT THE BON-GA AS WELL.
JIN-SOO TOOK CARE OF CHI-IN DAY AND NIGHT...
...WHENEVER HE WAS SICK.
YOU'RE BAD FOR TEASING LIKE THAT.
UH-HUH.
RIGHT, I'M THE...

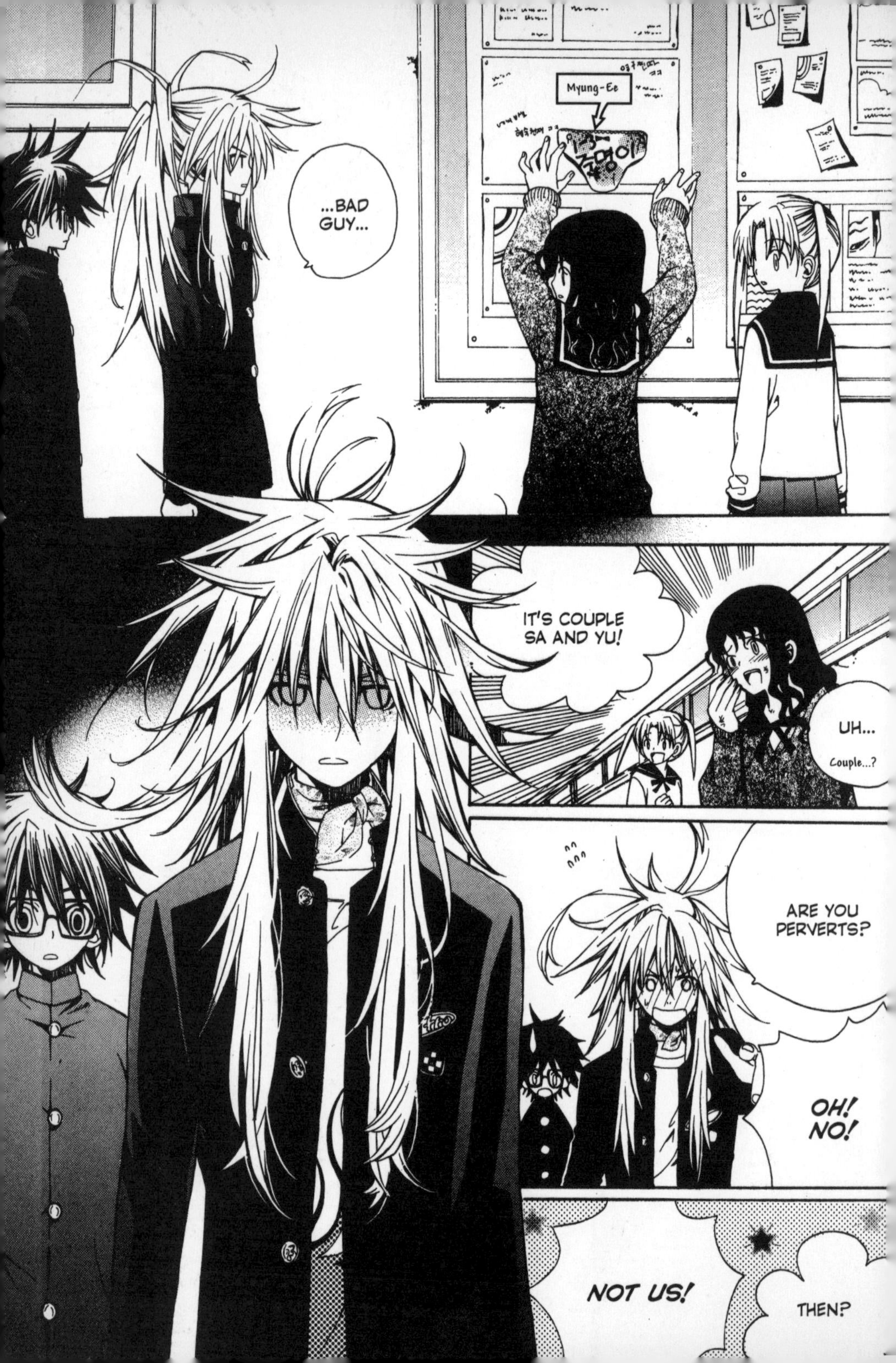
Myung-Ee
...BAD GUY...
IT'S COUPLE SA AND YU!
UH...
Couple...?
ARE YOU PERVERTS?
OH! NO!
NOT US!
THEN?

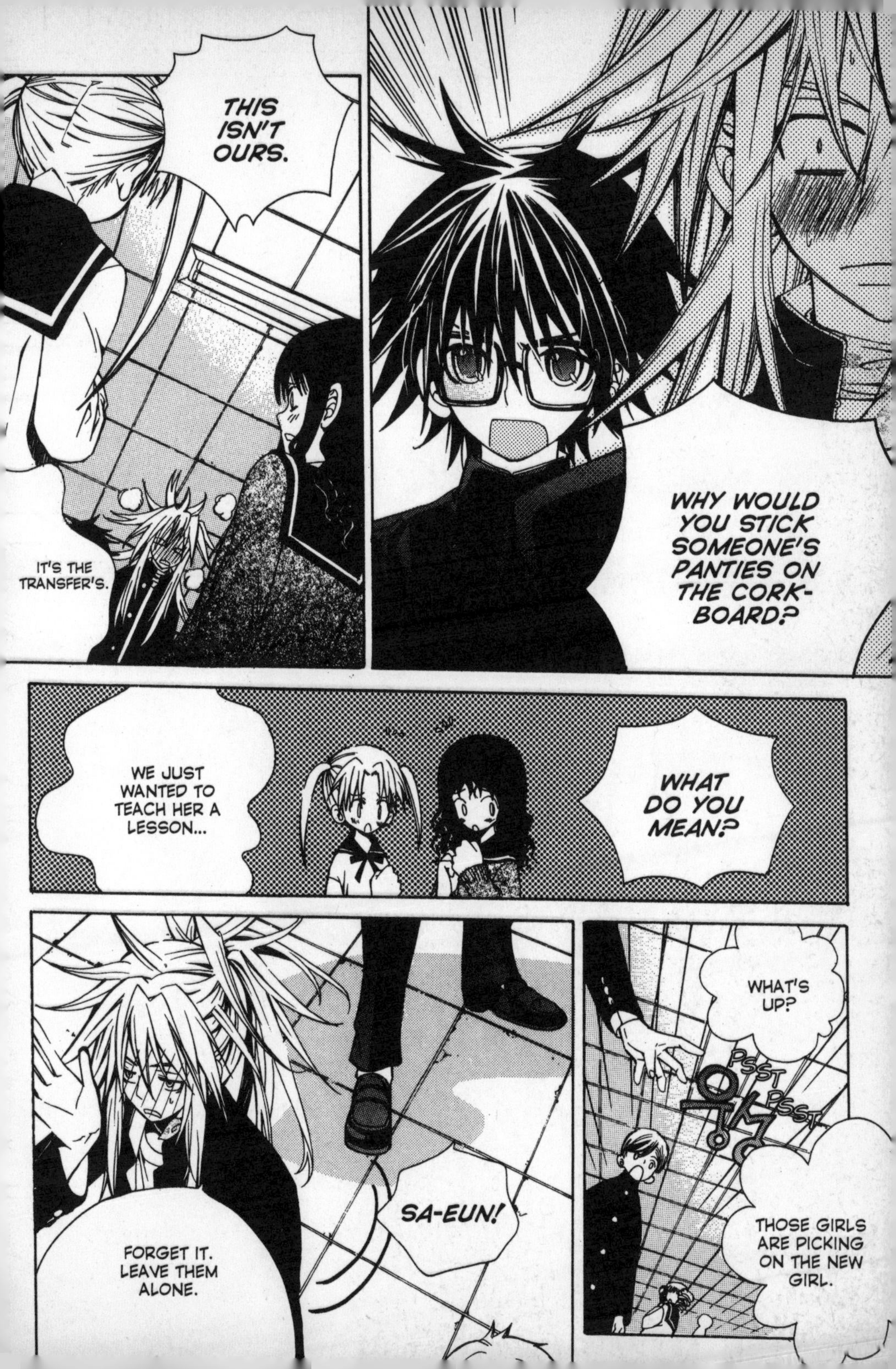
THIS ISN'T OURS.
IT'S THE TRANSFER'S.
WHY WOULD YOU STICK SOMEONE'S PANTIES ON THE CORK-BOARD?
WE JUST WANTED TO TEACH HER A LESSON...
WHAT DO YOU MEAN?
SA-EUN!
FORGET IT. LEAVE THEM ALONE.
WHAT'S UP?
PSST PSSST
THOSE GIRLS ARE PICKING ON THE NEW GIRL.

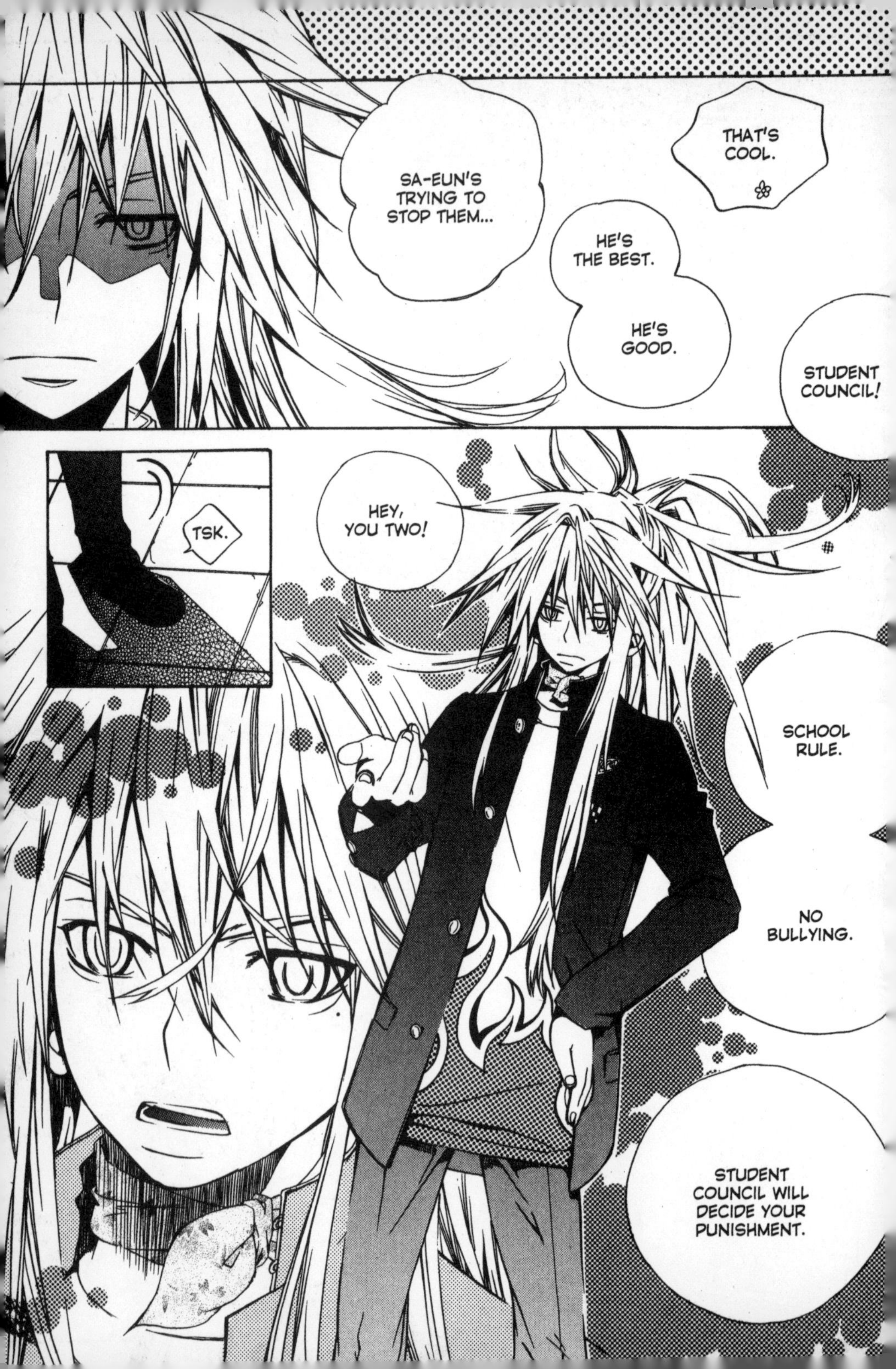
SA-EUN'S TRYING TO STOP THEM...
THAT'S COOL.
HE'S THE BEST.
HE'S GOOD.
STUDENT COUNCIL!
TSK.
HEY, YOU TWO!
SCHOOL RULE.
NO BULLYING.
STUDENT COUNCIL WILL DECIDE YOUR PUNISHMENT.

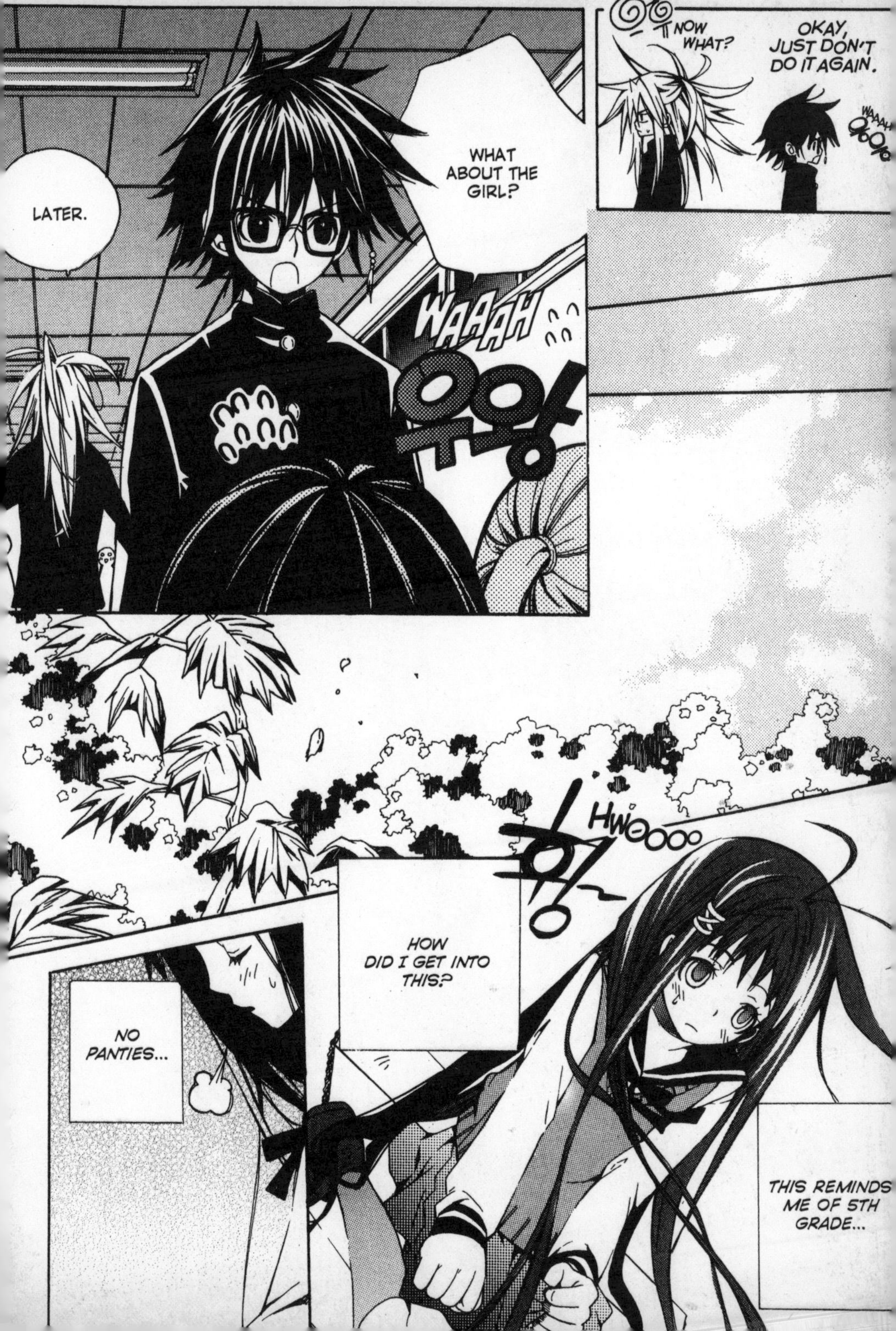

OKAY, JUST DON'T DO IT AGAIN.
WAAAH
NOW WHAT?
WHAT ABOUT THE GIRL?
LATER.
WAAAH
HWOOOO
HOW DID I GET INTO THIS?
THIS REMINDS ME OF 5TH GRADE...
NO PANTIES...

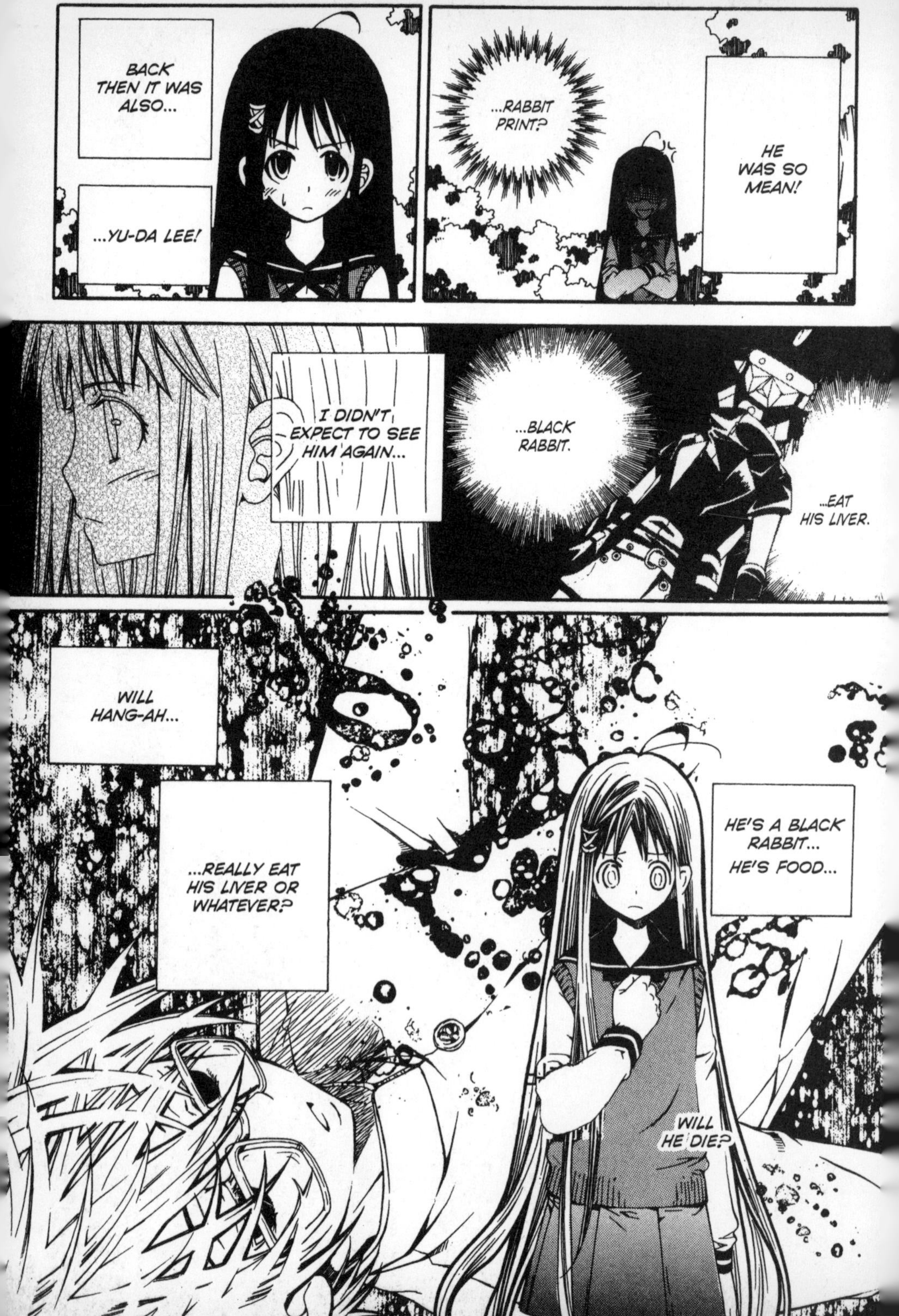
BACK THEN IT WAS ALSO...
...YU-DA LEE!
...RABBIT PRINT?
HE WAS SO MEAN!
I DIDN'T EXPECT TO SEE HIM AGAIN...
...BLACK RABBIT.
...EAT HIS LIVER.
WILL HANG-AH...
...REALLY EAT HIS LIVER OR WHATEVER?
HE'S A BLACK RABBIT...
HE'S FOOD...
WILL HE DIE?

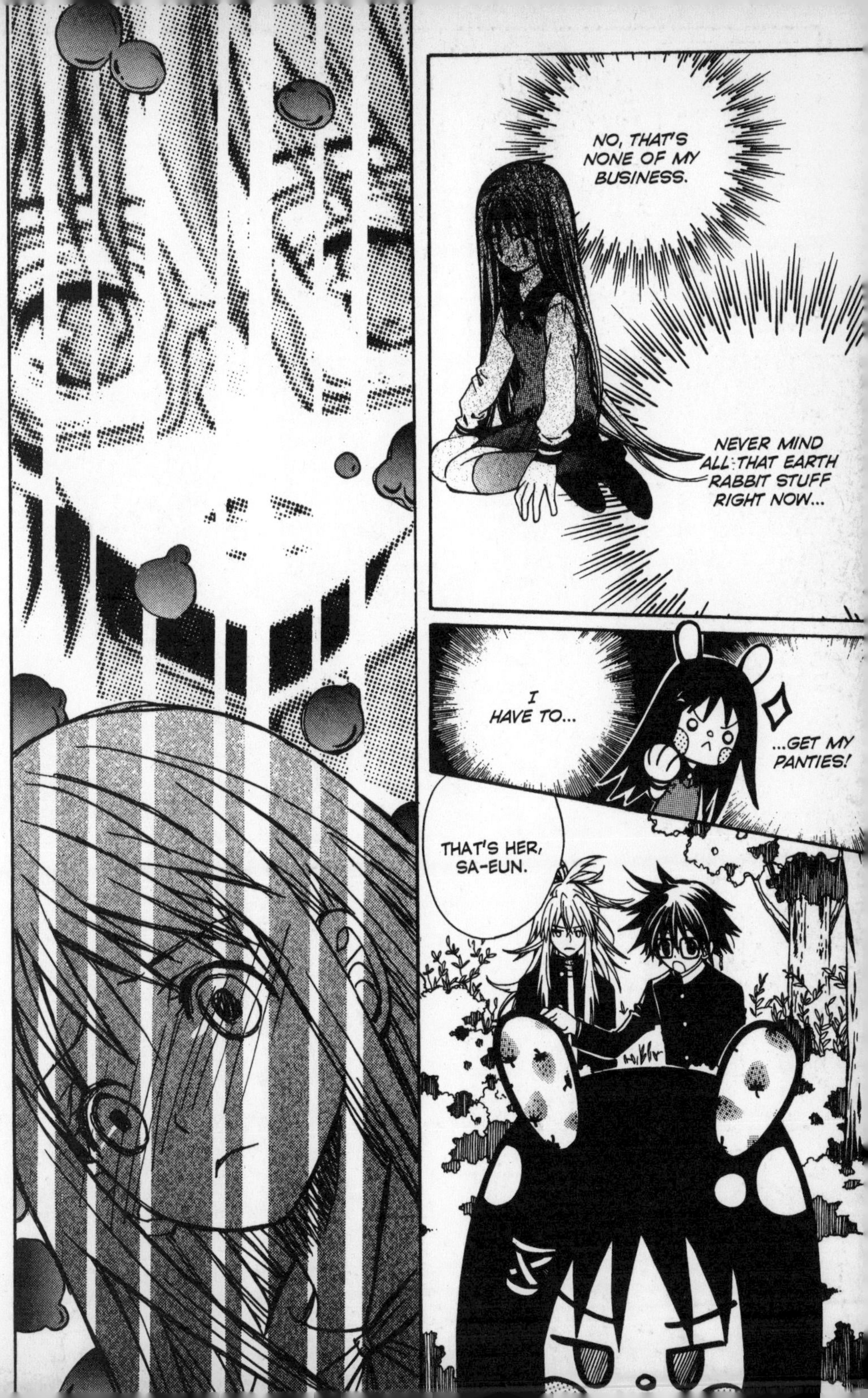
NO, THAT'S NONE OF MY BUSINESS.
NEVER MIND ALL THAT EARTH RABBIT STUFF RIGHT NOW...
I HAVE TO...
...GET MY PANTIES!
THAT'S HER, SA-EUN.

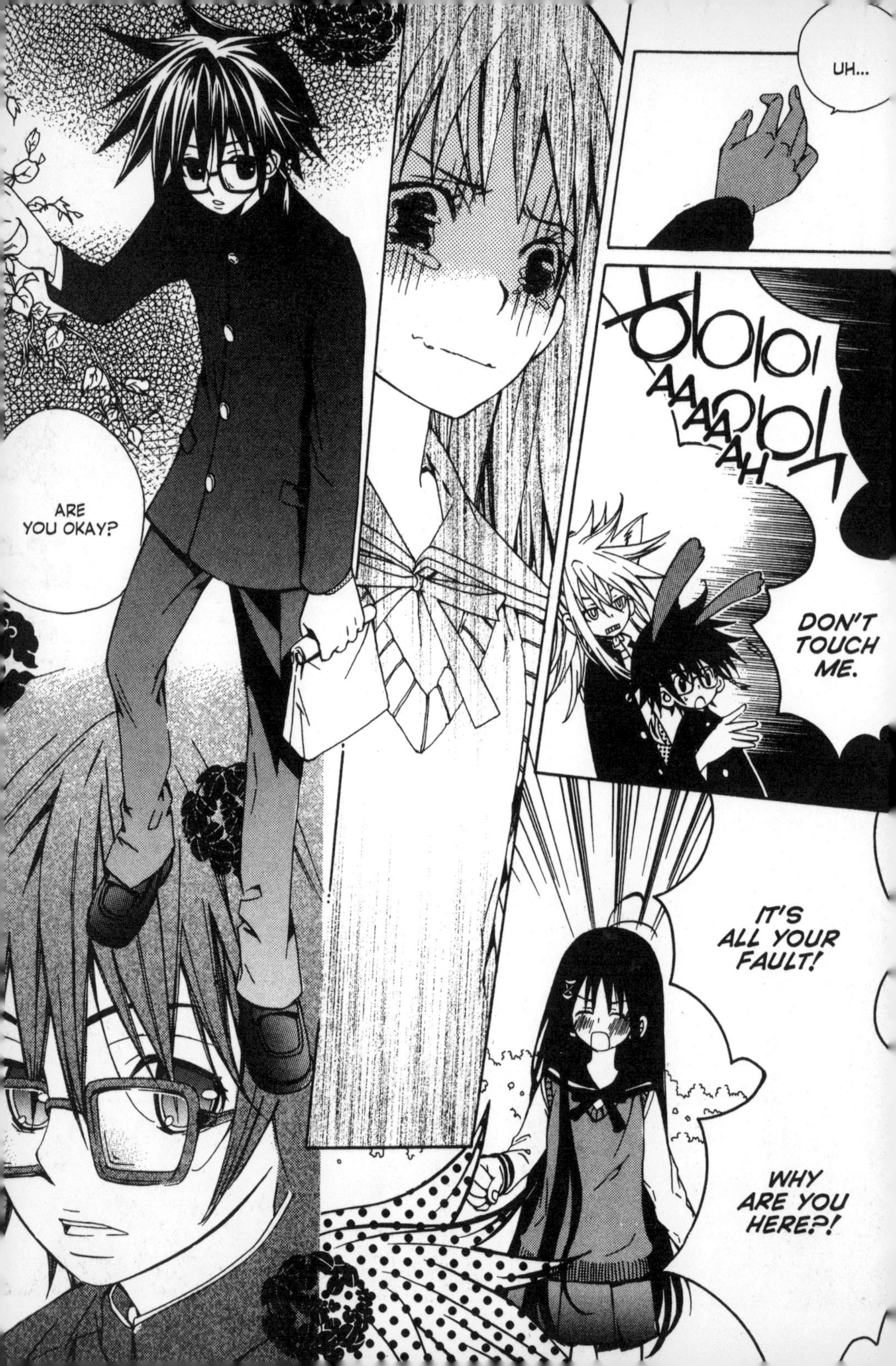
UH...
AAAAAAH
DON'T TOUCH ME.
ARE YOU OKAY?
IT'S ALL YOUR FAULT!
WHY ARE YOU HERE?!

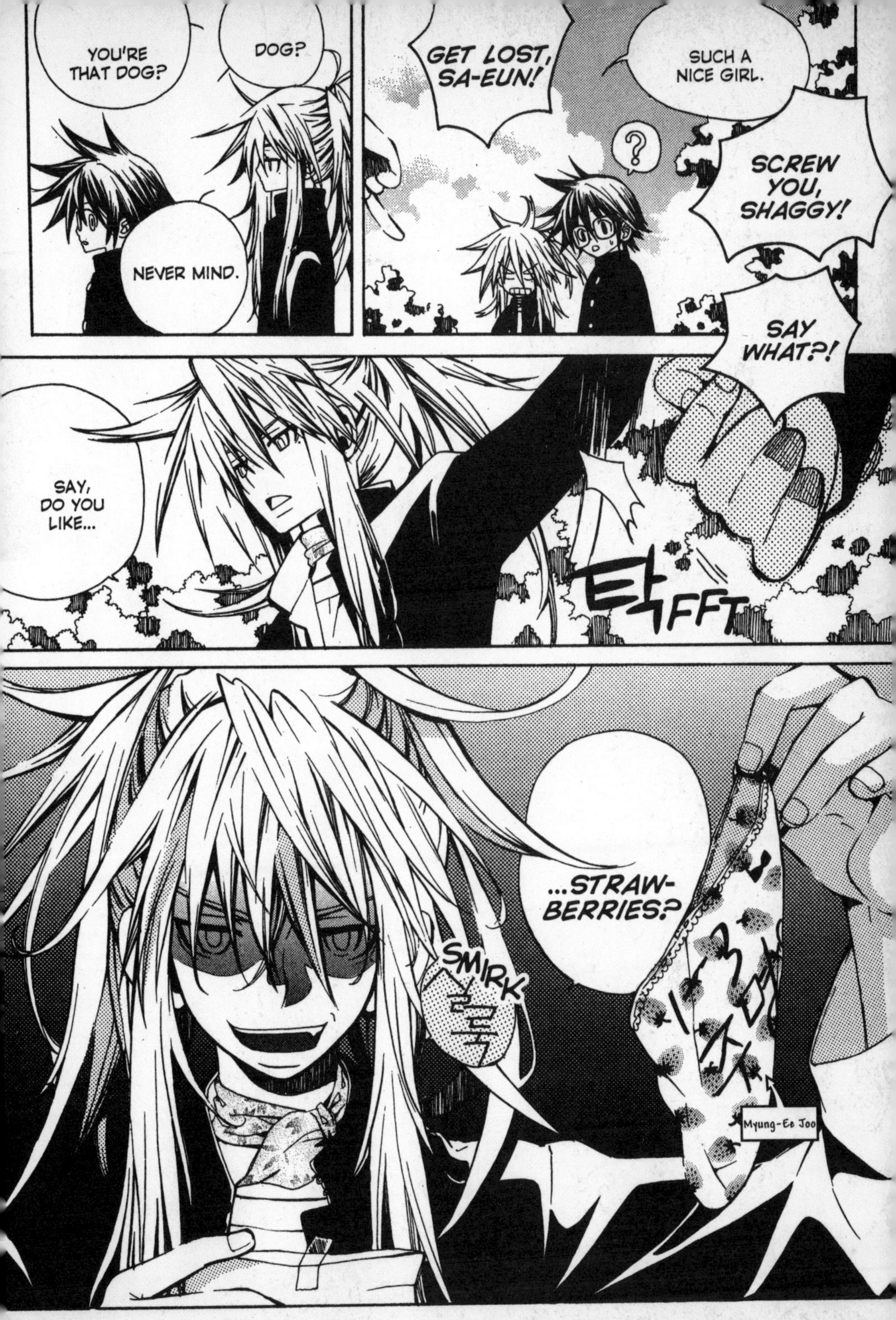
YOU'RE THAT DOG?
DOG?
NEVER MIND.
GET LOST, SA-EUN!
SUCH A NICE GIRL.
?
SCREW YOU, SHAGGY!
SAY WHAT?!
SAY, DO YOU LIKE...
FFFT
...STRAW-BERRIES?
SMIRK
Myung-Ee Joo

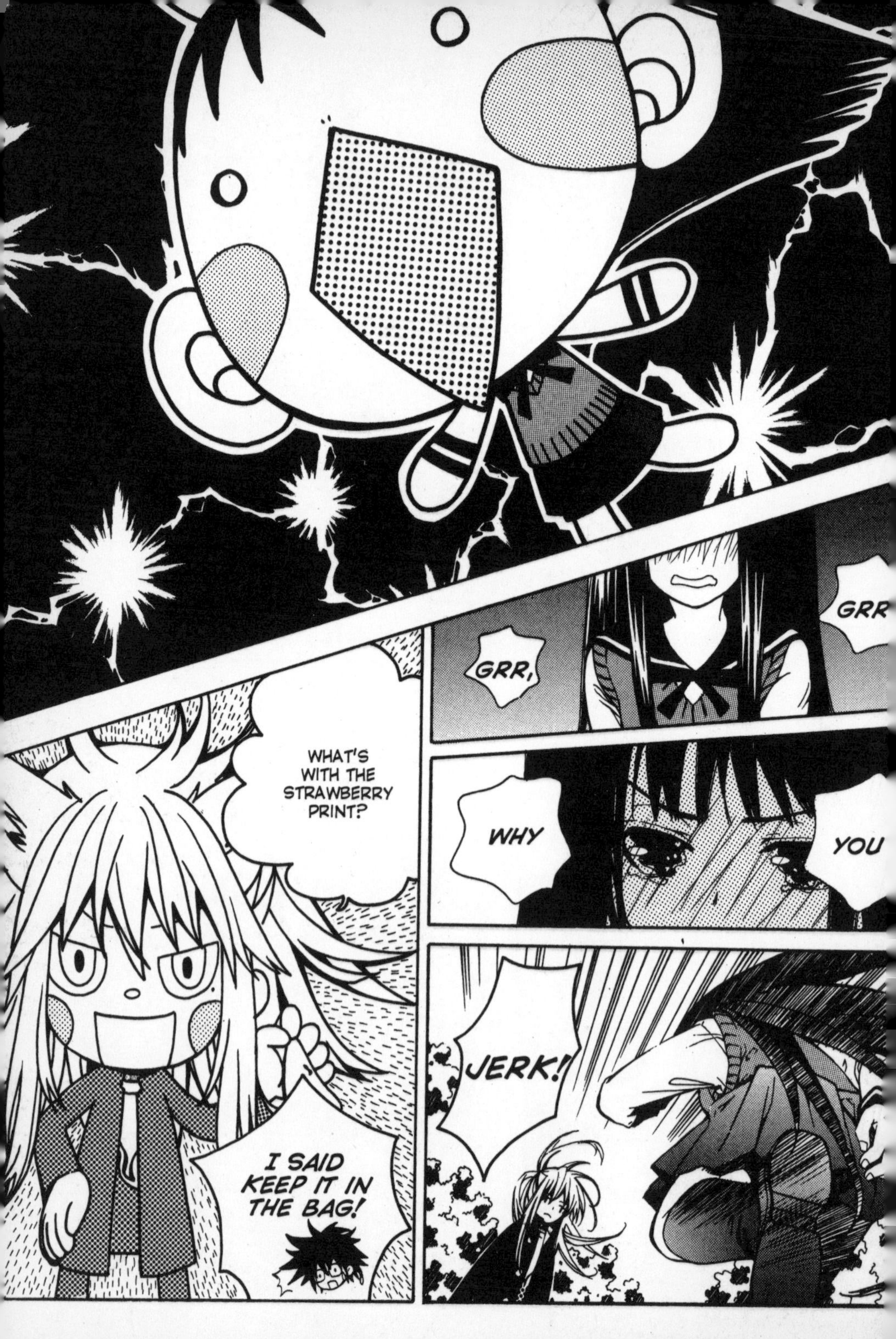
GRR
GRR,
WHY
YOU
JERK!
WHAT'S WITH THE STRAWBERRY PRINT?
I SAID KEEP IT IN THE BAG!

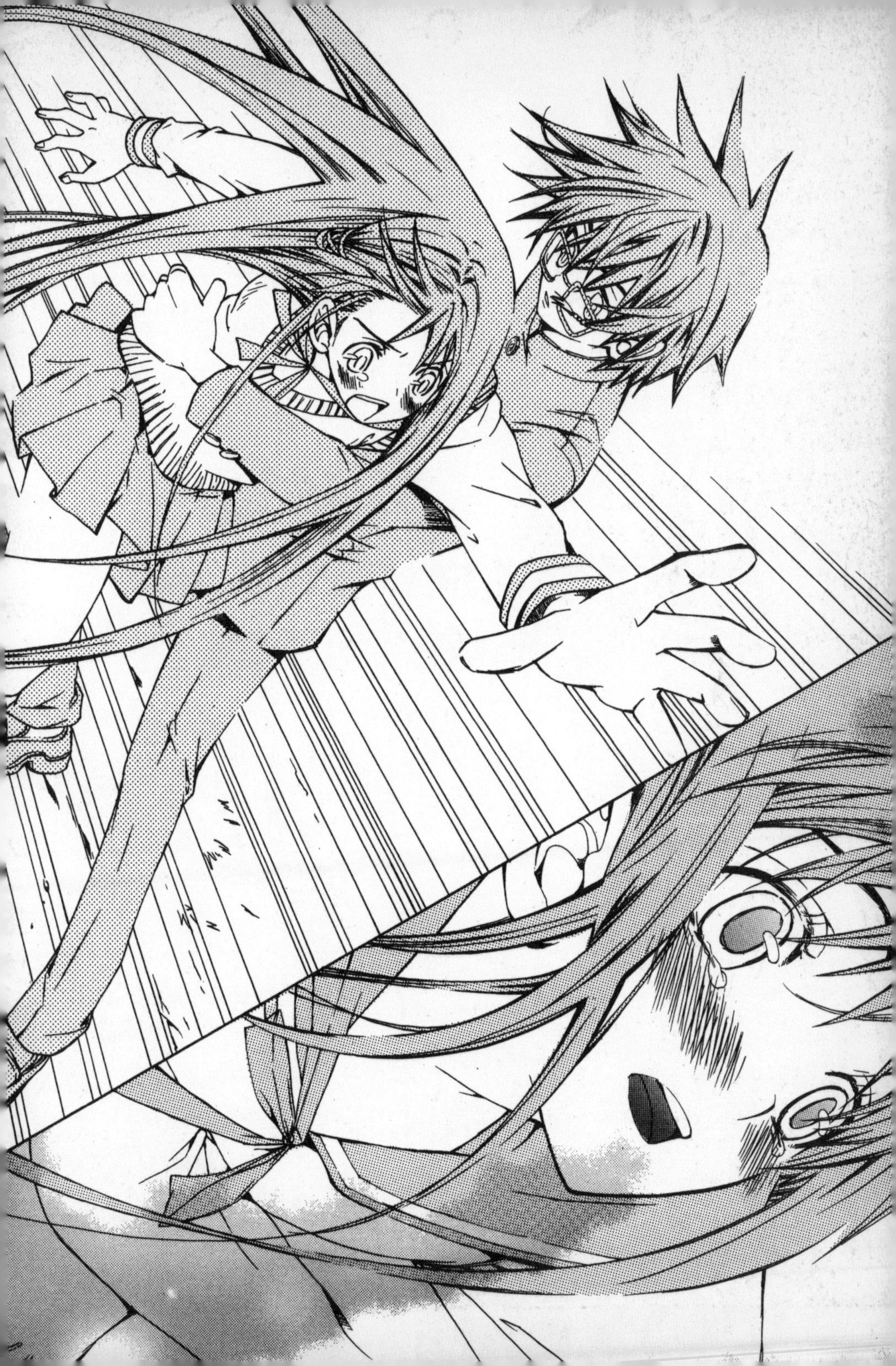

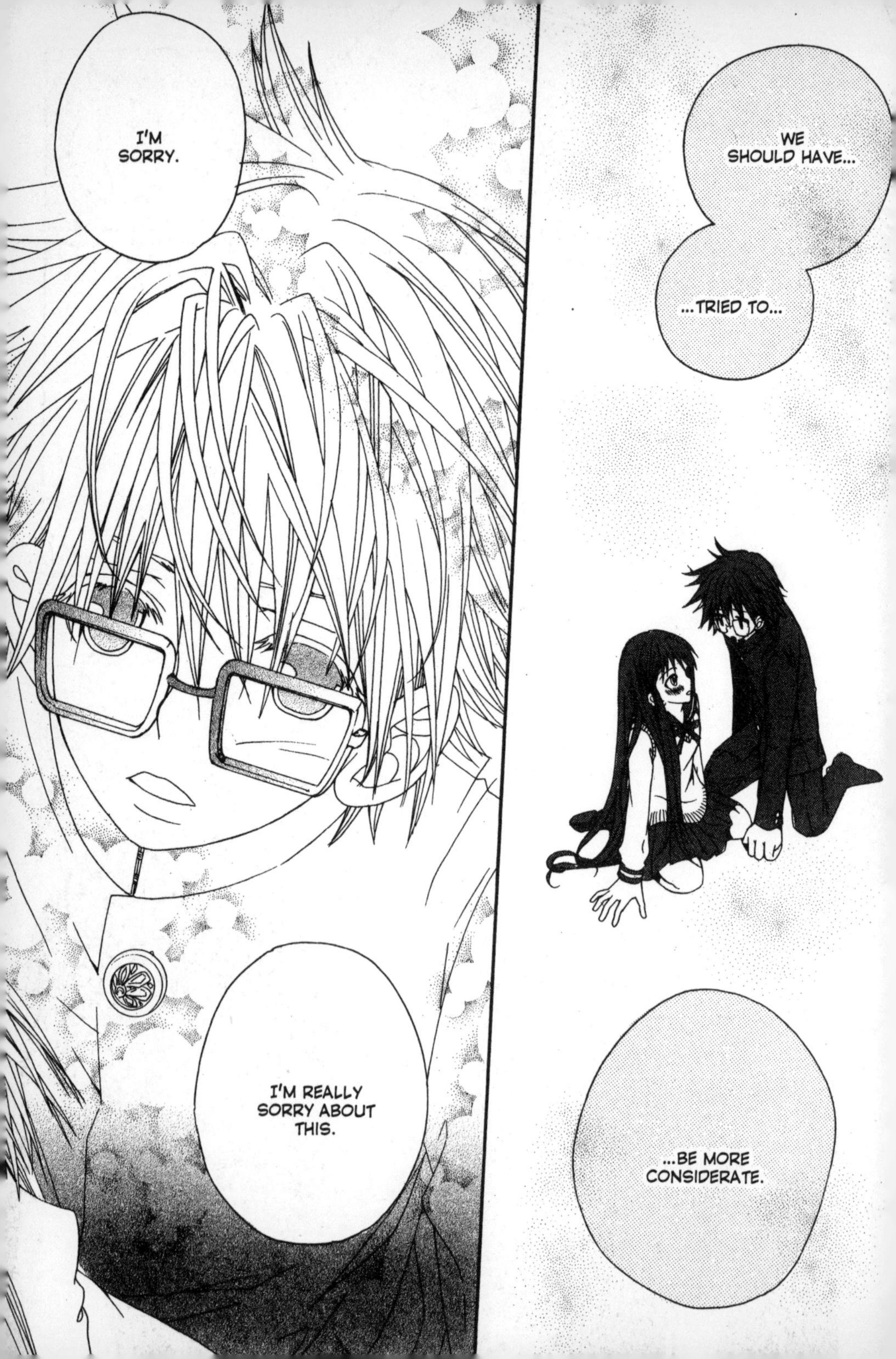
WE SHOULD HAVE...
...TRIED TO...
...BE MORE CONSIDERATE.
I'M SORRY.
I'M REALLY SORRY ABOUT THIS.

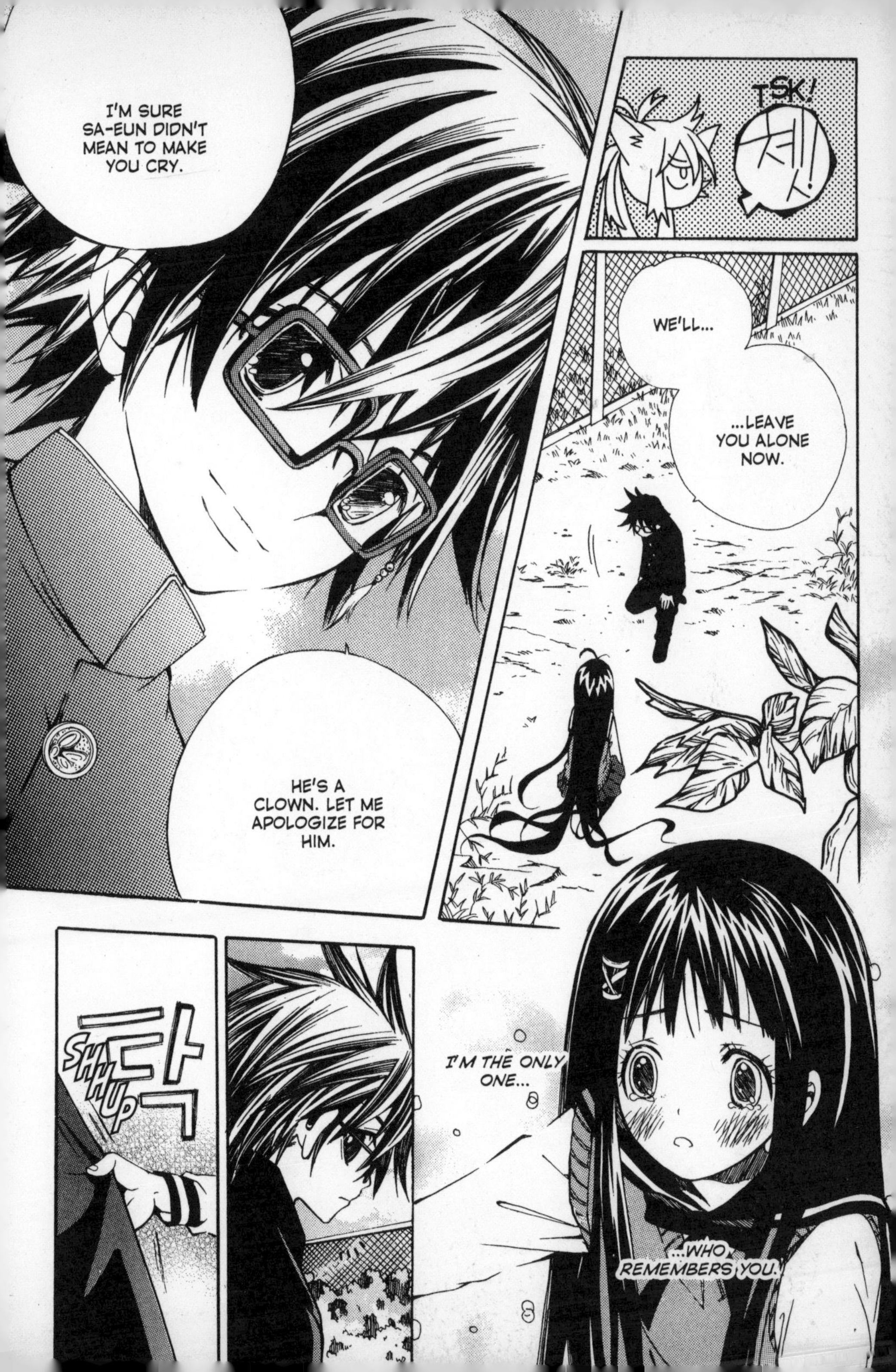
TSK!
체!
I'M SURE SA-EUN DIDN'T MEAN TO MAKE YOU CRY.
WE'LL...
...LEAVE YOU ALONE NOW.
HE'S A CLOWN. LET ME APOLOGIZE FOR HIM.
I'M THE ONLY ONE...
...WHO REMEMBERS YOU.
SHHUP
드락

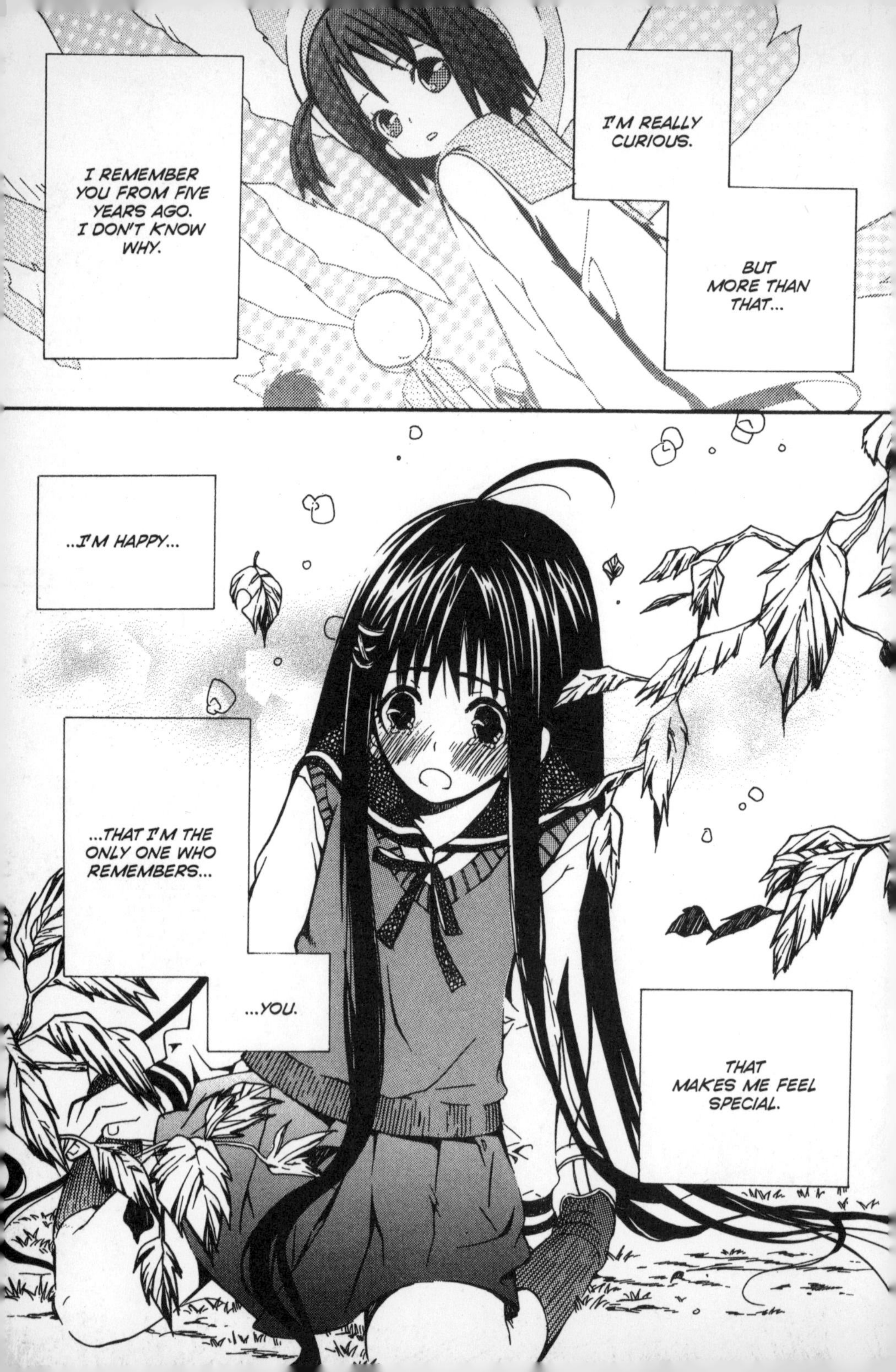
I REMEMBER YOU FROM FIVE YEARS AGO. I DON'T KNOW WHY.
I'M REALLY CURIOUS.
BUT MORE THAN THAT...
...I'M HAPPY...
...THAT I'M THE ONLY ONE WHO REMEMBERS...
...YOU.
THAT MAKES ME FEEL SPECIAL.

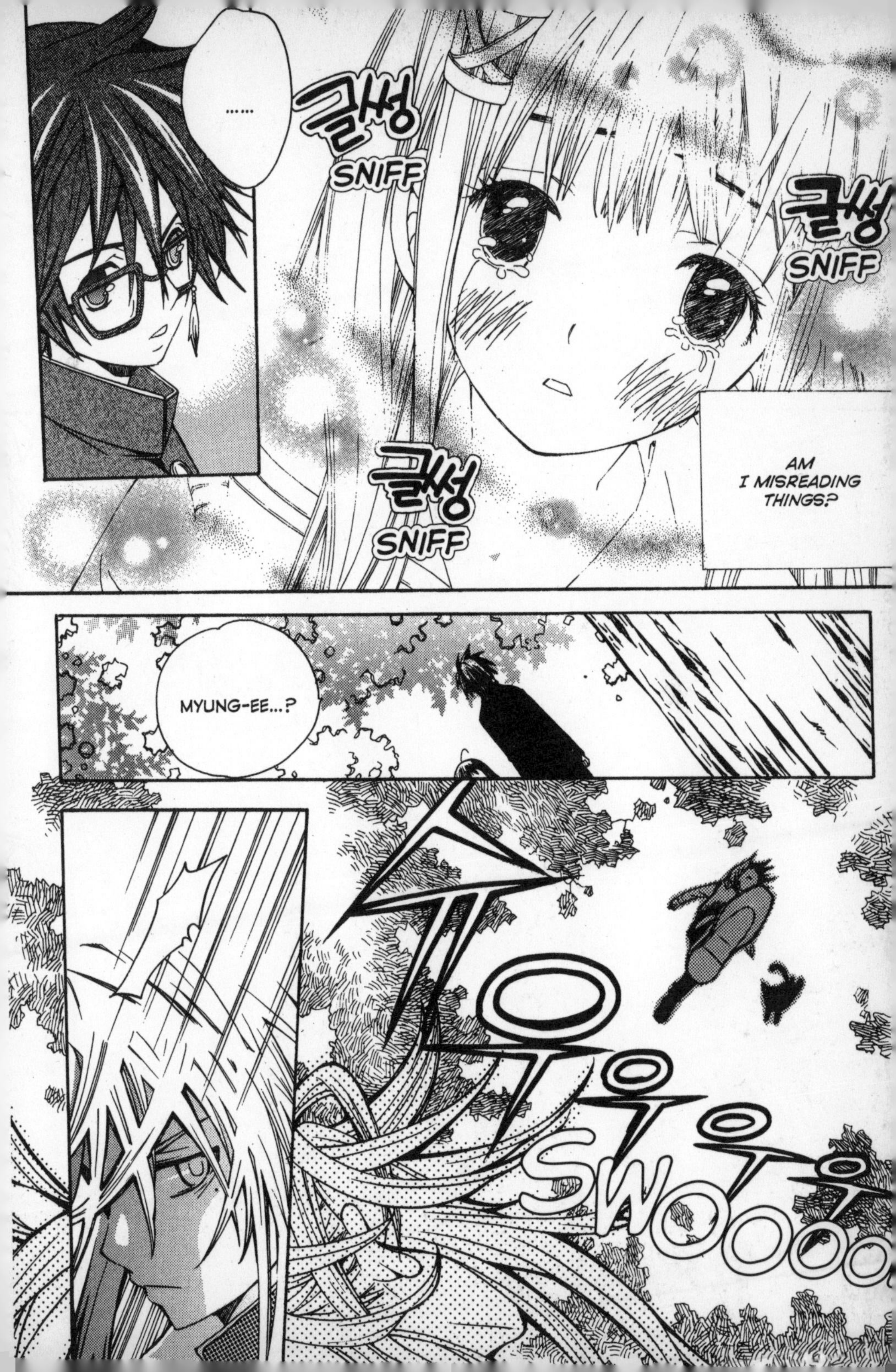
……
글썽
SNIFF
글썽
SNIFF
글썽
SNIFF
AM I MISREADING THINGS?
MYUNG-EE...?
SWOOOOO

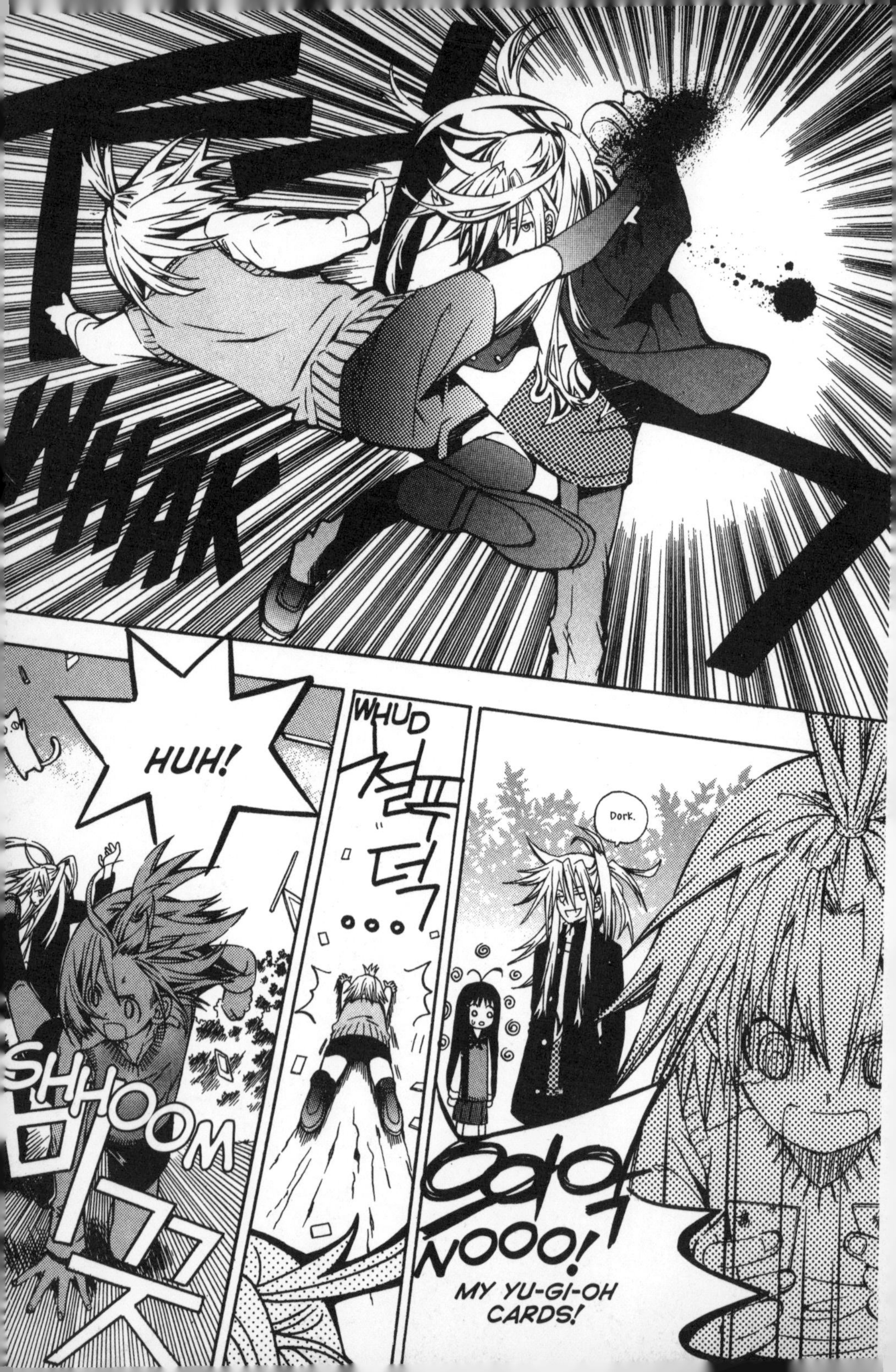
WHAK
HUH!
SHHOOM
WHUD
Dork.
NOOO!
MY YU-GI-OH CARDS!

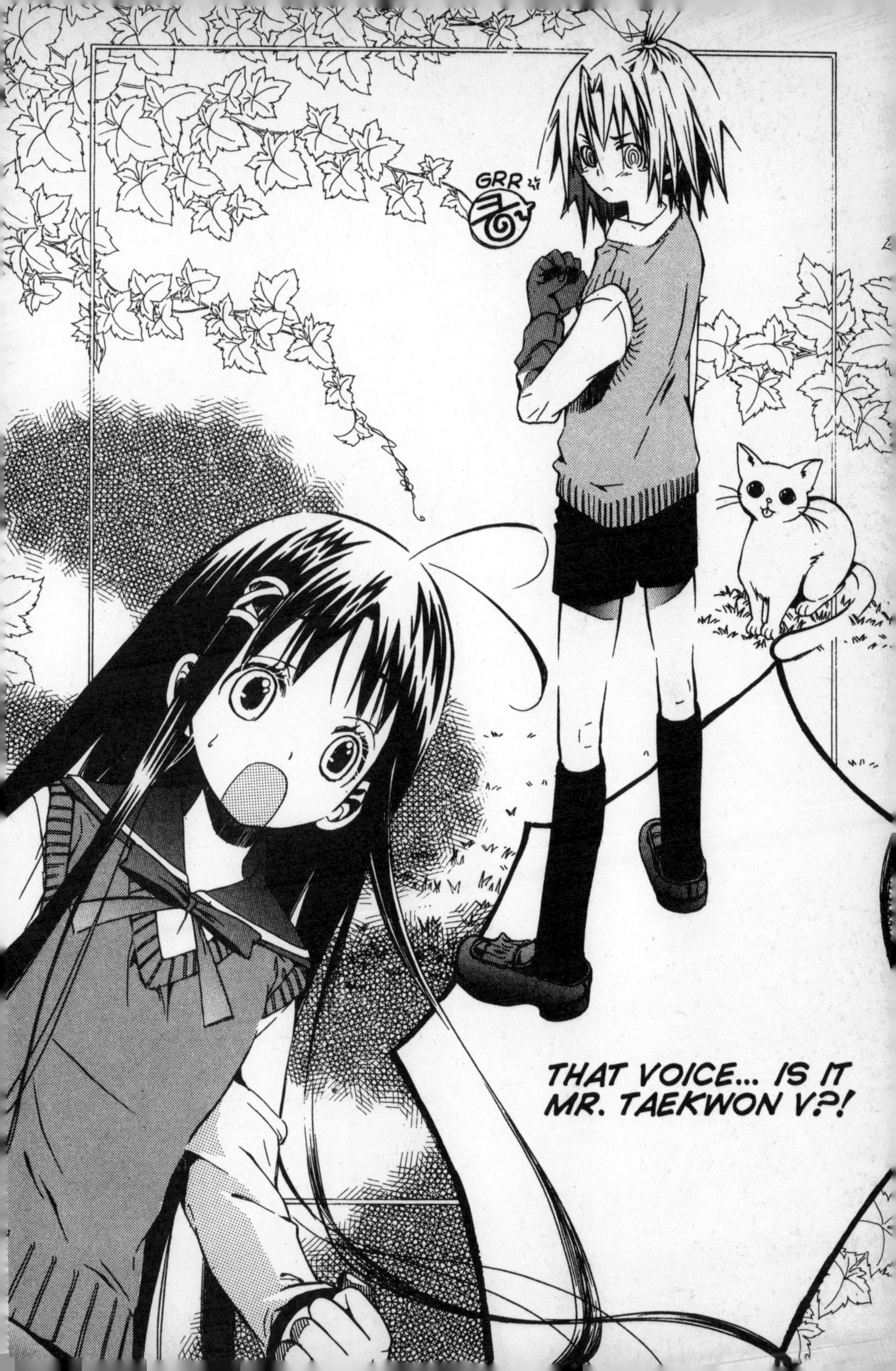
GRR
THAT VOICE... IS IT
MR. TAEKWON V?!

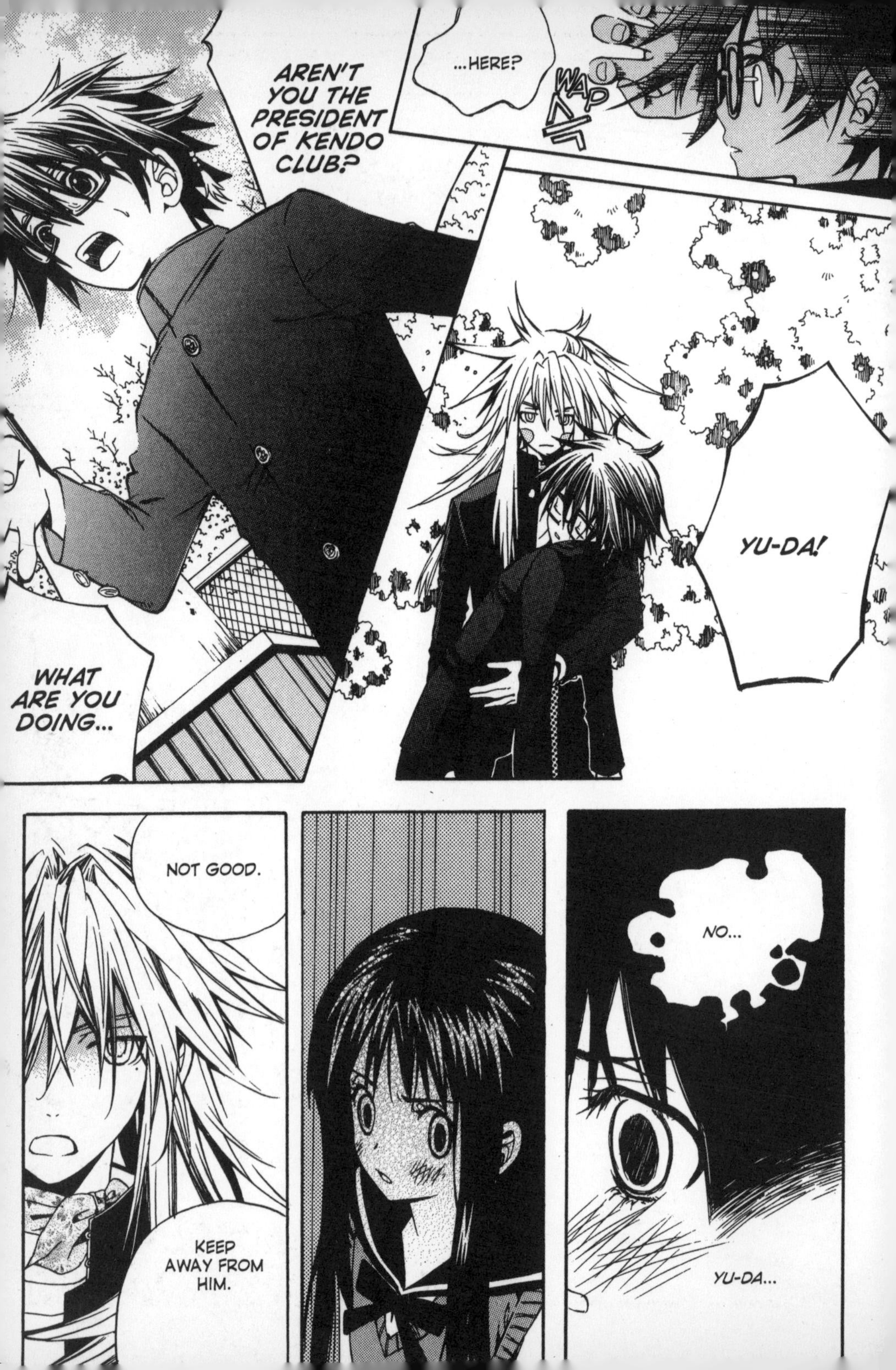
YU-DA!
WHAT ARE YOU DOING...
...HERE?
WAP
AREN'T YOU THE PRESIDENT OF KENDO CLUB?
NO...
YU-DA...
NOT GOOD.
KEEP AWAY FROM HIM.

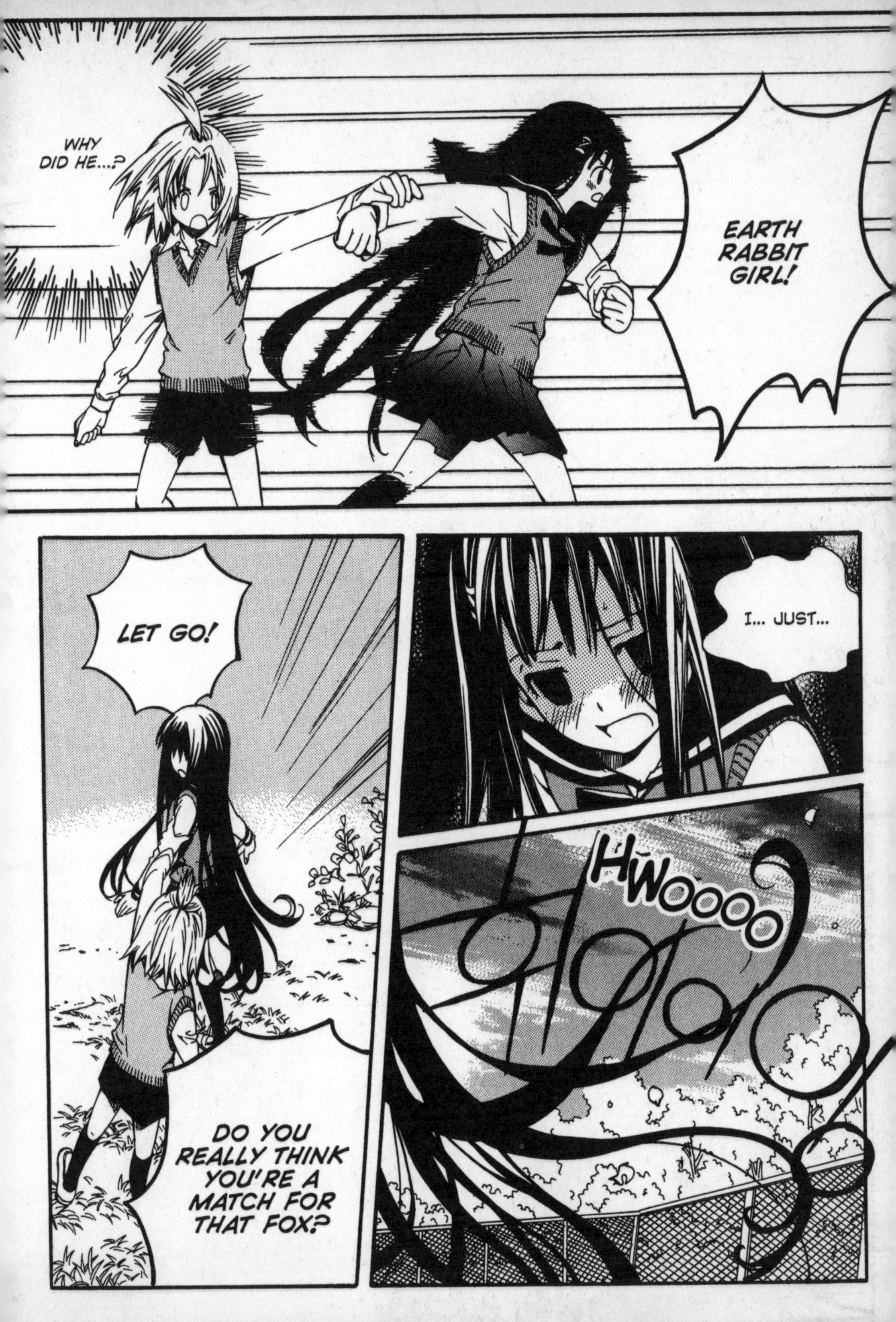
EARTH RABBIT GIRL!
WHY DID HE...?
I... JUST...
LET GO!
DO YOU REALLY THINK YOU'RE A MATCH FOR THAT FOX?
HWOOOO

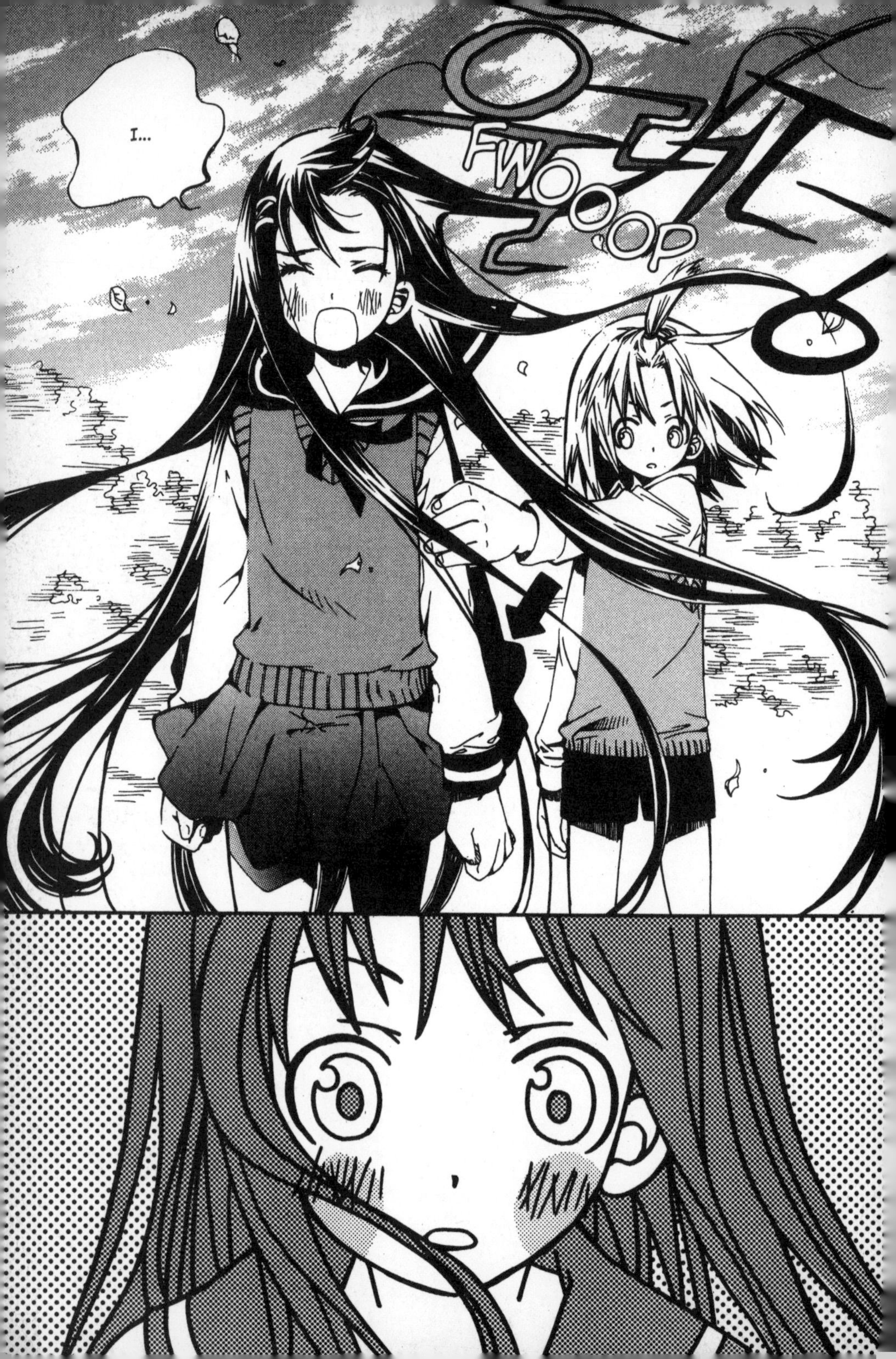

FWOOOOP
I...

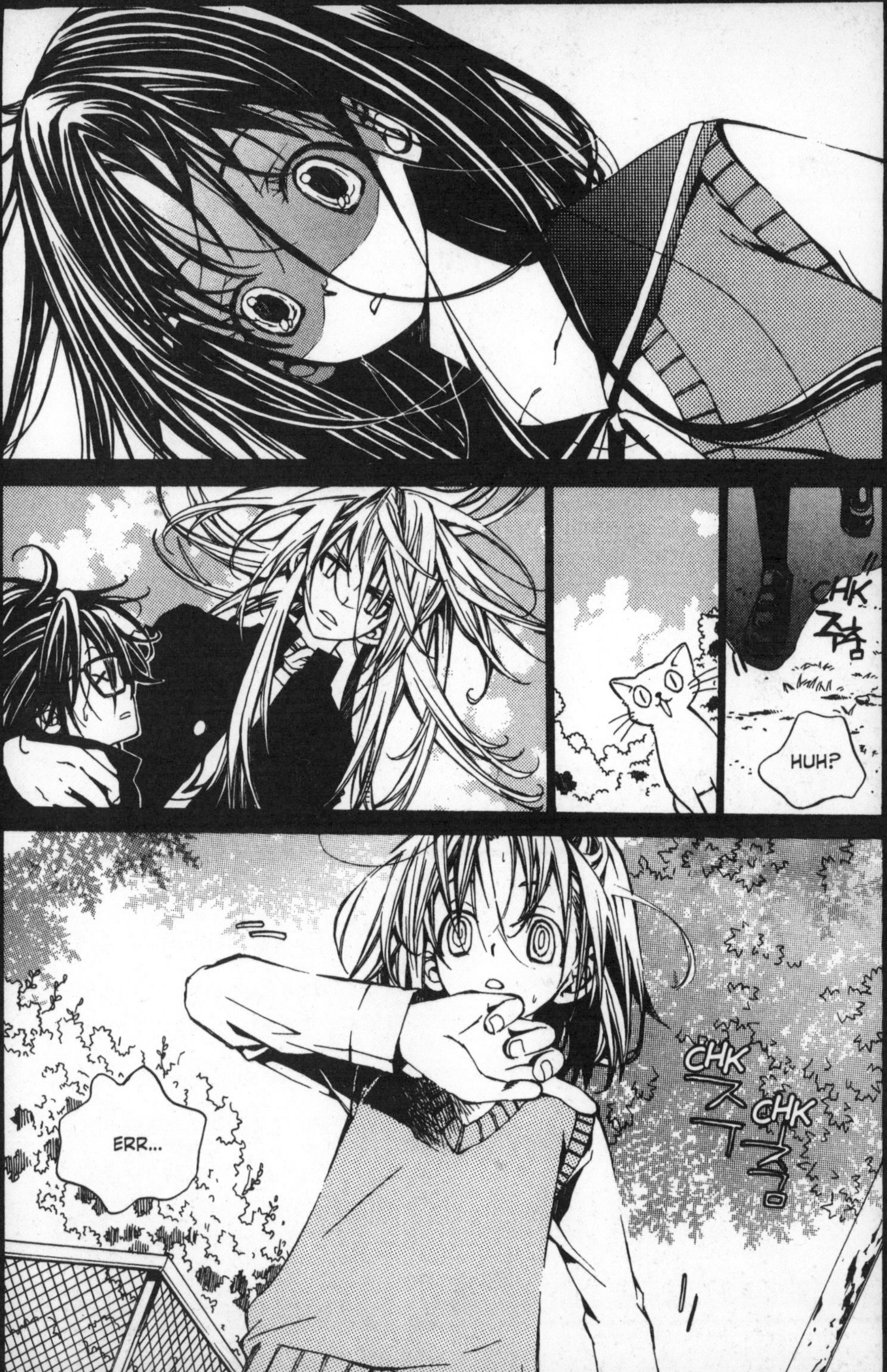
CHK
주춤
HUH?
ERR...
CHK
CHK

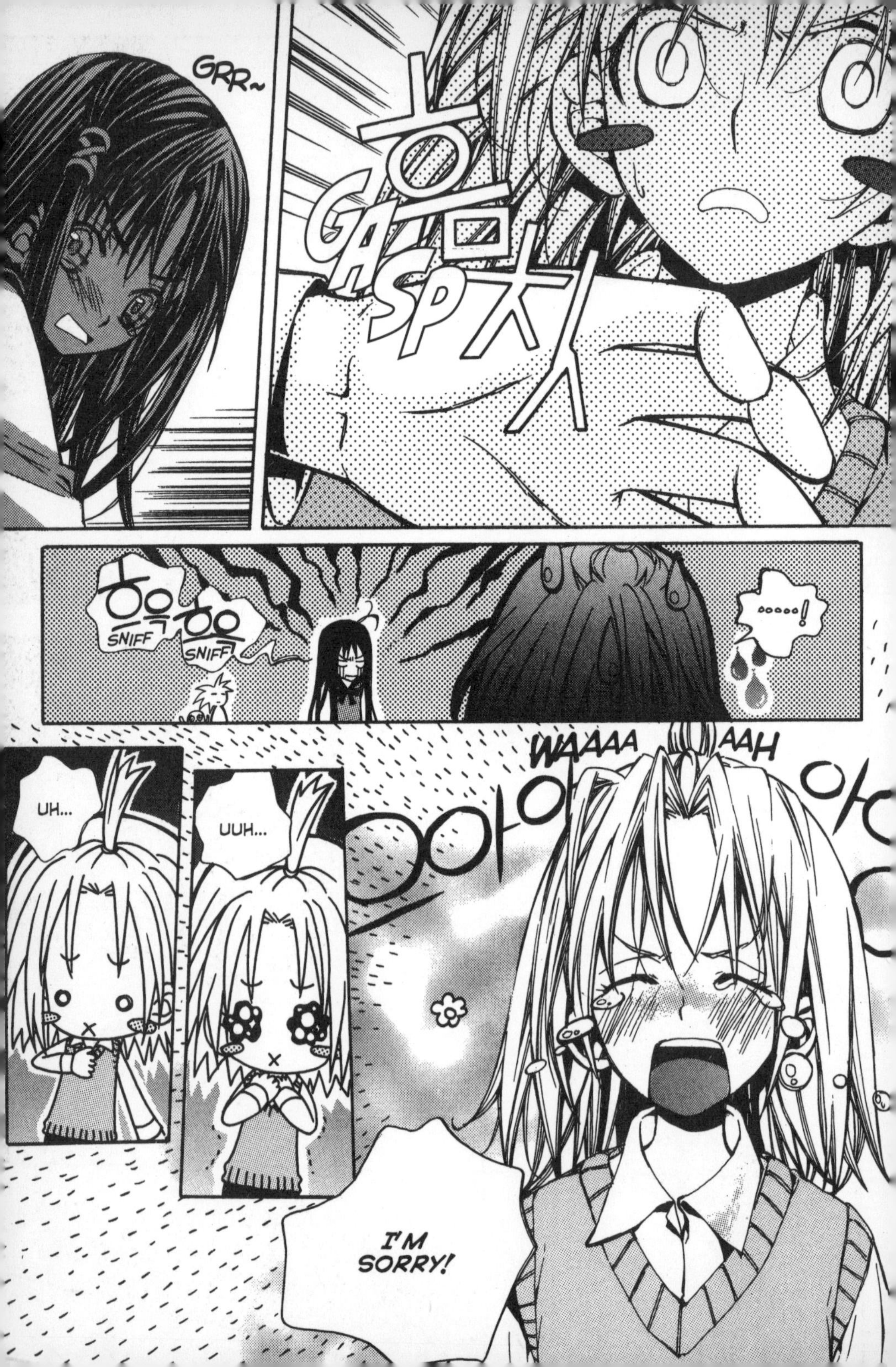
GRR~
GASP
SNIFF
SNIFF
.....!
UH...
UUH...
WAAAA AAH
I'M SORRY!

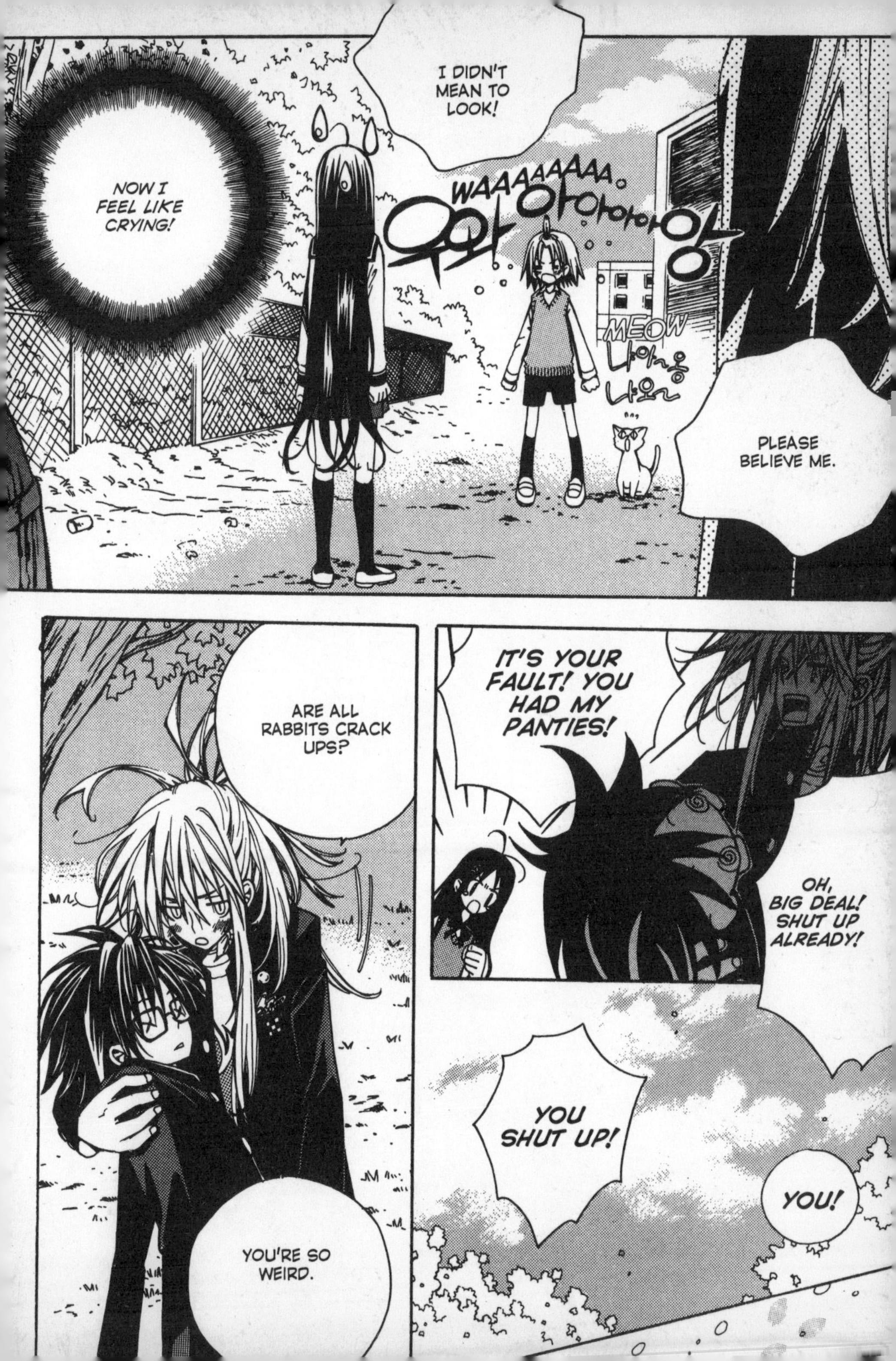

NOW I FEEL LIKE CRYING!
I DIDN'T MEAN TO LOOK!
WAAAAAAAA.
MEOW
PLEASE BELIEVE ME.
ARE ALL RABBITS CRACK UPS?
YOU'RE SO WEIRD.
IT'S YOUR FAULT! YOU HAD MY PANTIES!
OH, BIG DEAL! SHUT UP ALREADY!
YOU SHUT UP!
YOU!

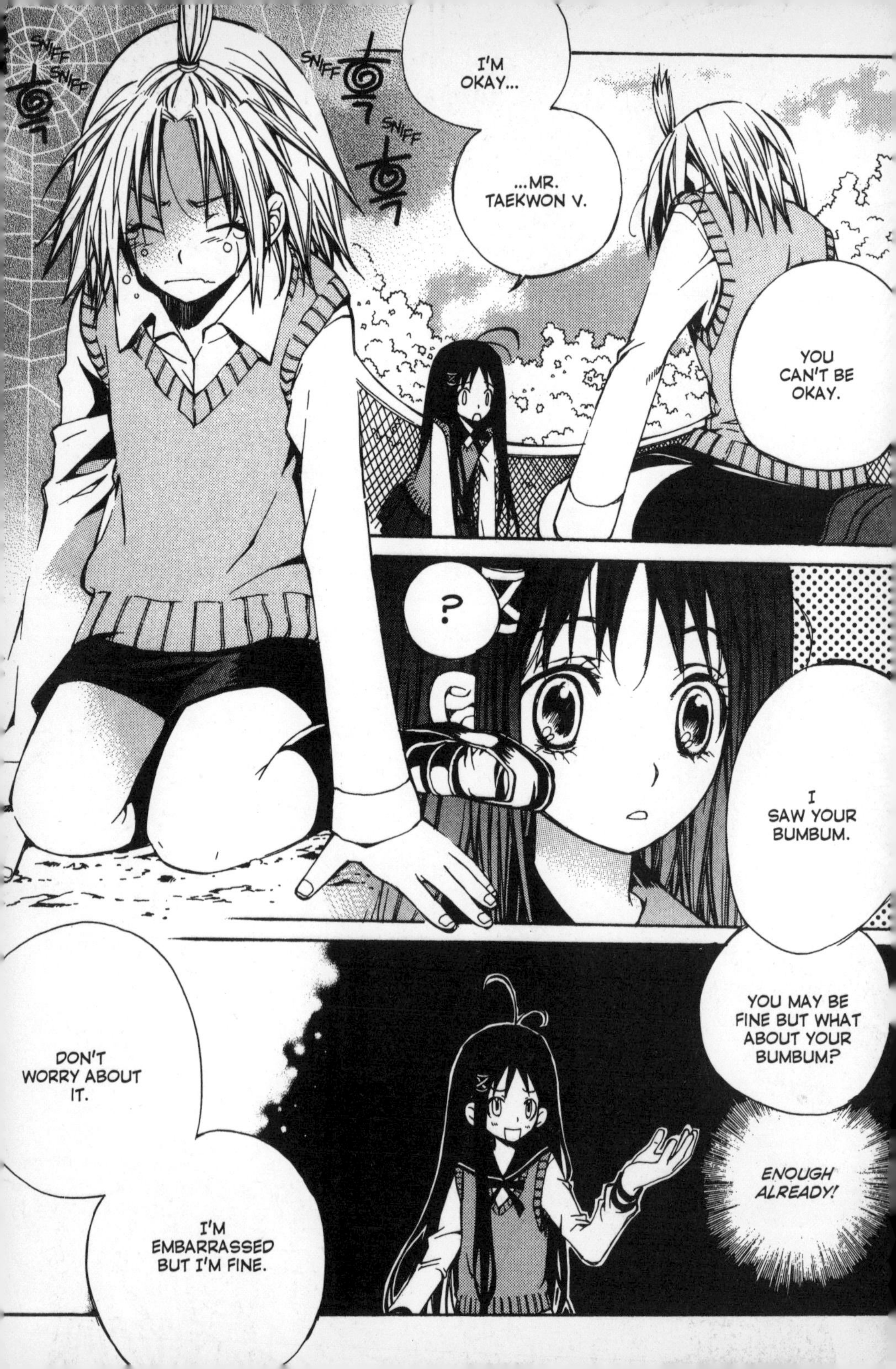
I'M OKAY...
...MR. TAEKWON V.
SNIFF SNIFF
SNIFF
SNIFF
YOU CAN'T BE OKAY.
?
I SAW YOUR BUMBUM.
YOU MAY BE FINE BUT WHAT ABOUT YOUR BUMBUM?
ENOUGH ALREADY!
DON'T WORRY ABOUT IT.
I'M EMBARRASSED BUT I'M FINE.

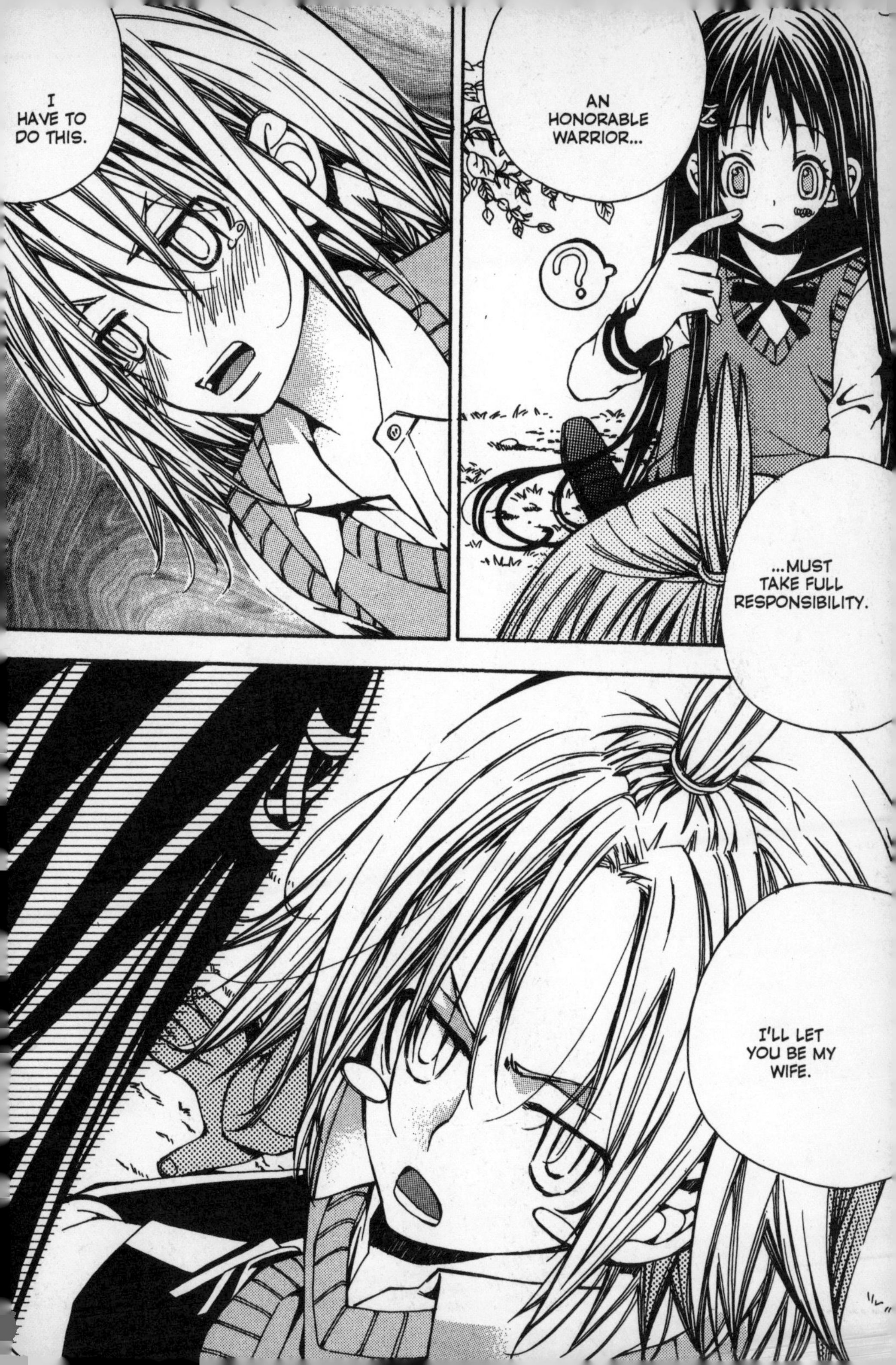
AN HONORABLE WARRIOR...
...MUST TAKE FULL RESPONSIBILITY.
I HAVE TO DO THIS.
I'LL LET YOU BE MY WIFE.

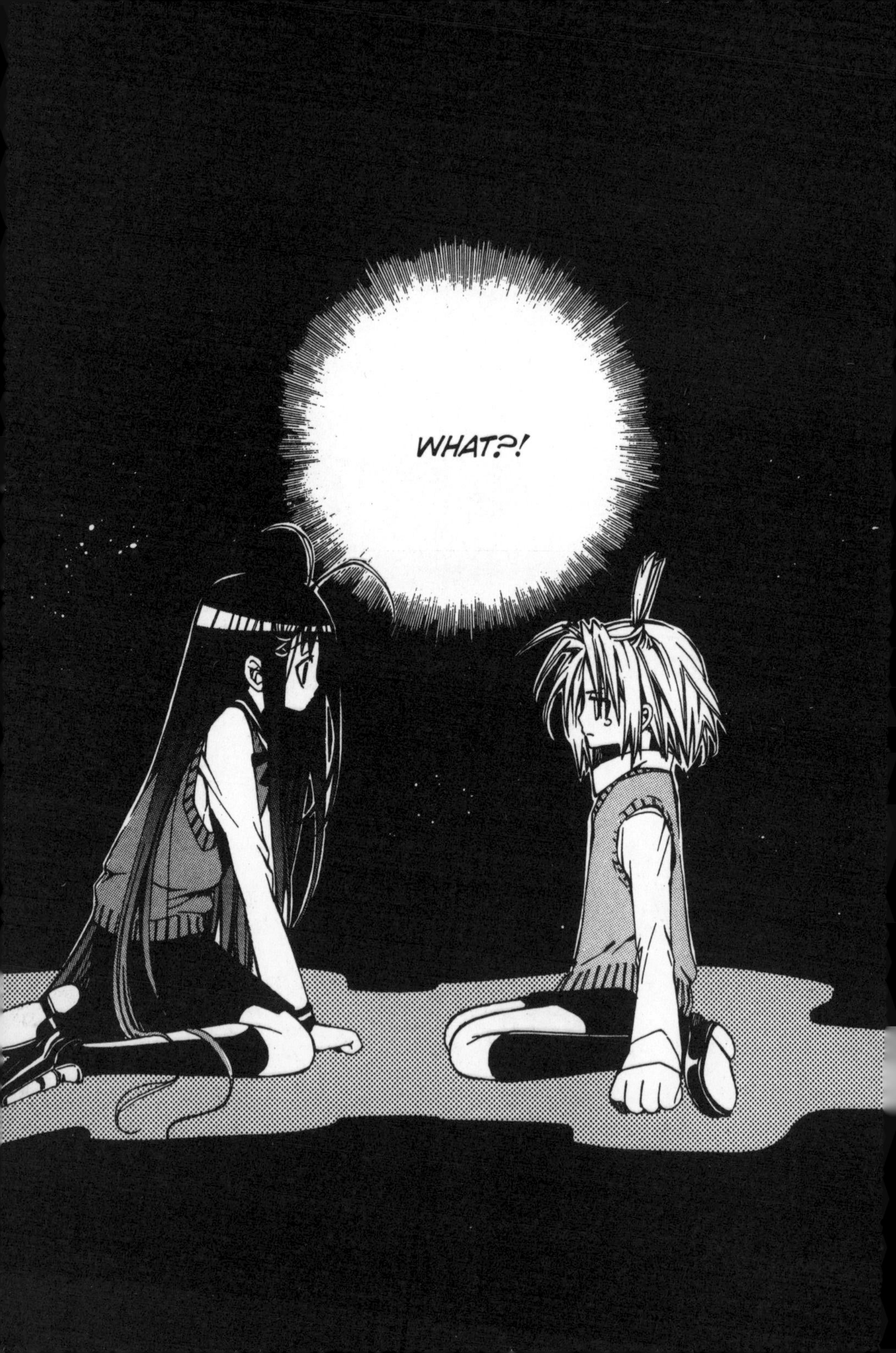
WHAT?!

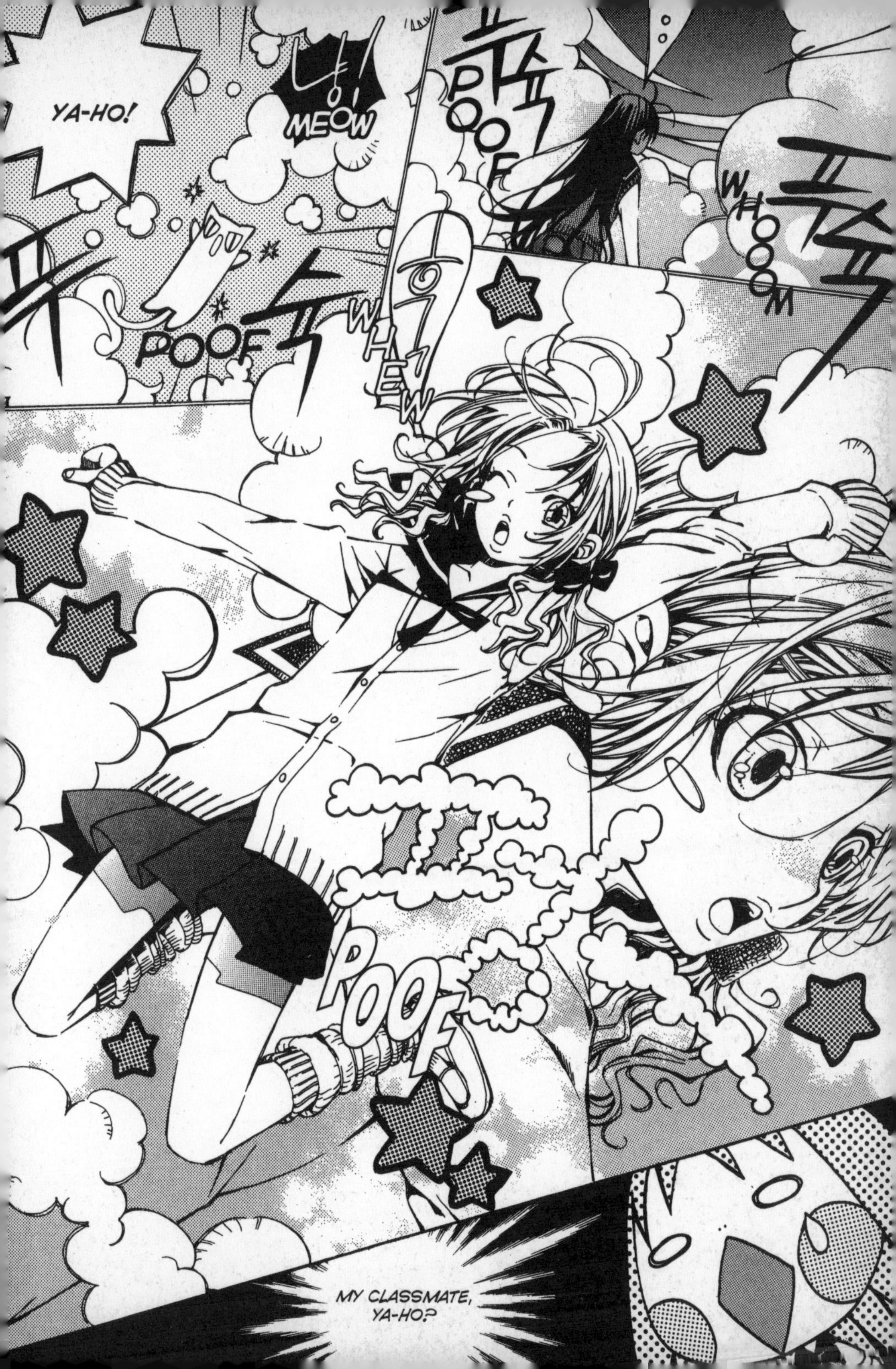
YA-HO!
냥!
MEOW
POOF
POOF
WHEW
WHOOOM
POOF
MY CLASSMATE,
YA-HO?

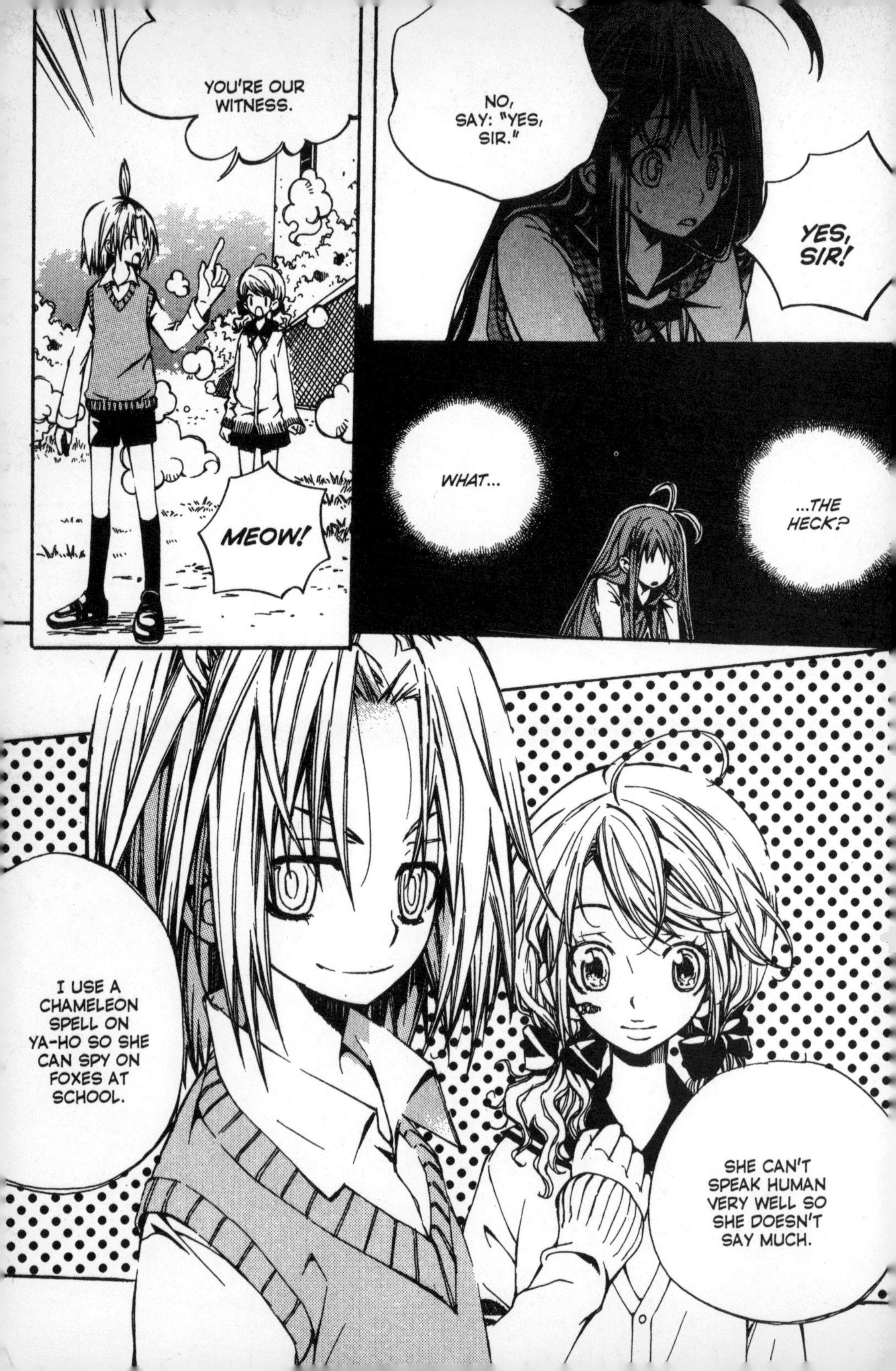
YOU'RE OUR WITNESS.
MEOW!
NO, SAY: "YES, SIR."
YES, SIR!
WHAT...
...THE HECK?
I USE A CHAMELEON SPELL ON YA-HO SO SHE CAN SPY ON FOXES AT SCHOOL.
SHE CAN'T SPEAK HUMAN VERY WELL SO SHE DOESN'T SAY MUCH.

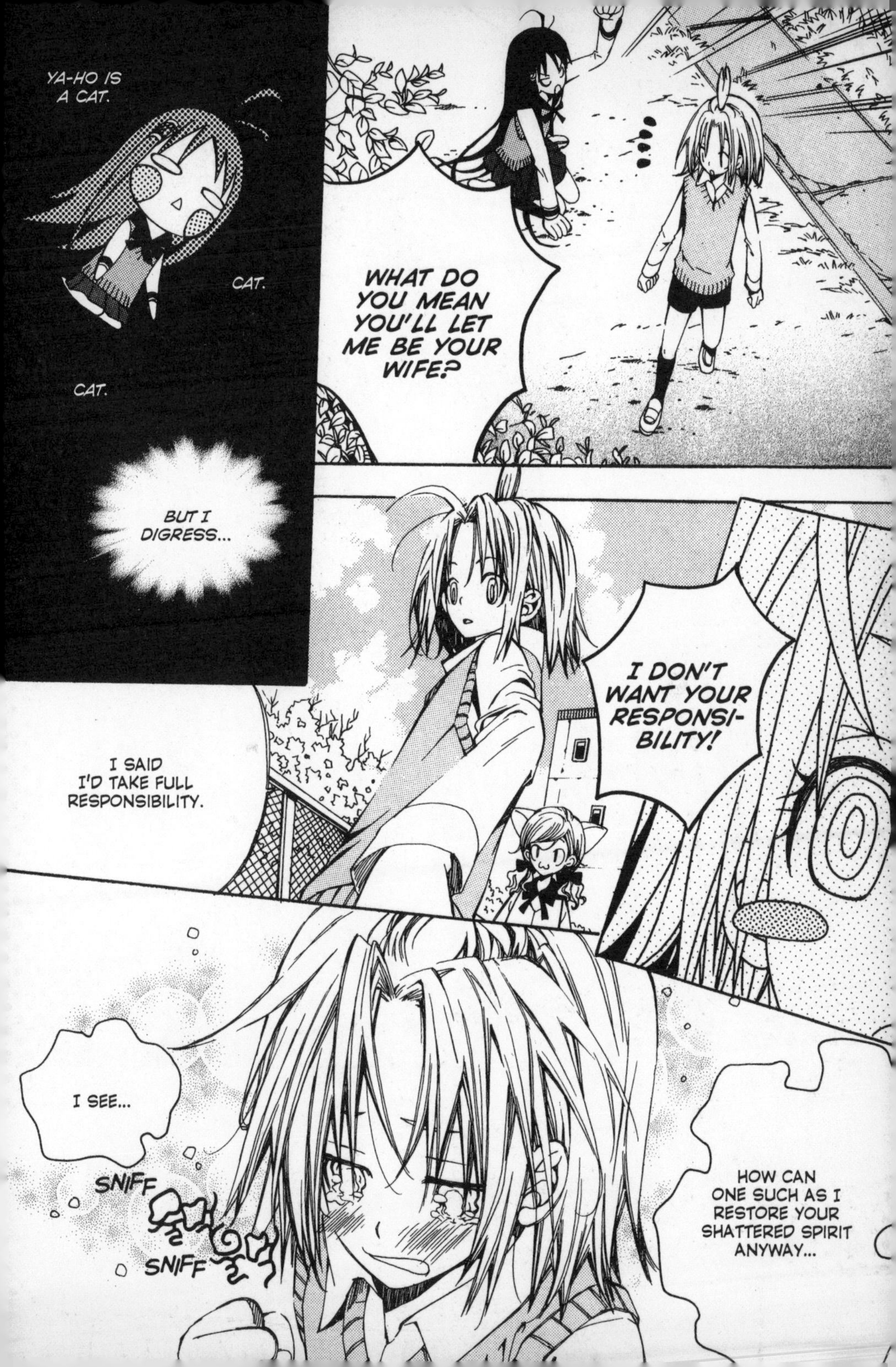
WHAT DO YOU MEAN YOU'LL LET ME BE YOUR WIFE?
YA-HO IS A CAT.
CAT.
CAT.
BUT I DIGRESS...
I DON'T WANT YOUR RESPONSI-BILITY!
I SAID I'D TAKE FULL RESPONSIBILITY.
HOW CAN ONE SUCH AS I RESTORE YOUR SHATTERED SPIRIT ANYWAY...
I SEE...
SNIFF
SNIFF

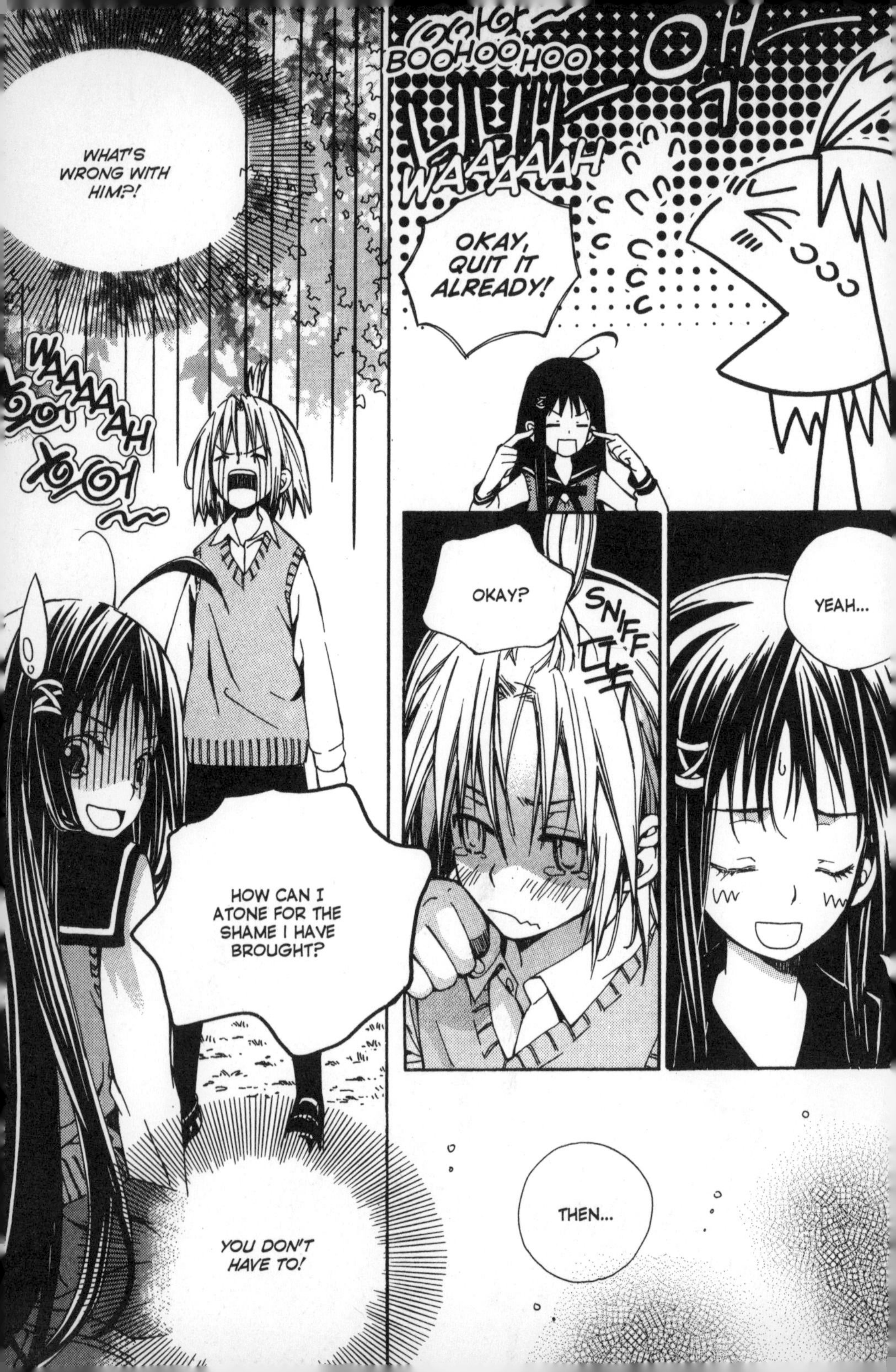
WHAT'S WRONG WITH HIM?!
WAAAAAAH
HOW CAN I ATONE FOR THE SHAME I HAVE BROUGHT?
YOU DON'T HAVE TO!
BOOHOOHOO
UUH
OH
WAAAAAH
OKAY, QUIT IT ALREADY!
OKAY?
SNIFF
YEAH...
THEN...

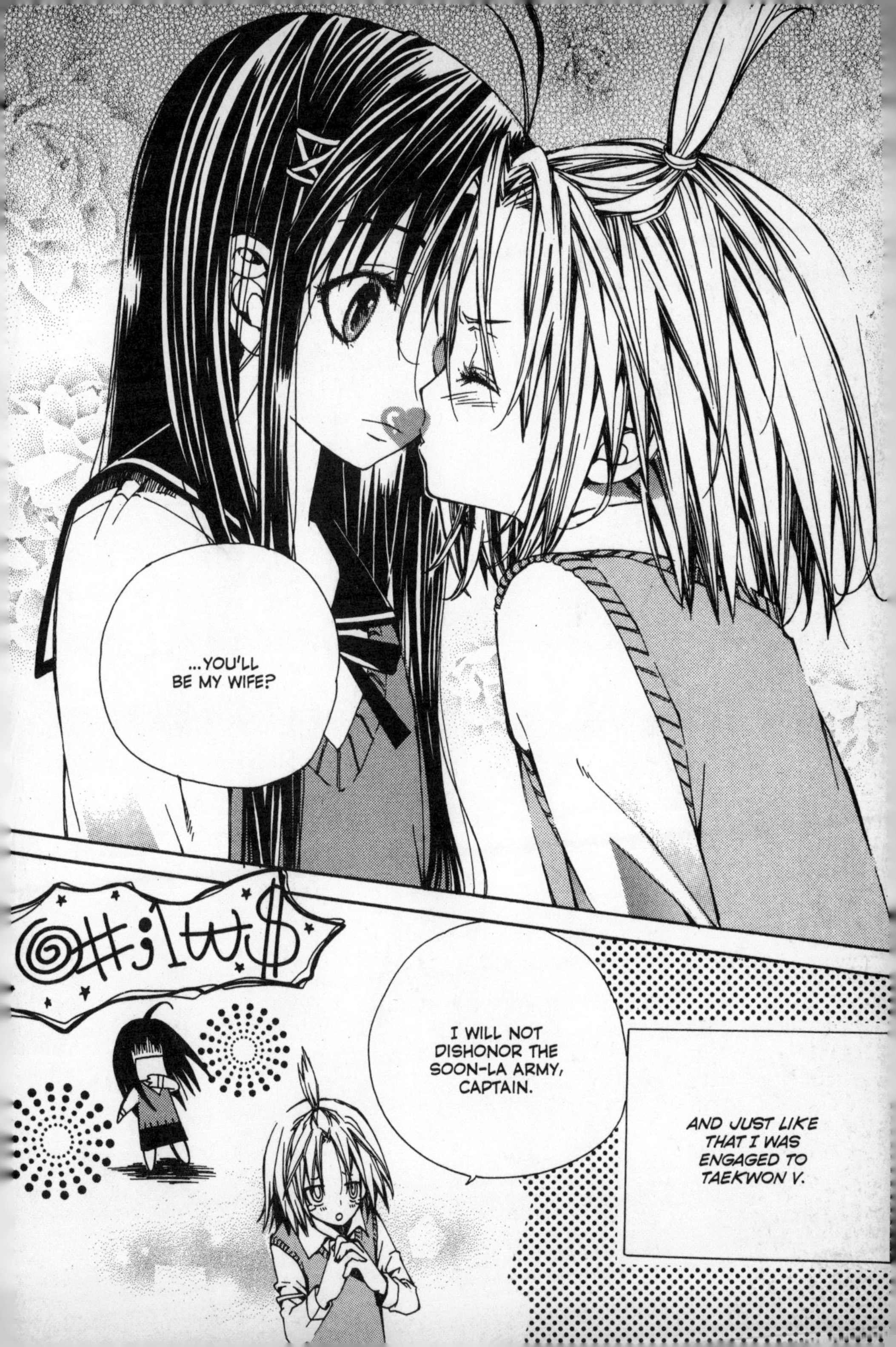
...YOU'LL BE MY WIFE?
I WILL NOT DISHONOR THE SOON-LA ARMY, CAPTAIN.
AND JUST LIKE THAT I WAS ENGAGED TO TAEKWON V.

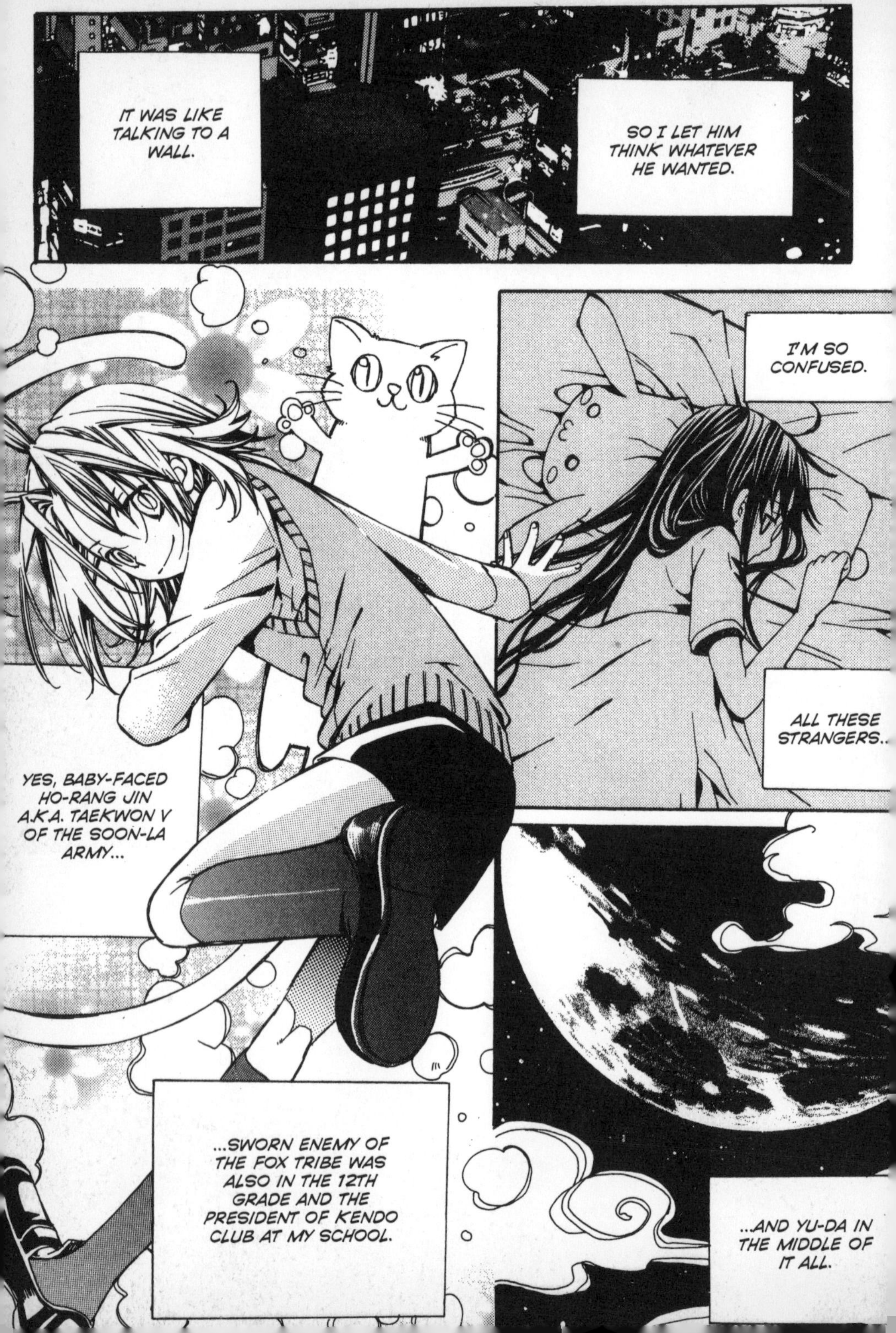
IT WAS LIKE TALKING TO A WALL.
SO I LET HIM THINK WHATEVER HE WANTED.
YES, BABY-FACED HO-RANG JIN A.K.A. TAEKWON V OF THE SOON-LA ARMY...
...SWORN ENEMY OF THE FOX TRIBE WAS ALSO IN THE 12TH GRADE AND THE PRESIDENT OF KENDO CLUB AT MY SCHOOL.
I'M SO CONFUSED.
ALL THESE STRANGERS...
...AND YU-DA IN THE MIDDLE OF IT ALL.

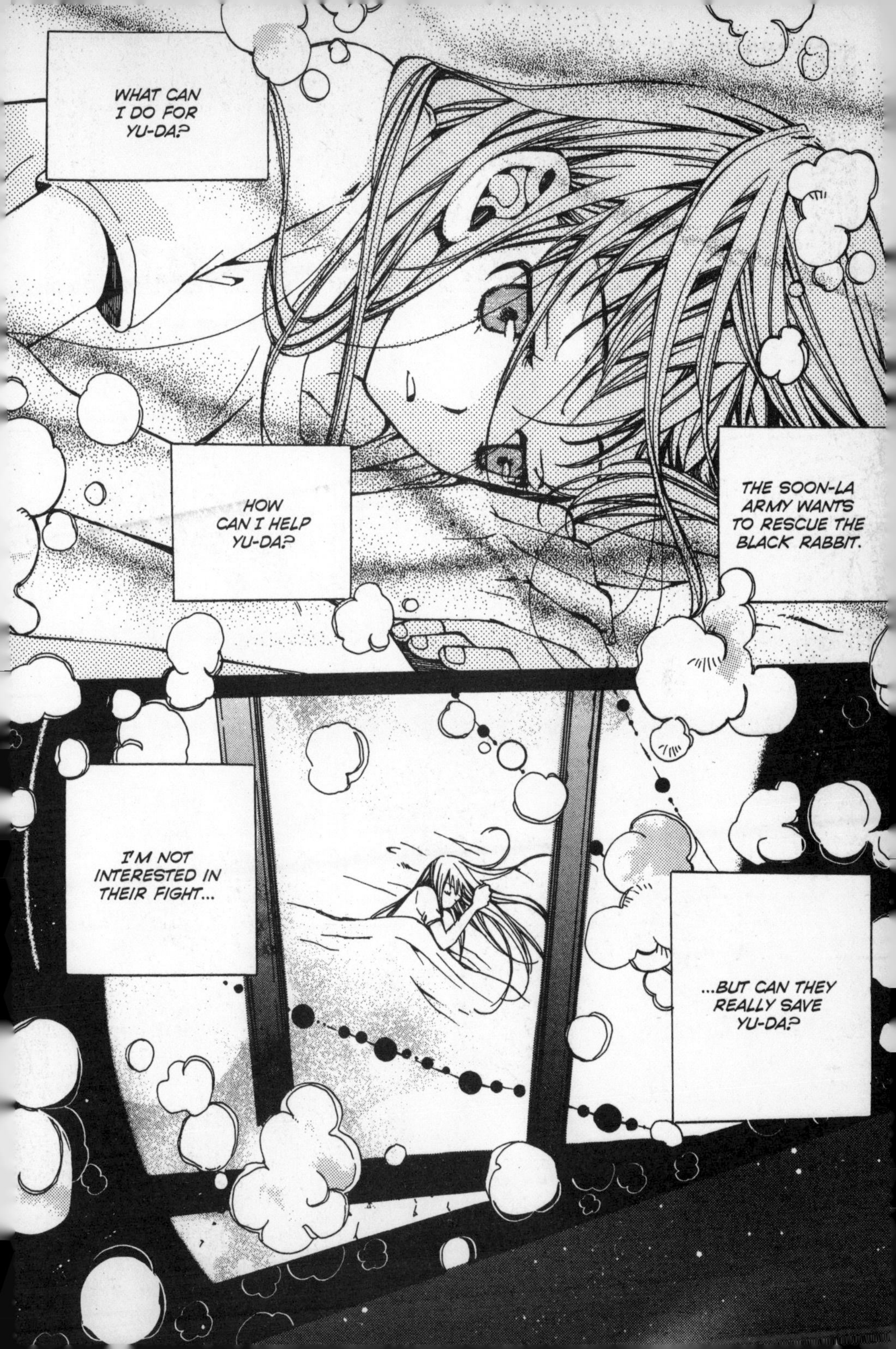
WHAT CAN I DO FOR YU-DA?
HOW CAN I HELP YU-DA?
THE SOON-LA ARMY WANTS TO RESCUE THE BLACK RABBIT.
I'M NOT INTERESTED IN THEIR FIGHT...
...BUT CAN THEY REALLY SAVE YU-DA?

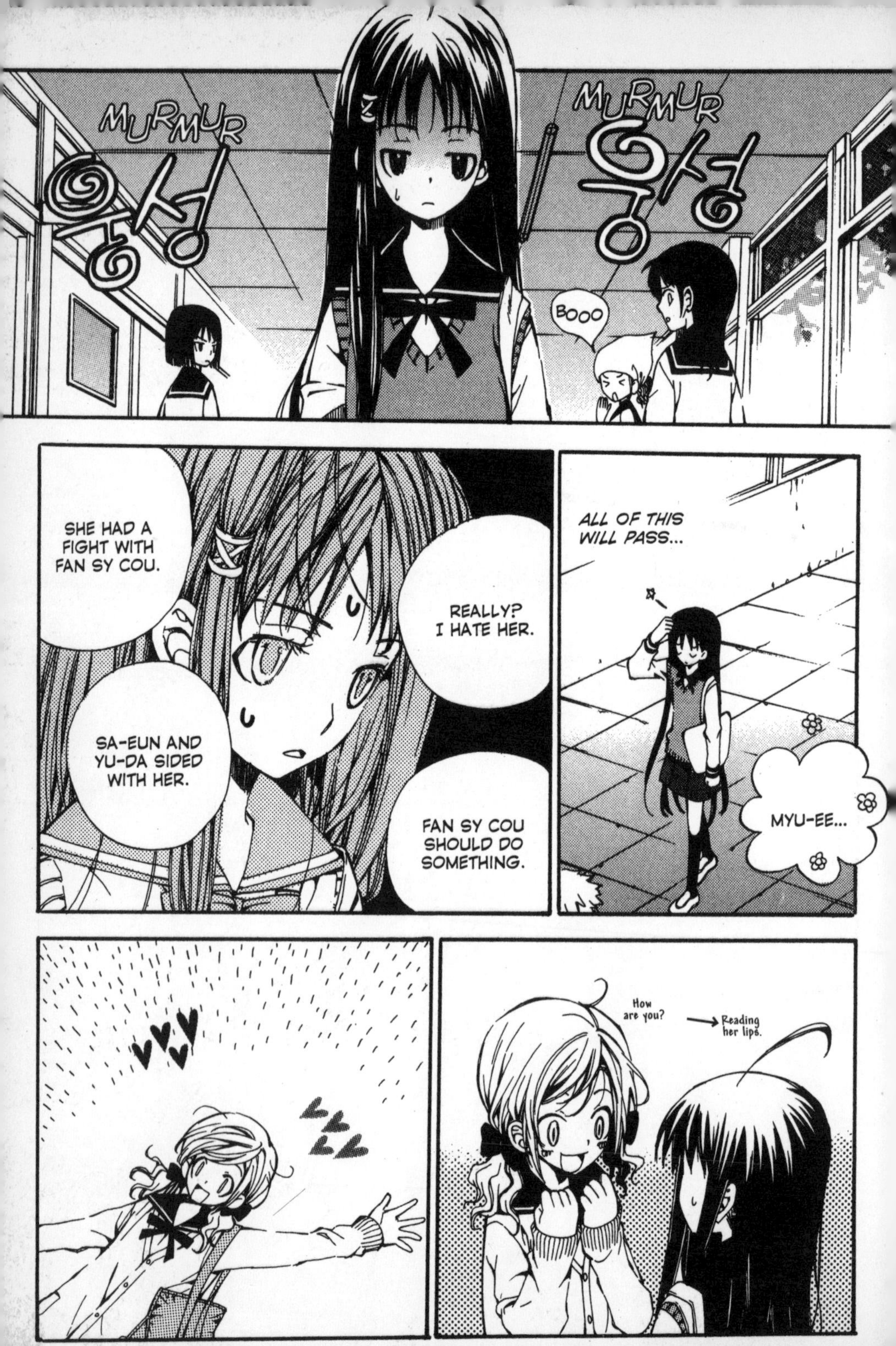
MURMUR
웅성
MURMUR
웅성
BOOO
SHE HAD A FIGHT WITH FAN SY COU.
REALLY? I HATE HER.
SA-EUN AND YU-DA SIDED WITH HER.
FAN SY COU SHOULD DO SOMETHING.
ALL OF THIS WILL PASS...
MYU-EE...
How are you?
Reading her lips.

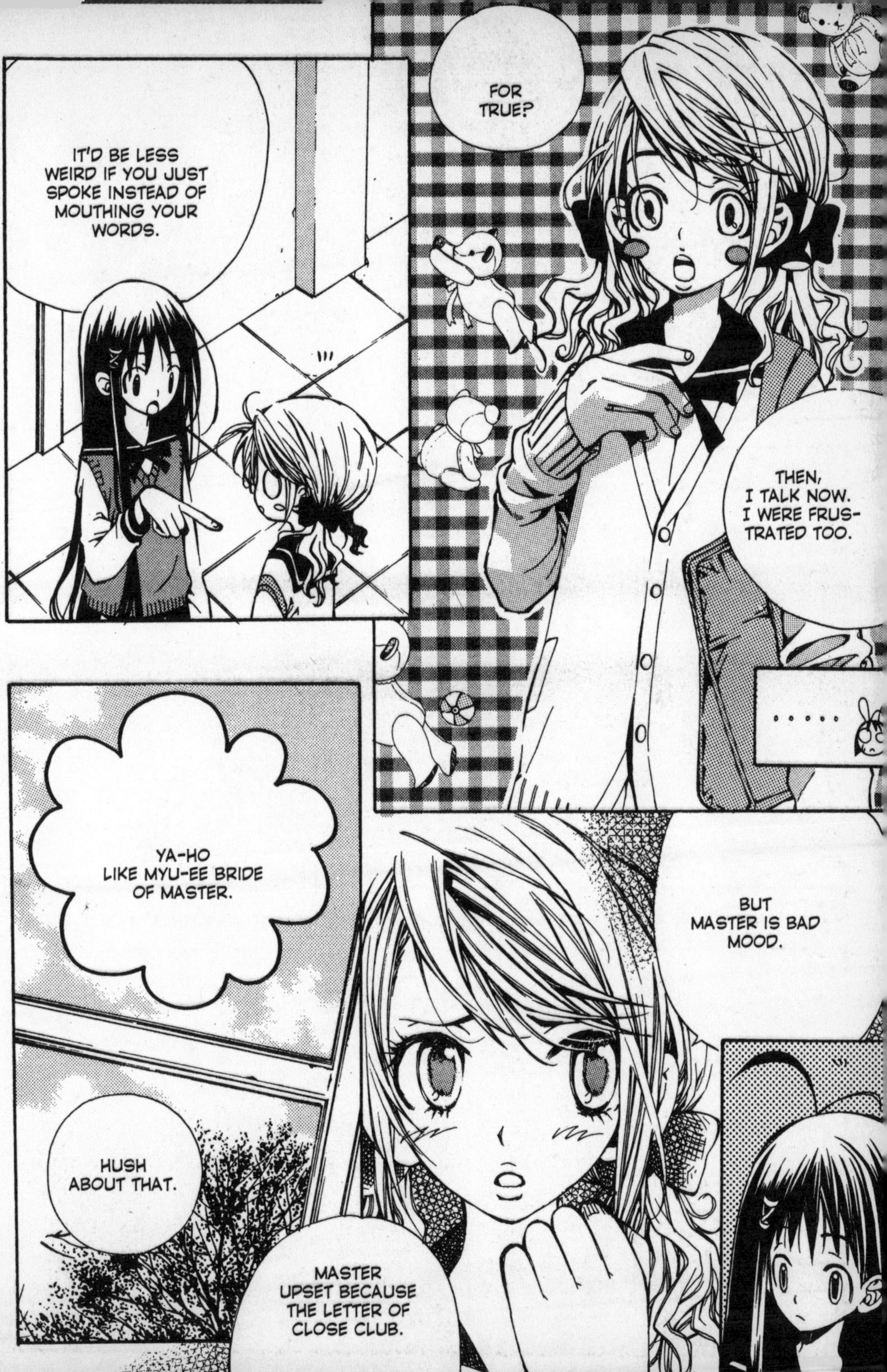
IT'D BE LESS WEIRD IF YOU JUST SPOKE INSTEAD OF MOUTHING YOUR WORDS.
FOR TRUE?
THEN, I TALK NOW. I WERE FRUS-TRATED TOO.
.....
YA-HO LIKE MYU-EE BRIDE OF MASTER.
HUSH ABOUT THAT.
BUT MASTER IS BAD MOOD.
MASTER UPSET BECAUSE THE LETTER OF CLOSE CLUB.

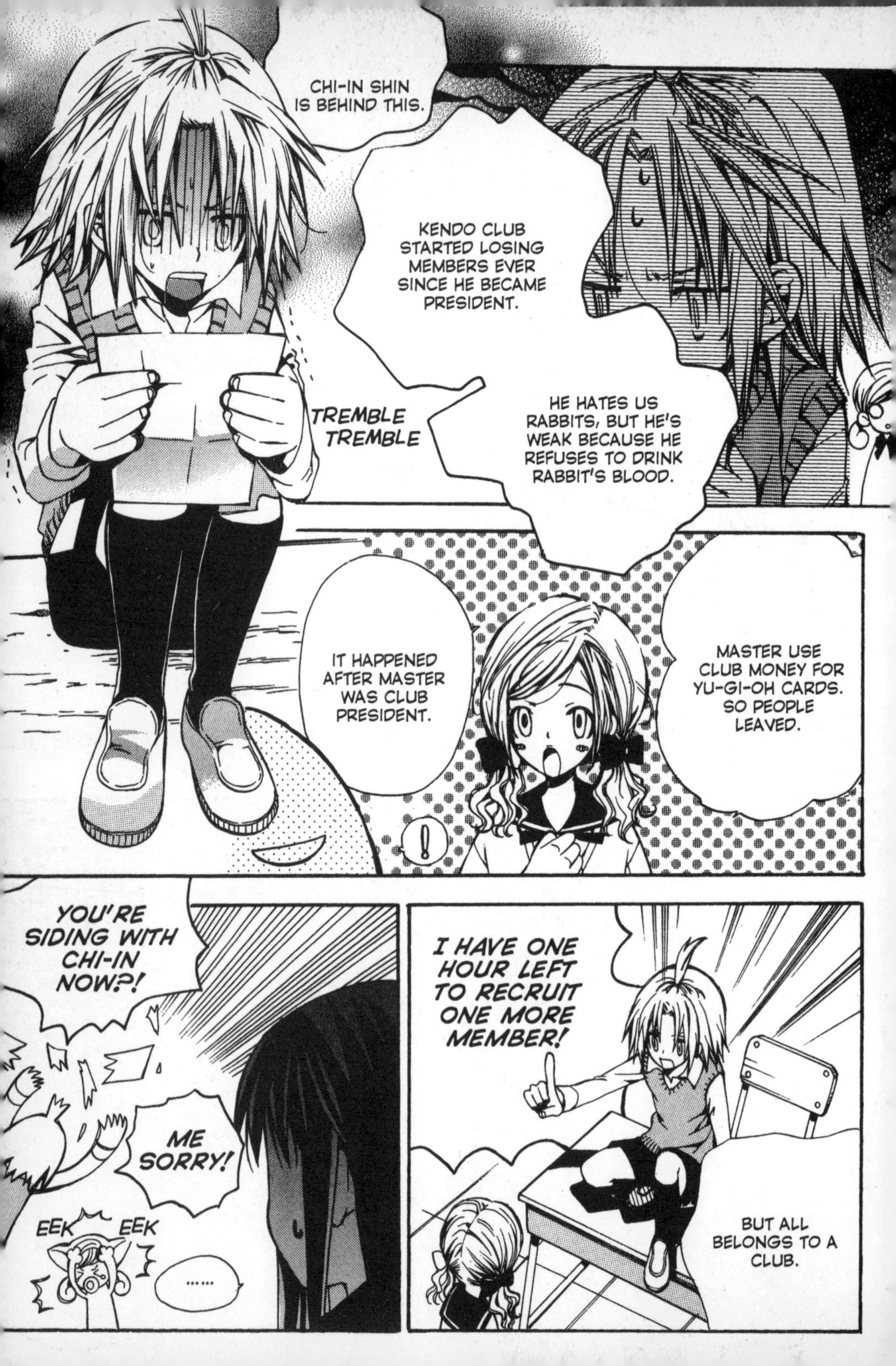
CHI-IN SHIN IS BEHIND THIS.
KENDO CLUB STARTED LOSING MEMBERS EVER SINCE HE BECAME PRESIDENT.
TREMBLE TREMBLE
HE HATES US RABBITS, BUT HE'S WEAK BECAUSE HE REFUSES TO DRINK RABBIT'S BLOOD.
IT HAPPENED AFTER MASTER WAS CLUB PRESIDENT.
!
MASTER USE CLUB MONEY FOR YU-GI-OH CARDS. SO PEOPLE LEAVED.
YOU'RE SIDING WITH CHI-IN NOW?!
ME SORRY!
EEK EEK
......
I HAVE ONE HOUR LEFT TO RECRUIT ONE MORE MEMBER!
BUT ALL BELONGS TO A CLUB.

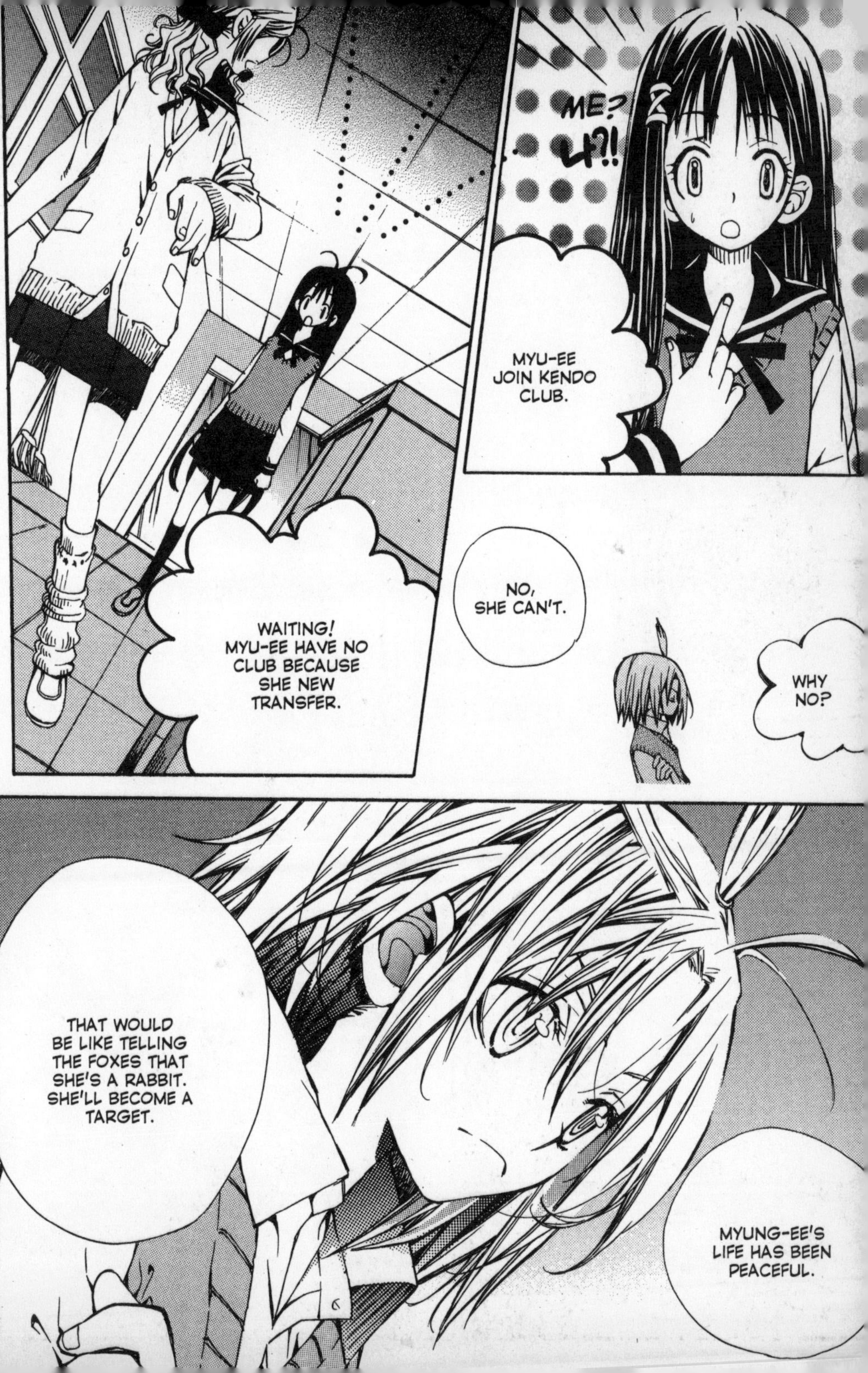

ME?
나?!
MYU-EE JOIN KENDO CLUB.
WAITING! MYU-EE HAVE NO CLUB BECAUSE SHE NEW TRANSFER.
NO, SHE CAN'T.
WHY NO?
THAT WOULD BE LIKE TELLING THE FOXES THAT SHE'S A RABBIT. SHE'LL BECOME A TARGET.
MYUNG-EE'S LIFE HAS BEEN PEACEFUL.

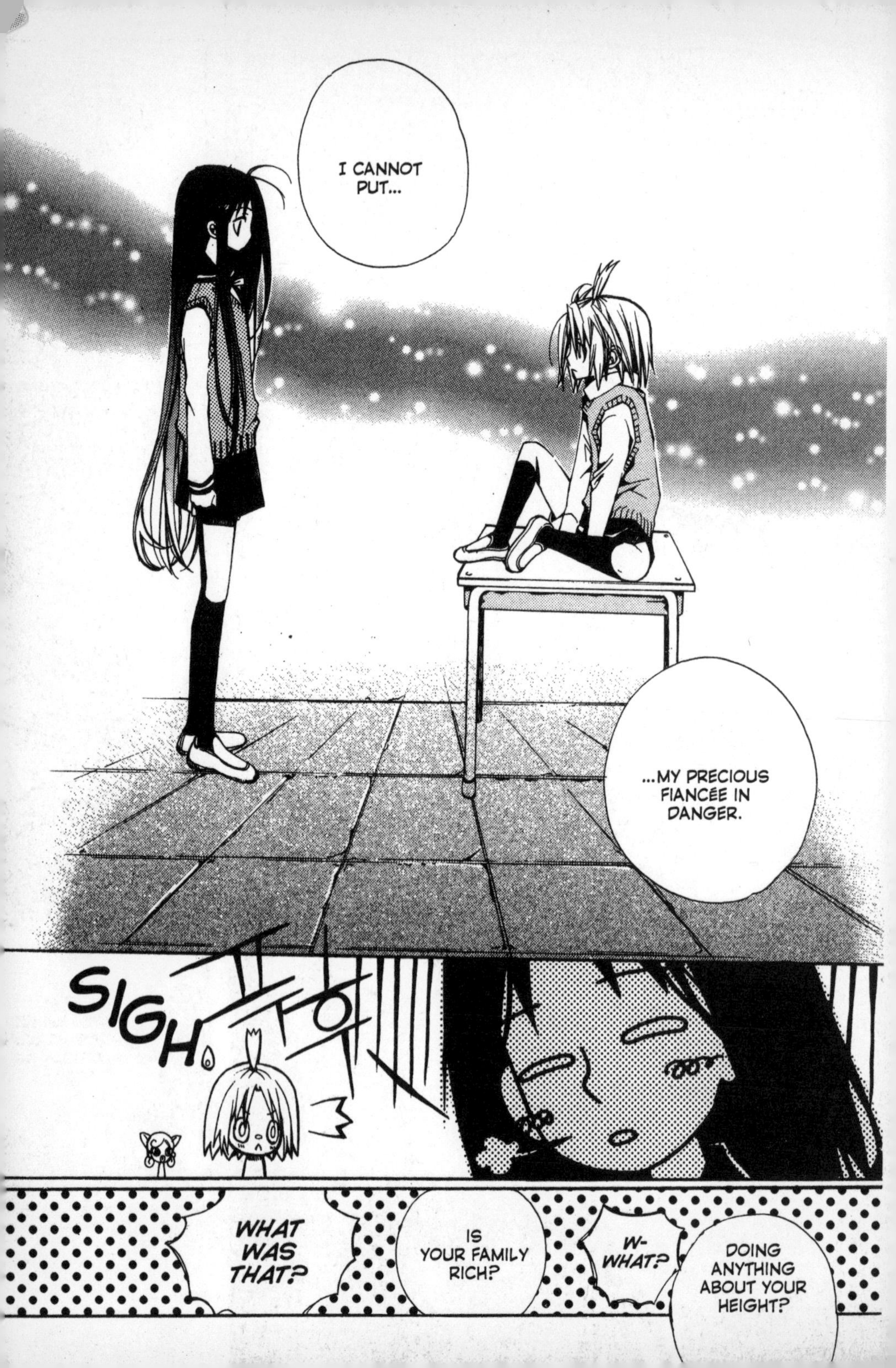
I CANNOT PUT...
...MY PRECIOUS FIANCÉE IN DANGER.
SIGH.
DOING ANYTHING ABOUT YOUR HEIGHT?
W-WHAT?
IS YOUR FAMILY RICH?
WHAT WAS THAT?

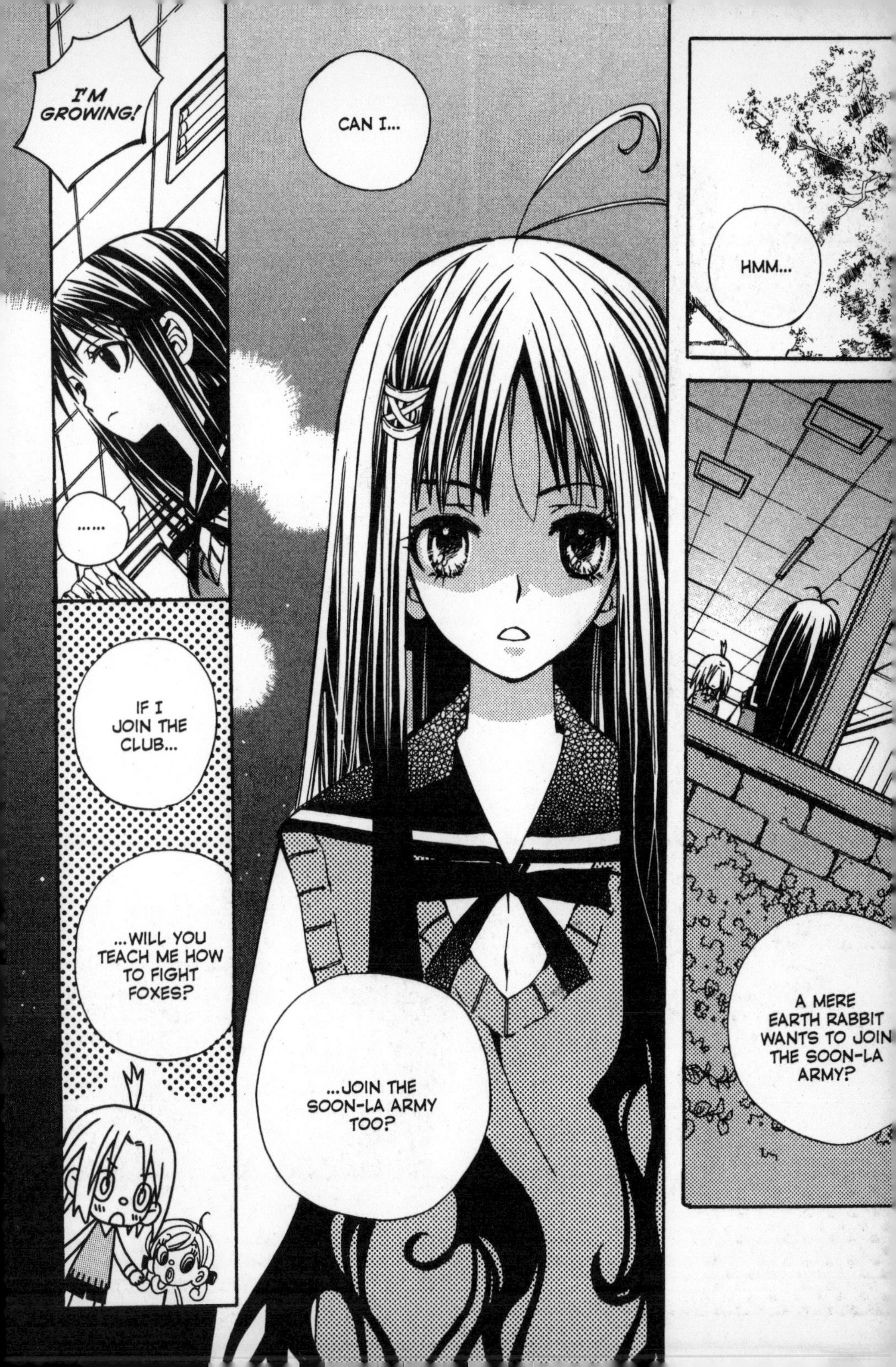
HMM...
A MERE EARTH RABBIT WANTS TO JOIN THE SOON-LA ARMY?
CAN I...
...JOIN THE SOON-LA ARMY TOO?
I'M GROWING!
......
IF I JOIN THE CLUB...
...WILL YOU TEACH ME HOW TO FIGHT FOXES?

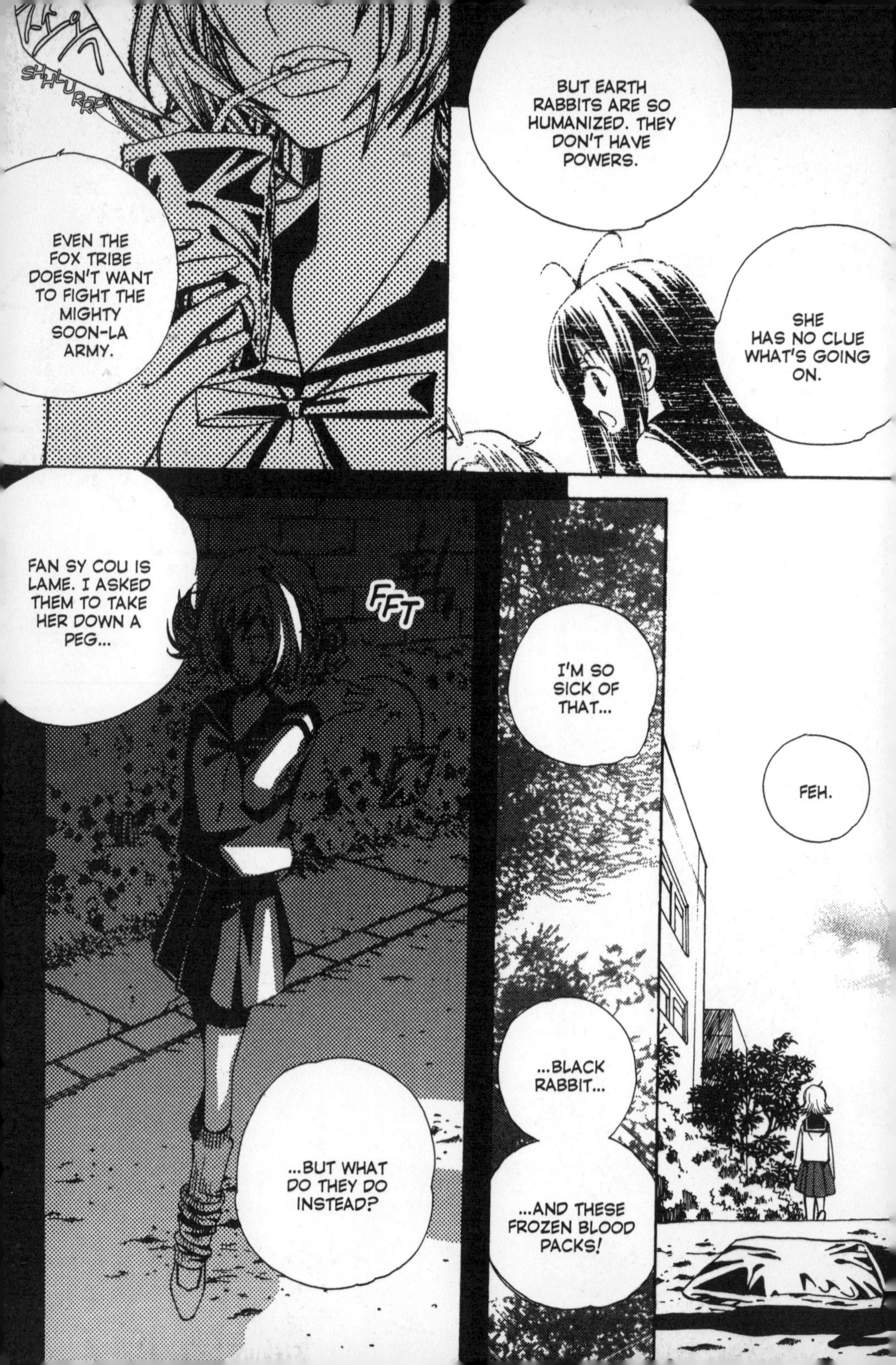
BUT EARTH RABBITS ARE SO HUMANIZED. THEY DON'T HAVE POWERS.
SHE HAS NO CLUE WHAT'S GOING ON.
SHHLURRRP
EVEN THE FOX TRIBE DOESN'T WANT TO FIGHT THE MIGHTY SOON-LA ARMY.
FEH.
I'M SO SICK OF THAT...
...BLACK RABBIT...
...AND THESE FROZEN BLOOD PACKS!
FAN SY COU IS LAME. I ASKED THEM TO TAKE HER DOWN A PEG...
FFT
...BUT WHAT DO THEY DO INSTEAD?

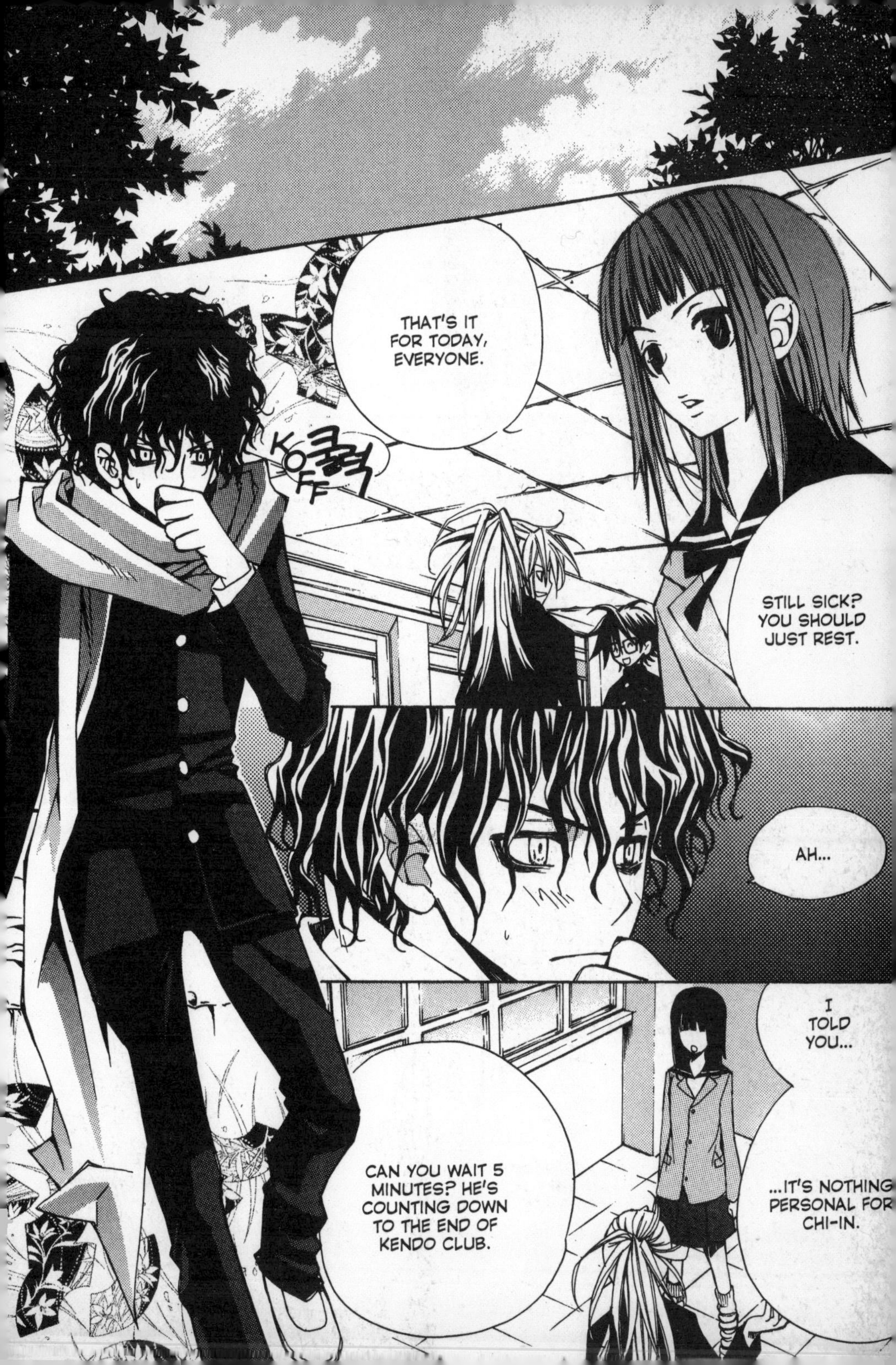
THAT'S IT FOR TODAY, EVERYONE.
KOFF
STILL SICK? YOU SHOULD JUST REST.
AH...
I TOLD YOU...
...IT'S NOTHING PERSONAL FOR CHI-IN.
CAN YOU WAIT 5 MINUTES? HE'S COUNTING DOWN TO THE END OF KENDO CLUB.

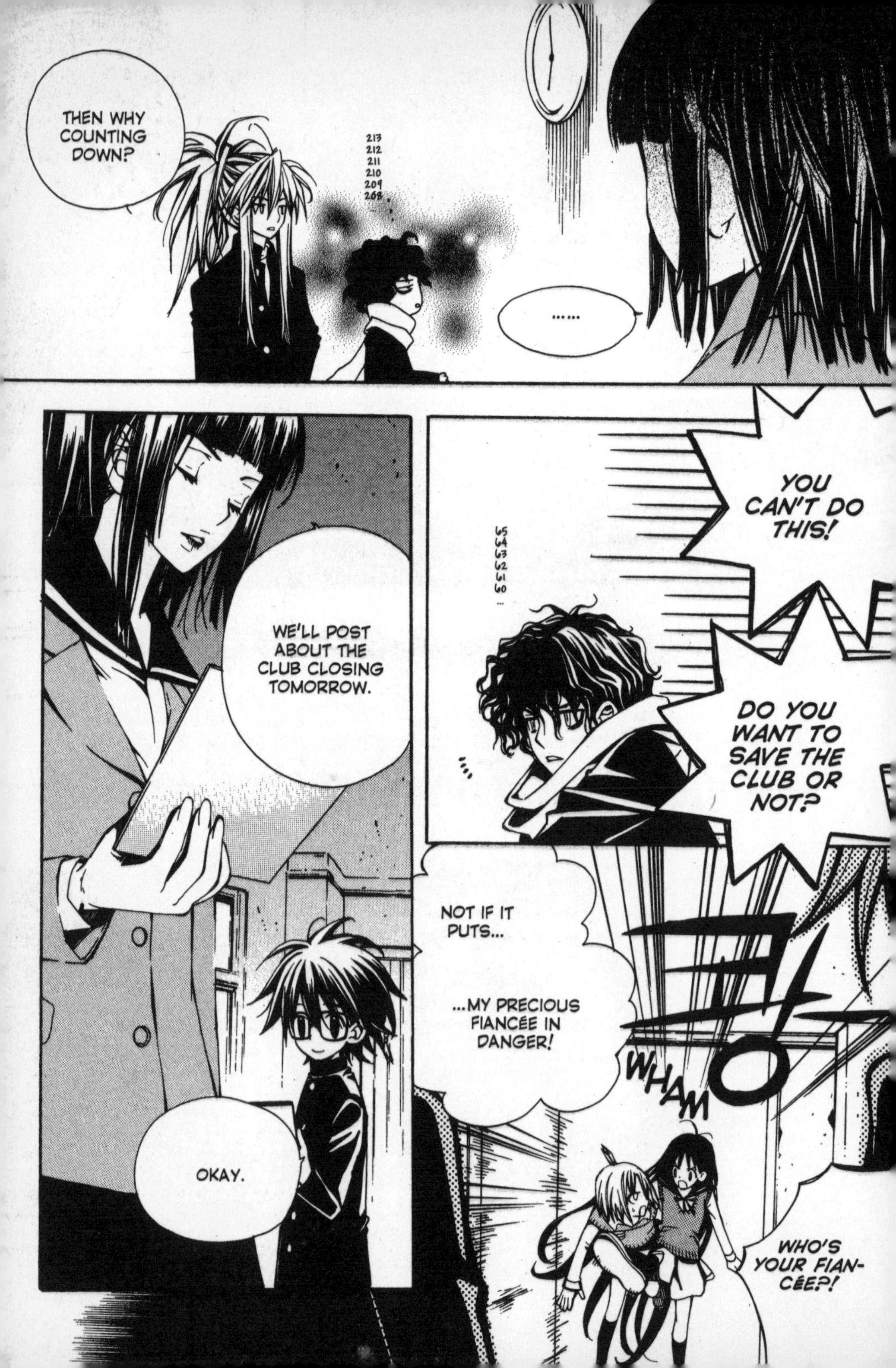

......
THEN WHY COUNTING DOWN?
213
212
211
210
209
208
YOU CAN'T DO THIS!
DO YOU WANT TO SAVE THE CLUB OR NOT?
65
64
63
62
61
60
...
WE'LL POST ABOUT THE CLUB CLOSING TOMORROW.
NOT IF IT PUTS...
...MY PRECIOUS FIANCÉE IN DANGER!
WHAM
WHO'S YOUR FIAN-CÉE?!
OKAY.

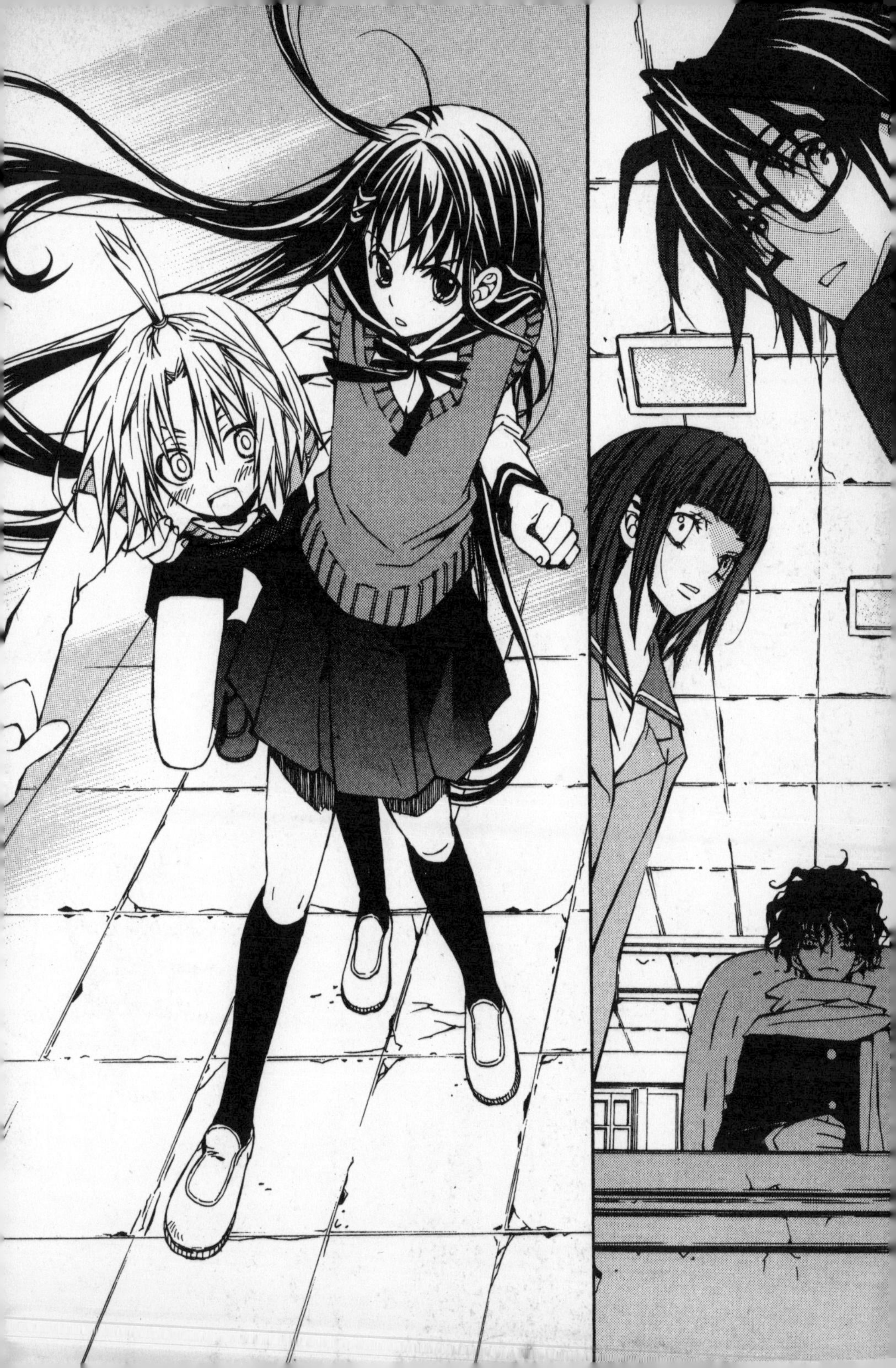

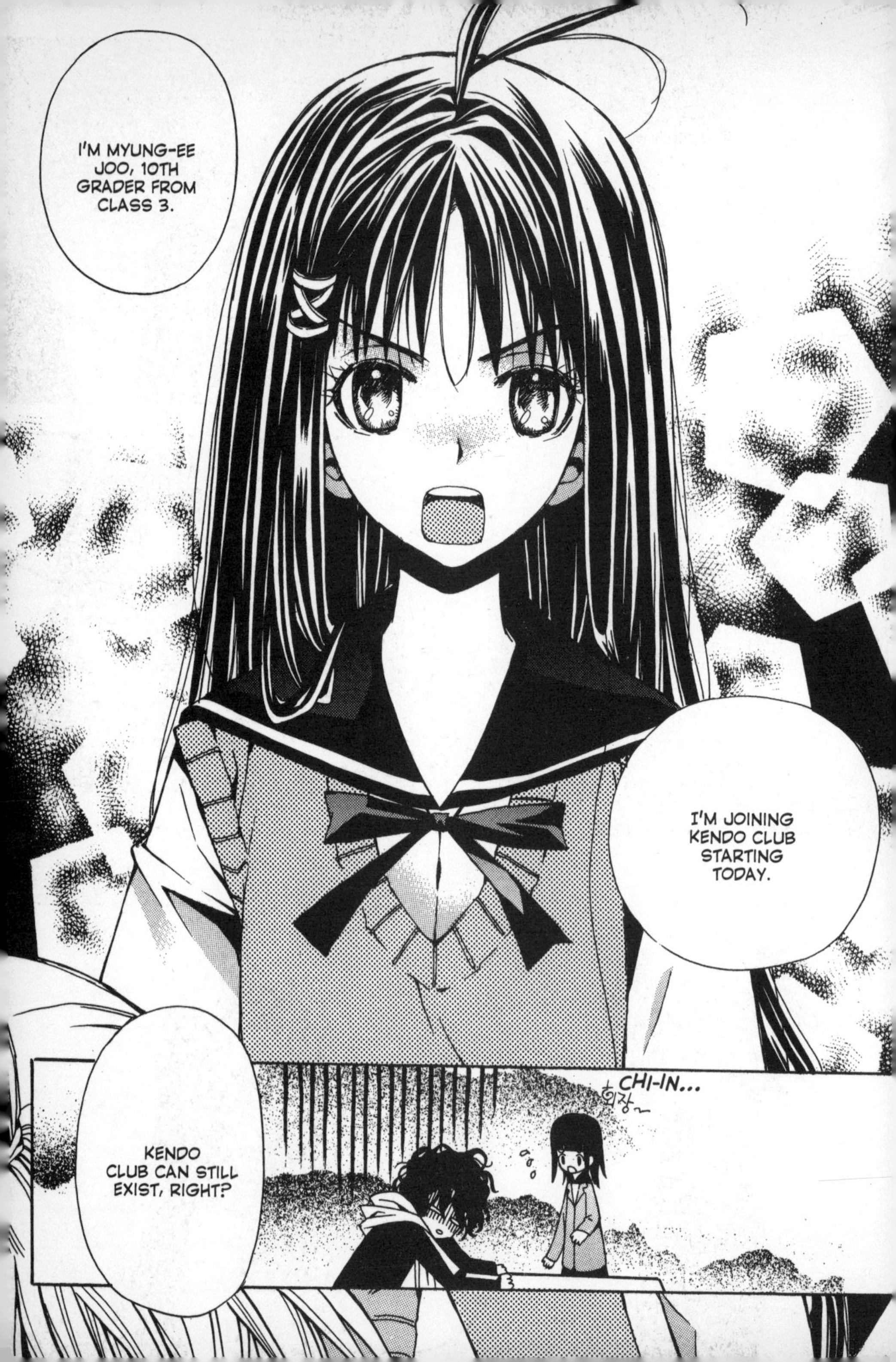
I'M MYUNG-EE JOO, 10TH GRADER FROM CLASS 3.
I'M JOINING KENDO CLUB STARTING TODAY.
KENDO CLUB CAN STILL EXIST, RIGHT?
CHI-IN...
회장~

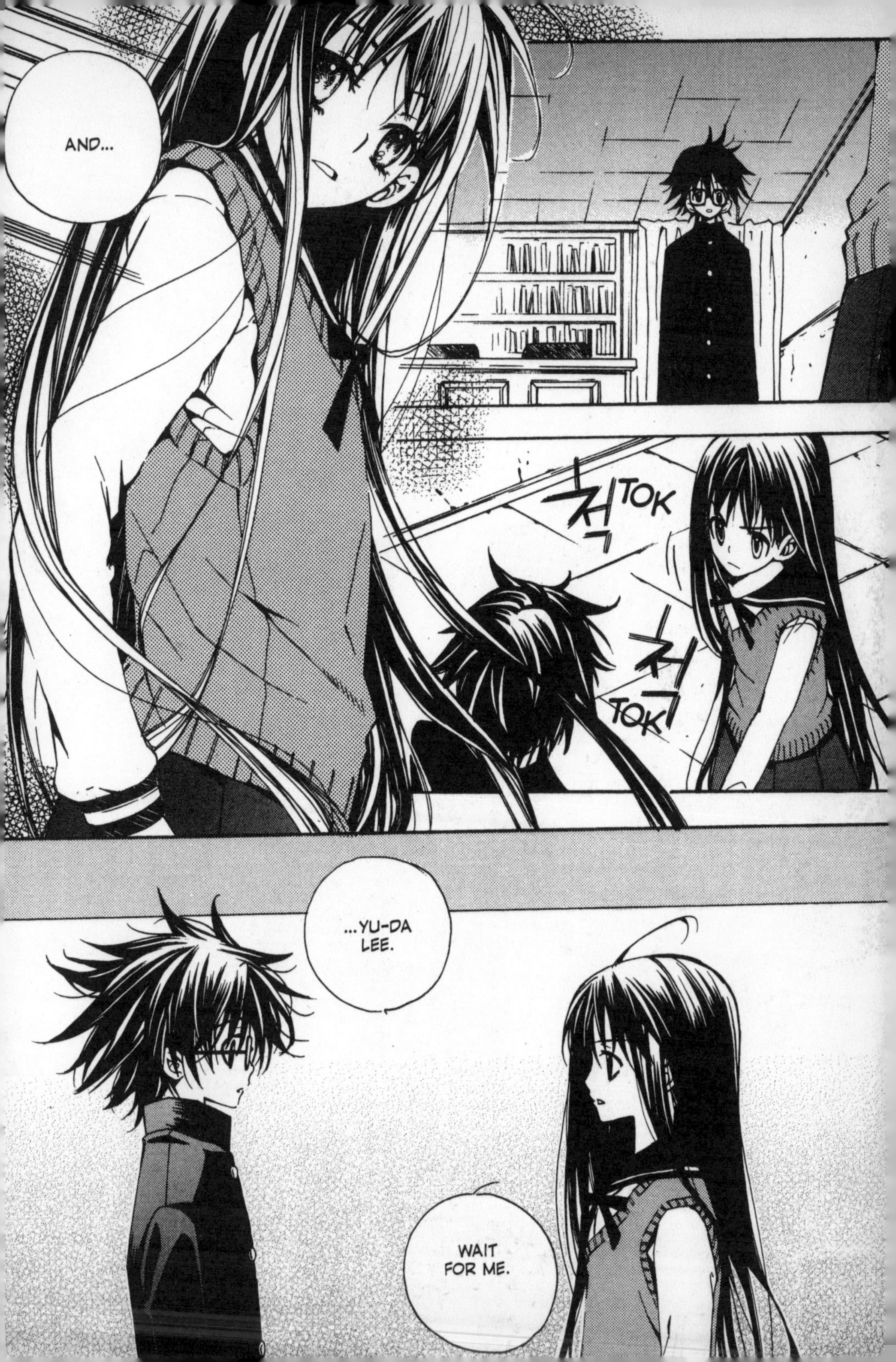
AND...
척 TOK
척 TOK
...YU-DA LEE.
WAIT FOR ME.

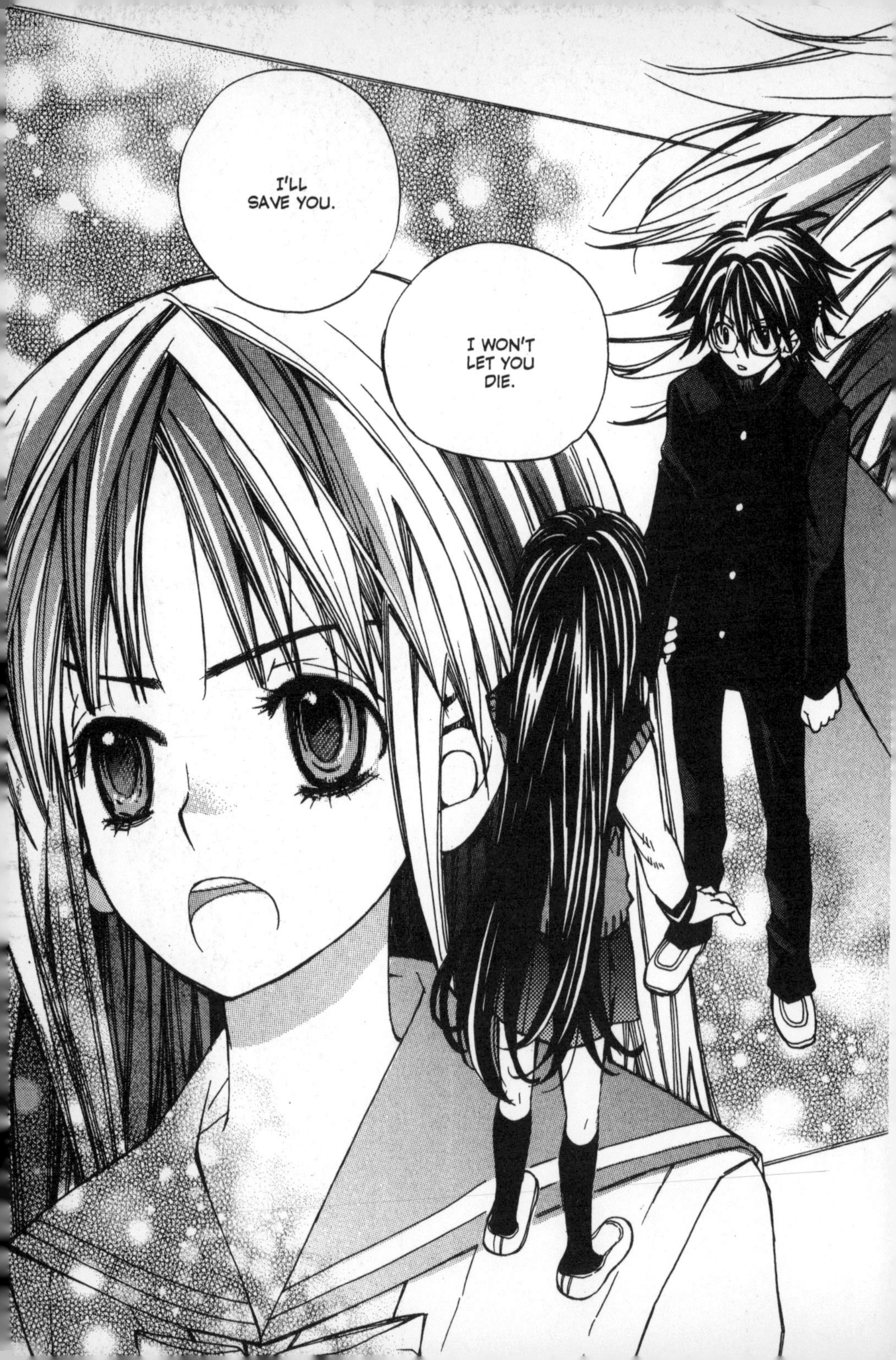
I'LL SAVE YOU.
I WON'T LET YOU DIE.

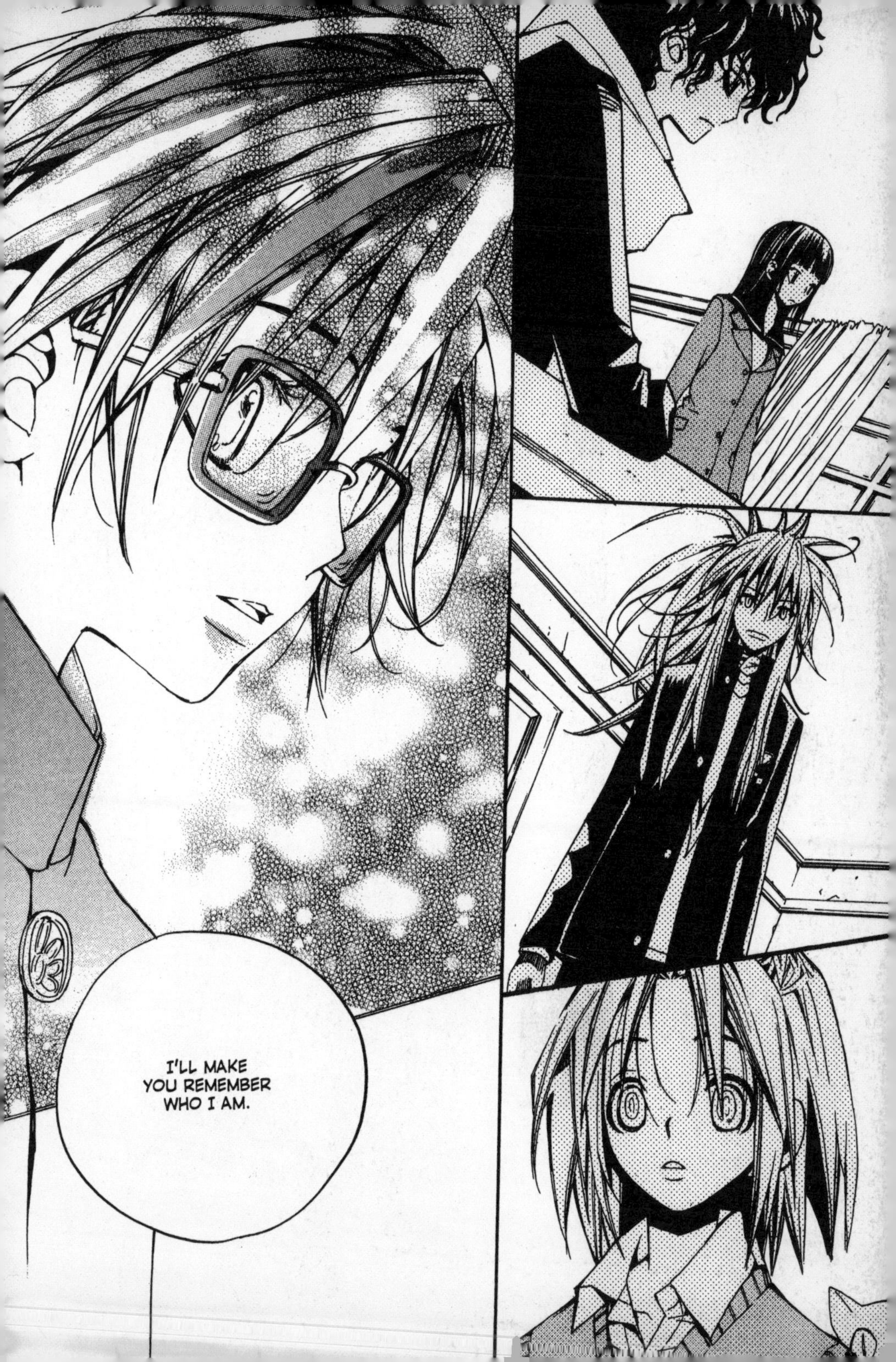
I'LL MAKE
YOU REMEMBER
WHO I AM.

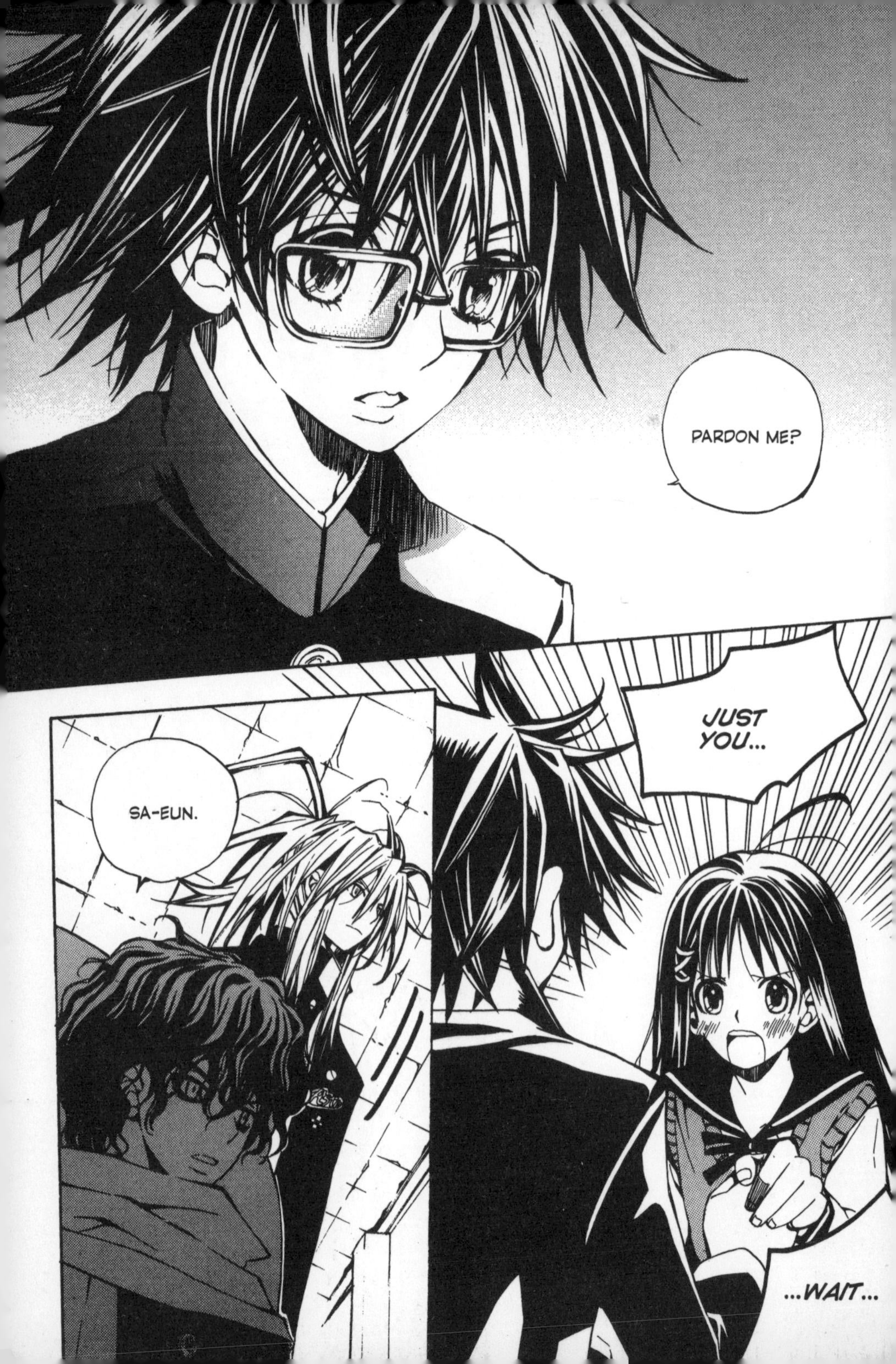
PARDON ME?
JUST YOU...
SA-EUN.
...WAIT...

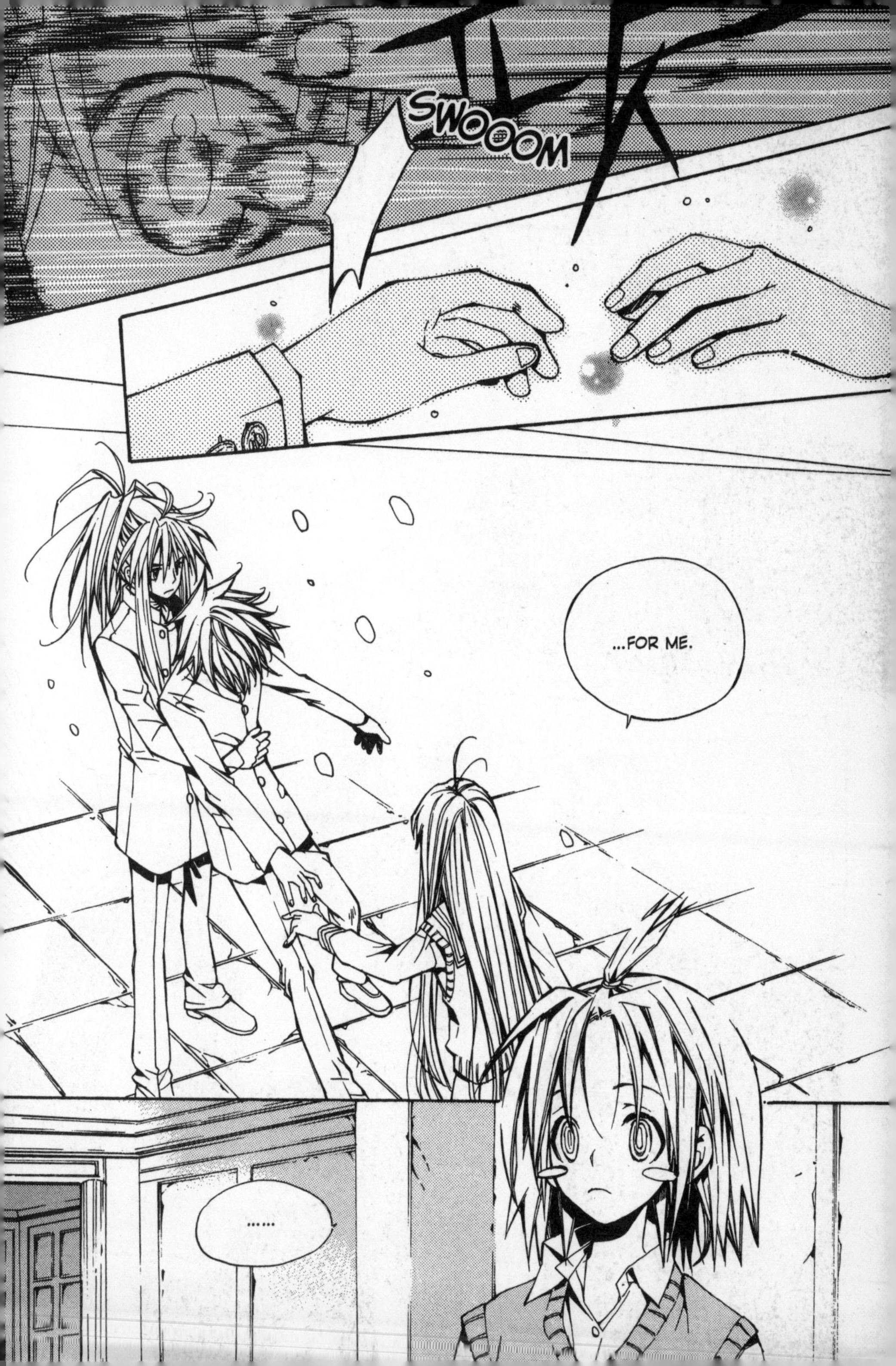
SWOOOM
...FOR ME.
......

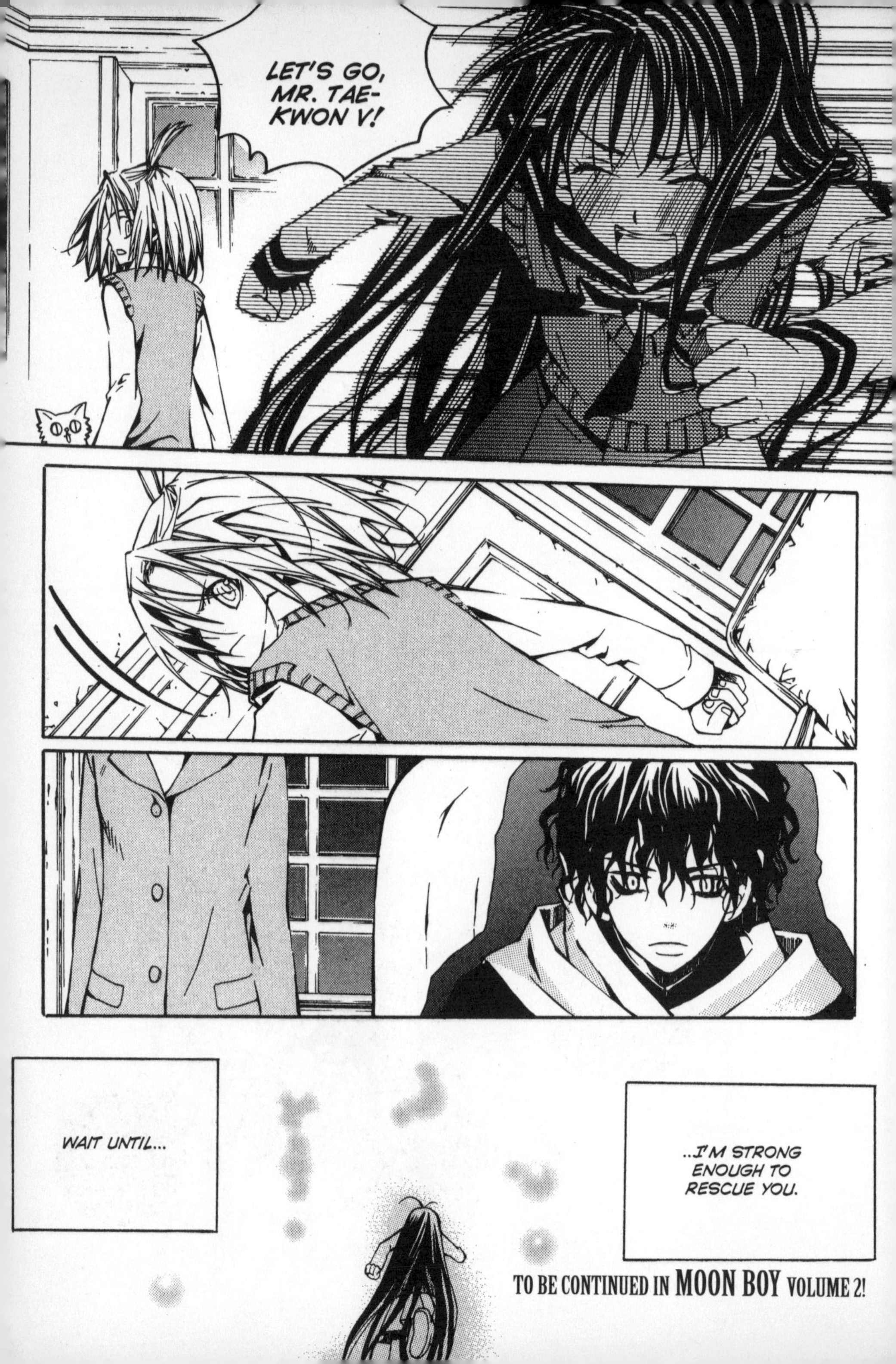
LET'S GO, MR. TAE-KWON V!
WAIT UNTIL...
...I'M STRONG ENOUGH TO RESCUE YOU.
TO BE CONTINUED IN MOON BOY VOLUME 2!

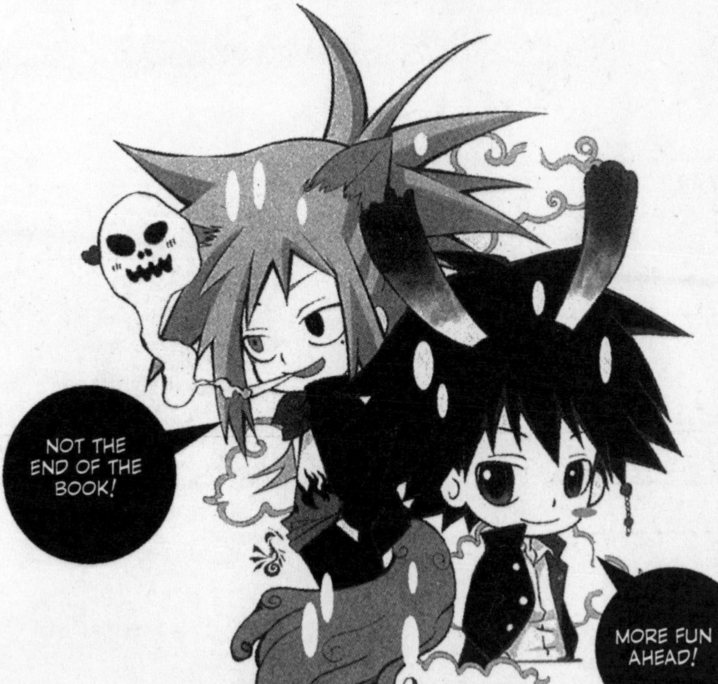
NOT THE END OF THE BOOK!
MORE FUN AHEAD!

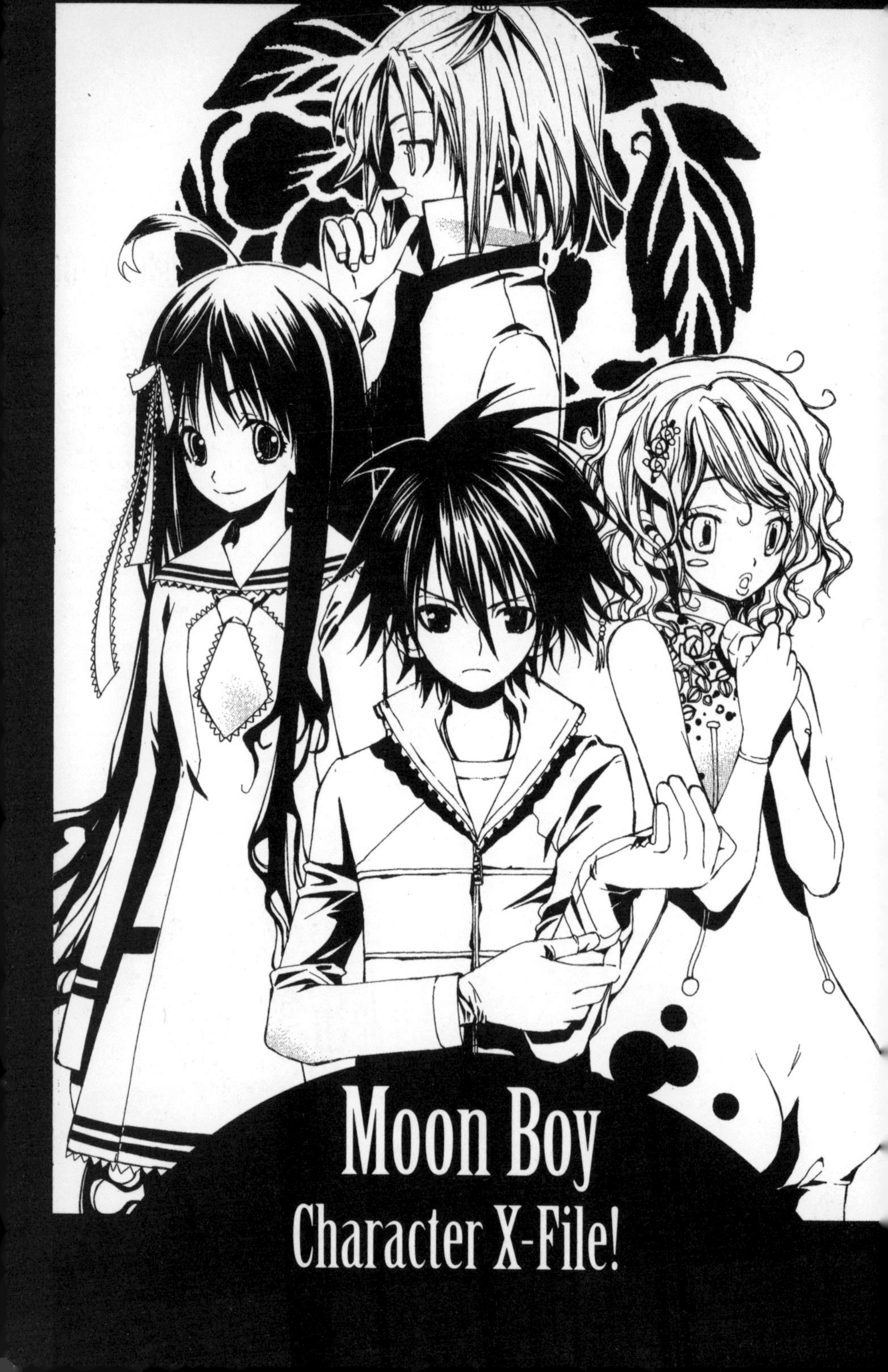

Moon Boy
Character X-File!

Moon Boy
Character X-File!

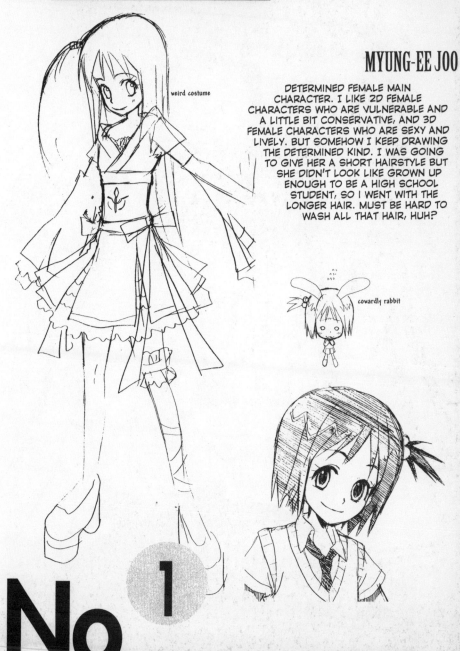

weird costume

MYUNG-EE JOO

DETERMINED FEMALE MAIN CHARACTER. I LIKE 2D FEMALE CHARACTERS WHO ARE VULNERABLE AND A LITTLE BIT CONSERVATIVE, AND 3D FEMALE CHARACTERS WHO ARE SEXY AND LIVELY. BUT SOMEHOW I KEEP DRAWING THE DETERMINED KIND. I WAS GOING TO GIVE HER A SHORT HAIRSTYLE BUT SHE DIDN'T LOOK LIKE GROWN UP ENOUGH TO BE A HIGH SCHOOL STUDENT, SO I WENT WITH THE LONGER HAIR. MUST BE HARD TO WASH ALL THAT HAIR, HUH?

cowardly rabbit

No 1

Moon Boy Character X-File!

YU-DA LEE

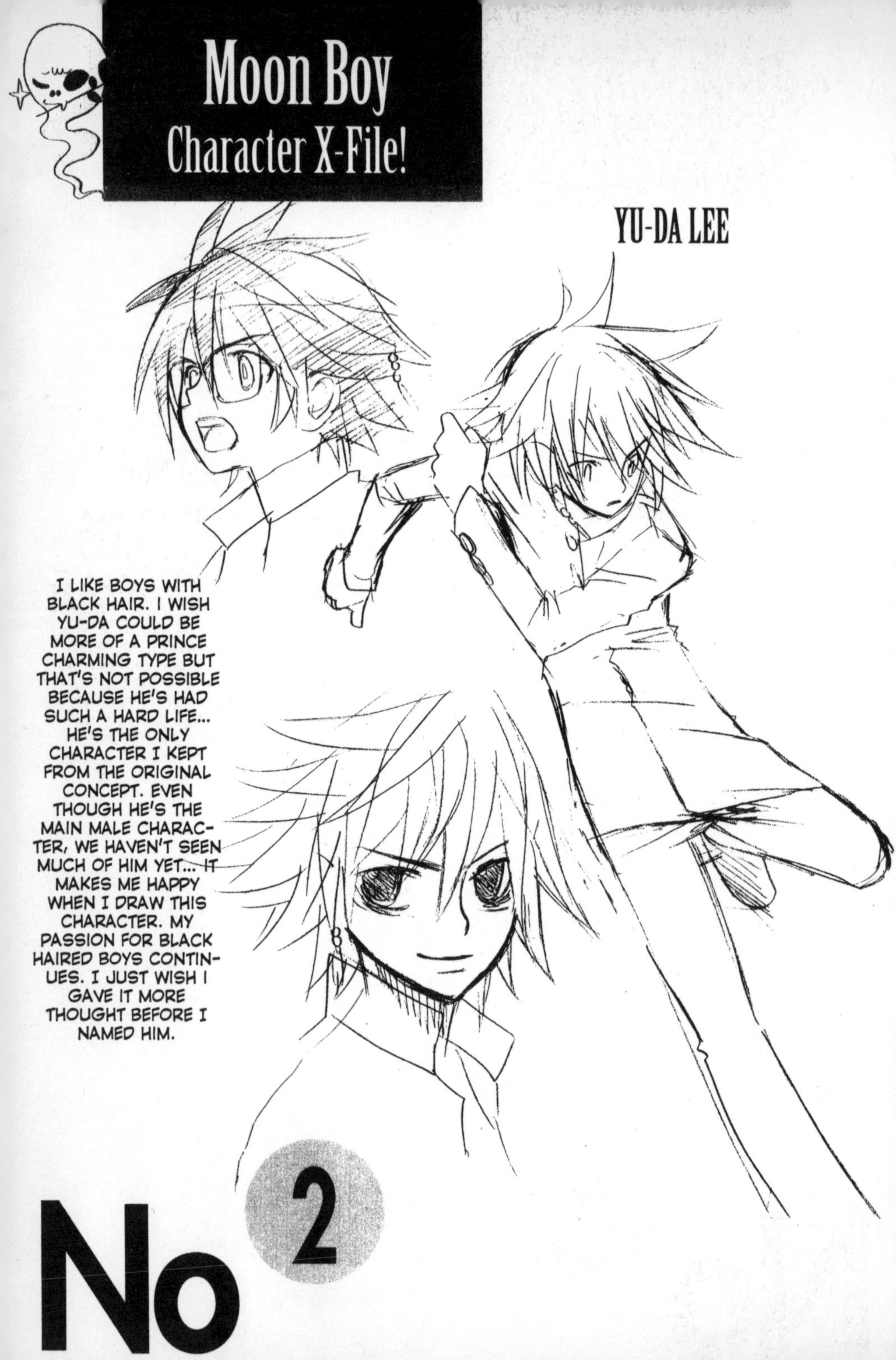

I LIKE BOYS WITH BLACK HAIR. I WISH YU-DA COULD BE MORE OF A PRINCE CHARMING TYPE BUT THAT'S NOT POSSIBLE BECAUSE HE'S HAD SUCH A HARD LIFE... HE'S THE ONLY CHARACTER I KEPT FROM THE ORIGINAL CONCEPT. EVEN THOUGH HE'S THE MAIN MALE CHARACTER, WE HAVEN'T SEEN MUCH OF HIM YET... IT MAKES ME HAPPY WHEN I DRAW THIS CHARACTER. MY PASSION FOR BLACK HAIRED BOYS CONTINUES. I JUST WISH I GAVE IT MORE THOUGHT BEFORE I NAMED HIM.

No 2

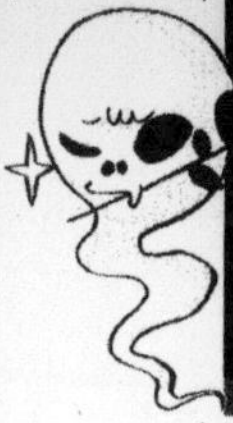

Moon Boy Character X-File!

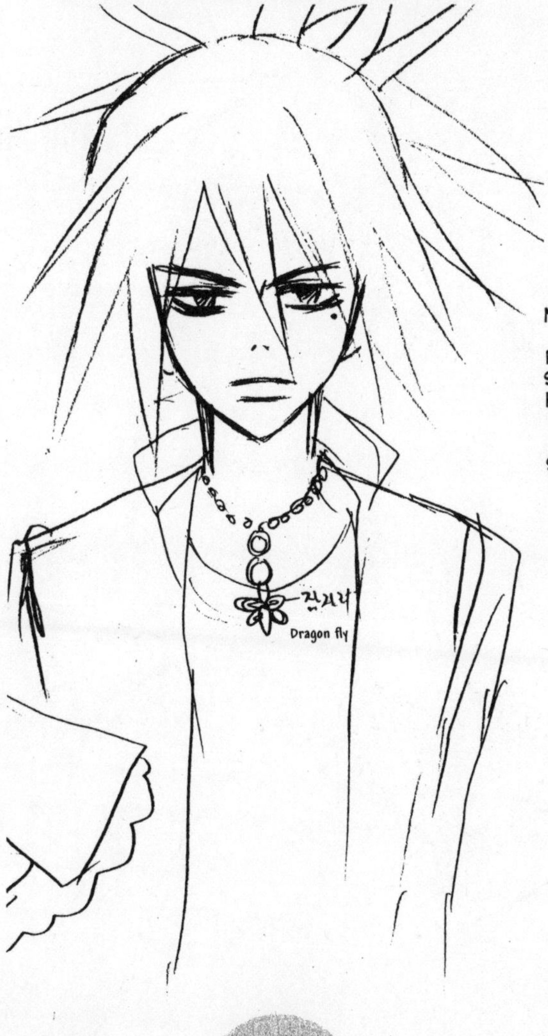

Dragon fly

SA-EUN WON

THIS MALE CHARACTER HAS A NOT-SO-POPULAR LONG HAIRSTYLE. HOW DARE I PUT A BOY WITH A FLOWER BOUQUET HAIRSTYLE IN THE STUDENT COUNCIL... PLEASE ACCEPT HIM BECAUSE THIS IS JUST A COMIC BOOK CHARACTER. I CREATED THIS LOOK BECAUSE I THOUGHT THERE SHOULD BE A WHITE HAIRED GUY TO CONTRAST THE BLACK HAIRED BOY. (WHY DO I ONLY KEEP TALKING ABOUT HAIR?) THIS CHARACTER REQUIRES MORE ATTENTION TO DETAIL BECAUSE OF HIS HAIR AND THAT MOLE UNDER HIS EYE.

No 3

Moon Boy
Character X-File!

HO-RANG JIN

THE PRESIDENT OF KENDO CLUB. I ORIGINALLY TRIED TO PORTRAY HIM AS SOMEONE WITH A BABY FACE BUT A BRUTAL CHARACTER, WHICH I ENDED UP MODIFYING. I REFERENCED HIS HAIRSTYLE FROM A JAPANESE POP STAR AND I'M HAPPY WITH HOW IT CAME OUT BECAUSE IT'S FUN TO DRAW.

No 4

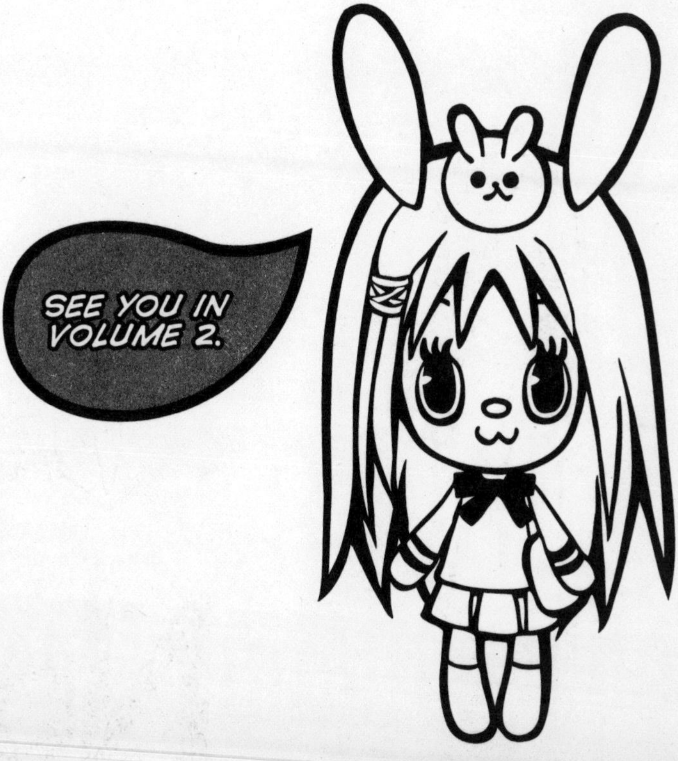
SEE YOU IN VOLUME 2.

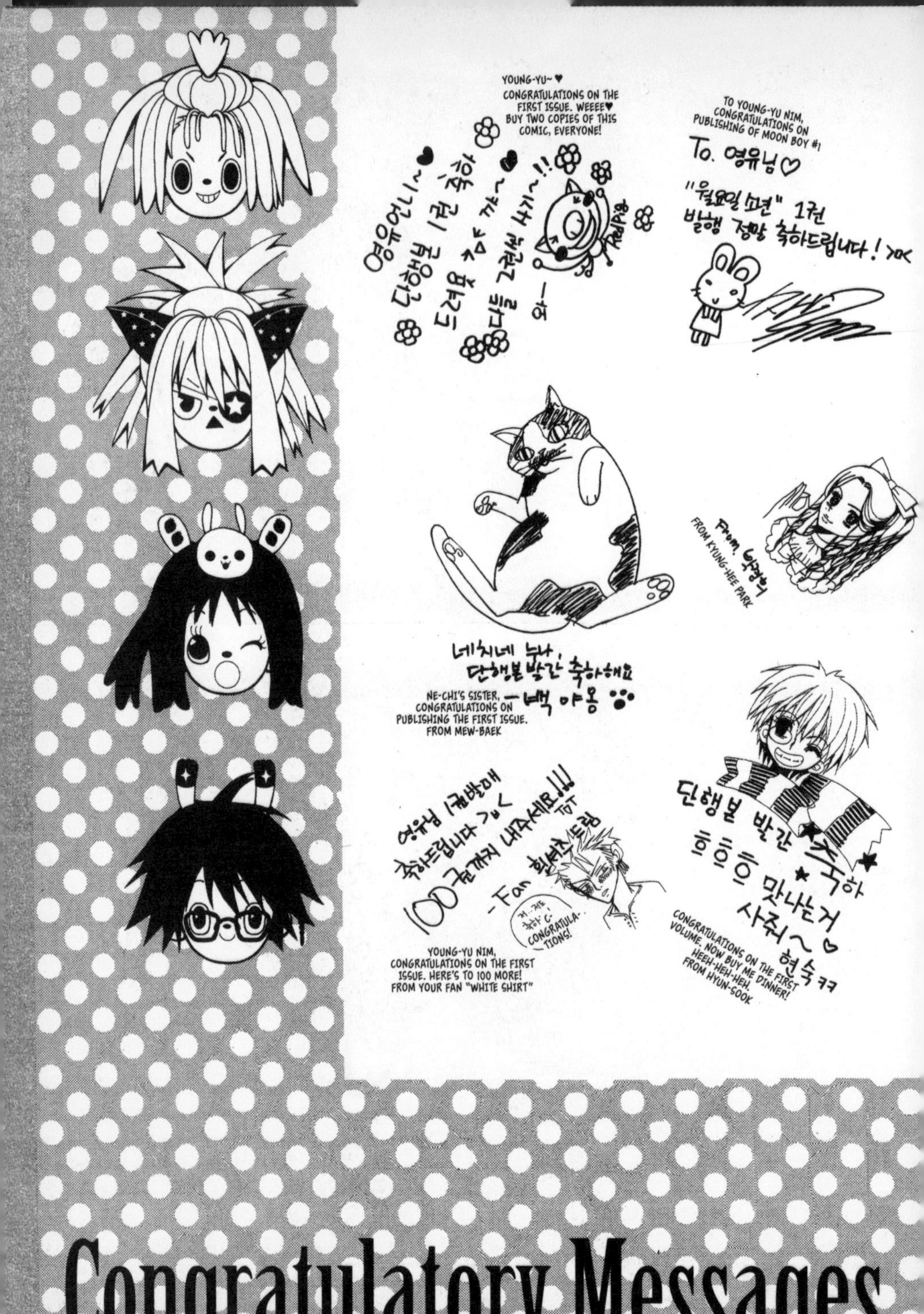
YOUNG-YU~ ♥
CONGRATULATIONS ON THE FIRST ISSUE. WEEEE♥ BUY TWO COPIES OF THIS COMIC, EVERYONE!
TO YOUNG-YU NIM, CONGRATULATIONS ON PUBLISHING OF MOON BOY #1
To. 영유님♡
"월요일 소년" 1권 발행 정말 축하드립니다!
From. 박경희
FROM KYUNG-HEE PARK
네치네 누나, 단행본 발간 축하해요 — 뱩 야옹
NE-CHI'S SISTER, CONGRATULATIONS ON PUBLISHING THE FIRST ISSUE. FROM MEW-BAEK
단행본 발간 축하 흐흐흐 맛나는거 사줘~♡ 현숙 ㅋㅋ
CONGRATULATIONS ON THE FIRST VOLUME. NOW BUY ME DINNER! HEEH-HEH-HEH. FROM HYUN-SOOK
CONGRATULATIONS!
YOUNG-YU NIM, CONGRATULATIONS ON THE FIRST ISSUE. HERE'S TO 100 MORE! FROM YOUR FAN "WHITE SHIRT"

Congratulatory Messages

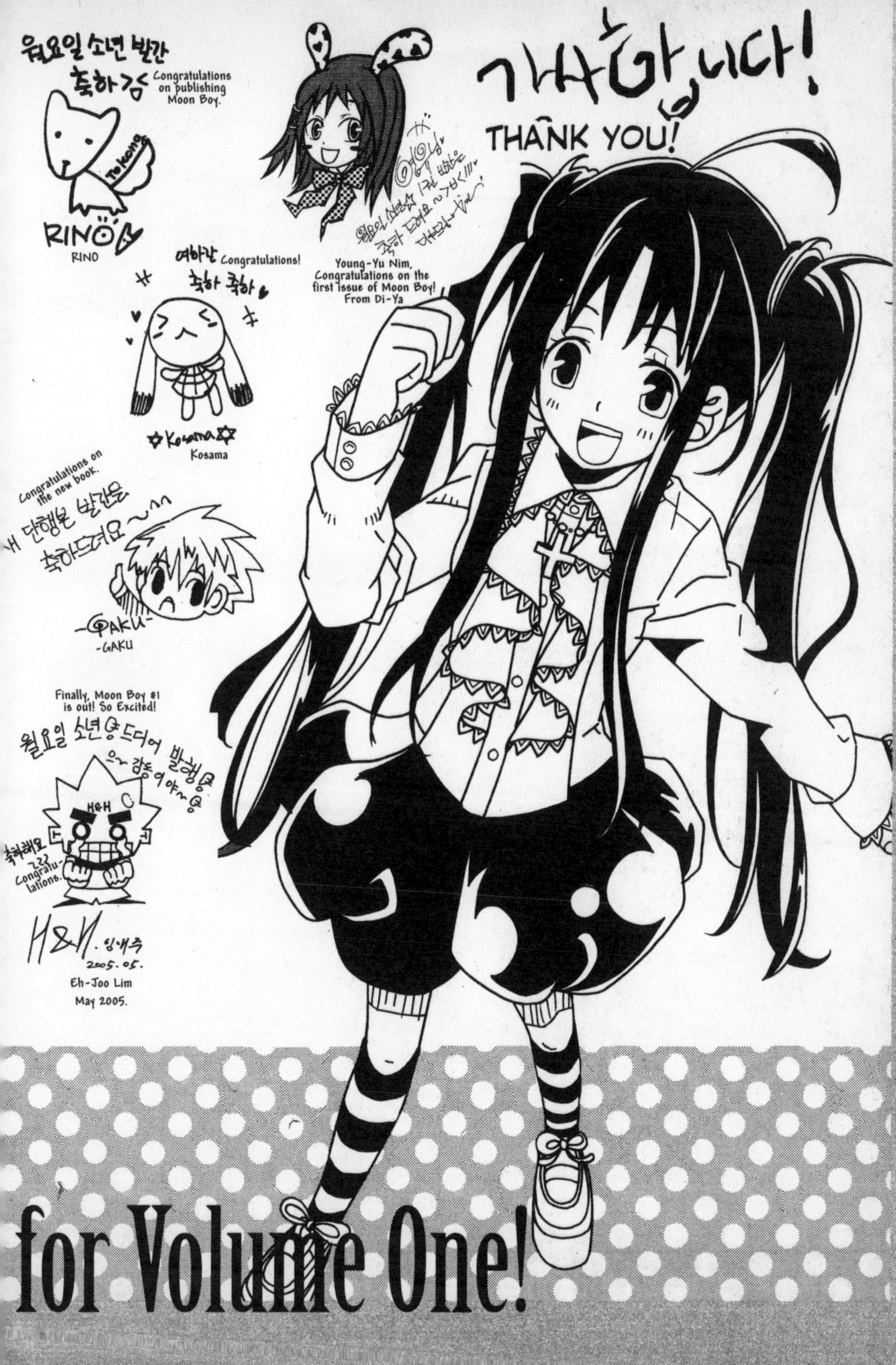
감사합니다!
THANK YOU!
월요일 소년 발간
축하감
Congratulations on publishing Moon Boy.
To kong
RINO
RINO
영유님
월요일 소년☆ 1권 발행을
축하 드려요~
Young-Yu Nim, Congratulations on the first issue of Moon Boy! From Di-Ya
여하랑
축하 축하
Congratulations!
Kosama
Kosama
Congratulations on the new book.
새 단행본 발간을
축하드려요~^^
-GAKU-
-GAKU
Finally, Moon Boy #1 is out! So Excited!
월요일 소년 드디어 발행
으~ 감동이야~
H&H
축하해요 ㄹㄹㄹ
Congratulations.
H&H. 임애주
2005.05.
Eh-Joo Lim
May 2005.
for Volume One!

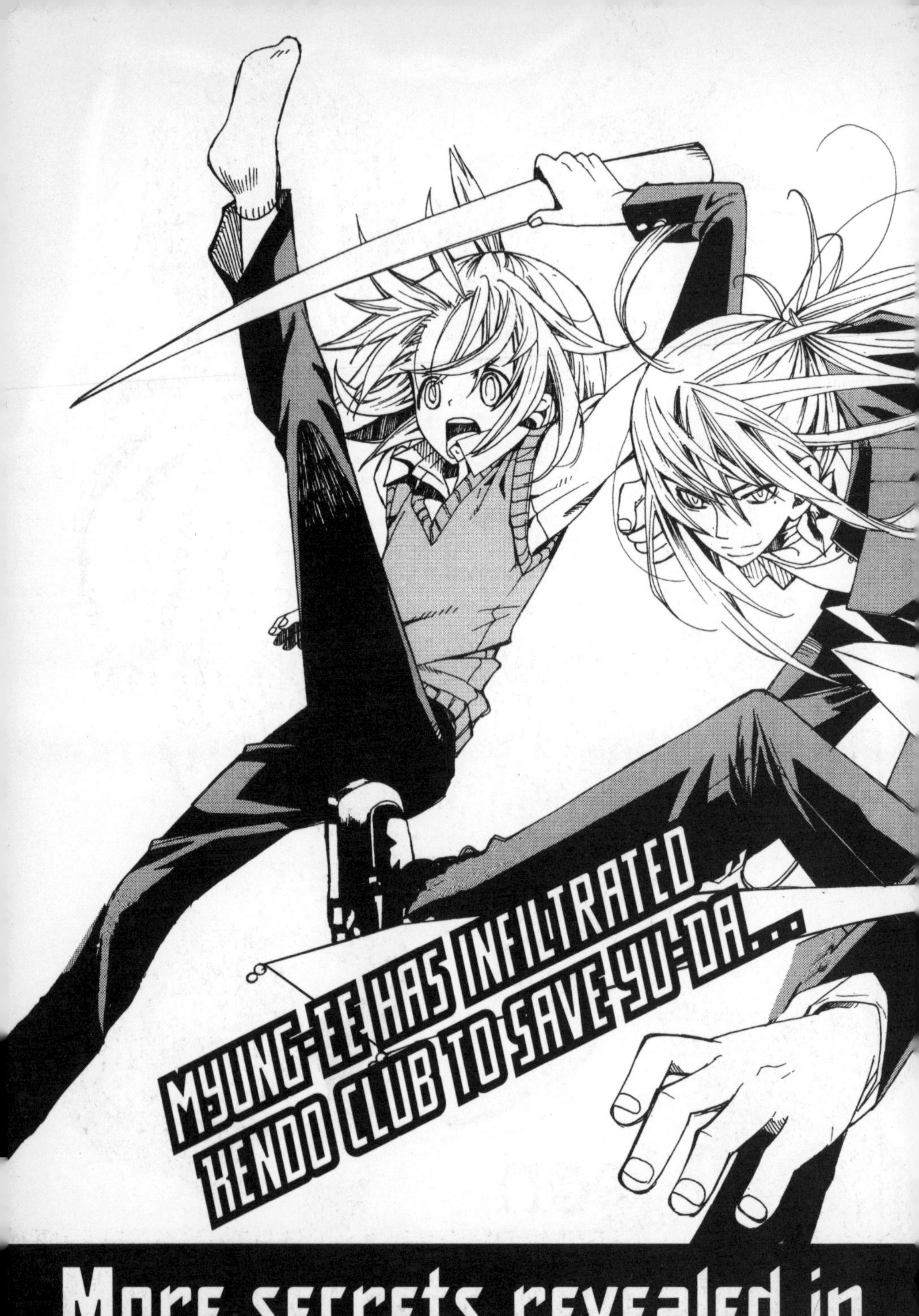
MYUNG-EE HAS INFILTRATED
KENDO CLUB TO SAVE YU-DA...

More secrets revealed in

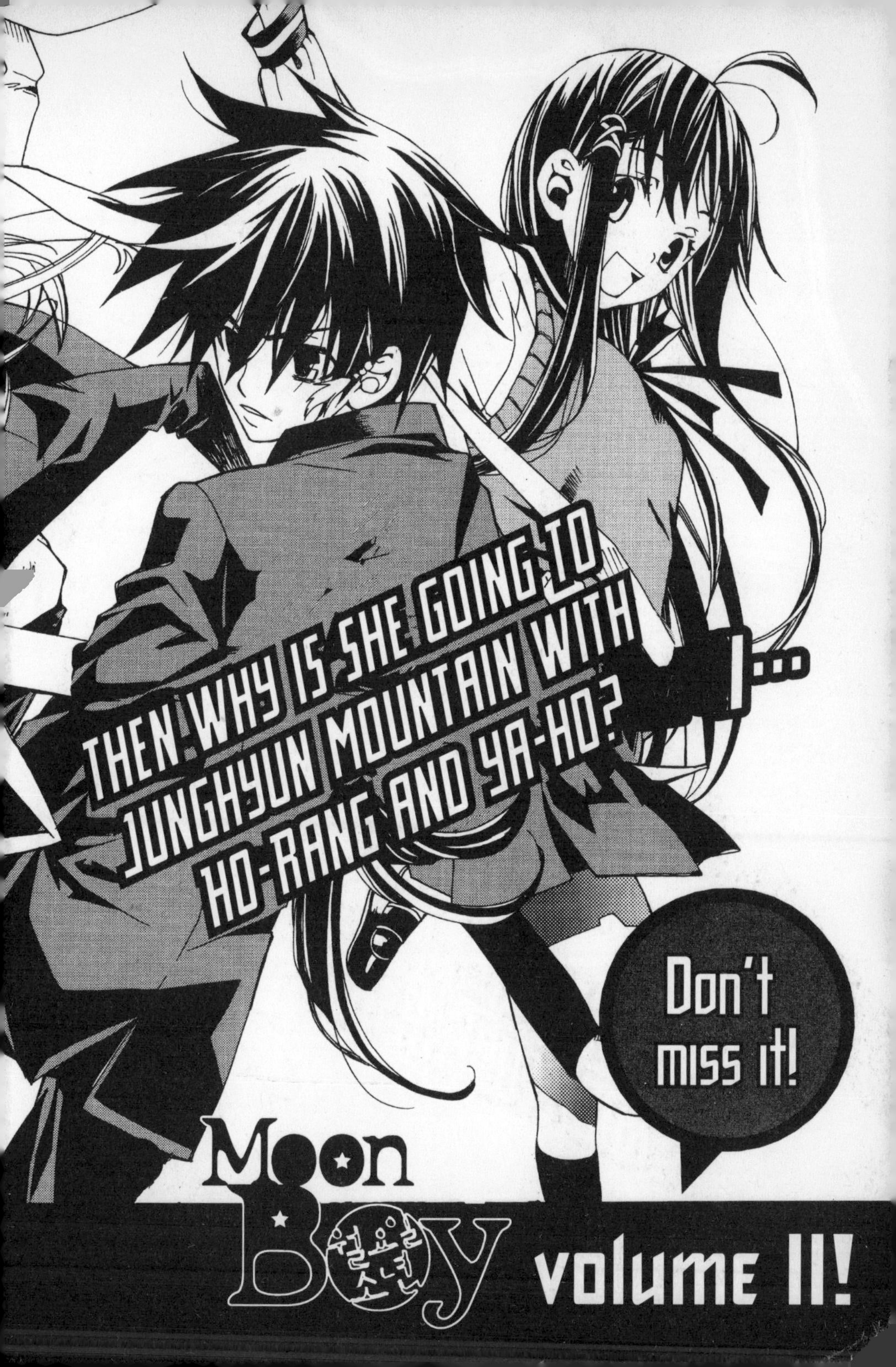
THEN WHY IS SHE GOING TO JUNGHYUN MOUNTAIN WITH HO-RANG AND YA-HO?
Don't miss it!
Moon Boy
volume 11!

Danbi Original

Moon Boy vol.1

Story and Art by YoungYou Lee

Translation HyeYoung Im
English Adaptation J. Torres
Touch-up and Lettering Terri Delgado · Marshall Dillon
Graphic Design EunKyung Kim

ICE Kunion

English Adaptation Editor HyeYoung Im · J. Torres
Managing Editor Marshall Dillon
Marketing Manager Erik Ko
Editor JuYoun Lee
Editor in Chief Eddie Yu
Editorial Director MoonJung Kim
Managing Director Jackie Lee
Publisher and C.E.O. JaeKook Chun

Moonboy Vol.1 © 2005 by Lee Young You All rights reserved.
This translated edition is published by arrangement with Haksan Publishing Co.,Ltd. in Korea.
English edition Vol.1 © 2006 by ICE Kunion.

Published by ICE Kunion.
SIGONGSA 2F Yeil Bldg. 1619-4, Seocho-dong, Seocho-gu, Seoul, 137-878, Korea

ISBN : 89-527-4604-X

First printing, May 2006
10 9 8 7 6 5 4 3 2 1
Printed in Canada

www.icekunion.com/www.koreanmanhwa.com